# HARD BARGAIN

## How FDR Twisted Churchill's Arm, Evaded the Law, and Changed the Role of the American Presidency

# ROBERT SHOGAN

D0018239

Westview Press

A Member of the Perseus Books Group

Printed in 1999 in the United States of America by Westview Press, 5500 Central Avenue, Boulder, Colorado 80301–2877, and in the United Kingdom by Westview Press,
12 Hid's Copse Road, Cumnor Hill, Oxford OX2 9JJ

Find us on the World Wide Web at www.westviewpress.com

A CIP catalog record for this book is available from the Library of Congress.
ISBN 0-8133-3695-3 (pbk)

The paper used in this publication meets the requirements of the American National
Standard for Permanence of Paper for Printed Library Materials Z39.48–1984.

10    9    8    7    6    5    4    3    2    1

FOR ELLEN

# Contents

# Preface to the Paperback Edition

## Paving the Road to Kosovo

It was the fateful spring of 1940. With Hitler at his throat, British Prime Minister Winston Churchill cabled a desperate plea for help to his new best friend, President Franklin Roosevelt, asking for the loan of 50 overage U.S. destroyers to fend off an anticipated cross-channel German invasion.

Eager to shore up the British against a common threat, Roosevelt was nevertheless fearful of isolationist opposition. Though the United States was still ostensibly neutral, Roosevelt secretly cut a deal with the British to trade the ships for U.S. naval bases on British possessions. To avoid congressional debate, he wangled the destroyers Churchill wanted via an executive order, in blatant disregard for the U.S. Constitution.

How big a role this transaction played in defeating the Axis is hard to measure. But FDR's destroyer trade sounded alarms in Berlin and Tokyo and locked the United States on course for World War II. Moreover, this momentous swap cast a long and troublesome shadow over U.S. foreign policy.

Roosevelt's flouting of constitutional principles was so flagrant that many years later Senator Daniel Patrick Monynihan contended that Roosevelt, "actually subverted the law" and "was clearly subject to impeachment." But the president suffered no legal retribution. Instead, his action established a precedent for unilateral presidential interventionism abroad, which having survived and flourished through wars hot

1

and cold manifested itself most recently in the bombs that rained down on Yugoslavia in the spring of 1999.

Traveling the road to Kosovo that Roosevelt paved, Americans have spilled blood in every corner of the globe in the last half of the twentieth century. But not once during the bellicose era since World War II has a U.S. president shown enough respect for the Constitution to ask Congress for a declaration of war.

The distinction is more than a mere legalism. By their overreaching, presidents have undermined respect for the rule of law and fostered public cynicism about the motives underlying their interventionism. This attitude did not escape Hollywood, as demonstrated by the motion picture "Wag the Dog": After the film's chief executive is caught making a pass at a teenage girl visiting the Oval Office, his image makers distract the public by staging a fake war on television against, eerily enough, Kosovo's next door neighbor, Albania.

"The movie . . . offers a vision . . . that would be chilling if it weren't so funny," the *New York Times* reviewer observed when the film opened early in January 1998. Within a few weeks, though, the film's satirical edge was blunted by the controversy over President Clinton's threats to bomb Iraq in the midst of an all-too-real White House sex scandal that had just engulfed him.

Undeclared wars also raise more substantive dangers. A formal proposal to Congress to declare war would reasonably be expected to generate a national debate on the ends and means of the proposed belligerency and would offer the president an opportunity to mobilize public support behind the war. Over the long run the absence of such a debate and such support forces our elected commanders-in-chief to rely on stealth and halfway measures, leading to stalemate, as in Korea, or defeat, as in Vietnam.

Clinton, as devoted to expediency as most of his predecessors, finds undeclared wars attractive because they spare him the necessity of explaining his purposes and the means by which he intends to achieve them. But conundrums not resolved in open debate often come back as nightmares. President Truman's failure to define U.S. objectives in the Korean "police action" ultimately led to frustration and massive discontent at home, wrecking his presidency just as Lyndon Johnson's devious escalation of the war in Vietnam ruined his dream of creating the Great Society.

Clearly, Clinton confronted similar difficulties in the Balkans. It soon became apparent that his stated purpose, halting the purging of the ethnic Albanians of Kosovo, could not be achieved by the means he had chosen, the bombing of the Serbs. As a result, rather than violate his pledge not to send U.S. ground troops into the cauldron of battle, Clinton agreed to a settlement that allowed freshly indicted war criminal Slobodan Milosevic to remain as ruler of Yugoslavia. Milosevic withdrew his troops from Kosovo, but retained sovereignty over that battered land, albeit accepting its occupation by an international military force.

After 10 weeks of undeclared war that cost the lives of thousands of people, Albanians and Serbs, and inflicted immense economic damage on Kosovo and Serbia, the United States and its allies faced the daunting task of returning to their homes 1.5 million Kosovars on whose behalf the war had supposedly been fought. And this in addition to the long-range problem of maintaining stability in the Balkans. The North Atlantic Treaty Organization (NATO) now had the mission of protecting five vulnerable little places—not only Kosovo, but Albania, Macedonia, Montenegro, and Bosnia as well—in the face of Milosevic's unrelenting ambition to forge a Greater Serbia.

Undeclared wars encourage the avoidance of accountability not only by presidents but also by members of Congress. Shorn of their clearly stated constitutional responsibility actually to declare war, presumably after due debate and deliberation, lawmakers too often tend to accept the inevitability of presidential war making, even when this runs counter to their better judgment.

While conceding "good reason to fear . . . that our mission is confused and our exit strategy a complete mystery," Republican Senator John McCain, a genuine war hero and all-but-announced candidate for his party's 2000 presidential nomination nevertheless went along with a Senate resolution approving the air strikes. If he opposed the president, the Arizonan claimed, "our adversaries around the globe will take heart from our inability to act in concert." Despite his initial misgivings about the U.S. role in Yugoslavia, McCain began leading the charge to send in U.S. ground troops, arguing that U.S. credibility is at stake in the struggle over Kosovo.

Others in the GOP upper echelons joined in the support of intervention, concluding, as the party's 1996 vice presidential candidate Jack Kemp put it in a position paper circulated among Republican leaders, "that no matter how weak the case for war in Kosovo may be on the merits, we are now inextricably involved and therefore must do whatever is necessary militarily to 'win.'" Kemp added: "The false premise on which the Establishment's line of reasoning rests is that peace around the world hangs on whether or not people believe America is prepared to go to war to preserve it."

The passive acceptance among Republicans, particularly on Capitol Hill, of Clinton's decision was reinforced by the failure of the War Powers Resolution, adopted in 1973 in the wake of Vietnam to curb presidential adventurism abroad. Presidents have ignored its cumbersome provisions and Congresses have failed to enforce them. Desert Shield, President Bush's massive military buildup in the Persian Gulf undertaken in 1990 without congressional authorization, demonstrated the law's inadequacy.

In announcing his destroyer deal with the British in war-torn 1940, Roosevelt described the transaction as an act of defense taken "in the face of grave danger." And when victory in World War II was followed by what John Kennedy called "the long twilight struggle" against Communism, nearly all of FDR's successors used similar claims of national peril to justify sending U.S. troops into harm's way, often with only dubious constitutional sanction and with little or no public debate.

What is striking and disturbing is that this presidential activism has persisted even after the collapse of Communism and the passing of any immediate threat to this nation's security. For even in the post–Cold War era, foreign policy holds the same allure that it offered for presidents in the preceding, and more dangerous, decades of the twentieth century. As a global statesman the president can hope to rise above the petty partisan discord and frustrations of the domestic scene and command the support of his fellow Americans as a symbol of the national interest.

Thus George Bush sought to use the Iraqi invasion of Kuwait in the summer of 1990 to transform the perception of himself as a temporizing caretaker, a weak and indecisive figure who was in danger of losing his grip on his own party, into that of a dynamic and forceful world leader. In this he had the considerable cooperation of the media caught up in the drama of the military crisis. Summing up a view widely expressed in the press at the time, the *Wall Street Journal* described the confrontation in the desert as presenting Bush with a "crucial opportunity to define his presidency," thus blotting out the deficiencies he had amply demonstrated during his first 18 months in the White House.

Goaded by British Prime Minister Margaret Thatcher into adopting a tough stance against Saddam Hussein—"This is no time to go wobbly, George," she famously instructed him—Bush nevertheless had difficulty explaining the reasons for massive U.S. commitment in the Gulf. Not until nearly six weeks after he had committed the United States to hold "a line in the sand" did Bush make a full scale address to the country on the crisis. "Out of these troubled times . . . a new world order can emerge," he promised, without explaining how that new order would differ from the old. And while he warned that "at home the material cost of our leadership can be steep," he did not say what that price might be or who would pay it.

In more concrete terms, Bush described the Iraqi threat to "the world's great oil reserves" as endangering "our way of life, our own freedom and the freedom of friendly countries." Political leaders trying to help Bush rally support for this far-reaching national commitment complained that the crassness of this rationale made their job harder. "I think that the American people are not willing to have their children in harm's way to protect cheap oil prices in the U.S.," said Democratic House Majority Leader Richard Gephardt of Missouri, who had been chosen by his party to pledge publicly its support for Bush's initial resistance to Saddam.

As the president moved closer to war, the country seemed divided and uncertain. The act of war itself, in January 1991, triggered a reflexive wave of public support for Bush, a mood sustained through the winter months as each night Americas viewed from the comfort of their living rooms their armed forces inflicting death and destruction on the enemy while suffering minimal casualties themselves. The one-sidedness fortunately extended into the brief ground war in which an outgunned and demoralized Iraqi army was quickly put to rout by the overwhelming might of the United States and its coalition allies.

Yet in victory, Bush allowed Saddam Hussein, the tyrant whom he had continually likened to Hitler, to remain in power. The president stood by while Hussein crushed attempted uprisings by Kurdish and Shiite minorities. Bush's nonresponse amounted to a repudiation of the high moral principles he had claimed as motives for the massive destruction the United States had unleashed on Iraq. His inaction in large part can be attributed to a lack of public resolve characteristic of undeclared wars, which raises doubts about whether Americans would be willing to back a conflict in which their own casualties rose above the triple digit levels of Operation Desert Storm. The losses that would inevitably have been suffered by prolonging the fighting and pushing on into the Iraqi homeland to destroy Saddam's regime would almost certainly have been of a different order and likely have produced a far less positive public reaction, a risk that Bush decided not to take.

Clinton, surprisingly enough given his own previous antipathy toward the military during Vietnam, has wielded the big stick around the world, from Iraq, where Saddam Hussein remains a threat nearly a decade after Bush's Desert Storm, and Bosnia to Haiti and now Kosovo, with Congress serving as little more than a rubber stamp.

Kosovo is not the first time Clinton has guessed wrong on military intervention. In 1993 he dispatched 15,000 U.S. troops into Somalia to reinforce a contingent sent there the year before on an ill-conceived "peace keeping" mission by President Bush. Troops commanded by Somali warlords killed 18 Americans in an ambush and then humiliated the world's only superpower by dragging the body of one soldier through the streets. But in the face of protests from Congress and public unwillingness to sacrifice more lives for what seemed a pointless and hopeless cause, Clinton pulled out all Americans in a few months. Said one U.S. official: "Foreigners can't make Somalis mount a government if they don't want one."

Much the same lesson was driven home in Haiti, where Clinton dispatched 20,000 troops in 1994, ostensibly to help establish a stable democratic government in that country where anarchy and despotism have long alternated in the driver's seat. Yet four and a half years later Haiti was still in such a state of turmoil that the security of the remaining contingent of the U.S. expeditionary force was at risk. This appraisal came from a top U.S. general who urged an end to the U.S. military presence, a development largely overlooked in the furor over Kosovo. "The unrest generated by political instability requires us to constantly reassess the safety and security environment in which our troops are living and working," Gen. Charles E. Wilhelm, chief of the U.S. Southern Command, told a House subcommittee.

Despite these miscalculations, Clinton pressed on with his Kosovo mission, energized by much the same vision that had captured many of his predecessors. Eight years after Bush viewed Operation Desert Storm as a chance to infuse his hitherto lackluster tenure with the grandeur of global conflict, similar thinking prevailed in the Clinton White House. John F. Harris, the knowledgeable White House correspondent of the *Washington Post*, reported that Clinton, following six scandal-tarnished years in power, now regarded Kosovo as the "defining moment for his presidency, and for American foreign policy at century's end."

In steering the destroyer deal to its consummation, Franklin Roosevelt flouted international law, as well as the laws of his own country. Clinton has been similarly cavalier. Choosing to ignore the United Nations—created by the nations that had fought and won World War II to be the chief arbiter of disputes among nations and punisher of wrong doers—because of the Russian presence on the Security Council, he instead carved out an unprecedented role for NATO. Established to guard its member states against attacks, NATO instead became the chosen instrument of the United States for mounting a war against another sovereign county.

For Clinton, NATO served another purpose, too. He sought to derive from that organization justification for the war, a justification that had been difficult for him to articulate following his failure to prevent the purging of the Kosovars. Unless NATO prevailed in the Balkans, the president, said, "it will not have meaning in the 21st century," suggesting in effect that the United States was now fighting a war to make the world safe for NATO.

In that same spirit, as they met in Washington to observe the 50th anniversary of the organization's birth, the leaders of NATO's member nations set the stage for more Kosovos by announcing they were prepared to use military force to prevent so-called human rights abuses everywhere in Europe. "We are moving into a system of international relations in which human rights, rights to minorities every day, are much more important, and more important even than sovereignty," NATO's Secretary-General Javier Solana declared. But that proclamation begged vital questions. Whose standards would be used in making judgments on human rights? And how would NATO's newly claimed authority to wage undeclared wars on a global scale impinge on U.S. constitutional safeguards on whose significance the Secretary General seemed to place little importance?

With the future clouded by the threat of continued escalation and expansion of the war, some members of Congress voiced their uneasiness, among them Republican Rep. Jim Leach of Iowa, a senior member of the House International Relations Committee. In a plea for more legislative involvement in Kosovo decision making, Leach wrote:

> If military intervention has the effect of deepening Serbian resolve, consolidating murderous leadership, escalating rather than quelling violence in Kosovo and expanding conflict in and outside the region, the case for its continuation on any grounds except a desire for a prideful exit is

dubious. For this war to be prosecuted further, constitutionality demands Congress take a definitive stand, and morality requires judgments be based on more than good intentions.

But Congress clearly had a difficult time deciding what stand to take. In one disjointed legislative day in April the House voted against formally declaring war on Yugoslavia, against pulling U.S. forces out, against supporting the air campaign, and against deploying ground troops without congressional consent. That left the lawmakers "maximum room" to remain uncommitted as Jerold Duquette, a political analyst at Virginia's George Mason University, pointed out. "It's a tie, nobody loses," he said.

But somebody does lose. To be sure, even critics of Clinton's policies concede that the world remains a dangerous place and that the United States must still fulfill its role in the community of nations. Yet past experience dictates that in meeting U.S. obligations abroad presidents must weigh the potential gains against the costs. Clinton has yet to pay a political price for the failure of the military missions he has launched to carry out their objectives in Kosovo, Haiti, Iraq and in Somalia before that, but that is largely because the U.S. casualty lists were blessedly small. But this calculus does not take into account the thousands of civilians who died during NATO's air onslaught on Serbia. And there is another cost to be reckoned in assessing undeclared wars—the harm to the workings of the political system as ordained by the Constitution, and on that score, a good deal of damage has already been done.

*Robert Shogan*
Chevy Chase, MD
June 1999

# Author's Note

Anyone who follows the presidency closely, as I have for more than thirty years, walks in the shadow of Franklin Roosevelt. This book examines the man who cast that shadow at a moment in history when events severely tested his fundamental beliefs and forced him to extend his skills to the utmost. Those who seek either to sanctify or demonize Roosevelt will find little support here. Neither angel nor devil, FDR emerges from these pages as a politician, seeking after the light as he saw it, but also seeking after reelection. This is not a story of villains against heroes, etched in black and white. The fundamental contest here is between principle and expediency, which can be glimpsed only in various shades of grey. It is my hope that the past seen through this prism can help to illuminate the future.

This book owes a primary debt to Kathleen Hall Jamieson, Dean of the Annenberg School for Communication of the University of Pennsylvania, who made it possible for me to spend an academic year on her campus as a professional-in-residence. The benefits included access to the stacks of Van Pelt Library and the assistance of two resourceful and resolute researchers, Robin Nabi and Sean Aday. I am grateful also to Mike Miller, national editor of the *Los Angeles Times*, to Jack Nelson, Washington Bureau chief, and Richard Cooper, his deputy, for helping to arrange leave time from the paper. Philip Ruiz and Steve Clark solved computer problems and Caleb Gessesse and Pat Welsh assisted in using the Washington Bureau library.

Larry Berman, Don Frederick, Joel Havemann, Tom Rosenstiel, and Brooks Yeager read portions of the manuscript and strengthened it with their suggestions. David Wigdor, assistant chief of the manuscript division of the Library of Congress, provided guidance to that division's collections, without which this book could not have been written, and Barbara Natanson of the prints and photographs division went well beyond the call of duty in helping me locate photos. At the Franklin D. Roosevelt Library, I owe special thanks to Robert Parks for his advice and encouragement. My work as a journalist has been enriched over the years thanks to the counsel of the academic community and I have to thank a number of its members, particularly James MacGregor Burns, Alonzo Hamby, and William Leuchtenburg, for advice and encouragement on this book. The British scholar John Charmley took the trouble to send me copies of relevant files from the Winston Churchill Memorial and Library at Westminster College where he was a visiting fellow. Amelia Ford Shogan researched the legal issues raised by Attorney General Jackson's opinion. John Robert Greene made available his own research into the early New Deal and arranged for the assistance of two of his students at Cazenovia College, Elizabeth A. Harwick and Dominic Jay Smith. Other assistance and advice came from Tom Allen, Katheye Anderson, R. W. Apple, Jennifer Burton, Robert Jackson, William Lasser, Laura Manning, Thomas J. O'Donnell, Ron Ostrow, Art Pine, Norman Polmar, Ted Van Dyk, Mary Wornley, my editor at Scribner, Hamilton Cain, who helped me to tighten and focus the original manuscript, and my agent, Philip G. Spitzer.

My wife Ellen provided editing and research help when I needed it most. In the case of this work, as with five previous books, my greatest debt is to her and to our daughters, Cynthia and Amelia, for their love and support.

Chevy Chase, Md.

June 1994

Put not your trust in princes.
*Psalms, CXLVI, 3*


You must understand that politics is not a profession
that rewards purity or perfection.
*Former Rep. Daniel J. Rostenkowski, Democrat of Illinois*

# HARD BARGAIN

# "I Want to Get My Hand in Now"

The cable followed a well established path. From the desk of newly installed Prime Minister Winston Churchill at Admiralty House, where he had until recently served His Britannic Majesty as First Lord and was still temporarily headquartered, it was hand carried by Naval courier to the United States Embassy, only minutes away at Prince's Gate on Grosvenor Square. Arriving there in late afternoon in its sealed envelope, it was immediately forwarded to the code room. In this sacrosanct chamber it was encrypted in the Gray code, one of the simplest and therefore one of the fastest ciphers. Then came the long telegraphic leap across the Atlantic, directly to the White House, where after being swiftly decoded it was placed at the right hand of the 32nd President of the United States, Franklin Delano Roosevelt. The date was May 15, 1940, eight months into a world conflict suddenly transformed from a phony war into a *blitzkrieg* which now threatened to engulf the Western democracies.

Roosevelt had no reason to expect good news from Churchill. Five days earlier Adolf Hitler's armies had swarmed across northern France and the Low Countries and all reports made clear that the Allies faced an epochal disaster. The morning's *Washington Post* recorded astounding new German victories. Rotterdam had fallen and the Dutch government announced the capitulation of its army, "to avoid the complete destruction of the country." Elsewhere Hitler's forces had reached the Meuse on a broad front from Liege to Sedan.

Even so, it took only a quick glance at Churchill's message to tell the President that Britain's plight was much graver than he had surmised. "The scene has darkened swiftly," Churchill wrote, emphasizing that the French had been stunned by the speed and force of the Nazi assault. "We expect to be attacked here ourselves," he wrote. "But if necessary we shall continue the war alone, and we are not afraid of that."

Then the Prime Minister, with no pretense at subtlety, appealed to America's own interest. "The voice and force of the United States may count for nothing if withheld too long," he warned the President, urging that Roosevelt declare the U.S. to be in a state of "non-belligerency." This would mean "that you would help us with everything short of actually engaging armed forces."

As the defender of an island nation under siege, it was only natural that Churchill should place ships first and foremost on his list. "Immediate needs are," the Prime Minister wrote, "first of all the loan of forty or fifty of your older destroyers. . . ." Churchill stressed that these destroyers, of World War I vintage, would merely "bridge the gap between what we have now and the large new construction we put in hand at the beginning of the war." He bolstered his case by pointing out that if, as he expected, Mussolini's Italy should enter the war, with its own submarine fleet to supplement Germany's undersea strength, "we may be strained to the breaking point." The Prime Minister asked for other help, too—aircraft, anti-aircraft guns and ammunition, iron ore and raw material. But it was the destroyers, as he would make plain time and again in the months to come, that were his country's greatest need.

With his own back against the wall, Churchill was forcing Roosevelt, in the midst of a presidential election year, to confront the most difficult decision of his presidency, during which profound turning points had already become almost commonplace. For Roosevelt to do what Churchill asked would clearly violate the tenets of international law and verge on being an act of war. It would require a commitment to the Allied cause from the United States far beyond anything Americans had previously countenanced or even considered. For him to refuse could mean the United States would be left without a single major power at its side to face the most dangerous foreign threat in its history.

Over the next four months Churchill's plea for warships would become the focal point of a momentous national debate. Those who believed the U.S. could not afford the risk of helping the British contended against those who said the U.S. could even less afford the risk of letting Britain perish. While this argument raged in public, the resolution of the issue was reached behind the scenes, largely shaped by the will of one man, Franklin D. Roosevelt.

His decision would set in motion a chain of events that ultimately plunged the U.S. into war and redirected its destiny. During the tortuous negotiations for the destroyers, Roosevelt's demands on the British caused them to complain that he was driving a hard bargain. Over the long run, though, the outcome would turn out to be an even harder bargain for Americans. For the destroyer deal ultimately levied an incalculable toll in blood and treasure expended on conflicts reaching into nearly every corner of the earth and stretching on for the rest of the century.

Beyond that, the challenge raised by Churchill's appeal would test Roosevelt's ability to lead the nation in crisis. He would be pitted against the system of politics and government which many believed he had rescued when he took office in 1933, in the midst of another type of crisis, the Great Depression. To deal with the economy's collapse he had vowed to seek power as great as "if we were in fact invaded by a foreign foe." He had then used the powers of the presidency in ways unimagined by any of his predecessors, redefining the nature of his office and transforming the relationship between Americans and their government.

Yet for all his skill, time and again, Roosevelt had been frustrated by the checks and balances devised by the Founding Fathers. The courts, the Congress, even his own party, had combined to stymie the President and erode his popular support. Now seven years after his first inaugural, danger from a foreign foe was not just a compelling metaphor, but also an all too real peril. Responding to the impending threat, Roosevelt would reach beyond even the new limits he had marked, matching his will and nerve against the system he had salvaged. In the interests of his country's security and of his own political ambitions, the President would find it necessary to twist the law, flout the Constitution, hoodwink the public, and distort the political process.

Roosevelt's handling of the destroyer deal with the British would set a pernicious precedent. His machinations would give impetus and legitimacy to the efforts of his successors to expand the reach of their powers, overriding constitutional guidelines and political principles, all in the name of national security. This syndrome would be exhibited by postwar chief executives confronted with supposed crises abroad, irrespective of party affiliation, from Harry Truman and the Korean conflict and Lyndon Johnson and the Vietnam War through Ronald Reagan and Nicaragua's Sandinista regime to George Bush and the Iraqi invasion of Kuwait.

But these consequences were still sleeping somewhere in the future. For the present, Roosevelt wanted to focus on the issues raised by Churchill's cable and on his relationship with the Prime Minister.

Churchill had good cause to feel comfortable about communicating with the President. Roosevelt himself had initiated their correspondence in the early days of the war, when Churchill had freshly returned to his old World War I post as First Lord of the Admiralty. "It is because you and I occupied similar positions in the World War, that I want you to know how glad I am that you are back at the Admiralty," the former assistant navy secretary wrote Churchill. "Your problems are as I realize complicated by new factors, but the essential is not very different," Roosevelt wrote. "What I want you and the Prime Minister to know is that I shall at all times welcome it if you will keep me in touch personally with anything you want me to know about."

Even with the diplomatic tip of his hat to Prime Minister Neville Chamberlain, this was an extraordinary proposal for a chief of state of one nation to make to the subordinate minister of another. The pretext was slim. In his subcabinet post in Woodrow Wilson's wartime administration, Roosevelt was more of a troubleshooter than a decision maker. To equate that role with Churchill's far-reaching responsibilities under Lloyd George might under other circumstances have been taken as a slight.

Roosevelt's duties under Wilson had taken him to England in 1918, bringing him and Churchill together for the first and so far only time. As it happened, the future President had taken an instant dislike to the future Prime Minister, who was then Minister of Munitions. "He acted like a stinker at a dinner I attended, lording it over us," Roosevelt had confided years later, in the first months of World War II, to Joseph P. Kennedy, his Ambassador to the Court of St. James. Still, looking into the future, Roosevelt discerned "a strong possibility" that Churchill might become the King's first minister. As he told Kennedy at the time: "I want to get my hand in now."

Not that FDR and his advisers did not harbor misgivings about Churchill. His long public career had been marked by erratic twists and turns which detracted from his occasional brilliance. He had been a soldier, journalist, historian, and until recently, in the view of most of his countrymen, a failed politician. Now, at age 66, Churchill had seized the opportunity offered him by the loss of confidence in his predecessor, Neville Chamberlain, to take charge of Britain's fortunes while the odds against her survival mounted at every toll of the clock. For all Churchill's talent, some found it hard to overlook his idiosyncrasies, among them his fondness for alcohol. Sumner Welles, the Undersecretary of State, had reported on his return from a visit to London the previous March that on the first evening he had seen Churchill, "he was quite drunk."

And when, on the day Churchill's appointment was announced, Interior Secretary Harold Ickes recorded in his diary that the President spoke of the new Prime Minister to his cabinet as "the best man that England had, even if he was drunk half of his time." Ickes himself supposed Churchill to be "too old."

Despite these concerns, Roosevelt had initiated his correspondence with Churchill because of his own resolve to be personally informed about a conflict whose impact on his country, he realized, would be far greater than he preferred to acknowledge publicly. With the telltale phrase, "the essential is not very different," the President had hinted to Churchill that he viewed the Second World War, during which he had publicly vowed to keep the United States neutral, as fundamentally an extension of the First World War. That the United States' ultimate entry into that war had clinched victory for Britain and its allies was a piece of history that Churchill kept stored away, never far from the forefront of his mind.

For months Churchill had carefully nurtured this relationship with Roosevelt, offering him occasional reports on British naval activities in the South Atlantic to keep up the President's interest. Now, the German armored spearheads which overwhelmed the French had created the desperate necessity for Churchill to exploit this channel of communication and whatever good will he had acquired.

As Roosevelt pondered his response to the new Prime Minister on this hot and muggy Wednesday in Washington, he had to consider first the attitude of the American people. So far during the war their attention was turned inward, as it had been for more than two decades since the end of World War I. As Roosevelt knew only too well, Americans had yet to recover economically or emotionally from the ravages of the Great Depression. Although conditions had improved since the early thirties, a sharp relapse late in 1937 had sent unemployment climbing again and eroded the sense of public confidence that Roosevelt had labored to build. For all of his New Deal's stirring rhetoric and brave promises, the jobless rolls in 1940 stood at eight million, meaning that nearly one worker out of seven was idle.

Millions who were not counted in the official tabulations of unemployment were barely eking out a living. Farmers were earning about $28 a month in 1940, as compared to $40 in 1929 before the booming Twenties went bust. The much vaunted programs established by the New Deal to revive the economy were still desperately needed to help the victims of the continuing hard times. On May 14, the night before Churchill's cable arrived, Eleanor Roosevelt, regarded as a symbol of

hope and compassion for the downtrodden, had joined a group of
unemployed women at the National Press Club for a five cent supper of
beef stew, an event intended to dramatize the plight of the "Daughters
of the American Depression." During dinner the First Lady chatted
with Mrs. Hughes Easley, wife of an unemployed St. Louis electrician,
chosen as "Welfare Mother of the Year." While she held her youngest
child in her arms, Mrs. Easley described how her family of ten got
along on $18 a month. Earlier, Mrs. Roosevelt had suggested a new
approach to encourage investment. "Perhaps it will be necessary," she
said "to risk what we are able to risk in order to give other human
beings a chance to exist."

Against this dreary economic backdrop, the country pursued its normal diversions. The baseball season, under way for a month, offered
surprising starts to both pennant races. In the American League a mys-
terious slump bedeviled the New York Yankees, while in the National
League, the usually hapless Brooklyn Dodgers had taken over first
place. Motion pictures, the most popular form of entertainment, were
selling tickets at the rate of 80 million a year. Ushered in by unprecedented ballyhoo, the film version of Margaret Mitchell's bestseller
*Gone With the Wind* at last was finding its way to neighborhood movie
houses for those who could afford the 20 cents price of admission. Walt
Disney's latest technicolor extravaganza for youngsters, *Pinocchio*, had
premiered at New York's cinema showplace, Radio City Music Hall, a
few weeks before. The products of Hollywood, which in wartime would
transform itself into a propaganda factory, as yet offered few allusions to
events abroad. But audiences watching *Balalaika*, a costume musical
set in pre-revolutionary Russia and starring Nelson Eddy and Ilona
Massie, might notice what *Time* referred to as "downright sinister Bol-
sheviks" lurking in the background, presumably Hollywood's revenge
for the Soviet Union's peace pact with Hitler and its aggression against
Finland.

The debut of a long-awaited product, stockings woven from a syn-
thetic fabric called nylon, brightened the day for women. The DuPont
company claimed nylon to be as sheer as silk, yet marvelously resistant
to runs. Trade sources estimated that only sixty-five dozen pairs would
go on sale around the country and predicted that none would be left on
the counters by noon. Nylon's introduction took on international significance, too. Manufacturers expected the new product would help tight-
en the boycott of Japanese goods organized in reprisal for Japan's
aggression against China by giving women an alternative to hose made
with silk imported from Japan.

Few Americans paid close attention to the stalemated Sino-Japanese war begun in 1937, or until recently to the European war either. Indeed the three-month border war between Soviet Russia and Finland had aroused more passion from Americans than the conflict between Germany and the Allies. "Gallant little Finland" stirred public sympathy not only because the Finns were up against the Communist hordes unleashed by the Kremlin but also because they had paid their World War I debts, in contrast, as some editorialists liked to point out, to the British and French.

Admiration for Finland inspired *There Shall Be No Night* by Pulitzer Prize–winning playwright Robert Sherwood, which starred Alfred Lunt and Lynn Fontanne. Premiering on Broadway two weeks before Hitler launched his attack in the West, the play depicted the impact of the Soviet invasion on a Finnish family. But Sherwood clearly intended his condemnation of aggression to reach beyond the Finnish war, which had ended two months before, to the struggle against Hitler. For this he was sharply attacked by the influential columnist Raymond Clapper, who called his work "inflammatory" and warned it would release "a suppressed urge" by Americans to intervene abroad. It seemed likely, though, that American views of the war would be less influenced by propaganda from either side than by the force of events abroad. Hitler's massive offensive commanded the nation's attention. In New York City an extra platoon of police directed Times Square traffic jammed by the great crowd that assembled to read the news bulletins flashing across the top of the *New York Times* annex. Headlines blared the news of German advances. "Nazis Fight Way Into France, Seize Sedan," proclaimed the *Washington Post*. Radios carried the static-ridden accounts of the fighting from correspondents stationed in the warring capital cities into the nation's living rooms.

The new techniques demonstrated by Hitler's troops, particularly the use of aircraft and tanks, had called into question previous U.S. assumptions about weapons and strategy, though Major General John K. Herr, the Army's chief of cavalry, defended the military usefulness of the horse. "Horses can still go where tanks and cars can't penetrate," Herr insisted. "Here in this country we have ten million horses and four million mules. We should make better use of that material so close at hand."

At the New York World's Fair in Flushing Meadows, the fog of war shrouded the bright hopes nurtured when the fair had opened in the ill-fated year of 1939 with the slogan "World of Tomorrow." The chief Belgian representative at the fair said his government would maintain his exhibit regardless of the war's outcome. On May 14, the day his country's capital surrendered, Reink Bekkering, manager of the Dutch exposition, vowed, "Holland will never cease to exist."

A similar note was sounded that same night by the Marquess of Lothian, Great Britain's ambassador to the U.S., in an address to the English-Speaking Union. "Despite all the murk and gloom of the time, I am not afraid," Lord Lothian told an audience of 1,500 that included, among other notables, J. P. Morgan. As he did in every speech he gave, Lothian emphasized the U.S. stake in the struggle abroad. A Hitler victory, he claimed, would "leave America isolated and alone to champion a free way of life."

Many Americans agreed. Earlier in the week, on the day following the start of the German offensive, Democratic Congressman Carl May of Kentucky, chairman of the House Military Affairs Committee, proposed easing the ban on American loans to Britain and France which had been enacted because they had defaulted on their war debts. "We ought to do everything we can to help the allies," he said. But Sen. Hiram Johnson of California, who had pushed the ban through Congress in 1934 with the quiet cooperation of Roosevelt, promised to fight any attempt to repeal his handiwork. "Experience in the last war taught us that the surest way to get into war is to let our money precede us." On the next day, May 13, Roosevelt's Secretary of State, Cordell Hull, warned in a speech to the American Society of International Law that the world was threatened by "an orgy of destruction" and called for "a wholly united opinion" to support the government's response.

Hull was notably vague about what this response might be. But whatever course the government chose, the evidence suggested that a united response would be hard to achieve. A basic conflict pervaded American views on the war. By a huge majority, about 85 percent according to a Gallup Poll taken in October of 1939, Americans wanted Britain and France to win the war; only 2 percent favored a German victory. But the sentiment against the U.S. entering the war was just as overwhelming; only about 15 percent interviewed by *Fortune* in December of 1939 were willing to enter the war on the side of the Allies, even if England and France were in danger of losing. This resistance to entering the war was all the more striking because, according to another survey, more than three out of five interviewed believed that if Germany defeated the Allies it would sooner or later go to war against the U.S.

Disillusionment with World War I powerfully influenced public attitudes. Nearly 70 percent believed that it had been a mistake for the

U.S. to enter that war. The dramatic events unfolding on the battlefields of France certainly might alter these attitudes. But how much and in what way? These were among the uncertainties that Roosevelt would have to reckon with if he sought to convince Americans to respond to Churchill's plea.

Yet another huge question he would have to resolve before he could take on this task had to do with his own political future. The economy's relapse had cut into the powerful political base which had won him a landslide reelection victory at the end of his first term. His second term had been marked by defeat and frustration. Now he had to decide whether to defy tradition and seek a third term in the White House. Roosevelt had carefully avoided revealing his intentions, unwilling either to lessen his influence by taking himself out of consideration, or to give ammunition to critics, who already accused him of lusting for power, by announcing he would run again. But the two national conventions that signaled the opening of the campaign were only a few weeks away and the pressure was mounting on him to announce his plans.

Whatever Americans thought of Roosevelt, none could deny his far-reaching impact on the country. Taking office with the nation's economy in ruins, its social and civic institutions undermined, its populace demoralized, and its government seemingly helpless, he had launched a program of reforms unprecedented in their scope. His achievements owed more to his character than his convictions. Often hazy and sometimes at cross purposes, these beliefs derived mainly from the traditional values of honor, fairness, and service passed on by his parents and reinforced in his prep school days at Groton. There, exposure to such spokesmen for the downtrodden as reformer Jacob Riis gave him the beginnings of a social conscience. From his father James, he inherited his allegiance to the Democratic party.

Groton also helped to shape his character, fostering the elusiveness which would become a dominant trait. He did not entirely fit in there, in part because his mother's reluctance to send her son away resulted in his admission at 14, not 12, which was the standard age. He was slow to develop, too. At 14 he was still a soprano; his willowy frame and unmarked features gave him a girlish appearance and his speech seemed stilted with a trace of an accent he had acquired from his travels abroad. To compensate and prove he was a regular fellow, young Franklin went well out of his way, once deliberately breaking the rules in class. "I have served off my first black mark today, and I am very glad I got it, as I was thought to have no school spirit before," he wrote his parents.

More constructively, he tried to prove himself an athlete. He tried out for football, baseball, hockey, and boxing but never made the varsity. Nevertheless, he still had a sense of apartness from his classmates, and he reacted by developing a shell over his innermost feelings which endured most of his life. Both at Groton and its almost inevitable sequel, Harvard, Franklin showed himself to be far more interested in the symbols of status than in intellectual attainment. His most significant accomplishment at Cambridge was becoming President of the *Crimson*, where his editorials focused mainly on whipping up "school spirit" and other parochial concerns.

Pursuing his early political ambitions first in the New York state legislature, then in the Wilson Administration, he assumed as his own the tenets of his party's progressive creed with its determination to use government to redress social and economic inequities. This formed the basis for the program of mild reforms he developed as governor of New York that helped him win a huge reelection victory in 1930 and put him on the road to the White House. Yet his performance as governor was uneven, providing ammunition to detractors, notable among them Walter Lippman. "Sooner or later some of Governor Roosevelt's supporters are going to feel badly let down," the columnist warned in one devastating critique.

> For it is impossible that he can continue to be such different things to such different men. . . . He is an amiable man with many philanthropic impulses, but he is not the dangerous enemy of anything. . . . A pleasant man who without any important qualifications for the office would very much like to be president.

Roosevelt's campaign for the Presidency in 1932 tended to bear out Lippman's assessment. He enjoyed stumping for its own sake. "To Roosevelt a good cause does not justify any trip, a good trip justifies any cause," wrote Raymond Moley, the architect of the early New Deal's "Brains Trust" who wrote many of FDR's 1932 campaign speeches. "Campaigning for him was unadulterated joy. . . . it was hands extended in welcome, voices warm with greeting, faces reflecting his smile along the interminable wayside."

Issues were another matter. Roosevelt brushed these aside unless they offered no risk. For the most part he sought to preserve his base of popular support while keeping his finger to the political winds. "No one who voted for him did it because he presented himself as learned or competent in all the matters he talked about," Rex Tugwell, a charter member of the Brains Trust, later pointed out. "They voted for the big easy smiling man who had no fear of failing at anything, who seemed capable even of saving sinners from themselves." In view of his healthy margin of victory—he won 57 percent of the popular vote and all but six states—Tugwell thought it a waste that Roosevelt had not been bolder and more explicit as a candidate. "The fact was that Franklin was continually accused by Hoover and others on the Republican side of intentions that were precisely those he should have proclaimed," he wrote. "He denied the accusations, only to reverse himself embarrassingly later on."

But for Roosevelt it was more important that he preserve the utmost flexibility. "It is a little bit like a football team that has a general plan of game against the other side," Roosevelt said early in his presidency in explaining his approach to economic policy to a group of White House reporters.

> Now the captain and the quarterback of the team know pretty well what the next play is going to be and they know the general strategy of the team, but they cannot tell you what the play after the next play is going to be until the next play is run off. If the play makes ten yards, the succeeding play will be different from what it would have been if they had been thrown for a loss. I think that is the easiest way to explain it.

Whatever Roosevelt lacked in ideological consistency he tried to make up for with the force of his personality. "A second-class intellect, but a first-class temperament," was the famous judgment rendered by Oliver Wendell Holmes when he first encountered FDR as president-elect in 1933. It was Roosevelt's personality that came to define his presidency. For more than seven years Roosevelt had adjusted his personality to his office and at the same time tailored his office to match his personality until now it was difficult for most Americans to tell where one left off and the other began.

At 58, his handsome, patrician features, regal bearing, and strong, resonant voice all reflected his invincible self-assurance. "He must have been psychoanalyzed by God," a spellbound aide once remarked. This self-confidence stemmed not from therapy but rather from breeding. It was rooted in a privileged upbringing as the only child of an indulgent father, and a doting and domineering mother. His father, James, who was 53 when Franklin was born in 1882, rode to hounds and hosted afternoon teas and formal dinner parties at Springwood, his Hyde Park estate. Franklin's mother, Sara Delano Roosevelt, a tall and stately beauty, was proud of her Huguenot Delano forebears who had set foot in the New World even before the Dutch Roosevelts. "In the past—on both sides of your ancestry—they have a good record and have borne a good name," Franklin was reminded by his father. James Roosevelt was worth about $300,000, hardly more than petty cash when compared to the holdings of some of his Hyde Park neighbors. These included Frederick W. Vanderbilt, who had inherited from his grandfather Commodore Vanderbilt, the shipping and rail tycoon, an estate of more than $70 million, including a lavish Italian Renaissance mansion which dwarfed the seventeen-room home of the Roosevelts. With the exquisite snobbery that comes with old money, the Roosevelts looked down on such *nouveau* ostentation. When he turned down an invitation to the Vanderbilts, James had only to tell Sara: "If we accept we shall have to have them at our house."

Still, the family's own life style was scarcely austere; Franklin had governesses and tutors to polish his manners and drill him on his lessons, and yachts and ponies to enliven the carefree hours at Springwood. By the time he was 15 he had been to Europe eight times, and had been introduced to the likes of Mark Twain and President Grover Cleveland, not to mention his frequent visits with his fifth cousin, Theodore.

By his startling swift ascent of the political heights TR, who was 24 the year Franklin was born and had already won a seat in the New York legislature, demonstrated to Franklin that for a Roosevelt no political goal was unattainable. The trail TR blazed on his way to the White House charted a course for his young cousin to follow—state legislature, assistant secretary of the Navy, governor of New York. In 1907, as a 25-year-old law clerk in New York, while his cousin was finishing his second term in the White House, Franklin confided to his colleagues that he did not intend to pursue the law as a career, but instead had his eye on the presidency. "Any one who is Governor of New York has a good chance to be President with any luck," he remarked.

FDR's equanimity was sustained by an iron will, a quality he had exhibited over and over again in a political lifetime of overcoming adversaries foolish enough to underestimate him. This trait he demonstrated most graphically by refusing to submit to the polio which had threatened to destroy his career. Many believed that his illness, which struck him down when he was approaching his fortieth birthday, heightened his sense of compassion. Whether or not that was actually the case, it did force him to become more focused and less frivolous.

Three years after the onset of the disease he marked his return to national politics, delivering the address nominating New York

Governor Al Smith for President. Roosevelt had slowly made his way down the aisle in Madison Square Garden to the back of the speakers' platform, leaning on his son James and on a crutch. When the time came for FDR's introduction, James handed his father the other crutch and he started for the podium. Roosevelt struggled step by step, his eyes riveted on the floor, sweat running down his forehead. The delegates and galleries watched in silence, remembering the dashing figure Roosevelt had cut four years earlier, when he had been the party's vice-presidential candidate. At last he reached the lectern, set down the crutches, threw back his leonine head and flashed a smile of triumph. Electrified, the crowd gave him a thunderous salute.

The speech itself, memorable chiefly for his dubbing Smith "the happy warrior of the political battlefield," though warmly received, was almost an anti-climax. The presidential election was a disaster for the Democrats but the convention had made Roosevelt one of his party's heroes.

Above all else, he was a master of indirection and misdirection, a gift that helped him to escape the normal penalties for inconsistency and self-contradiction, to appease and assuage his friends and to befuddle and frustrate his foes. "His mind does not follow easily a consecutive chain of thought," his Secretary of War Henry Stimson once noted in his diary, "but he is full of stories and incidents and hops about in his discussions from suggestion to suggestion and it is very much like chasing a vagrant beam of sunshine around a vacant room."

After vainly trying to get a straight answer out of the President on a key appointment, his Interior Secretary Harold Ickes exploded. "You won't talk frankly even with people who are loyal to you and of whose loyalty your are fully convinced," Ickes told Roosevelt. "You keep your cards close up against your belly. You never put them on the table."

Roosevelt cloaked his guile with a personal charm reputed to be so overpowering that some political foes were said to shrink from private encounters with him lest they succumb to his wiles. At Harvard, editor Roosevelt got along so well with other *Crimson* staffers that his co-editor recalled "in his geniality was a kind of frictionless command." His distant cousin, Anna Eleanor Roosevelt, was so captivated by his gaiety and natural ease that she married him in 1905, soon after his graduation from Harvard.

But after a while some found his personality began to wear thin; Tugwell thought that Roosevelt's charm ultimately became "part of a whole apparatus of defense" designed to conceal his true beliefs. "He had a trick of seeming to listen, and to agree or to differ partly and pleasantly, which was flattering," he recalled. "This was more highly developed as he progressed in his career and it was responsible for some misunderstanding. Finally no one could tell what he was *thinking*, to say nothing of what he was *feeling*." (Emphasis in original.)

Among those he shut out of his life was his wife, who discovered that while Franklin was serving as assistant secretary of the Navy, he had been conducting a romance with her part-time secretary, a woman named Lucy Mercer. When Eleanor confronted her husband and threatened him with divorce, he tried to make little of the problem. "Don't be a goose," Roosevelt told his wife.

"I was a goose," the newly awakened Eleanor replied, and refused to back down.

To clinch matters, Roosevelt's mother, Sara, warned she would cut him off financially if he left his wife and children. Roosevelt broke off the relationship, preserving his marriage and his political prospects.[*]

Contributing to Roosevelt's tendency to deceive was his disability, the extent of which he managed to keep from the public. Before his inauguration his longtime political operative, Louis Howe, had inspected the hallways and doorways of the White House, with an eye for avoiding locations where the President in his wheel chair might be exposed to view and to photographs by visitors. He sent Roosevelt's press secretary, Steve Early, to consult with the Chief of Secret Service, Colonel Ed Starling, a veteran of the last months of Woodrow Wilson's presidency when he too had been in a wheel chair. Howe's arrangements helped to insure that most Americans had no more than a dim idea of the severity of the President's condition, that he actually spent most of his waking hours in a wheel chair, that even with his braces he could not stand erect without support, and that even with assistance he could walk only a few yards at the most, usually along a well planned route. A complaisant press corps submitted to the White House ban on pictures of the President in a wheel chair, being lifted out of an auto, or being carried up stairs. When Roosevelt fell in the mud at Philadelphia's Franklin Field, as he was about to deliver his address accepting his party's renomination to the presidency in 1936, Secret Service agents and aides quickly surrounded him, shielding his sprawling figure from the 100,000 onlookers. Pool reporters knew about the incident, but never reported it.

---

*But decades later, after Roosevelt had become President, his old flame, since married and widowed and now known as Lucy Mercer Rutherfurd, came back into his life. The two began seeing each other again in 1941, without Eleanor Roosevelt's knowledge. She was with FDR in Warm Springs, Ga. when he died April 12, 1945.

By the time he ran for a second term, FDR had managed to sweep most complaints about his policy contradictions aside with the power of the beliefs and loyalties that he embodied in his own person. When he met with Moley in May of 1936 to map strategy for the forthcoming campaign, he shrugged off Moley's questions about one of his tax proposals. "That's a detail," Roosevelt said. "There is one issue in this campaign. It's myself, and people must be either for me or against me."

He waged the campaign accordingly. As FDR stumped the country, he forged an emotional bond between himself and his audiences, appealing to their deepest hopes, fears, and resentments, and Roosevelt himself seemed infused by the passion he generated. The apotheosis of Roosevelt as the tribune of the masses came in his last campaign address at Madison Square Garden when he declared. "I should like to have it said of my first administration that in it the forces of selfishness and of lust for power met their match." The response was so thunderous that the President had to shout for silence, before delivering his punch line: "I should like to have it said of my second administration that in it these forces met their master."

In November, his 46-state landslide defied any comparison. Yet his huge majority was built on a quicksand of charisma and contradictory promises. And now Roosevelt had a new adversary, his own hubris. He felt empowered by his victory to confront the Supreme Court which had continually thrown roadblocks in the path of his legislative program. Many had expected this, but no one was prepared for the way Roosevelt went about it. His court-packing scheme, giving him the power to add a new justice to the Court for every one who did not quit after age 70, betrayed two hallmarks of FDR's character: his obsession with secrecy and his bent for artifice. By keeping the strategy to himself he forfeited the chance to mobilize popular support. Then he presented his scheme as a prescription for judicial inefficiency, when everyone knew its real purpose was to reverse the Court's obstinate conservatism. Under these circumstances, the personal appeal which he had relied on was no match for his foes on the Court and in the Congress, each defending their institutional prerogatives.

In the wake of the Court defeat he found himself awash in a tide of misfortune that mocked his reelection triumph. Having successfully defied the supposedly invincible FDR on the court-packing scheme, Congress balked more and more often at the New Deal agenda. Meanwhile, the economy turned down, and before long the dismal statistics gave currency to an ominous new term: Roosevelt Recession.

With his prestige crumbling, FDR struck back. As the 1938 elections approached, he launched a purge against the conservatives in his own party who had been frustrating him in Congress. Throwing all the resources of his office into the struggle, he sought to enlist party professionals in his cause. However, in the 1936 campaign, he had done nothing to lay the groundwork for such an effort. Now he had only his personal appeal to depend on and that was nowhere near enough. Not only did Roosevelt fail in nearly every case to recast his party, the internecine battle weakened the Democrats in the fall struggle against the Republicans, who took full advantage. In November their candidates gained eight Senate seats and 88 more in the House, nearly doubling their strength in that body.

Late in 1938 historian Walter Millis delivered a somber verdict on the New Deal. It had been, he wrote, "reduced to a movement with no program, with no effective political organization, with no vast popular party strength behind it, and with no candidate." As for Roosevelt himself, he seemed nothing more than a lame duck politician who had lost his grip, facing the dead end of his career. In the spring of 1939 a *Fortune* magazine survey showed that little more than one-third of the electorate would support Roosevelt if he ran again.

Then, before the next year was out, the war in Europe erupted, slowly but steadily altering the American political landscape. Now, in the final spring of the second term of Roosevelt's presidency, as the war reached some climactic stage, a critical decision about his country's involvement had been forced upon him by Churchill's appeal for the Navy's old destroyers. In one sense this decision complicated his political future, yet in another sense it offered a breathtaking opportunity. The cause of freedom, intertwined with patriotism, could serve as surrogate for the domestic goals of the early New Deal and kindle the intellectual and emotional spark needed to revitalize his presidency. And the threat of war and aggression could provide the strongest of all possible reasons to justify breaking the third term tradition. To carry this off, he would have to reconcile the conflicting demands of international affairs and domestic politics, never an easy task. What made it even harder was that in all his years in the White House, Roosevelt had done little to prepare the country to deal with the dangers it now faced from abroad.

# The Corkscrew Trail

From room 1702 at Chicago's Congress Hotel one could look out at the splendor of the shops on Michigan Avenue, at the greenery of Grant Park, and beyond that at the gleaming waters of Lake Michigan. But on the first day of July, 1932, the gnarled and wizened figure who was that room's registered occupant had neither time for nor interest in this magnificent view. He was Louis McHenry Howe, a man renowned for his ill temper and slovenly appearance, his political astuteness, and, most important, his total devotion to the advancement of Franklin D. Roosevelt. These last two traits had earned him influence, unmatched by anyone else, even Roosevelt's campaign manager James Farley, with the man whose ambition to be President of the United States had absorbed the past two decades of Howe's sixty-one years on earth.

To visitors to the room it seemed that now that he had come so close to his goal, Howe might not survive to reach it. His shriveled body, racked by asthma and heart disease, was stretched on the floor much of the time as he gasped for air in the stifling Midwest heat. One of his secretaries who encountered him thus fled in tears, crying: "He is dying, the little boss is dying." But a reporter who had known Howe for years reassured her. "Louis Howe has come this far, half alive," he said, "and you know damned well he isn't going to die until he sees Franklin Roosevelt nominated for President."

Though Howe could hardly speak above a whisper, he always answered the phone by his side. It was the sole contact between Roosevelt's forces at the convention and the candidate back in the governor's office in Albany, providing him with a measure of control over the action. Even near extremis, no detail touching on his candidate's fortunes was too trivial to escape his notice. In the midst of the hubbub on the floor, Howe seized the phone and croaked out a new order to one of Roosevelt's whips on the floor: "Tell them to repeat 'Happy Days Are Here Again.' "

It would take more than a song, even an anthem as rousing as the one

Howe himself had selected as FDR's theme song, to bolster the New Yorker's flagging candidacy. All during the months preceding the convention, Howe had charted his candidate's progress on a huge wall map that depicted in various colors the states pledged to the competing candidates for the Democratic nomination. The dominant color on that map even now was the crimson assigned to front runner Roosevelt. While his strength was literally all over the map, trouble loomed for the governor at the trash-littered floor of the convention hall across the street. The root of the problem was the rule requiring that the party's nominee must get not just a simple majority but two-thirds of the votes of the delegates. Established at history's first Democratic convention in 1832, it had been preserved ever since to protect the interests of the South, in effect giving Dixie veto power over the nominee. Intended to assure unity, it had provoked discord. This rule had prevented Al Smith's nomination in 1924 and dragged the convention on for 103 ballots, leading to the compromise choice of corporate attorney John W. Davis and to his subsequent overwhelming defeat. Now this same procedural barrier stood between Roosevelt and the nomination.

The New York Governor had entered the convention far in front of the field with 661 and a half votes out of a total of 1,154. He needed more than 100 additional votes, though, and after three ballots he had gained a mere twenty or so. The anti-Roosevelt alliance, supporting either FDR's old ally and current foe, Al Smith, the party's 1928 standard-bearer, House Speaker John Nance Garner of Texas or several favorite sons, showed no signs of yielding. Waiting in the wings was Newton Baker, Woodrow Wilson's Secretary of War, known for his dedication to Wilson's unfulfilled dream of a League of Nations, now ready to capitalize on Roosevelt's loss of momentum.

This difficulty had been foreseen in advance. Before the first ballot was cast, Louisiana Governor Huey Long, an ardent Roosevelt backer, had phoned the New Yorker's advisers in Albany. "Get him to take a stand in favor of a soldier's bonus," the Kingfish urged. "Otherwise, you haven't got a chance for the nomination." Roosevelt, who was opposed to the bonus as a spendthrift scheme, turned the idea down. Long, never one to mince words, retorted: "You are a gone goose."

In the wake of the results of the first three ballots, the unspoken thought crossed the mind of Sam Rosenman, Counsel to Governor Roosevelt and his chief speech writer, stationed at Roosevelt's side in Albany "that perhaps the Governor was right." To Raymond Moley, with the Roosevelt forces in Chicago, it seemed probable that when the convention was resumed, "a pretty general crackup of the Roosevelt forces would occur." Howe and Farley, though, had a plan for just this exigency. They knew that the man who held the balance of power at the convention was William Randolph Hearst. That aging lord of the press, still driven by imperial ambitions, could sway two large delegations which between them had just enough votes to put Roosevelt over the top. Hearst's own state of California had 44 delegates pledged to Hearst's own choice for the nomination, Speaker of the House, John Nance Garner, while Texas had 46 votes of its own, naturally enough committed to "Cactus Jack" Garner, its favorite son. The key to unlocking those delegations, Howe and Farley reasoned, was Hearst's antipathy to the League of Nations, which he was convinced would lead the U.S. into deleterious entanglements abroad, and consequently to the League's longtime proponent, Newton Baker. The Roosevelt managers got word to Hearst that unless Texas and California switched to FDR, his candidacy would collapse, the convention would likely turn to Baker, and the Democratic Party would fall under his internationalist spell.

To help seal the deal, his managers gave to Hearst a promise that would resonate through Roosevelt's first years in the White House. Roosevelt, they assured the publisher through his agent in Chicago, Joseph Willicombe, would not meddle in Europe, would steer away from the temptations of international agreements. For good measure, they pledged to give the vice-presidential nomination to Hearst's own favorite, "Cactus Jack" of Texas. The bargain was struck, and just before dinner, Howe phoned the news to Albany. FDR muttered only a few words into the phone—"Good, fine, excellent"—and hung up. As he sat back to listen to events in Chicago unfold, his secretary, Missy Lehand, remarked: "F.D., you look like the cat that swallowed the canary."

In Chicago, the fourth roll call of the states soon reached the California delegation, whose chairman, William Gibbs McAdoo, came forward to the podium. "California came here to nominate a President of the United States," he said. Then, in an allusion to the 1924 debacle, he added: "She did not come here to deadlock this convention." Shouting over the boos of Roosevelt's foes, McAdoo declared: "California casts forty-four votes for Franklin D. Roosevelt."

"Good old McAdoo," Roosevelt cheerfully remarked in Albany, as the Californian's words boomed out over the radio. He might have added: "Good old Hearst."

The assurances to Hearst not to get involved in European affairs foretold the pattern that Roosevelt would follow throughout his presidency of tailoring his stands on foreign policy to serve his immediate political interest, causing him increasing difficulty in the years to come. By the time of the convention that pattern was already well established. It had begun with another and more explicit concession Roosevelt provided to Hearst months before, without which the deal at the convention probably could never have been consummated.

That compromise sacrificed the League of Nations, which FDR had stoutly championed as Democratic vice-presidential candidate in 1920 and which Hearst had bitterly fought since Woodrow Wilson first proposed it. As the 1932 campaign approached, Hearst could readily see that thanks to the Great Depression, circumstances favored the Democrats winning the White House for the first time in the postwar era. Fearful that the election of the wrong Democrat might rekindle efforts to enlist the U.S. in the dreaded League, Hearst cast about to find a Democrat to his own liking.

He settled on Garner of Texas. Not only did Cactus Jack vehemently oppose American involvement in the League, he was also against such other internationalist fallacies as canceling the World War I debts of Britain and France, former allies now hard pressed by the global Depression. Not content with the power of his national chain of newspapers, Hearst bought radio time to boost his candidate. "Unless we Americans are willing to go on laboring indefinitely merely to provide loot for Europe," he declared, "we should personally see to it that a man is elected to the Presidency this year whose guiding motto is 'America First.' " That man, he said, was Garner—"a loyal American, a plain man of the plain people."

In the editorial barrage that followed, while heaping praise on Garner, Hearst also denounced Roosevelt, citing Roosevelt's enthusiastic support of the League when he campaigned for Vice President in 1920. In Georgia, Roosevelt supporters sent word to Farley that Hearst had instructed his local staffers "to get up interviews against Roosevelt" with a particular eye on appealing to "the old Tom Watson element" in the party, whose hearts still beat in tune to the xenophobia of nineteenth-century Southern populism. At first Roosevelt tried to overlook the assaults. Howe, though, feared Hearst could not be ignored. His newspapers reached 16 million readers in every large city across the land; his magazines sold 30 million copies. "This is bad ball," Howe warned Roosevelt. "You may have to make a public statement before we get through, if this thing gets any more violent."

Adding to the pressure on FDR, Wilson's old ally and longtime backer of the League, Newton Baker, had publicly declared that he would not seek to introduce the question of U.S. membership into the

League into the forthcoming campaign. While he still maintained his support of the League, Baker promised that even if he were President, he would not take the U.S. into the League, until there was "a convinced majority sentiment" backing the idea. The net result of this bit of sidestepping, the *New York Times* observed, was to render Baker "much more available as a candidate with the practical Democratic politicians." That fine point did not escape Roosevelt, either. Hoping to dispose of the problem quietly, he dispatched Farley to assure the editor of Hearst's flagship paper in the East, the New York *American*, that the charges of internationalism against FDR were false. Hearst was unimpressed. "If Mr. Roosevelt has any statement to make about his not now being an internationalist he should make it to the public publicly, and not to me privately," he insisted in a page one editorial.

Three days later, FDR caved in. In his response to Hearst, which he managed to sandwich into a speech on boosting agricultural exports to the local grange, the Governor recalled his vigorous support of American participation in the League during the 1920 campaign. For this, he had no apology. "But the League of Nations today is not the League conceived by Woodrow Wilson," Roosevelt contended. Instead of the force for world peace that Wilson had foreseen, the League had become "a mere meeting place for the political discussion of strictly political national difficulties."

So much for the League. What the world needed today, asserted Roosevelt, was greater recognition of the importance of honoring international agreements, most certainly including war debts. Then, in a conclusion calculated to race the heart of every jingoist, he declared: "Europe owes us. We do not owe her." His statement appeared to grant Hearst exactly what he had wanted, as skeptical journalists quickly noticed. Liberal commentator Elmer Davis called Roosevelt "a man who thinks that the shortest distance between two points is not a straight line but a corkscrew." Taking a harsh view of Roosevelt's "acrobatics," the *New York Herald Tribune* contrasted FDR's repudiation of the League with the milder thrust of the statement by Baker who, the paper argued, "certainly showed more sincerity and we suspect lost less by his realism than has the Governor by his recantation."

Roosevelt did pay a short-term price for his *volte face*. He had to endure the sarcasm of Republicans like the isolationist bulwark Idaho Senator William Borah, who was reminded of the biblical admonition: "Repent ye, for the kingdom of heaven is at hand." Borah added: "I presume the Governor is seeking the Kingdom of Heaven in the Presidency." In addition, he had certainly upset some of his own early supporters, particularly longtime Wilsonian loyalists like Colonel Edward M. House, who had been the closest of all confidantes to the last Democratic President. House was even more perturbed by word from Howe that to ingratiate himself further with Hearst, Roosevelt was prepared to follow up his renunciation of the League with a similar statement about U.S. membership in the World Court, which like the League he had long advocated. House warned FDR about the reaction to such a move among "your most ardent and influential friends." The League statement, House said, "has already strained their loyalty and many of them have told me that if you take the same position on the World Court they cannot support you."

As it turned out, FDR refrained from disavowing his previous support of U.S. membership in the Court, Hearst did not press the matter, and House and other supporters stuck with Roosevelt. After all, the controversy over the League stirred up by Hearst was somewhat hypothetical. No practicing politician thought there was a realistic chance of the U.S. entering the League any time in the near future.

What were the results of this bargain? On the credit side, by rejecting the League, the New York governor had gained support for his candidacy among Democrats in the South and West where the foundation of his strength was emerging. Montana Senator Burton K. Wheeler, who in later years would bitterly oppose FDR's efforts to aid Great Britain against Hitler, but who in 1930 had been the first prominent Democrat to endorse Roosevelt for President, now found fresh reason to praise him. Kudos also came from Tennessee Senator Kenneth McKellar who hailed Roosevelt for "speaking out plainly."

Meanwhile Roosevelt's budding liaison with Hearst was generating significant long-term side effects. During the pre-convention period in 1932, the role of his emissary to Hearst had been assumed by one of Roosevelt's new supporters from the ranks of business, Joseph P. Kennedy. In May, the *New York Times* noted that a Kennedy meeting with Roosevelt, hard on the heels of a Kennedy visit with Hearst in California "had excited some attention." As well it might. For Kennedy had brought back encouraging word from Hearst, whose isolationist views he shared and who greatly admired Kennedy's achievements as a financier. Mollified by Roosevelt's February assault on the League, Hearst gave Kennedy to understand that as long as Roosevelt avoided any statements on foreign affairs which might offend the publisher's sensibilities, Hearst would not lash out against the New Yorker. That eased the concern among Roosevelt's strategists that Hearst would seek to mobilize the Garner delegates in California and Texas in a drive to stop Roosevelt. To maintain this detente with "W. R.," Kennedy kept in touch with the publisher for the rest of the spring and early summer. At the convention in Chicago, among all the Roosevelt agents trying to reach Hearst it was Kennedy whose call got through. "If Roosevelt cracks on the next ballot," he warned Hearst, "it'll be Baker." And later it was Kennedy to whom Hearst entrusted his contribution to the Roosevelt campaign treasury. Although many people helped to pave the way for Hearst's support of Roosevelt, Kennedy was characteristically immodest about his own role. The debt he established with FDR would ultimately lead to his appointment as ambassador to the Court of St. James at a fateful hour in the relations between the U.S. and Great Britain.

Neither Roosevelt nor Howe could have foreseen all these events back in February when the Grange speech was delivered. But the potential implications of Roosevelt's words were clear even then. He was striving to ensure that if the struggle for the Democratic nomination should deadlock, Hearst, rather than join the anti-Roosevelt forces, would regard him as an acceptable compromise. It was a shrewd calculation. Roosevelt's reward for rejecting the League, and turning his back on his Wilsonian past, was the smoothing of his path to the White House.

But the other side of the equation, though harder to calculate was nevertheless also of importance. By giving in to Hearst on the League of Nations, Roosevelt lost a major opportunity. He could have rebutted the growing suspicion voiced by Lippman and others that he was too ready to sacrifice principle on the altar of expediency. Moreover, had he been willing to risk Hearst's ire, Roosevelt could also have used the occasion to argue that American self-interest was dependent on the welfare of other nations, particularly its longtime friends in Western Europe. This was an assertion that would have stood him in good stead throughout the 1930s.

Though the speech to the Grange was only one address in a year filled with rhetoric, Roosevelt's rejection of the League presaged the direction he would take in the campaign to come and for his early years in the White House. With the nomination in hand, FDR had little more to say on foreign policy and nothing of comfort to offer to apostles of Wilson's version of internationalism and the League.

Political realities ruled out a major Roosevelt foreign policy speech in the view of his campaign advisers. "Public interest was at a low point," they reasoned, as Raymond Moley recalled, and any statement of his beliefs "would likely cost him more undecided votes than it would make for him." Their candidate was already sure of the West and Middle West, where his neo-isolationist views "would be immensely popular," while as Moley pointed out, "there was no advantage in alienating those Eastern elements which would shy at his policies."

This stance on foreign policy sharply contrasted with the basic outlook that had been a hallmark of Roosevelt's first two decades in public life derived from his early upbringing. From childhood on he had been deeply absorbed by geography, an interest encouraged by his stamp collection, and his travels. Even before he reached adulthood he had toured Europe several times, the first when he was three years old, more often than he had been to the Midwest of his own country. By the time he ran for the presidency he had visited twenty-nine foreign countries and had lived nearly three years of his life abroad. Long before he became assistant secretary of the Navy, the sea had captured his imagination. This fascination, which began with toy boats he had sailed as a child gained an intellectual framework from the works of Alfred Thayer Mahan who constructed a strategic *Weltanschauung* built on sea power. Roosevelt was 11 when he first read Mahan's *History of Sea Power* and he pored over the work intensively until, his mother recalled, "he practically memorized the whole book." He was so caught up with the bold new talk of American expansionism that when the Spanish-American War broke out, though he was still at Groton, he tried to run away and enlist but his plans were foiled by an outbreak of the measles.

At Springwood, the family estate in Hyde Park, European periodicals were always in evidence and visitors familiar with Europe and Asia were often on hand. The youthful Roosevelt could claim command of French and German along with a smattering of Italian and Spanish. His forebears on his mother's side had been celebrated maritimers, in the forefront of U.S. trade with China, and FDR's pride in their exploits engendered a feeling of kinship with the Chinese. This was the explanation he offered privately when, as president-elect, he made a rare departure from his avoidance of problems abroad by tacitly supporting outgoing Secretary of State Henry Stimson's policy of denying recognition to the Japanese seizure of Manchuria from China. "I have always had the deepest sympathy for the Chinese," he told a startled Raymond Moley. "How could you expect me not to go along with Stimson on Japan?"

A far more important family influence, of course, was cousin Theodore, whose own expansionist view of America's world role seemed to serve as a coda to FDR's early career. "Whether we wish it or not," the first President Roosevelt had declared, "we are a great peo-

ple and must play a great part in the world." Running for the vice presidency in 1920, Franklin Roosevelt sought to mimic TR both in style
and substance, not always with great success. Many viewed the 38-
year-old FDR as merely a jejune facsimile of his distinguished relative,
who had passed away the year before. "Franklin is as much like
Theodore as a clam is like a bear cat," jeered the *Chicago Tribune*. "If
he is Theodore Roosevelt, Elihu Root is Gene Debs and Bryan is a
brewer."

In his eagerness to emulate TR's Big Stick diplomacy, FDR sometimes forgot his idol's admonition to also speak softly, causing himself
considerable embarrassment on at least one occasion. Trying to promote the League of Nations, Roosevelt argued that if the U.S. joined, it
would be able to count on the support of its smaller neighbors in the
Caribbean. And in a clumsy effort to emphasize his point, he bragged of
the influence he had wielded as assistant secretary of the Navy. "You
know I have had something to do with the running of a couple of little
Republics," he asserted. "The facts are that I wrote Haiti's Constitution
myself and, if I do say it, I think it's a pretty good constitution."

Aside from its crudity, Roosevelt's boast was off the mark. Assistant
Navy Secretary Roosevelt's involvement in Haiti had been limited to a
brief visit there during the U.S. occupation in 1917. And he had never
contributed as much as a comma to the Haitian national charter.
Republican standard-bearer Warren Harding called Roosevelt's statement "shocking," and Roosevelt in his discomfort could think of no better response than to claim he had been misquoted by the Associated
Press. This only worsened matters when supporters of both parties who
had been present signed a statement backing the AP's story.

Haiti aside, Roosevelt's role at the Navy Department allowed him to
demonstrate the activism that characterized his famous forebear and
which would be tested a quarter of a century later. Shortly after the U.S.
entered World War I, in April of 1917, the U.S. Navy learned from the
British Admiralty that German U-boats were sinking Allied merchantmen faster than they could be replaced. Though the British Isles were
on the verge of starvation and defeat, the Royal Navy did not have
enough destroyers to assign to convoy duty without putting its own
warships in grave jeopardy. At meetings with Allied missions that
month Roosevelt urged America's new allies to prod Wilson into giving
them all the help they needed, just as he himself would be urged by
Churchill a generation later. Ultimately Assistant Navy Secretary
Roosevelt promised the British thirty U.S. destroyers to combat the U-
boat menace at the Western approaches. Though he made his pledge

with nothing more than his own none too magisterial authority as a sub-cabinet official, the promise was kept.

On the campaign trail in 1920, Roosevelt and Democratic standard-bearer James Cox went all out for U.S. membership in the League. This delighted the Republicans, who were convinced Americans detested the idea. The truth was that most voters were indifferent. The dominant issue of the election—and the main reason for Warren Harding's land-slide victory—was not the League, but the public's weariness with Wilson after eight years. At any rate, by 1924 the Democrats had backed away from their commitment to the League. Instead the plat-form merely called for a national referendum on the issue. Ducking the League issue, however, was of small help given the Democrats' other troubles that year. Their national convention was bitterly divided over prohibition and the Catholicism of New York Governor Al Smith, whose name Roosevelt had placed in nomination. It took 103 ballots to select an ineffective compromise candidate, corporate lawyer John W. Davis, who went down to an ignominious defeat.

Similarly in 1928 Smith, after finally gaining the nomination, chose to steer clear of further controversy. He had little to say about foreign policy. Roosevelt, though, had different priorities that year. His cam-paign for Governor of New York signaled the rebirth of his presidential ambitions and endowed his views on foreign policy with new signifi-cance. Responding to an invitation from *Foreign Affairs* to offer "A Democratic View" on foreign policy, Roosevelt without directly advo-cating American membership in the League nevertheless praised it as "the principal agency" for settling international disputes. "We Democrats . . . do not believe in the possibility or the desirability of an isolated national existence," he declared.

This view represented a moderation of the beliefs espoused by vice-presidential candidate Roosevelt in 1920. But it was a far greater shift from his 1928 article, with its praise for the League and its stress on international cooperation, to his 1932 Grange speech with its sharp rejection of the League and its harsh insistence that America's old allies clear up their debts. At the time, Roosevelt sought to minimize the sig-nificance of his rejection of the League, arguing that he was still devot-ed to the internationalist principles espoused by Woodrow Wilson. "Have you ever stopped to consider that there is a difference between ideals and the methods of attaining them?" he wrote one querulous admirer. "Ideals do not change but methods do change with every gen-eration and world circumstance." Roosevelt's method of responding to Hearst, however, had been chosen not to fulfill ideals but rather to attain power. And once in power, it would become increasingly difficult to see the connection between his methods and the ideals on international affairs to which he still professed loyalty.

Roosevelt's shift on the League of Nations drummed up support from many isolationists—not only from his own party, such as Montana's Wheeler and Tennessee's McKellar, but also from Republican ranks. Weary of President Hoover's stubborn passivity in the face of the Depression, Republican Senators Robert La Follette of Wisconsin, Hiram Johnson of California, and George Norris of Nebraska, all with strong ties to the old Progressive Party, backed Roosevelt outright. Others, such as the redoubtable Borah of Idaho, who had mocked Roosevelt's reversal on the League earlier in the year, and Gerald P. Nye, a combative Senate newcomer from North Dakota, indirectly boosted Roosevelt's candidacy by refusing to endorse Hoover. Though campaign year pressures forged the alliance between Roosevelt and the isolationists in both parties, this marriage of political convenience endured well beyond election day. For most of his first term no group backed the New Deal president more dependably and to no group was he more responsive than to the coalition dedicated to the proposition that America should keep its distance from the rest of the world.

Rooted deep in the country's history, American isolationism was buttressed by the Monroe Doctrine. This self-centered outlook on the world prevailed well into the nineteenth century when it gained new adherents with sometimes sharply contradictory beliefs. Most embittered were the populist farmers from the South and West, resentful of the British financial interests whom they viewed as allied with the much-reviled Eastern bankers. More benign but no less impassioned were the pacifists and social reformers who saw international involvement as leading to war. Not only did they regard war an evil in itself but they also denounced it as a corrupting influence on society and a diversion from the efforts to deal with social and economic problems at home. From these two groups in both parties Roosevelt found his first-term isolationist allies. Their votes helped transform into law New Deal plans to benefit farmers, small businessmen, and workers and to restrain the excesses of big business and finance through regulations and taxes. They freely lent support on domestic issues, in large part because they knew they could usually count on having Roosevelt as a silent, and sometimes reluctant, partner on foreign policy.

Enactment of the Johnson Act of 1934, banning Americans from making loans to nations that had defaulted on war debts, typified the collaboration between FDR and the isolationists. By the time Roosevelt

entered the White House, Johnson, then in his late sixties, had been a
towering figure in American politics for more than two decades. His
only defeat had come as vice-presidential candidate on Theodore
Roosevelt's Bull Moose ticket in 1912. In 1916 he won election to the
Senate where he had remained ever since, a thorn in the flank of those
whom TR had branded as "malefactors of great wealth." Johnson's proposed loan prohibition was born more out of his zeal for curbing the
power of the bankers and financiers, who he believed had profited
greatly from World War I, than from the widespread resentment of
Britain and France's failure to pay off their World War I debts.

While the debate on the measure swirled around Capitol Hill, the
President kept his silence. Although Johnson and other backers avoid-
ed saying that they had the President's support, they believed, as
Johnson put it privately, that Roosevelt "really favored the bill" to use
"as a weapon in dealing with these European welshers." The British
Ambassador Sir John Lindsay reached the same conclusion after
Johnson's proposal. As Sir John reported to London, the bill had passed
"without any opposition, with perfecting amendments proposed by the
State Department and with the Administration leaders of the Chamber
standing by in favorable neutrality, all circumstances combining to indicate an absence of opposition by the White House." Few doubts about
the President's real position remained when, shortly after signing the
bill in April 1934, he invited Johnson and his wife to the White House
for dinner and later favored Mrs. Johnson with an autographed picture
of himself.

For all of that good feeling, Johnson and Roosevelt soon found themselves nominally on the opposite side of another foreign policy controversy, one that had even more importance, at least symbolically: the
issue of U.S. membership in the World Court, which Roosevelt had
long favored but which he had considered abandoning in 1932 in order
to placate Hearst. By the end of his second year in the White House he
was ready to make a fight for the Court, but only up to a point. In fact,
even as he gave the State Department the green light to press for membership when the 69th Congress convened in 1935, he confided to
Senator Johnson, who of course bitterly opposed the idea, that he was
acting mainly to avoid conflict with his party's platform.

That was all Johnson had to hear. He took the field against the Court
and soon gained as allies Hearst, who pulled out all the editorial stops
in his newspapers against the Court, and the fiery Father Charles
Coughlin, who appealed to millions over the radio from his headquarters in a Detroit suburb. When the final vote came on January 29, 1935,

the World Court resolution fell seven votes short of the two-thirds majority it needed. Defeat left Roosevelt duly resentful. If the Senators who voted against the Court ever got to Heaven, he wrote Senate Foreign Relations Committee chairman Joseph Robinson, "they will be doing a great deal of apologizing, for a very long time—that is if God is against war and I think he is." Such high-minded indignation had a nice ring to it. But if Roosevelt saw the defeat of the Court proposal increasing the threat of war, as his letter to Robinson suggested, he might have sounded the alarm publicly. He had not. Instead, he had sent a message to the Senate backing the Court resolution only five paragraphs long and framed in legalistic terms.

In addition to aiding the isolationists by default on the World Court, Roosevelt was directly instrumental in their greatest triumph of his first term, the Senate probe into the munitions industry. This three-year-long inquisition, conducted by North Dakota's Gerald Nye, dramatically reflected and reinforced public disillusionment with the U.S. role in World War I. Nye's beliefs were shaped by the activist tradition of LaFollette style progressivism in Wisconsin, where he was born and raised, and by the agrarian radicalism of the Non-Partisan League of North Dakota, where his political career was launched. Entering the Senate in 1925 as a Republican when he was in his early thirties, he had rebelled against the conservatism of GOP Presidents Coolidge and Hoover and found more attractive the liberal reforms of Democrat Roosevelt. No stodgy Plainsman, Nye was known in the Senate for his well tailored dark suits and flashy ties, his energy, and his boldness. He was recruited by pacifist groups to launch the investigation in part because of his critical view of big business and in part because he was the only senator willing to take on the challenge. Where his colleagues saw risk, Nye saw opportunity. With Roosevelt's help, he cashed in.

As always Roosevelt was loath to give offense to the isolationists and reluctant to ignore the public agitation for some such inquiry. Early in 1934, he told the Senate that he was "gratified" that the committee had been appointed, recommended that it "receive the generous support of the Senate" and promised the full cooperation of the executive branch. The president was as good as his word, ensuring that the committee got nearly all the government records it wanted, including income tax returns. And in a lengthy private meeting he told committee members that he sympathized with their cause, even adding, according to some accounts, that he favored the elimination of the aviation industry because of its potential for destructiveness if a new war should break out.

With this backing, the hard-driving Nye sent his hearings into high gear, calling scores of witnesses from the ranks of corporate America, among them the DuPonts and J. P. Morgan, and earning reams of newspaper coverage. Nye himself went on the lecture circuit, where time and again he underlined what he considered the main lesson of the hearings: "The profits of preparation for war and the profits of war itself constitute the most serious challenge to the peace of the world." Ultimately Nye devised a twelve-point plan to tax the profits out of war, which Roosevelt in part endorsed.

Nothing came of the war profit taxes proposal but the powerful impact of the hearings did lead to the enactment, starting in 1935, of so-called neutrality legislation, which, as Hull later wrote, would tie the Administration's hands as the threat of war emerged abroad. "It tangled our relations with the very nations whom we should have been morally supporting," the Secretary of State complained. The early debate on neutrality legislation was shaped by mounting pressure from isolationists for a ban on arms shipment abroad in the event of war. Roosevelt proposed that Congress give him the right to impose the ban only on aggressor nations while continuing to supply countries acting in self-defense. The isolationists on Capitol Hill refused to grant this discretion, however, and Roosevelt signed the bill anyway, reasoning that it could be amended in six months when the embargo provision expired. More important than the details of the law was its signal that the U.S. would stand aside from the world's turmoil. Two months after the embargo went into effect, in August 1935 Italy invaded Ethiopia, aided by imports of U.S. oil and other raw materials not covered by the embargo on arms.

Roosevelt's hopes of gaining discretionary power over the embargo in 1936 were dashed and he had to settle for a simple one-year renewal of the all inclusive ban. A week after the President signed the embargo extension, Hitler repudiated the 1925 Locarno Treaty under which Germany and France had pledged not to attack each other. The Führer sent German troops into the Rhineland in violation of the Treaty of Versailles. As Hitler had foreseen, Britain and France did nothing. In the U.S. these events heightened cynicism about European affairs and strengthened the isolationist position. Certainly the Roosevelt Administration offered no argument to the contrary. Hull refused a French appeal to condemn Hitler's action on moral grounds. That June the platform adopted by the Democratic convention that renominated Roosevelt might have been written by Gerald Nye himself. It pledged "to work for peace, to take the profits out of war, to guard against being drawn, by political commitments, international banking, or private trading, into any war that may develop anywhere."

This was the foreign policy route Roosevelt had been following since his Grange Speech four years before, amidst the domestic successes of the New Deal climaxed by his triumphant reelection in 1936. But soon after his second term began, events at home and abroad forced him to veer off course into uncharted seas. On the domestic front his misguided effort to recast the Supreme Court undermined his alliance with the progressive isolationists. They were repelled by what they regarded as a dangerous aggrandizement of executive power. At the same time, the economic slump and the failed purge of conservative Democrats robbed the New Deal of the momentum for domestic reform which had been the underlying justification for Roosevelt's isolationist policies and which had cemented his alliance with the isolationists. But the greatest pressure on Roosevelt came from the growing threat of aggression overseas. In his response Roosevelt followed no consistent set of beliefs or values. Many of his actions and much of his rhetoric seemed superficial, guided mainly by short-term political interests, and occasionally by personal whim. Now and then he displayed an awareness of the profound problems that were developing abroad, but only rarely did he offer a coherent response. It was a harum-scarum approach that left the country confused and divided by the ominous march of events abroad.

The danger was worldwide and loomed across both oceans that guarded U.S. neutrality. While Hitler hastened his military buildup in Europe, following his unchallenged thrust into the Rhineland, in the East Japan struck at China, igniting a struggle that was to last nearly a decade and spread across the Pacific before its apocalyptic end nearly a decade later. Meanwhile the U.S. handcuffed itself with yet another Neutrality Act, signed by Roosevelt in May of 1937, which once again reflected the influential impact of the Nye Committee. The law banned not only arms shipments to belligerents but loans to warring nations as well as making it illegal for Americans to travel on their ships. To ease the blow on American exports, the 1937 act contained a so-called cash-and-carry provision, giving the President authority to allow sales of nonmilitary material to belligerents who paid for it in advance and hauled it on their own ships. Mocking the retrospective reasoning underlying the legislation, the New York *Herald Tribune* called it "an act to preserve the United States from Intervention in the War of 1914–18."

In October of 1937, groping for a more effective answer to the new war in Asia and to the escalating threat from Hitler, Roosevelt delivered his first major foreign policy address since his reelection, accusing a few unnamed countries of "threatening a breakdown of all international law and order." Likening this to "an epidemic of physical disaster," he seemed to call for "a quarantine" of aggressor nations.

It was by far the most dramatic foreign policy pronouncement of Roosevelt's presidency until that time and captured attention around the world. At the League of Nations in Geneva, where a response to the Japanese attack was under debate, "its effect was instantaneous and put an end to considerable shilly shally that was going on," Jay Pierrepont Moffat, head of the State Department's newly created division of European affairs, recorded in his diary. The next day, the League General Assembly voted to condemn the Japanese attack and issued a call for a multi-nation conference on the Far East.

At home the early reaction was also favorable; Moffat likened it to "a burst of applause." Of the first flood of letter and telegrams to the President, 423 supported the speech whole, only 74 were in opposition. Major newspapers across the land, from the *Los Angeles Times* and the *San Francisco Chronicle* to the *Christian Science Monitor* and the *New York Times*, welcomed the speech as a sign of a stronger U.S. foreign policy. The *Chicago Tribune* and the Hearst press were hostile, but they were clearly in the minority.

The problem was, though, that neither the President's supporters nor his critics nor apparently the President himself knew exactly what he meant by "quarantine." Many people supposed that what he had in mind at the least was some form of economic sanctions against the Japanese, since anything less would render his statement meaningless. Roosevelt himself scotched that idea, though, during an off-the-record exchange with reporters the day after his speech.

"Look, 'sanctions' is a terrible word to use," he said. "They are out of the window."[*]

What about a peace conference? he was asked.

But that idea, too was "out of the window," the President said. "You never get anywhere with a conference."

---

[*]Two months later, after Japanese bombers attacked and sank the U.S. gunboat *Panay* in the Yangtze River, Roosevelt took a different view of the meaning of quarantine, in the privacy of a Cabinet meeting. When Vice President Garner argued that only force would make an impression on the Japanese, Roosevelt said economic sanctions could be effective. "We don't call them economic sanctions; we call them quarantines," he explained. "We want to develop a technique which will not lead to war. We want to be as smart as Japan and as Italy. We want to do it in a modern way."

When pressed, he referred reporters to the concluding words of his speech: "America hates war. America hopes for peace. Therefore America actively engages in the search for peace."

This of course explained nothing. But the President dropped the subject, disheartening and disillusioning his early supporters and leaving the field to Hearst and other isolationists who continued to denounce the speech.

As the world drifted toward war in his second term, Roosevelt's responses to foreign policy challenges lacked any unifying framework. Instead the President's actions and rhetoric reflected his penchant for personal dealings, behind-the-scenes maneuvering and grandiose schemes. Thus, right after the failure of the quarantine speech, he seized upon an idea advanced by Undersecretary of State Sumner Welles: to summon all the diplomatic representatives in Washington to a meeting with the president on Armistice Day to hammer out the fundamentals of a plan for international peace.

Hull, who resented Welles's influence with FDR anyway, was convinced that the plan, which made no provision for advance consultation with the British or French, was unrealistic and tried to squelch it. But FDR pursued the idea with British Prime Minister Neville Chamberlain. As he noted in his diary, Chamberlain thought the idea was "fantastic and likely to excite the derision of Germany and Italy." Fearful of offending the United States with an outright rejection, Chamberlain tactfully dragged his feet until Roosevelt finally abandoned the notion.

Even the inhibitions of the Constitution did not impede Roosevelt's imagination. Later in 1937, after the Japanese attack on the U.S. gunboat *Panay* in December, FDR raised the possibility with the British of mounting a joint blockade of Japan as a way to stop Japanese aggression without going to war. Ambassador Lindsay, who told London that Roosevelt was in "his worst inspirational mood," pointed out that the Japanese, instead of docilely knuckling under, would likely regard a blockade as an act of war, in accordance with the tenets of international law. Roosevelt claimed, on what grounds he did not explain, that doctrines about what constituted war were changing, allowing one nation to blockade another without officially becoming a belligerent. He also advanced the dubious contention that ordering such a blockade would be within his prerogatives as Chief Executive.

By the fall of 1938 the flashpoint of war had shifted to Central Europe where Hitler, having swallowed up Austria by imposing *Anschluss*, was menacing Czechoslovakia, demanding that the tiny country yield its heavily German Sudetenland to the Third Reich. Once again Roosevelt had a plan, or rather two alternative plans, intended to combat the threat from Hitler, which he passed on to the British. If war over the Sudetenland could be averted, Roosevelt proposed a world conference to lay the groundwork for long-term peace. He himself would attend if the conference could be held outside Europe, say in the Azores. If Britain and France did go to war, FDR suggested that the Allies limit their operations to blockading Germany, perhaps not even formally declaring war. As Roosevelt explained to Ambassador Lindsay, if such a strategy could be presented as a "humanitarian" move, designed to avoid the normal toll of war, it would win the favor of the American public. This in turn would help him to circumvent the Neutrality Act's ban on selling arms to belligerents so that he could ship arms to the allies. Roosevelt added the warning to Lindsay that if word of his plan leaked out, "he would almost certainly be impeached and the suggestion would be hopelessly prejudiced." This secret ploy also came to naught.

Whatever the merits of these hypothetical schemes, Roosevelt displayed more boldness and imagination in concocting them than he did when he confronted a real crisis in the fall of 1938 over Hitler's demands on Czechoslovakia. In the course of a message to the Führer urging the continuation of negotiations between Germany and Britain and France, the President assured the dictator that the United States had "no political involvements in Europe" and "would assume no obligations for the conduct of the present negotiations." This made clear to Hitler that he had nothing to fear from the nation that had fought World War I to keep the world safe for democracy. The next day, responding to word that Chamberlain had accepted Hitler's invitation to meet with him at Munich, Roosevelt sent the British Prime Minister a two-word cable of congratulations: "Good man." Once the Munich parley concluded with the agreement by Britain and France to allow Hitler to dismember Czechoslovakia, all the President's concern about the threat of German aggression seemed to melt away. "I fully share your hope and belief that there exists today the greatest opportunity in years for the establishment of a new order based on peace and law," he cabled Chamberlain.

The optimistic glow generated by Munich soon faded, however. Within a month of the signing of the agreement Roosevelt was asking a visiting British politician to assure Chamberlain when he returned to London that he could count on having "the industrial resources of the American nation behind him in the event of war with the dictatorships," depending of course on the President's ability to manage this. He wanted Chamberlain "to know that privately," the President said, but he "couldn't say it publicly." Chamberlain, taking the assurance for what it was worth, did not put great stock in it.

The subsequent tension-filled months would provide other examples of discrepancies between Roosevelt's public approach to the threat of war and what he said and did privately. His most emphatic public statement came in his message to Congress in January of 1939 when he called for "methods short of war but stronger and more effective than mere words" in meeting the threat of aggression. He offered no specifics, though, nor did he follow up to heighten public reaction to his tough language.

Meanwhile, though, he had assigned Treasury Secretary Henry Morgenthau to conduct secret negotiations for warplanes with the French. They wanted to purchase 1,000 aircraft from the U.S. to help make up for their numerical disadvantage against Hitler's *Luftwaffe*. That idea drew protests from the War Department, which was desperately trying to build up the United States' own puny air force. But pressed by Morgenthau, who argued that the French along with the British made up "our first line of defense," in late December of 1938 Roosevelt approved the idea of dealing with the French, provided their orders did not interfere with shipments to the U.S. Army Air Corps. This, he stressed to Morgenthau, "for reasons of state should be kept as confidential as possible," a point Morgenthau impressed upon Jean Monnet, the head of the French purchasing mission. Monnet readily agreed.

A month later, the veil of secrecy was torn away in spectacular fashion. A newly designed Douglas bomber, which the French were interested in buying, crashed on a test flight in Los Angeles, killing the pilot and badly injuring a French observer. A great outcry went up as the press and Congress demanded to know why the Frenchman was on the plane, since Federal law prohibited the sale of U.S. military aircraft to foreign powers. Technically the ban did not cover the destroyed plane since it was still the property of Douglas. That was a distinction, though, not likely to matter much to outraged isolationists on Capitol Hill. They grasped the fact that the President was going behind the back of Congress to entangle the U.S. abroad and was putting into foreign hands warplanes needed for America's own defense, to boot.

To still the uproar, Roosevelt invited the members of the Senate Military Affairs Committee, which had launched a full-scale probe of the incident, to an extraordinary meeting at the White House.

Signifying the importance and sensitivity of the meeting, Roosevelt took the highly unusual step of ordering that the discussion be transcribed. During its lengthy and rambling course, the President asserted that the United States had to confront "a policy of world domination between Germany, Italy and Japan," which he traced back to the signing of the anti-Comintern pact in 1936. The key to defense against the Japanese, the President said, was the ability of the armed forces to hold a chain of islands in the Pacific. On the other side of the world, he said, "our first line is the continued independent existence of a very large group of nations," and he ticked off nearly a score of countries, stretching from Britain and France on the west across Poland in Central Europe all the way to Turkey and Persia on the east.

Of these, the two most important to the United States were Britain and France. "We don't want France to have to yield to this, that and the other thing, because if France yields and England yields, there won't be any independent nation in Europe or Africa or anywhere else," the President told his guests. Getting down to cases, FDR weighed the chances of Britain and France in a war against Germany and Italy. "We cannot assume they will defeat Germany and Italy," he said. "It is a fifty-fifty bet that they would be put out of business and that Hitler and Mussolini would win." If the two Axis powers prevailed, he said, it would be primarily because of their vast superiority in air power. Therefore, the President said, it certainly behooved the U.S. to help build up France's air force. In the first place, Roosevelt contended, as he told the French, "our factories at the present time are idle. If you put your orders in now they will be substantially completed before our orders get in this spring to come." In the second place, Roosevelt continued "it is to our interest, quite frankly, to do what we can, absolutely as a matter of peace, peace of the world, to help the French and British maintain their independence."

"Mind you, this must be confidential," Roosevelt had said at the outset of the meeting. The "one thing we don't want to do," he said, is to "frighten the American people at this time or any time. We want them to gradually realize what is a potential danger."

This hope was to turn out to be in vain, which even Roosevelt himself half expected. "I know the rule of every President is that if you tell more than two senators it gets out," he said. In this case, the word was out the next day, when a number of major newspapers reported that Roosevelt had told the senators that America's frontier was either on the Rhine or in France. Actually the White House transcript had not used those exact words, but Roosevelt had mentioned France and countries well to the east of the Rhine. Nevertheless, at his press conference Roosevelt denounced the report, attributed to an unnamed senator, as a "deliberate lie," and denied that the "frontier on the Rhine" phrase summed up what he had actually said. Of course it had. But Roosevelt was not about to admit that, even to himself. The fact remained that the President had tried to get around the law and had been found out. And his efforts to extricate himself had heightened his embarrassment. The net result of all this was to sharpen the mistrust between Roosevelt and the Congress, to undermine his credibility with the public, and to reinforce his natural inclination to indulge in Machiavellian tactics.

Now was the time to follow up on his suggestion to revise the Neutrality Law. Instead of leading the charge himself, however, he turned that task over to the chairman of the Senate Foreign Relations Committee, Key Pittman of Nevada, a legislator known as much for his fondness for alcohol as for his statesmanship.[*] Pittman sat on his hands for two months until March when Hitler sent his armies into what was left of Czechoslovakia, shattering whatever illusions remained about the Munich agreement and reminding Roosevelt of the flaws in the Neutrality Law. "If Germany invades a country and declares war, we'll be on the side of Hitler by invoking the act," Roosevelt told Texas Senator Tom Connally, a senior member of the Foreign Relations Committee. And in his March 17 press conference Roosevelt said the time for action on Neutrality Act revision was past due.

Prodded into action, Pittman drafted legislation which repealed the arms embargo and put all trade to belligerents on a cash-and-carry basis, an approach that he claimed would protect American ships from harm but still allow help to the British and French. Instead of pushing the legislation to the floor, though, Pittman conducted lengthy hearings which dragged on into the summer. Frustrated but still cautious, Roosevelt had Hull send to Congress a lengthy statement urging repeal of the arms embargo, but avoided making a direct appeal to the public himself. He did plead privately with Senate leaders at a last-ditch meeting in the White House in the oval room of the second floor of the White House, which the President used as an informal study. The room was crammed with seascapes, ship models, and stacks of papers. A dark

---

[*]When after the fall of France in June 1940 Pittman publicly suggested that, since "the probability of Hitler's domination of Europe is evident," the British had best, without further ado, send the Royal Navy to the New World to carry on the war from there, Lothian advised the Foreign Office not to take this "outburst" seriously. "He was almost certainly intoxicated when he made it," the Ambassador explained.

green chenille rug covered the floor and the walls were lined with mahogany book cases. The windows looking to the south offered a view of the dome and columns of the new Jefferson Memorial. A tray of drinks stood in one corner.

The President introduced a solemn tone by opening the meeting with a prayer. Seated by the fireplace in one of the worn leather sofas, some of which dated back to his cousin Theodore's presidency, in grim, but moderate language, he outlined the threat of war, its consequences, and the reasons for repealing the embargo. After an hour, he concluded, "Right now, I've fired my last shot. I think I ought to have another round in my belt," he said.

"Mr. President," Republican Senate Leader Charles McNary of Oregon interjected, "Am I right in understanding that you believe there is a probability of war between now and the next regular session of Congress?"

Roosevelt did not want to overplay his hand. "I don't say there's a probability," he told McNary. "But I am certain there is a very strong possibility."

"Nobody can foretell what may happen," said Borah of Idaho, perhaps the most intransigent of the opponents of repealing the embargo, "My feeling and belief is that we are not going to have a war," Borah said, "Germany isn't ready for it." Finally, Vice President Garner, ever the realist, took a quick head count of those in the room and then turned to the President. "Well Cap'n," he said, "we may as well face the facts. You haven't got the votes."

Roosevelt, leaning back in his sofa as he smoked a cigarette, nodded and told Garner he felt that he had done his best. No one in that company ventured to suggest that the President would have had a better case for that assertion if he had risked his own prestige more directly to build public support for repeal. At any rate, Roosevelt said, now the Senate would have to take responsibility. There would be "no difficulty about that," Borah snapped.

Six weeks after Vice President Garner's head count in the White House study, on September 1, 1939, the President was awakened before dawn by William Bullitt, his Ambassador to Paris, telling him that the German invasion of Poland had launched World War II.

"This nation must remain a neutral nation," the President told the country two days later after Britain and France had formally declared war. But in pointed contrast with Wilson, who in a celebrated phrase called on Americans to be "neutral in thought as well as deed," Roosevelt said: "I cannot ask that every American remain neutral in thought as well. . . . Even a neutral cannot be asked to close his mind and conscience." Nevertheless, the President added comfortingly, "I hope the United States will keep out of this war. I believe that it will. And I give you assurance and reassurance that every effort of your government will be directed toward that end."

Robert Sherwood, the playwright and presidential speech writer, later would concede that this contention "may be denounced as at worst deliberately misleading or at best as wishful thinking. The inescapable fact is that this is what the President felt compelled to say in order to maintain any influence over public opinion and over Congressional action."

But Sherwood's argument could not be proven, since Roosevelt had never really tried any other way. The President might have been more influential in the tense months ahead, as the fortunes of war turned against the European democracies, if he had been more willing to argue publicly as he had privately why isolationism was against the nation's interest. In the absence of such candor, Roosevelt seemed absorbed by the fatalism he had expressed to the Senate leaders over drinks in the White House study. This same attitude was reflected in his remarks to his Cabinet, when they met a few hours after the start of the war on September 1. Roosevelt said the sense of crisis that pervaded Washington reminded him of the start of World War I, twenty-five years earlier, when he had also been in Washington as assistant secretary of the Navy. "The same rush messages were sent around, the same lights snapped on in the nerve centers of government," he recalled, then added somberly: "Unless some miracle beyond our present grasp changes the hearts of men, the days ahead will be crowded days, crowded with the same problems, the same anxieties that filled to the brim those September days of 1914. For history," Roosevelt concluded, "does in fact repeat."

# CHAPTER THREE

# "A Good Stiff Grog"

Shortly after the consummation of the Munich pact, in October of 1938, the Marquis of Lothian, whose appointment as His Britannic Majesty's next ambassador to Washington had been decided upon but not yet announced, embarked on a sort of reconnaissance trip to the United States. This was a country where Lord Lothian, born Philip Kerr, had traveled often and widely, as Director of the Rhodes Scholarship Trust, where he had many influential friends, dating back to his days as private secretary to Lloyd George, and where he invariably found his spirits lifted. "I always feel fifteen years younger when I land in New York," he once remarked. For their part Americans generally liked Lothian, not only for his admiration for their country but also for his direct and relatively unaffected manner, which belied the stereotype in their minds of the British elite as stiff-necked and condescending.

But Lothian's personality had another, troublesome side. He was at times overly intense, given to bursts of enthusiasm for one cause or another and inclined sometimes to thrust himself into situations he could not appropriately handle. One senior foreign office official uncharitably dismissed him as "an incurably superficial Johnny-know-it-all." In this instance Lothian, distressed about the continuing threat Hitler posed to Britain, had assigned himself a task that was bound to put a strain on the normal ease of his contacts with Americans. His purpose in his visit to the U.S. was to find out how Americans were reacting to Munich, but beyond that, "to make some of them understand that if they want to avoid catastrophe themselves" they could not simply rely on the efforts of their Allies from the last war.

Lothian could think of no better place to start than at the top, so he called on the President in January 1939. Before Lothian could get his message to the President, however, he had to endure a certain amount of needling from Roosevelt, related to statements that Lothian had made not so long before, expressing his confidence in Hitler. As a Briton known to be sympathetic to Germany because of what he regarded as its unfair treatment by the Versailles Treaty, Lothian had been granted two audiences with Hitler. After the most recent meeting in 1937, which had lasted for two and one-half hours, Lothian came away with the conviction, which he was not shy about expressing, that Germany was not concerned with dominating other nations, just with protecting her own interests. "Hitler should be allowed his head in order to repair the crime of Versailles," was the gist of his advice as Roosevelt heard it. Later Lothian explained that he had not read the unexpurgated edition of *Mein Kampf* until 1939, when his eyes were thus opened to Hitler's real intentions. Whatever the reasons for Lothian's myopia, it was not a deficiency unique to him, but was in fact shared by many other Britons of his set. At any rate by the time he met with Roosevelt he had confessed the error of his ways.

With that behind him, Lothian sought to impress upon Roosevelt the notion that the United States would have to play a larger role in world affairs. "Britain has defended civilization for a thousand years," he told the President in a burst of rhetoric. "Now the spear is falling from her hand and it is up to you to take it and carry on," a metaphor that Roosevelt did not want to hear. In the privacy of a cabinet meeting, the President was prepared to acknowledge that he regarded Britain as the U.S.'s first line of defense and, therefore, that the U.S. should do what it could to help bolster the British cause. Not in public, though. And neither in public, nor even in private would he accept the enlarged responsibilities that Lothian sought to thrust upon the United States.

Instead, he countered by telling Lothian that the British needed to stiffen their collective backbone. The U.S. was willing to help "all it could," but it would do nothing "if Great Britain "cringed like a coward," Roosevelt told Lothian.* The President sought to drive this point home to Whitehall, and he did so at the first opportunity when a letter arrived from one of his former Harvard professors, Roger B. Merriman, enclosing a gloomy assessment of Britain's prospects from the historian George M. Trevelyan. The President's response dripped with sarcasm and disdain. "I wish the British would stop this, 'We who are about to die salute thee,' attitude," he began, then mentioned Lothian's remarks on his visit and recalled his response.

> I got mad clear through and told him that just so long as he or Britishers like him took that attitude of complete despair, the British

*This language may have been somewhat embellished by the President in the course of recounting the conversation to Harold Ickes. Lothian in his accounts of the meeting stressed how cordial the President had been.

would not be worth saving anyway. What the British need today is a good stiff grog, inducing not only the desire to save civilization but the continued belief that they can do it. In such an event they will have a lot more support from their American cousins—don't you think so?

Knowing Roosevelt well enough to assume that the President had not vented this outburst for his eyes alone, Merriman sent a copy on to his friend Trevelyan, who of course passed it along to *his* friends at the Foreign Office. There it provoked much head shaking among those who had never approved of Lothian's appointment in the first place. But when Roosevelt was asked directly by the British about his opinion of Lothian as ambassador, he made plain he had no objection. And Lothian subsequently took up his post in the sprawling British Embassy on Massachusetts Avenue, replacing Sir Ronald Lindsay, arriving just four days after the German–Soviet nonaggression treaty cleared the way for world war and three days before Hitler hurled his armies at Poland.

The fundamental purpose of FDR's letter had far more to do with policy than personality. In his own circumlocutious way Roosevelt was sending a message to the British, advising them to square their shoulders, and even more pointedly not to depend too much on "their American cousins." The President's attitude on this point, based on what he considered to be the political realities confronting him at home, would exacerbate the tensions between Washington and London during the opening months of the war, obscuring the common interest the two nations had in blocking the advance of Hitler's war machine.

British diplomats and politicians viewed such warnings from Roosevelt as confirmation of negative impressions already formed. "It is always best and safest to count on nothing from the Americans but words," Prime Minister Neville Chamberlain had written in 1937. These misgivings, like the resentments widely held among Americans, could be traced back to World War I and its aftermath. As the British remembered events, Woodrow Wilson had been for nearly four years "too proud to fight," while a whole generation of Britons shed their blood from Gallipoli to Ypres. With victory, Wilson imposed his own unrealistic view of the postwar world on Europe through the League of Nations, which his own country then rejected and reverted to its traditional isolationism under the Republican administrations of the 1920s. Moreover, in the 1930s, the policies of the resurgent Democrats under Roosevelt, notably the Johnson Act's ban on loans to nations that had defaulted on their war debt loans and the Neutrality Act's embargo on arms sales to all belligerents, aggressor and victim alike, reinforced this stance. Meanwhile, American industry and commerce, enjoying the fruits of the World War I victory for which the British had paid such a high price, expanded at home, and American merchants flourished abroad, carving out for themselves a sizable share of markets long dominated by the British.

Roosevelt's personal style did little to improve British feelings for the Americans. They were unsettled by his flamboyance, suspicious of his complicated schemes, and dubious of his political leadership skills. "Mr. Roosevelt is notoriously inaccurate as to detail, especially where the detail hampers his pet schemes," Ambassador Lindsay cabled home after hearing out FDR's pre-Munich blockade proposal.

On the American side of the Atlantic, the impression given by the Nye Committee hearings was that the British, in league with American bankers and "merchants of death," had ensnared the United States in the Great War. And though Americans themselves shunned involvement in European affairs, nevertheless London's failure to curb Hitler's aggressive impulses had hardened their cynicism toward the British.

For his part, the President seemed in many ways to feel a bond with America's "cousins" across the Atlantic. He owned a complete file of *Punch* going back to 1841, had once served as a vice president of the English-Speaking Union, and during World War I had been close friends with Sir Cecil Spring Rice, the British Ambassador, and with other British diplomats. Still, his attitude also reflected a family tradition of rivalry with the British dating back to the eighteenth century, when the Roosevelts of that day were deeply involved in the sugar trade in the West Indies. "That is what made them revolutionists rather than Tories in 1776," Roosevelt later contended. He often carped at the British Empire for pursuing its own selfish interests to the detriment of other nations and took a sour view of the British aristocracy's influence on the country. "The trouble with the British is that they have for several hundred years been controlled by the upper classes," FDR told Jim Farley in the summer of 1939. "The upper classes control all trade and commerce; therefore the policy of the British government relates entirely to the protection of this class."

In this atmosphere, each side viewed every proposal of the other with abundant suspicion. This was the case in June of 1939, when Roosevelt, months after his pre-Munich blockade plan had evaporated, devised yet another highly unorthodox gambit for collaborating with the British that once again ignored international law, contradicted his public professions of neutrality, and strained the constitutional limits on

executive power. This particular idea would assume broader significance a year later when it became relevant to negotiations stemming
from the appeal Churchill had made for U.S. destroyers. What
Roosevelt proposed to Ambassador Lindsay was an arrangement under
which the U.S. would secretly lease air and naval bases on the three
British West Indies islands, Trinidad, Santa Lucia, and Bermuda. In the
event of war, these vantage points would help the neutral U.S. Navy
patrol that portion of the West Atlantic, "with a view toward denying
them to warlike operations of the belligerents." In sum, it amounted to
another variation of the quarantine concept, which Roosevelt had first
broached so enigmatically in his Chicago speech.

Always fond of an historical precedent, even if he had to extend his
reach to find one, Roosevelt said that when the time came for him to
disclose this scheme, he would defend it to the American public by citing the operations of the U.S. Navy in 1798 when its men-of-war drove
French privateers out of these same waters. This was a dubious analogy,
however, since President John Adams ordered this action only after
authorization from the House of Representatives. If all this worked out
as Roosevelt envisaged it, the bases would help relieve the Royal Navy
of the burden of convoy duty in the West Atlantic, a considerable
advantage. But because of the sketchiness of his proposal to the British
and their general misgivings about the President, the idea raised at
least as many doubts as hopes. Ambassador Lindsay, while supporting
the general thrust of the plan, described himself and his embassy staff
as "aghast at the light-hearted manner in which the President was
preparing to defy all ordinary conceptions of neutrality at the very outset of a war." And in London, the Foreign Office's legal experts
ridiculed the President's eighteenth-century precedent as irrelevant,
contending that the U.S. had no legal right to patrol waters hundreds of
miles from its coast. They fired off a barrage of pointed questions
intended to find out just what Roosevelt had in mind. Where would the
boundaries of the patrolled area be drawn? What steps would the U.S.
take to guard against the quarantined zone becoming a sanctuary for
German raiders? Would the U.S. pass on to the British whatever intelligence it gained from its patrol?

Finding these queries overly demanding and specific, Roosevelt
stiffly advised the British that they should understand that he could
only "move as his own public opinion would allow." For example, he
mentioned that he had already postponed inaugurating the patrol as
soon as war was declared, as he had initially intended, and would wait
until some eruption of hostilities on the high seas would agitate

Americans enough to make them receptive to his plan. In the meanwhile, without committing himself firmly, the President was willing to
guide and reassure the British on the points they had raised. While the
limits of the patrol area would have to be defined in consultation with
the other American countries, he thought it could conceivably stretch
"down the whole west side of the Atlantic." Within this broad strip the
warships of Germany, and its Axis partner Italy, would be treated differently than British or French ships, since the Axis powers, unlike Britain
and France, had no possessions in the Western Hemisphere. And any
Axis warship suspected of trying to use the zone as sanctuary would be
sent on its way within 24 hours. In regard to passing on intelligence to
the British, the President managed to convey the vague impression that
the British could count on the Americans relaying whatever they had
learned.

All this was sufficiently satisfying for the British to set aside their misgivings and go forward with negotiations. By the end of August, within
hours of the outbreak of war, sites for naval and sea plane bases had
been selected. The agreements reached between the two countries covered the smallest detail, including even the stipulation that on St. Lucia
the U.S. Navy would pay ten dollars for every coconut tree it cut down
in the course of clearing the land. This parleying was cloaked in the
utmost secrecy from start to finish. By Lindsay's reckoning no more than
six or eight officials in the White House, State and Navy departments
were aware of the proposal. To safeguard against the threat of leaks
abroad, Roosevelt turned down Lindsay's suggestion that the French be
drawn into the talks. And Lindsay himself, at Welles's request, even
burned his written notes of Roosevelt's reply to the British memorandum. The arrangement remained hidden from public knowledge for a
long time to come, in large part because the Navy did not use the bases.
Roosevelt was reluctant, particularly in the midst of the battle over
amending the Neutrality Act in the fall of 1939, to act in any way that
might give the isolationists ammunition. Moreover, the Navy lacked the
resources to man and develop its new strongholds. Finally, the anticipated thrust into the region by German submarines did not materialize
until long afterward, when the U.S. was already in the war.

None of this prevented Roosevelt from going forward with a broader
plan for a Western Hemisphere "Neutrality Zone," patrolled by the
navies of all the American states, averaging about three hundred miles
in width around the two American continents. In marked contrast to
the secrecy shrouding the island leases, this plan was widely heralded
as an example of inter-American cooperation and of the vigorous asser-

tion of neutral rights. Soon after the start of the war, a Pan-American conference issued the Declaration of Panama, which embodied Roosevelt's plan almost word for word. Addressing the delegates to the Conference, Sumner Welles proclaimed the manifesto to be "a declaration of the inalienable right of the American Republics to protect themselves . . . from the dangers . . . of a war which has broken out thousands of miles from their shores and in which they are not involved."

While Welles publicly promoted the plan as a shield against the warring powers, Roosevelt privately sold the idea to the British as a boost for the Allies. In June of 1939, when England's King and Queen visited the United States, Roosevelt told George VI that U.S. ships would fire on any German submarine that ventured into the neutrality zone. In the President's first meeting with Lothian after the new Ambassador's arrival in August, the President emphasized that the neutrality patrol "would be of great assistance to England and France because it would relieve strain on their navies." As Roosevelt explained, food and war materials could be shipped from U.S. and Latin America to Halifax or some other Canadian port and there transferred to British freighters for the trip to Europe.

The plan had skeptics on both sides of the Atlantic, including the Secretary of State. Hull's antipathy may well have been reinforced by the fact that one of its biggest boosters was Welles, whom he had good reason to view as a threat to his own ostensible status as the president's chief foreign policy adviser. Personal feelings aside, as Hull later pointed out, Roosevelt's idea "had no precedent in international law and could therefore be validly objected to by the belligerents." If its legality was dubious, so was its feasibility. Belligerent ships were cruising in the zone even as the delegates met in Panama. And on the day before the delegates put the finishing touches on the Declaration of Panama, a British merchant ship was sunk within the zone by the German pocket battleship *Graf Spee*. Eight more kills were recorded by the *Graf Spee* before she was hunted down by the Royal Navy and crippled, forcing the Germans to scuttle her outside the Uruguayan port of Montevideo in December of 1939.

This spectacular episode was probably the most significant action in the West Atlantic during the first year of the war and was of course a flagrant violation of the neutrality zone. Roosevelt joined in a protest from the signatories of the Declaration of Panama. Churchill, then First Lord of the Admiralty, responded directly to the President. Earlier, as Hull had anticipated, the Admiralty had rejected the Declaration of Panama contending that "no country can properly claim jurisdiction of large areas of oceans," that went beyond the generally accepted three-mile limit for territorial waters. Now Churchill, dealing directly with Roosevelt after expressing his regrets for the "trouble about recent incidents," claimed that as a result of the destruction of the *Graf Spee,* "the whole South Atlantic is now clear and may perhaps continue clear of warlike operations." He added: "Trust matter can be allowed to die down and see no reason why any trouble should occur unless another raider is sent which is unlikely after fate of first." To assuage the President's feelings, Churchill sent along detailed accounts of the *Graf Spee's* last battle, which Roosevelt found "tremendously interesting."

As the months wore on, and the British along with the French assumed nearly all the burden of patrolling the South Atlantic, the British gradually took the view that Roosevelt's Neutrality Zone was not merely an oversold benefit to their war effort but also potentially a downright hindrance to their postwar economy. Apart from keeping the war away from America, its main purpose, the Foreign Office suspected, was to assist in U.S. "economic and political penetration in Latin America" where in the past the British had enjoyed economic superiority.

Even the repeal of the arms embargo, which was probably Roosevelt's most significant contribution to helping the Allied cause early in the war, left something to be desired from the British point of view. With the outbreak of the war, the President had renewed his efforts to revise the Neutrality Act. But in appealing to Congress on September 21, he justified the change on the innocuous grounds of "returning to the ancient precepts of the law of nations." Most of all, though, he was careful to depict his proposal as a way to help keep America at peace rather than to aid Britain and France. He called the current embargo "most vitally dangerous to American neutrality, American security and above all American peace." His plan, which included a ban on U.S. citizens and ships from entering combat zones, would provide, the President said, "far greater safeguards than we now possess or have ever possessed to protect American lives and property from danger."

The isolationists were not fooled. "I hate Hitlerism and Nazism and Communism as completely as any person living," wrote Senator Arthur Vandenburg of Michigan, one of the leading Republican foes of repealing the embargo.

> But I decline to embrace the opportunist idea—so convenient and so popular at the moment—that we can stop these things in *Europe* without entering the conflict with everything at our command, including men and money. There's no middle ground.

Vandenberg, along with Nye, Johnson, LaFollette, and Borah led the charge against repeal on Capitol Hill. LaFollette proposed establishing a national committee to rally public support for maintaining the arms embargo and prominent advertising man Chester Bowles, co-founder of the Benton and Bowles agency, offered to help.* But the idea was rejected because of the fear by some foes of repeal that such a campaign would seem too contrived and artificial. Roosevelt had no such compunctions. Reluctant to take on the battle himself, he got opponents of the embargo to persuade the revered Kansas newspaper editor William Allen White, who had solid Republican credentials, to set up an organization called the Nonpartisan Committee for Peace through Revision of the Neutrality Law. Within a few weeks White's group formed chapters in thirty states with a host of prominent sponsors, including Al Smith, Henry L. Stimson, Frank Knox, and Rabbi Stephen S. Wise. For once, the isolationists were outgunned. After more than six weeks of impassioned debate, on the air waves and on Capitol Hill, Congress voted on November 3 to repeal the arms embargo and at the same time approved a cash-and-carry provision which was greatly to the advantage of the Allies as long as they controlled the seas. Roosevelt signed it into law the next day.

Looking back on the battle, Roosevelt wrote to an aide to King George VI that while much of the opposition to repeal was based on "mere political partisanship," much of it "also reflected an honest belief that we could build a high wall around ourselves and forget the existence of the rest of the world." But nothing the President himself said after the outbreak of war directly contradicted that concept. Instead he presented the lifting of the embargo as a way to help Americans live in safety, regardless of what happened in the rest of the world, thus fostering an illusion which as he must have known would ultimately be rudely shattered.

From Chamberlain the action brought the President a note of gratitude. Not only were the British and French buoyed by the assurance they could draw on "the reservoir of great American resources," the Prime Minister wrote, "but they drew profound moral encouragement" from the American action. Yet it did not take the British long to realize that under the cash-and-carry rules of the revised Neutrality Act, tap-

*Later wartime head of the Office of Price Administration under Roosevelt, a Democratic congressman and Governor of his state of Connecticut, briefly Undersecretary of State in the Kennedy Administration, and then Ambassador to India, Bowles would become an enthusiastic proponent of an activist U.S. role in the world.

ping into the American reservoir was imposing a severe strain on their own hard currency resources. Accordingly, they cut back on purchases of other items, notably tobacco, with painful consequences in parts of the U.S. "Our war purchases have dislocated the American economy," a Foreign Office survey of the American mood pointed out in February. "A starving farmer and a ruined shopkeeper cannot be expected to refrain from bringing pressure to bear on the Administration and the Administration inevitably have to press us."

Americans also complained bitterly about the impact of the British blockade of Germany. Under its rules all neutral ships were required either to get advance certification from the British that their cargos were not bound for Germany or else submit to search of their cargoes, including mail, in British ports. "I would not be frank unless I told you that there has been much public criticism here," Roosevelt wrote Churchill in February of 1940. "The general feeling is that the net benefit to your people and to France is hardly worth the definite annoyance caused to us."

Whether or not Churchill passed that letter on to Chamberlain is not known, but the Prime Minister had already had his fill of grumbling from the Americans. "Heaven knows I don't want the Americans to fight for us," he wrote his sisters late in January of 1940. "We should have to pay too dearly for that if they had a right to be in on the peace terms. But if they are so sympathetic they might at least refrain from hampering our efforts and comforting our foes."

In gauging American public opinion, not only did the British draw on newspaper editorials and radio commentary, but they also carefully read and analyzed the overseas mail on the U.S. ships. One study noted the number of envelopes emblazoned with such slogans as "Neutrality First" and "No Entanglements" and concluded that while most Americans "are violently anti-Hitler, anti-Stalin and pro-Ally, they are at the same time violently neutral." Although unwilling to make any commitments to the Allied cause, Americans were "full of advice" about steps that might lead to peace. One popular notion was for "a United States of Europe" which would erase the military fortifications and tariffs separating the European nations; another was to choose some prominent personage to serve as a "mediator" of the grievances that touched off the war.

This wishful environment helps to explain President Roosevelt's announcement, to the great consternation of the British, that he was dispatching Undersecretary Welles on a fact-finding tour of Europe. His itinerary would take him to the Axis capitals of Berlin and Rome, as well as to London and Paris. The official announcement on February 9, 1940, said only that the purpose of the trip was to advise the President and Hull on conditions in Europe. But the British, well aware of Roosevelt's fondness for high-level diplomacy that involved no risk for himself, suspected that Welles's real assignment was to push Britain and France into reaching a negotiated peace, a development that would of course greatly enhance Roosevelt's prestige at the start of the presidential election year.

"The President and those surrounding him think we can't win," David Scott, undersecretary of the Foreign Office's American department, concluded. "If the President can somehow stop the war his own domestic position will be enormously strengthened."

The British feared that this gesture coming from a supposedly friendly neutral and potential ally undercut their own position at a crucial point. "I must frankly admit to a good deal of anxiety lest the effect of this move, however carefully presented, should be to cause embarrassment to the democracies, from which Germany, still unconvinced of the failure of the policy of force, will reap advantage," Chamberlain wrote the President.

Roosevelt stood firm, though, and Welles departed on his grand tour, bearing with him presidential letters of introduction to Mussolini, Chamberlain, and French Premier Edouard Daladier. Roosevelt described Welles as "an old boyhood friend," and offered assurances that whatever was said to him would be repeated only to Roosevelt himself and the Secretary of State. From his first meeting, with Mussolini, Welles drew some hope, perhaps reflecting the Italian mistrust of Germany. Following his audience with Hitler, Welles knew better. "I believe that German might is such as to make the triumph of Germany inevitable," Hitler told FDR's emissary. "But if not we will all go down together." Still Welles went through the motions of completing his trip by visiting the Allied capitals, stops which the President now privately described as "window dressing." In Paris, the undersecretary encountered the defeatist mood that foretold the debacle that would soon overtake the Third Republic.

In London, Welles was struck with the contrasting determination of the British to carry on the fight. Chamberlain, 71, brimming with energy and spirit, spoke of the Nazis "with white hot anger," and told Welles he saw no chance for peace as long as the Nazis held power. Churchill received Welles "sitting in front of the fire, smoking a 24-inch cigar and drinking a whiskey and soda." To Welles, "it was quite obvious that he had consumed a good many whiskeys before I arrived." Nevertheless, Churchill launched into a soliloquy on the war and its causes lasting nearly two hours, "in the course of which he became quite sober." One point Churchill stressed: The German aim of world supremacy threatened the U.S. as much as it did Britain.[*]

On his return to Washington late in March Welles briefed Hull and Roosevelt. Hull concluded that it all boiled down to what most people had already assumed: There was no reasonable hope for peace. As Welles himself later wrote, the only thing that could possibly stand in the way of Hitler unleashing devastation upon the world was the conviction that the U.S. would enter the war to fight against him. But probably the most significant consequence of Welles's implausible quest for peace was to demonstrate to Hitler that any decisive action by the United States was far removed from the thinking of its president.

Meanwhile Roosevelt had realized the futility of the trip as a peace mission, and privately sought to minimize its initial purpose. The whole idea had come to him as "an impulse," he told Assistant Secretary of State Breckenridge Long—one that "could not do any harm and might do good." In reality it contributed to tension and unease between the U.S. and the British at a critical moment. In an effort to salvage something from the affair, Roosevelt declared that while there was "scant immediate prospect" for peace, Welles's efforts would be of "the greatest value" when the time to make peace finally came.

Within a few days, on April 9, 1940, Hitler suddenly stepped up the pace of war, attacking Norway and Denmark. The Danes collapsed within 24 hours and within a few weeks the *Wehrmacht* had conquered most of Norway. These defeats reverberated in the United States, setting back British efforts to win over American opinion. At first, Roosevelt was "hopping mad" at the failure of the British fleet to stop the German invasion. "It is the most outrageous thing I ever heard of," he told Morgenthau, who was himself equally indignant.

"To let them walk in quietly and take Oslo seems ridiculous," the treasury secretary said. "After all, the Germans had 50 ships to group there, and where was the British blockade?"

While these and other questions begged an answer, Roosevelt clung

---

*Afterward, Welles told officials at the U.S. Embassy that Churchill was one of the most fascinating people he had ever met, and the Foreign Office considered telling that to Churchill. But Undersecretary Alexander Cadogan, known for his tart tongue, saw no need to take the trouble to get authorization from some higher authority just to tell Churchill that he had made "a unique impression on Mr. Welles," adding: "I take comfort from the fact that Mr. C. will already have that conviction, so nothing is lost." At any rate Churchill might have cared less about the impression he had made on Welles if he had known that, on his return from the trip, Welles told Morgenthau that Mussolini was the greatest man he ever met.

to the public stance of neutrality. "Your Government is keeping a cool head and a steady hand," he told the Young Democratic Clubs of America, when the war in Scandinavia was ten days old. "We are keeping out of wars in Europe and Asia." Gibing at the opposition party, while also offering a vague sop to the internationalists, Roosevelt said he did not agree with "the preachment of a Republican aspirant for the presidency," an apparent reference to the outspoken isolationist, Senator Vandenberg, that the U.S. "should do nothing to try to bring about a better order, a more secure order of world peace when the time comes." What the U.S. should or could do, Roosevelt did not say.

By the end of the month, as the Allied military situation in Norway steadily worsened, Roosevelt's initial anger turned to anxiety and depression. Lunching with Morgenthau on April 29, Roosevelt was "very worried about the English situation and glumly forecast that "the English are going to get licked." "I can't get out any orders telling everybody to take a very, very gloomy and serious attitude toward this matter," he told Morgenthau. "But I feel that's what we should do."

Though Morgenthau was himself deeply distressed about the British defeats, he felt Roosevelt was overstating the case. "Well frankly, Mr. President, I don't see why you want us to take that attitude," Morgenthau replied.

"By taking the attitude that England is going to get licked," Roosevelt explained, "we prepare sentiment in this country."

Morgenthau left, determined to urge Eleanor Roosevelt to help him alter the president's outlook. He need not have bothered. Roosevelt's natural buoyancy lifted him out of this despondency. The outburst however betrayed the anxiety he would exhibit in the weeks to come, not about preparing public sentiment but rather adjusting his own actions to follow what he perceived to be the tides of public opinion.

At first the British hoped that the German assault in Norway, by ending the so-called Phoney War, would improve their standing with the American public. "Assuming that this war remains genuinely active from now . . . it is reasonable to suppose that we shall be permitted to take whatever steps are necessary to secure a victory without undue criticism and even with American sympathy," a Foreign Office analysis suggested after the war came to Scandinavia. But these hopes were dashed when the German juggernaut forced withdrawal of the Allied expeditionary force sent to help the beleaguered Norwegians. "In Norway, the Allies let time slip through their fingers," the *Washington Post* declared. "The Allies have missed the bus again," said the *Philadelphia Inquirer*. "If the Norwegian expedition could not be undertaken and carried through in sufficient force, it should not have been undertaken at all," contended the *Boston Transcript*.

"American public was almost totally unprepared for British withdrawals from Norway," the British Library of Information reported to London early in May in one of its periodic surveys of American opinion. "Increasing anxiety and concern over general war situation and possibility of German victory arousing serious considerations of America's future policy." Far from making Americans more willing to intervene, Lord Lothian reported that the Norwegian defeat had intensified U.S. anxiety about being "dragged into the war." He found the country to be "dominated by fear of involvement and incapable of positive action." The British could do little themselves to alter these attitudes, the Ambassador believed, recalling that the British themselves had decided to stand firm against Hitler only after he swallowed up what was left of Czechoslovakia in March of 1939. "The point at which they will be driven to say as we did after Prague, 'This far and no further' depends mainly on the dictators and the events they precipitate."

As it turned out, events moved more swiftly than Lothian probably expected. The massive German offensive against France and the Low Countries, launched only a month after the assault on Scandinavia, appeared to provide the test of American will that Lothian had anticipated. But U.S. ambiguity persisted. On May 13, three days after the blitz began, the President sent his Ambassador Joseph P. Kennedy, whom the British had little reason to regard as a friend, to call on Foreign Secretary Halifax.

The German assault had made "a most profound impression upon the United States." Kennedy stated, so much so that Americans were now prepared "to go to almost any lengths to help Allies, except," he added, "to send men." Asked what the British should do to take advantage of this situation, Kennedy was vague. That would depend on what they needed, he said. Anyhow, he remarked, if the Germans did not gain "immediate success," he personally did not think Britain would need U.S. help to win the war.

Halifax who had already seen enough bad news from the front to think otherwise, pressed Kennedy further, asking what the U.S. reaction would be if the British were to find themselves in "extreme difficulty" in the near future.

Once again Kennedy was hazy. He mentioned the possibility of extending economic credits, but said he had concluded that the British really did not need them, adding "it would only be bad tactics and create suspicion" if the British raised that subject.

Would the U.S. consider loaning the Royal Air Force some of its own military aircraft right away, Halifax asked, to be replaced eventually by planes the British had on order?

Take that sort of request directly to the President, Kennedy replied. In parting, the ambassador offered Halifax a piece of advice drawn from the ethos of an old-fashioned Irish wake. "You must pass the hat now," he said, "while the corpse is warm."

# "Those Bloody Yankees"

The British hardly needed urging from Kennedy or anybody else to seek American help. Earlier that spring the British and French had placed orders for 4,600 U.S. aircraft with every intention of buying more in the future. In May, a few days before Hitler launched his blitz, T. North Whitehead, the head of the Foreign Office's American section, noted that Britain was already receiving "substantial" shipments of U.S. arms and acknowledged that without these supplies, "we probably could not win this war." But his analysis added: "Nor is it probable that we shall win it without considerably more help from America than we received today." It was only two days after Kennedy's visit to the Foreign Office that Churchill's cabled request for fifty U.S. destroyers, along with several hundred airplanes and anti-aircraft guns, landed on the President's desk. For the British also realized, as Kennedy had pointed out, that ultimately their chances for getting the destroyers and other armaments they badly needed depended mainly on one man, Roosevelt.

Trying to track and adjust to the shifting currents of public opinion, Roosevelt faced the problem that while events in Europe commanded everyone's attention, responses to them varied wildly. Internationalists sounded ominous warnings and demanded support for the Allies. Hitler's victory, asserted the *New York Times*, "will mean the end of freedom and democracy and culture throughout all Europe in our time." Frank Knox, Alfred Landon's vice-presidential running mate in 1936 and publisher of the *Chicago Daily News*, called upon the U.S. to help "in every way short of war itself those who are now fighting the bestial monster." Dark-horse Republican presidential contender Wendell L. Willkie declared that if the GOP should take the position that "what is going on in Europe is none of our business, then we might as well fold up." And some Americans warned that Hitler's success in Europe would lead Japan to advance its own imperial plans in Asia by seizing British Malaya and the Dutch East Indies.

In the opposite corner, the various factions that made up the isolationist movement wanted no part of the trouble abroad. On the left,
among pacifists, pro-Soviet labor unions, and various youth organizations, the heating up of the war only stiffened their determination to
stay out of it. In New York, a local public employees' union bulletin proclaimed, in contravention of the "over there" spirit of World War I:
"Yanks are NOT Coming." In Rochester, the United Shoe Workers
passed a resolution opposing "all steps leading to war." In Los Angeles a
group of young businessmen calling themselves "We Who Would Not
Die" launched a nationwide campaign to mobilize youth against the
war, and editors of thirty-five college newspapers around the country
sent a "Stay Out of War" letter to the White House.

On the right a good many conservative isolationists displayed intense
new concern about the ability of the country to defend itself against a
threat which most had previously denied existed; some, notably the
Hearst press and Senator Vandenberg, now preferred to call themselves
"insulationists." And with each day bringing news of new German gains
in France, the opposition of the so-called insulationists mounted to
sending aid that could be used instead to bolster America's own defenses. "The war is on our threshold," warned the *Omaha World-Herald*.
"U.S. defense precautions are like a $1,000 insurance policy on a mil-
lion dollar concern." To some degree that attitude was shared at the
War Department, which according to the British Embassy was "giving
out some very gloomy stuff" about the course of the battle in France,
intended to create the impression that any aid would be wasted and
might simply fall into German hands. As the Embassy's biweekly
Washington letter to the Foreign Office glumly concluded: "The same
people who used to say the Allies could win without any American help
are now saying that no possible American help could have any effect."

In responding to this turmoil, Roosevelt sounded an uncertain trumpet, his tone varying from day to day. Addressing the Pan American
Scientific Congress in Washington, on the night of May 10, hours after
Hitler launched his assault against France and the Low Countries,
Roosevelt said "the tragic news" from Europe had "shocked and
angered" all Americans. Speaking from the podium in Constitution
Hall, with the painted battle flags of the American Revolution as a backdrop, the President denounced those who sought to use the achievements of science "to dominate hundred of millions of human beings." If
these forces, which he did not name, met with success, Roosevelt
warned, they would "enlarge their wild dream to encompass every
human being and every mile of the earth's surface."

This indignant rhetoric trailed off into a murky peroration. Could the Pan American nations live in peace, "if all the other continents embrace by preference or by compulsion a wholly different principle of life?" Roosevelt asked. "I think not," he said, but then seemed to cast doubt about his own answer. "Surely it is time for our Republics to spread that problem before us in the cold light of day, to analyze it, to ask questions, to call for answers . . . and above all to act with unanimity and single-ness of purpose . . ." *Time*, whose own approach to the war was vigor-ously pro-Ally, complained: "Like many a Presidential speech on foreign affairs it clarified little, influenced public opinion far less than events."

The next week, Roosevelt drove through a spring rain down Pennsylvania Avenue to address a joint session of Congress. Two days earlier, the Dutch Army had capitulated. On this day, May 16, the British and French were in full retreat in the face of the German advance and Churchill had rushed to Paris to stiffen the backbone of the French General staff. Warning that "new powers of destruction" harnessed by "ruthless and daring" aggressors now mocked the American faith in the oceans that bordered each coast as safeguards, Roosevelt asked Congress for an unprecedented $2 billion in defense spending. This would buy 50,000 airplanes, an army of one million men, and, with a measure of luck, the time to prepare for an attack on the United States itself.

The President certainly got the nation's attention and received what Ickes graded as "the finest reception he has been accorded by a joint ses-sion of Congress in five or six years." Even if a minority of members "sat silent and hostile in their seats," Ickes reasoned that the "Republicans will have to go along on this program because the country is for it, and they dare not do otherwise." It was no difficult feat for Roosevelt to argue that the U.S. had to bolster its defenses against the threat from abroad. As Ickes observed, that was as plain to most Americans as the grim headlines in their newspapers. The tougher and more urgent question was how much help the U.S. should give the British, an issue the president dealt with in only two brief sentences. "I ask the Congress not to take any action which would in any way hamper or delay the delivery of American-made planes to foreign nations which have ordered them, or seek to purchase new planes," he said. "That, from the point of view of our own national defense, would be extremely short sighted." Nowhere in the speech did he provide a justification for such help that would counter the isolationist argument that any arms shipped abroad would be a drain on the resources America needed to protect herself.

In fact, when, on the same day that he addressed Congress, he responded to Churchill's May 15 request for the fifty destroyers, Roosevelt seemed to accept those arguments. It was easy to see why Churchill thought Roosevelt had destroyers to spare. When the United States entered World War I, the Navy, desperately trying to catch up with the fleets of the other powers, embarked on a building binge, constructing 273 destroyers, only a few of which were completed in time to actually see action. In the years between the wars, a lean period for the Navy, some were lost to accident and others were scrapped. Those that remained were smaller than newer ships, antiquated in design, but still serviceable. No fewer than 62 were still in commission at the start of the war, when the President ordered the overhauling and recommissioning of more than 100 others. Combined with newer vessels, the U.S. had a destroyer fleet of more than 200 ships. By contrast, Great Britain could count only about 130 destroyers commissioned in its home waters, and only about half of these were judged fit for service.

Nevertheless, in his message to Churchill the President sounded like a rich man replying to a request for a loan from a poor relative by proclaiming his own poverty. Advising the Prime Minister that nothing could be done about the destroyers "without the specific authorization of the Congress," an assertion that he himself would later go to great lengths to undermine, the President expressed his misgivings about seeking such approval "at this moment." Given the requirements for the United States' own defense, its commitments elsewhere in the Western Hemisphere, and its obligations in the Pacific, Roosevelt thought it "doubtful" whether the destroyers could be spared "even temporarily." At any rate, the President said, even if they could be made available it would take six or seven weeks before the ships could go into active service under the Union Jack.[*]

In the face of such a rebuff, a lesser person in Churchill's position

---

[*]The same arguments were used that same day in a cable from Secretary Hull to Ambassador Bullitt in Paris, turning down a French request relayed by Bullitt for twelve old destroyers that the French wanted to use to patrol the Mediterranean. But the French persisted. On June 7 the French Ambassador, Count René Doynel de Saint-Quentin, asked Welles for an interview with Roosevelt to take up the destroyer issue. The President sent word through Welles that no such meeting was necessary, repeating the reasons previously given for refusing the destroyer request. The Ambassador, "deeply chagrined," told Welles he would be considered persona non grata by his government unless he gained an audience with the President. Roosevelt thereupon agreed to see the Ambassador, although their meeting did not alter the negative decision on the destroyer request.

might well have abandoned his quest, but Churchill was both stubborn and desperate. On May 19, five days after his initial request for the destroyers, and four days after Roosevelt had turned him down, he tried again. His patience was clearly running thin. "Here's a telegram for those bloody Yankees," he told his secretary John Colville. "Send it off tonight." Colville, startled by Churchill's departure from his usually conciliatory tone toward the United States, did as he was told and then went to bed. To Colville's annoyance, Churchill awakened him at 2:20 in the morning and had him get the telegram back from the Embassy before it could be dispatched to America. Once again Colville followed orders, though he noticed that after Churchill had reread the telegram he sent it off again, without making any changes. "I understand your difficulties, but I am very sorry about the destroyers," the Prime Minister cabled Roosevelt. "If they were here in six weeks, they would play an invaluable part."

Then he referred to a conversation between the President and Lord Lothian, in which the President expressed concern about the future of the British fleet. In the worst case, if Hitler conquered England, the President suggested that the fleet might take up harbor in the Western Hemisphere. Churchill sought to drive this notion from the President's mind. His government was determined to fight on against Hitler, whatever the odds, to the bitter end if necessary, the Prime Minister assured the President. But should the Churchill regime be driven from office by defeat, "and others came to parley amid the ruins," he warned:

> . . . You must not be blind to the fact that the sole remaining bargaining counter with Germany would be the fleet, and if this country was left by the United States to its fate no one would have the right to blame those then responsible if they made the best terms they could for the surviving inhabitants. Excuse me, Mr. President for putting this nightmare bluntly.

On the same day that Churchill issued that stark warning, German troops seized Amiens and Abbeville, and finished driving a corridor 20 miles wide from the Ardennes to the English Channel, splitting the Allied front in two. Two days later Hitler's forces on the Channel coast thrust north toward Calais and Boulogne. Yet in the face of Churchill's warning and the calamitous news from France, Roosevelt maintained a notable silence on the issue of aid to the Allies for a critical month. The President's professed belief that Britain and France were crucial to U.S. security, which he had confided to the Armed Services Committee a year earlier in the privacy of the White House, remained unspoken in public.

He rejected an opportunity to make that point at his May 21 press conference when he was asked if he approved of a proposal introduced by Democratic Senator Claude Pepper of Florida, perhaps Britain's most outspoken supporter on Capitol Hill, to allow the U.S. Government to sell first line military aircraft directly to the allies. The President replied that he had not heard of it until that very morning when Pepper had informed the White House of his proposal. "No comment was requested," Roosevelt added elliptically. Three days later the resolution was rejected by the Senate Foreign Relations Committee by a 12-to-1 vote, with the opposition arguing that it would amount to direct intervention by the U.S. in the war in Europe, violating international law.

Roosevelt's next major address, his Fireside Chat of May 26, departed from the sense of crisis and urgency that had infused his address to Congress. Certainly the President himself was concerned. When he was joined by a small group of advisers in his study before the speech there was none of the usual levity. Reading dispatches from the battle front brought to him by a White House usher, the President attended to the mixing of drinks, normally one of his favorite rituals, "rather mechanically," Sam Rosenman thought, "as though his mind were thousands of miles away." "All bad, all bad," Roosevelt muttered as he handed the bulletins on to Mrs. Roosevelt, who read them and silently passed them on to the others in the room.

Nevertheless the speech itself seemed designed mainly to reassure rather than inspire action. While he deplored the plight of millions of civilians fleeing the havoc of war engulfing France and Belgium, the President's only mention of aid to these countries was a plea to give to the American Red Cross to support its relief efforts abroad. His most immediate objective was to defend himself against criticism that he was to blame for the nation's lack of preparedness, which was a theme that isolationists were now trumpeting with increasing vigor. Thus Democratic Senator Bennett Champ Clark of Missouri had alleged that the $8 billion appropriated for defense during Roosevelt's presidency had been "poured down a rat hole," and complained that the Army Air Corps had "only 58 planes that aren't obsolete."

". . . Let us not be calamity howlers and discount our strength," said Roosevelt, boasting that prudent spending and wise management by his Administration had produced "the best equipped and best trained peacetime military establishment in the whole history of this country." This came at a time when, as Roosevelt well knew, the Army and Navy were both so hard pressed for material that they claimed they had none to spare for the embattled Allies.

This speech, according to the British Embassy's Washington Letter, "did not arouse much enthusiasm privately among the press." And *Time* grumbled: "In the tension of Washington Franklin Roosevelt showed no noticeable inclination to lead the apparently growing public desire to lend all aid short of war to the Allies."

At a press conference two days later Roosevelt went out of his way to correct any impression that the crisis he had adumbrated earlier that month would cause undue inconvenience to the electorate. "I think people should realize that we are not going to discombobulate or upset any more than we have to, a great many of the normal processes of life," the President volunteered. He pointed to a report in journalist Doris Fleeson's widely read "Capitol Stuff" column, which speculated that the defense effort might mean an end to production of new cars and luxury items. In an attempt at humor that was heavyhanded in its sexist tone even for that time, FDR remarked that "one of the ladies in the room . . . wanted to know whether things that could be put into the luxury class would have to be foregone by the population," and added: ". . . The answer is that this delightful young lady will not have to forego cosmetics, lipstick, ice-cream sodas. . . ." Amid the ensuing laughter, Fleeson protested: "That really wasn't what I was going to ask." But the President ignored her to make his point. "We do not want to upset the normal trend of things any more than we possibly can help."

In his May 15 cable asking for the fifty destroyers, Churchill had placed second on his list "several hundred of the latest type of aircraft of which you are now getting delivery." The Prime Minister suggested that these could "be repaid by those now being constructed in the U.S. for us." Next he had asked for anti-aircraft guns and ammunition, "of which again," he had assured Roosevelt, "there will be plenty next year, if we are alive to see it."

In contrast with the cold water he had splashed on the destroyer proposal, the President told Churchill that "we are doing everything within our power" to get the British the aircraft they sought. As for the request for anti-aircraft guns, the President said, that would get "the most favorable consideration," but added the caveat, "in the light of our own defense needs and requirements."

This last loomed as a substantial problem for several reasons. The President's Army and Navy chiefs resented any effort to bolster the British when their own stocks of arms were inadequate. Many in Congress also opposed aid, as the overwhelming defeat of Senator

Pepper's resolution demonstrated. Still another roadblock was the pre-vailing legal opinion, adamantly adhered to by Secretary of War Harry Woodring, that for the U.S. government to sell any war materials to a belligerent power would violate Federal law. On top of all that, Roosevelt had created an odd administrative arrangement to supervise the supplying of the Allies with armaments. The man in charge was the Secretary of the Treasury, the high-strung and sometimes high-handed Henry Morgenthau, the Cabinet officer to whom Roosevelt felt proba-bly felt greater kinship than any other, a man he was confident he could trust completely and manipulate whenever he chose.

At the outset of the war, following the revision of the Neutrality Act which allowed the Allied purchase of munitions, Roosevelt sought to bar the big Wall Street banking houses from filling the lucrative and subsequently controversial middleman role they played in World War I. He turned that task over to the Treasury department. Instead of using the House of Morgan, as they had done twenty-five years earlier, the Allies were obliged in effect to work through the House of Morgenthau. Under Roosevelt's arrangement, the British and French opened special accounts in the Federal Reserve Bank of New York, with Morgenthau in charge of coordinating their transactions. The Treasury Secretary thus became the President's agent for dealing with the Anglo-French pur-chasing commission sent to the United States to acquire munitions.

By the time he had assumed this task, the forty-nine-year-old Morgenthau had been Treasury secretary for six years. More important-ly, he had known Roosevelt longer and better than anyone else in the Administration. They met back home in New York State in 1915, where Morgenthau, the scion of a prominent German Jewish family, had attempted to free himself from his domineering father's influence by setting himself up as a highly successful gentlemen farmer in Dutchess County, not far from FDR's Hyde Park. Their common interest in New York Democratic Party politics cemented their friendship, and during Roosevelt's governorship, Morgenthau served as an adviser on agricul-ture and farming. When Roosevelt entered the White House, Morgenthau joined the Administration as head of the Federal Farm Board, moving over to Treasury when a vacancy developed there.

Both were wealthy patricians who could afford to look beyond mate-rial concerns, a bond that helped them share confidences. "To Henry, from one of two of a kind," FDR inscribed a photo of himself and Morgenthau.

Not everyone shared FDR's affection and regard for his old neigh-bor. Morgenthau's colleagues found him too often displaying the brusqueness and arrogance associated with his class. And he took every advantage of his intimacy with the President. Once when the President was directing where he wanted paintings placed on his office walls, Marvin McIntyre, an old Roosevelt hand himself, pointedly remarked: "You are right, Mr. President, you ought to have them hung to suit yourself. After all, you are in this office more than anyone else except Henry Morgenthau."

In contrast to his chumminess with Morgenthau, Roosevelt had little in common and little contact with Navy Secretary Edison and Secretary of War Woodring, yet he preferred to let them linger on in their jobs rather than face up to the problem of getting them to leave. The son of the legendary wizard of Menlo Park, Edison, like his father, had a severe hearing loss which tried Roosevelt's patience. "Between you and me it's rather difficult to work with him because he is so hard of hearing," Roosevelt once complained to Jim Farley. After a Cabinet meeting, Farley himself noted in his diary that Edison seemed to talk about matters in his department "without knowing some of the details, and that the President was growing somewhat annoyed." Edison moved up to Navy secretary at the start of 1940 after running the department for months from his post as assistant secretary during the illness of his predecessor, while Roosevelt did nothing to find a more suitable department chief. Finally, soon after Edison was sworn in to his new job, Roosevelt gracefully eased him out; he persuaded him to resign so he could run for governor of his home state of New Jersey.

He was similarly hesitant to get rid of Woodring, who bitterly opposed aid to the allies which he saw as violation of the Neutrality Act, despite the nagging of his other Cabinet members. "You've just got to do something about your War Department," Morgenthau urged him in late April. "You are right," the President said, "you are right," and went on to discuss possible replacements. But he held off from actually making a change.

"He has promised a dozen people to get rid of Woodring but makes no move," Ickes, no friend of Woodring's, grumbled in his diary in early June. The frustration of other cabinet members reached the point that Harry Hopkins suggested to Ickes that all of them, led by Secretary of State Hull, offer their resignations, in hopes of prying Woodring loose. In early June, amidst a Cabinet discussion of the crisis abroad and preparedness efforts at home, Morgenthau sent Ickes a note: "Dear Harold, you are still my *favorite* candidate for Sec. of War. Henry." The amusing part of this, Ickes thought, was that it was Woodring who passed on Morgenthau's note.

Ignoring this friction as much as he could, Morgenthau threw himself eagerly into his assignment, which aroused his deepest feelings. "We should learn the lesson which the past seven years have taught us," Morgenthau had written Roosevelt a few weeks after Munich. "The current claim of an aggressor power is always its last—until the next one."

After meeting with the President to review the requests in Churchill's cable, Morgenthau summoned to his office the Army's new Chief of Staff, George Catlett Marshall, to see what could be done. Marshall at this point had been in charge of the Army for less than a year. His forcefulness and clearheadedness were not yet appreciated outside the military and he had yet to establish the relationship with his Commander-in-Chief that would win him Roosevelt's boundless trust. But as an orderly and rational man, when first confronted a few days earlier with the President's haphazard management style, Marshall had reacted accordingly; he respectfully but firmly lectured his Commander-in-Chief about the urgent need to expedite preparedness efforts.

"I don't quite know how to express myself about this to the President of the United States," Marshall had remarked at one point in the discussion, "but I will say this, *you have got to do something and do it today.*"*

"He stood right up to the President," Morgenthau, who was "tremendously impressed," had noted in his diary. "You did a swell job, and I think you are going to get about 75 percent of what you want," Morgenthau told Marshall a few hours after the encounter.

To the President, Morgenthau wrote two days later:

> In view of my experience with the Army during the last couple of days, I am taking the liberty of making a suggestion. Let General Marshall, and only General Marshall, do all the testifying in connection with the bill which you are about to send up for additional appropriations for the Army.

Now as they faced the problem of sorting out priorities between the armament needs of the Allies and of the United States itself, Morgenthau told Marshall: "If I was the president, I would make you make the decision." And that is in effect what happened.

Dealing with the British requests item by item, Marshall vetoed the plea for aircraft, desperate as it was, because it would set back United

---

*The emphasis is in the original.

States efforts to train its own pilots. "It is a drop in the bucket on the other side, and it is a very vital necessity on this side and that is that," he told Morgenthau. The request for anti-aircraft guns met the same fate. "The shortage is terrible and we have no ammunition for anti-aircraft and will not for six months," he told Morgenthau on May 22, 1940. "So if we gave them the guns, they could not do anything with them."

But based on a quick survey conducted by the Chief of Army Ordnance, Marshall did produce an inventory of material that the Army could afford to do without. For the time being, Marshall told Morgenthau, he had set aside legal and political considerations, addressing only the issue of "what might we spare if means were found of getting it over to the allies." His was a far more extensive tally than previous estimates of surplus material—500,000 Enfield rifles, 35,000 machine guns, 500 75 mm field guns, 500 mortars with 50,000 shells, and 100 million rounds of rifle and machine-gun ammunition. Marshall compiled these figures only through creative bookkeeping. At Marshall's order, the list had been based on what would be surplus to a army of 1.8 million, about six times the present size of the Regular Army, taking into account the amount of equipment that would supposedly be produced before the Army reached the higher level.

Understanding this, and realizing how difficult this process was for Marshall, Morgenthau asked him: "How's your conscience on this?" His conscience would be satisfied, Marshall said drily, as long as he could get to church before he formally declared the arms to be surplus.

Informed of Marshall's list, Ambassador Lothian called on Sumner Welles to underline the British need for munitions. With the haughtiness which would become all too familiar to Lothian in the weeks ahead, Welles told him that Marshall's list was tentative, that legal issues remained to be resolved "and that the question therefore was one of the highest policy which could of course could be determined only by the President in consultation with the highest appropriate members of the Administration."

But a week later no arms had been released. And with Britain's fortunes darkening every hour, Arthur Purvis, the head of the British purchasing mission in the U.S., arrived at the Treasury building around the corner of Pennsylvania Avenue from the White House to argue his case. A Scotsman born in London, Purvis had been sent to the U.S. twenty-five years earlier to buy naval supplies during the First World War. In the interim he had crossed the Atlantic again to take over a Canadian munitions company, eventually becoming one of the giants of the Canadian business world. Purvis's burr, and his ample store of jokes in which Englishmen invariably came off second best to Scotsmen, charmed the Americans he encountered. He was a tenacious negotiator, though, determined to wring all the weapons he could out of the Americans.

"What is really the essence of the difficulty?" he wanted to know.

"It's against the law," Morgenthau told him, explaining that the lifting of the arms embargo applied only to private companies, not the government itself. "It's absolutely against our Neutrality Act to sell these guns to belligerents and he's been fussing with it ever since last Saturday," Morgenthau said of the dilemma facing Marshall. Also, prospects for changing the law, Morgenthau thought, were nil. "We can't get it through Congress." But in this case, as in others to follow, for a government trying to reconcile the needs of the British with the pressures of politics, the law was not necessarily an insurmountable obstacle, as Morgenthau duly noted. "It's a question of can we do it *illegally*," [emphasis added] the Treasury Secretary remarked, a comment that could have served as a motto for the Roosevelt Administration's efforts to aid the British.

Reassuringly, though, Morgenthau added that General Marshall was trying to find a solution. To boost Purvis's spirits, Morgenthau extolled Marshall's resourcefulness. As a young officer in Tientsin, Morgenthau said, Marshall had wanted his troops to learn Chinese but lacked the money to pay for language lessons. Instead he traded manure from the Army's stables to anyone who would teach his men. Morgenthau had suggested to Marshall that if he could get language lessons for his soldiers for manure, he could find a way around the neutrality law. "I said, 'Use the manure deal,' " Morgenthau told Purvis.

"You're very reassuring," Purvis replied.

Largely because of Secretary Woodring's opposition, Marshall spent nearly another full week finding a way around the law. Finally, Marshall, with the help of a squad of government lawyers from Treasury, State, War, and the Justice Department invented a legal basis for avoiding the ban on government sales to a belligerent, derived from a 1919 law governing the disposal of surplus materials. Under this statute, the lawyers decided, the Army could sell a range of surplus items, including trucks, guns, ammunition, and planes to private manufacturers who could then in turn legally sell them to British or French. The proceeds from the sales to the private companies would accrue to the Treasury. To expedite matters, the government lawyers contended, the arms sales did not need to be advertised.

With that ruling, the logjam broke. Asked to select from Marshall's surplus list, Purvis asked for "the whole damned lot." The windfall was well timed. On June 4, the last British soldier had departed the beaches of Dunkirk, leaving behind in German hands a vast arsenal that British factories would need months to replace.

"I am delighted to have that list of surplus matériel which is ready to roll," Roosevelt wrote Morgenthau on June 6. "Give it an extra push every morning and every night until it is on board ship." Writing to Lewis Douglas, his former budget director, who was in the forefront of those urging aid to the Allies, Roosevelt rejoiced over the "excellent ruling" which had cleared the way for sales of surplus equipment. "I have a sneaking suspicion that the old material which we are turning in will be on its way to France in a few days," he said slyly. But, Roosevelt added, "I am not talking very much about it because a certain element of the press . . . would undoubtedly pervert it, attack it and confuse the public mind."

As shipments abroad mounted, though, the Roosevelt Administration had to devise new subterfuges to justify its largesse. On June 6 the Navy disclosed it was sending fifty Hell Diver scout bombers, assigned to reserve squadrons, back to the Curtiss-Wright company for resale to the British. The fifty Hell Divers were "temporarily in excess of requirements," according to the Navy's laborious explanation, because the pilots who would normally fly them were serving instead as instructors in the Navy's expanded training program. In time, these planes would be replaced by aircraft "of a superior type" with leakproof gas tanks and pilot armor. The Navy described the planes it was sending back, carrying two machine guns and 1,000 pounds of bombs, as aging, even though some had been in service for only three months. "As you know, a plane can get out of date, darned fast," Roosevelt explained at his June 8 press conference, a remark that was greeted with knowing laughter from reporters.

Impressed by the potency of German Stuka bombers in Europe, the Army had asked for one to three squadrons of the supposedly surplus Navy Hell Divers, a fact that was not disclosed to the public. But to Morgenthau, the British came first. "Nuts on the Army," he told Admiral John H. Towers, the chief of naval aviation.

Towers agreed, but he was worried about congressional reaction. "You realize we are subject to attack on the Hill?" he asked the Treasury Secretary.

"So are we all," Morgenthau replied prophetically.

Isolationists were indignant. "It is just a question of time until your sons will follow to man the planes and the ships," warned Democratic

Senator Homer Bone of Washington. "Some persons in this Administration are hell-bent to get us involved in this war. The method itself is hypocrisy and backdoor strategy."

Some newspapers disagreed. and struck back at the isolationists, The Youngstown, Ohio *Daily Vindicator* described the opponents of the aid to the Allies "as mistaken and downright traitorous." The Atlanta *Constitution* said "The people want action," and complained of delay on Capitol Hill. And the Charlotte *Observer* reported that "a large majority" of the letters received by North Carolina's two U.S. Senators favored immediate aid to the Allies.

For his part, Roosevelt refrained from debating the issue on its merits. Instead, when the subject of the surplus shipments arose at his press conference, the President described the transactions as if they merely illustrated good business sense. "The world situation has developed a demand for this deteriorated material, the sale of which would not have been possible a short time ago, but now it has an immediate value," he claimed. "Today we have more buyers. In other words it's a buyer's market."*

Two days later, on June 10, the President temporarily abandoned such attempts at flim-flam when Italy, as expected, declared war on France, already on the verge of collapse under the weight of the German assault. Even before the official news arrived from Rome, a telegram from Churchill to Canadian Prime Minister Mackenzie King had disturbed Roosevelt. Churchill's telegram, a copy of which Roosevelt had received from the Canadians, offered no assurances that the British fleet would not be turned over to the Germans if Britain were to be defeated. Instead Churchill raised the possibility, as he had in his May 19 cable to Roosevelt, that he might have to turn His Majesty's Government over to Britons who, unlike himself, would be willing to bargain over the fleet with the Germans.

This of course was just what Churchill wanted Roosevelt to worry about. FDR took the bait. He instructed Jay Moffat, his new Ambassador to Canada, to urge the Canadians to get assurances that the British would never surrender their fleet. Also Roosevelt wanted the Canadians to help persuade London that the United States "could give almost as much help as a neutral as if she became a belligerent."

Clearly, Roosevelt decided, Britain needed a boost. Mindful that Mussolini was to speak in a few minutes, fully expecting what Il Duce

---

*Carried away by his enthusiasm, Roosevelt misspoke. As one alert reporter pointed out, he should have said "seller's market"

would say, Roosevelt talked to Moffat about the commencement speech he would give that afternoon at the University of Virginia in Charlottesville. The address would be a "tough one," Roosevelt said, drawing the issue between the democracies and the fascist powers "as never before." During the two-hour train ride through the Virginia foothills to Charlottesville later that day, the President pondered a cable from Ambassador Bullitt, repeating French Premier Paul Reynaud's caustic comment on learning that Italy was about to declare war: "What really distinguished, noble and admirable persons the Italians are to stab us in the back at this moment."

This bitter metaphor, penciled into the President's text at the last minute, would be fashioned into the most memorable phrase of the strongest speech the President had yet delivered on the war.* His visage grim under his cap and gown, his voice steely and laced with contempt, Roosevelt told the graduates: "On this tenth day of June 1940, the hand that held the dagger has struck it into the back of its neighbor." In Washington "an audible gasp of surprise combined with whistles of astonishment" could be heard from the crowd of reporters gathered around the radio at the National Press Club. Calling for "effort, courage, sacrifice and devotion" in a time of national peril, in words that were directed as much at Britons as at Americans, Roosevelt came closer than ever before to linking the security of the United States directly to England's fate. "To the opponents of force," he promised to extend "the material resources of this nation," at the same time as he vowed that the U.S. would speed up its own rearmament. "All roads leading to the accomplishing of these objectives must be kept clear of obstructions," he declared. "We will not slow down or detour. Signs and signals call for speed—and full speed ahead."

Despite the President's rhetoric, obstacles blocked the road, some, in a sense, of his own making. A week after his University of Virginia speech, Lothian suggested to him that the time might very well have come for him to make "a completely frank statement" about the consequences to the United States of British defeat, so that the American public might then conclude "that assistance to the British in every pos-

*Reynaud had used the "stab-in-the-back" phrase before, and it had been repeated in previous Bullitt cables. In fact it was contained in an early draft of Roosevelt's speech, but taken out because Sumner Welles argued that using it would make it impossible to get Mussolini's cooperation when the time came to make peace. But on the trip to Charlottesville the President evidently decided that Mussolini's services as a peacemaker could be dispensed with and reinserted the phrase.

sible way was its own best defense." Roosevelt refused. He and Hull worried that if they put too much stress on the threat to Britain, the public would demand that he shift the United States fleet, then stationed at Pearl Harbor, to guard against Japanese attack, to the Atlantic. In view of the danger from Tokyo, such a move, they told Lothian, would have "disastrous effects."

Lothian thought that argument far fetched. Whatever the reasoning, it was clear that Roosevelt preferred to rely on sleight-of-hand to ship arms to the British, rather than risk a public confrontation with the isolationists over the issue of aid to Britain.[*] This approach had worked with Enfield rifles, machine guns, mortar, and even dive bombers. When applied to warships it backfired, however, forcing the President into a retreat which cast a cloud over the entire effort to bolster Britain.

The train of events began in London well before Roosevelt's Charlottesville speech, on May 25, with an analysis by Britain's Joint Planning Committee submitted to the Chiefs of Staff, of the situation that would face the British if France should be defeated while Italy entered the war on Germany's side. Along with doing "our utmost" to get U.S. aircraft, the report urged "immediate steps . . . to obtain destroyers and motor torpedo boats." A note appended to the recommendations warned: "If we allowed any note of panic or hysteria to appear in our messages, the effect might be to convince the administration that they would be wiser to concentrate on the defence of the U.S. than to dissipate their resources in support of what would appear to be already a lost cause."

Under the circumstances, though, Arthur Purvis, Britain's purchasing chief in Washington, had little time to spare for such niceties. On May 29, the same day that he braced Morgenthau about Marshall's list of army ordinance, Purvis handed the Treasury Secretary a list of "naval priorities." Its chief items were the destroyers that Churchill had already been refused and "as many as possible" of a group of twenty-three motor torpedo boats then under construction for the Navy.

"The destroyer thing is out," Morgenthau told him immediately, "because somebody went to the President about that." "Somebody" apparently referred to Admiral Harold Stark, the Chief of Naval Operations, who would resist giving destroyers to the British to the bit-

---

[*]He had even gotten the Congress to go along part way with him, by authorizing the government to directly exchange the surplus material it turned back to the manufacturer for newer equipment, instead of reselling it and having to go to the Treasury for funds to buy the new equipment.

ter end. Stark claimed he needed every ship he had to patrol the Eastern seaboard and the Caribbean. Destroyers were in short enough supply so that Roosevelt was considering recommissioning the remaining thirty-five of the World War I vintage craft at a cost of $6 million.

Lunching with Ickes on June 4, Roosevelt found even more reasons for not turning the destroyers over to the British than he had already given to Churchill. First, he did not think they would be of much use because of their age and limited armament; the old ships carried only four guns, and had no anti-aircraft weapons. Besides, Roosevelt added, sending the ships might serve to "enrage Hitler" without doing the Allies much good. "We cannot tell the turn the war will take, and there is no use endangering ourselves unless we can achieve some results for the Allies."

As Ickes saw it, the President would lose no matter what he did. "If you do send some help with bad consequences to ourselves the people will blame you, just as they will blame you if you don't send help and the Allies are crushed."

Giving up on destroyers for the time being, Purvis concentrated on obtaining the torpedo boats. These the British intended to use for much the same purposes served by destroyers, to guard against invasion and hunt down submarines. In contrast to the British plea for destroyers, this request seemed to offer little difficulty. Roosevelt and his advisers failed to foresee that the torpedo boats would set off such a storm as to make any possible destroyer deal more remote than ever.

No sign of trouble loomed on May 30, when Morgenthau informed the British that they would be able to get 20 of the 23 torpedo boats under construction. The Navy would get 20 boats of its own, six months later. The Navy justified the deal on the grounds that the later models could be improved based on the performance of the older boats in combat under the British flag. Then, too, the boats carried tubes for 18-inch torpedoes, which the Navy had ruled obsolete in favor of 21-inch missiles.

While some people might raise eyebrows about the legality of these rationales, the President himself apparently had little patience for such quibbling. At the June 4 Cabinet meeting, while the torpedo boat deal was going forward, Navy Secretary Charles Edison mentioned to Roosevelt that the Navy's Judge Advocate General had said that the transaction was illegal. FDR scoffed. He described the Navy's top legal officer as "a sea lawyer," and "an old admiral whose mental capacity I know personally," from the President's days as Assistant Secretary of the Navy. Better send him on vacation, he advised Edison, and if the man next in line didn't know any better, he should also go on vacation.

Edison, who knew his days at the Navy Department were numbered, kept repeating his initial objections until finally, the President told him: "Forget it and do what I told you to do."

While Roosevelt pursued his schemes to aid them, the British monitored the American mood. "U.S. public opinion is on the fence and the next few days or weeks it will be on one side or the other," T. North Whitehead, one of the Foreign Office's American specialists, had noted on May 31. On that day, the British were in the midst of the Dunkirk evacuation which was to conclude on June 4 with the evacuation of about 338,000 British and Allied troops.

It was hailed as a miracle. Churchill himself wryly noted: "We must be very careful not to assign to this deliverance the attributes of a victory; wars are not won by evacuations." The Prime Minister calculated that Britain would need three to six months to replace the equipment left behind on the bomb-torn beaches. He and his advisers realized that Americans questioned whether Britain could survive Hitler's war machine. While the American public wanted to "see the Nazi regime smashed," Whitehead noted, Americans had yet to make up their minds as to whether the Allies could win, even if they got the U.S. help they asked for. "If we are judged unable to meet the German forces, our supplies of aeroplanes etc. will be curtailed in favor of the U.S. armed forces."

Hitler's forces underlined the point. On June 5, the day after Roosevelt had scoffed at Edison's objections at the Cabinet meeting, the Germans launched a massive new offensive, spearheaded by their swift Panzer divisions. The latest French defense line on the Somme was broken the next day. By June 9 the Germans had smashed their way to the Seine and seized Rouen.

British concern about the reaction of Americans to these defeats mounted. John Balfour, head of the Foreign Office's American department, cautioned Foreign Secretary Halifax that in their eagerness to get American supplies the British must avoid heavy-handed tactics. "The isolationists still command powerful forces in Congress," which if given some pretext by the British, could "raise a storm in public opinion which might well paralyze all effective U.S. action."

Events would soon lend substance to Balfour's anxiety. The triggering episode was a June 13 hearing by the Senate Naval Affairs Committee on proposed legislation to build up the fleet. With rumors swirling around the capital, California's Hiram Johnson asked the Naval officer testifying on behalf of the bill whether it was true that the Navy had agreed to transfer some of its destroyers to the British.

Nothing had been done about transferring destroyers, the officer replied truthfully. No one asked a question about motor torpedo boats, which would have required a different answer. Still Senator David Walsh, the Massachusetts Democrat and militant isolationist who chaired the committee, was not fully satisfied. Without much difficulty he pushed through the committee a resolution to investigate the whole issue of disposal of so-called surplus property by the Navy.

That spelled trouble, as the witness from the Navy Department realized. As soon as the hearing had concluded, the officer, whose name is lost to history, hurried back to the department's headquarters next door to the White House. There he alerted Assistant Navy Secretary Lewis Compton, who had been steering the torpedo boat transfer through the bureaucratic shoals. Hoping to limit the damage, Compton phoned Walsh the next morning to tell him of the torpedo boat transfer and immediately found himself summoned before the committee. In a few hours the committee learned about other negotiations as well, which Walsh later described as dealing with "the transfer or release of Naval property of one kind or another . . . of which no member of Congress had the slightest information or knowledge."

That same day Navy secretary Edison scribbled a note to the White House, headed "important." It would have taken a man of great character not have felt some degree of self-satisfaction to see that the course of action he had earlier counseled against, and had been derided for so doing, now threatened to blow up in the President's face. But if Secretary Edison had such feelings, he kept them to himself. Instead he merely warned the President of trouble ahead. "Sen. Walsh is reported to me as in a towering rage about sale of Navy stuff to Allies," Edison wrote. "He is threatening to force legislation prohibiting sale of anything. Whole committee in lather."

While this storm brewed in Washington, in London an increasingly hard-pressed Churchill cabled Roosevelt yet another plea for destroyers:

> If we have to keep as we shall, bulk of our destroyers on the east coast to guard against invasion, how shall we be able to cope with a German-Italian attack on the food and trade by which we live? . . . Here is a definite practical and possible decisive step which can be taken at once and I urge most earnestly that you will weigh my words.

The President did not respond, except to indicate to Ambassador Lothian his desire to help Britain in her hour of need. Told of this Churchill bluntly cabled Lothian:

I am deeply sensible of President's desire to help us. Please tell him that the most effective thing he can do is to let us have the destroyers immediately.

Following instructions, Lothian tried to prod Roosevelt into action. But the President told him that he was already having "the greatest difficulty" getting Congress to agree to release the torpedo boats he had promised the British and that it would be "impossible" to get approval for transferring the destroyers. In fact, as Lothian and Churchill would soon come to realize, as a result of the torpedo boat scheme, the stakes in the conflict between Roosevelt and the isolationists in Congress had been raised. Now all possible aid to the British was at risk, including of course the badly needed destroyers. And in this confrontation the President could hardly have found a more formidable adversary.

By the time he lifted his bulky six-foot frame to the Senate floor to challenge the President on the torpedo boat issue, David Walsh had made his mark on his state and his country, his career reflecting the cross currents that accounted for how Franklin Roosevelt's Democratic Party viewed America's role in the world.

Walsh's manner and appearance established him as nearly a caricature of the Irish pol. "He votes wet and drinks wet," *Time* magazine had once observed. He paid attention to his dress, affecting silk shirts in bright colors and stripes. But a regular regimen of exercises failed to restrain his stomach from bulging over his belt or his double chin from jutting out over his stiff collar. At the podium his voice was husky, his manner earnest; in full flight he often rubbed his hands together vigorously and tugged his right ear.

The son of a $12-a-week laborer, Walsh had had a career that touched the pride of the Massachusetts Irish, a rising new breed in that state's democratic party. Denied the gloss of Harvard, he instead worked his way through the grittier terrain of the College of the Holy Cross in Worcester in three years, then studied for the law at Boston University. In 1913, just before his fortieth birthday, he became the first Irish Catholic elected governor of his native state and moved up to the Senate in 1918.

Working-class voters flocked to his banner in Massachusetts, and Walsh steadfastly backed most of Roosevelt's economic reforms and in 1938 co-authored the Fair Labor Standard Act of 1938, the last of New Deal's landmark achievements. But now on foreign policy the two men differed sharply, with Walsh adhering to an isolationism strongly rooted in his Irish origins. More than decades earlier, in October of 1919, he had urged the Senate to reject Wilson's League of Nations, complaining of the British oppression of Ireland. Wilson typically never forgot or forgave this betrayal from a fellow Democrat. When Walsh was seeking reelection to the Senate in 1924, Wilson denounced him from his deathbed and, many felt, helped to bring about Walsh's defeat by a narrow margin.

But Walsh bounced back, regaining his seat in the Senate, where he dedicated himself to building up the fleet. In 1935 during debate on a proposal to increase Naval spending, Senator Nye, in opposition, challenged Walsh, now chairman of the Naval Affairs Committee, to define foreign policy. "It depends on the state of mind of the President and State Department at any given time," Walsh said. "We have simply got to trust the patriotism and the genius of the President," he added loyally.

Now, from what he had learned about the navy's torpedo boat transaction, Walsh had decided that it was time to stop relying on the President and instead look to Congress to exercise its own prerogatives. On June 19, as word came that the Navy was prepared to go ahead with its plans, Walsh denounced the deal as "a grievous wrong" to young Americans who might be summoned to defend their country. Disposal of these speedy craft would leave the U.S. coast vulnerable to enemy attack, he warned. At the White House, Roosevelt's press secretary Stephen Early stood behind the Navy's claim that it would benefit from the trade in the long run.

But the President was concerned and turned the matter over to his attorney general, Robert Jackson. While Jackson pondered, he got some advice from the man who had became Roosevelt's closest adviser on a broad range of issues, Harry Hopkins. No lawyer, Hopkins had won a reputation for finding fresh solutions to old problems but in this predicament he appeared overmatched. "Assuming we are in a jam over those ships to the British," Hopkins proposed a way out to Jackson, based on a somewhat lame explanation: "The British tell the Navy that for some appropriate reason, they do not want the ships."

It was too late for such flimsy pretexts. The Administration, on shaky legal ground to begin with, now found that the tide of battle in Europe was eroding its position. On June 21, two days after Walsh's initial attack on the torpedo boat deal, a French delegation received armistice terms from the Germans in the same railway car at Compiègne forest where twenty-two years earlier World War I had ended in German defeat. No discussion of the German demands was permitted. In Washington, the isolationists had a field day on the floor of the Senate, citing the French collapse as evidence of FDR's folly in seeking to bolster the Allied cause. Far from helping, they complained that by promising the French support, the President had led them on to disaster with promises of arms he could not deliver.

"We have suffered a humiliation in foreign affairs the like of which has never happened in all of the history of these United States," declared Senator Nye. "Our President on his own responsibility may have encouraged a great and friendly power to ruin." In view of what had happened, Nye proposed that Roosevelt should retire and turn the presidency over to Hearst's old hero, Cactus Jack Garner. "In this crisis of national disaster," Nye said, "there is no one but the Vice President who can now restore the national unity and national confidence in governmental leadership."

The dominant figure on the floor that day, though, was Walsh of Massachusetts, as he set about reasserting congressional authority in the wake of the torpedo boat disclosure. "When these vessels leave the country, if they do," he warned, "there will not be another modern vessel of that type in case we are engaged in war." Walsh had a remedy in mind for the future, far-reaching in its scope. To establish the groundwork for his proposal, Walsh recalled that he had asked Assistant Navy Secretary Compton upon what authority he had acted in arranging the torpedo boat deal. In reply, Compton mentioned the recognized right of government agencies to modify contracts. "Who in God's name," Walsh thundered, "in the Congress or in the country thought that when such a power was given that these contracts . . . would be changed to assist one side or the other of belligerents at war?"

"Now Senators, see how careful we shall have to be in our legislation?" Walsh pointed out. "They have a right to modify or change their contracts."

Then Walsh offered as his plan to prevent any such thing from happening again a sweeping restriction, embodied in a new section of the naval appropriations bill then before the Senate. It applied to all U.S. military equipment and supplies, banning their disposal "in any manner whatsoever" except on the condition that the Army's chief of staff or the Navy's chief of naval operations certified that such material "is not essential to and cannot be used for the defense of the United States." As Secretary Edison had warned, Walsh was determined to ban the sales of "*anything*." (Emphasis added.)

Although the Senate immediately approved the amendment, some Senators complained that Walsh's revenge on the Navy would contravene the Senate's action taken only ten days before to legitimize Roosevelt's procedure for sending surplus equipment to the Allies.

"Under that provision not a single plane would be transferred to the Allies," Republican Senator Frederick Hale of Maine told Walsh. Lister Hill, Democrat of Alabama, took the floor to point out that a considerable difference existed between the phrases "not essential" and "cannot be used," which were both in Walsh's amendment. "Nearly anything could be used, as I construe it," Hill said. Even an old musket, though it might be obsolete, Hill argued, "would almost have to be so rusty or so broken or so worn that it could not be fired before any man could honestly certify that it could not be used."

In his years in the Senate Walsh had learned when to be stubborn and when to give ground. His main concern was in preserving the fleet, and his own authority as chairman of the Naval Affairs Committee. Now he saw no point to quibbling over details when he was getting the essence of what he wanted. "I think the distinguished Senator has called attention to language which might well be stricken out as too exacting." In response to Walsh's own request, the Senate quickly agreed to delete the objectionable phrase "cannot be used."

Walsh could afford to be generous. The President was in full retreat. On June 24, three days after the Senate approved Walsh's restrictive amendment, Roosevelt abruptly canceled the torpedo boat deal. By way of explanation, the President cited an "informal opinion" by Attorney General Jackson. Having found Hopkins's suggestion unhelpful, Jackson ruled that the transfer of the ships to Britain appeared to violate a Federal law banning an American company from selling warships to a belligerent.

Unwilling to confront the issue of aid directly, within the framework of the political system, the President had tried to evade its limitations. In the end he had been caught by Senator Walsh and forced to pay a price. For the British, now left alone to face Hitler, it was another piece of bad news. After talking to Welles, Lothian cabled home that the Undersecretary agreed that the collapse of the torpedo boat deal was "extremely unfortunate," but said the President "had no other option."

Not only was the torpedo boat transaction dead, but Walsh had appeared to all but end any hope for such future deals for American ships, including the much sought-after destroyers. It was true that at the last minute Walsh had relented, and by modifying his amendment had left the door open a crack. The narrow aperture, though, would be difficult for Roosevelt to exploit. Moreover, this was an election year. For the time being the President would be obliged to shift the focus of his attention from Britain's fate to his own political future.

# "He's Fixed It
# So Nobody Else Can Run"

Traveling in Europe with his family in July 1939, James Farley, Roosevelt's longtime campaign manager, was startled when, during a twenty-minute audience with Pope Pius XII, his Holiness asked if FDR would run for President for a third time.

"If he does, he would be breaking unwritten law, because no one has ever done so within our party system."

The Pope smiled. "You know I am the first Italian Papal Secretary of State to be elected Pope."

Like the Pope, Roosevelt was not overly impressed by precedent. In making the most important decision of his political career he was more concerned with events, particularly with the war in Europe. No one will ever know when Roosevelt finally decided to seek a third term in the White House. What is clear is that from the beginning of his second term he did all he could to keep the option of reelection open.

Roosevelt did have a fall-back plan, in case he should decide to choose the other option and retire. In January of 1940, four months after the start of World War II, he had signed a three-year contract with *Collier's* magazine under which he would become a contributing editor, writing twenty-six articles a year. In return *Collier's* would pay him $75,000 a year, since he declined to take more than his pay as chief executive, and provide office space and a staff. Thomas Beck, the publisher of the magazine, doubted that Roosevelt would ever fulfill the contract because he expected him to run for president. The progress of the war in 1940 would confirm Beck's skepticism as it steadily pushed Roosevelt further away from retirement and closer to another term in the White House.

The war made it easier for Roosevelt to maintain his flexibility because it gave him a good reason for delaying the announcement of his intentions, on the theory that ruling himself out as a candidate would restrict his ability to influence other nations. Equally important, the war also offered a justification for breaking the third term tradition. Taking every advantage of these circumstances, Roosevelt sought to demonstrate that while his leadership was essential to prepare the nation for war, he also was the man best suited to keep the nation at peace. Helping Britain could fit into this strategy only if he could persuade voters that doing so would strengthen the United States without increasing risk of war. To carry off this balancing act, the President set out first to throttle any challenge to his renomination within his own party and then to win bipartisan backing to disarm the Republican opposition.

Outside forces complicated his task. In the Congress Senator Walsh had created a forbidding new legal roadblock to British aid in general and the destroyer deal in particular. The French collapse in Europe, meanwhile, had fostered defeatism in the United States and increased the political risks of helping the beleaguered British. "The defeat and capitulation of France threw confusion in the Aid the Allies camp, discouraging enthusiasm and causing a sharp recession of the tide previously flowing strongly in that direction," a British survey of the American press noted late in June. Even strong supporters of the Allies like the columnists Dorothy Thompson and Walter Lippman "concentrated on arousing America to her own peril . . . instead of continuing to demand a specific program of action to defeat Hitler in Europe."

Even before the fall of France, some in the Foreign Office, sensitive to the American mood and the pressures on the President, had concluded that desperate begging for help would likely be counterproductive. "We must not over-stress our dire necessity, that would only show weakness," T. North Whitehead minuted at the end of May as the Nazi forces engulfed France. "If we can only persuade the Americans that we are confident of our success *and show reason* we shall get American help." (Emphasis in the original.) No less a personage than King George VI pursued this approach in a letter to the President in the week after the fall of France. Conceding that his country had endured "a series of disasters," His Majesty contended nonetheless that the "spirit here is magnificent." His subjects, the King said, "are inspired by the thought that it is their own soil which they now have to defend against an invader." Then the King came to the point, reminding the President of Britain's need for U.S. destroyers, "which is becoming greater every day if we are to carry on our solitary fight for freedom to a successful conclusion."

When nothing came of that Royal effort, Churchill considered trying to make another plea himself. "It has now become most urgent for you to give us the destroyers and motorboats," the Prime Minister began a cable on July 5 which became even more importunate as it went on: "It seems to me very hard to understand why this modest aid is not given now at the time when it could be decisively effective. Pray let me know if there is no hope." When the first draft could not pass muster with Foreign Secretary Halifax, Churchill gave up on the idea. Except for a courtesy notification that the Duke of Windsor would be posted as Governor of the Bahamas, the Prime Minister did not correspond directly with the President until the end of July.

This uncharacteristic exercise of restraint was probably Churchill's most important contribution to Anglo-American relations during that bleak period. Having concluded, as he confided to Jim Farley, that the British had only "about one in three" chances of surviving Hitler's onslaught, Roosevelt would scarcely have been receptive to further British requests for help. He wanted to be free to concentrate on his most immediate problem, the unfolding presidential campaign.

The most evident obstacle was the third term tradition, which had been established by Washington and confirmed by Jefferson. Yet it was a custom, not a law, and though no one had ever broken it, some Presidents had come close to trying. In the case of Andrew Jackson, ill health and advancing age may have had as much to do as tradition with his retirement after two terms. In FDR's own view, the first Roosevelt in the White House, his cousin Theodore, had at the least bent the tradition since he had served all but a few months of William McKinley's term and then had been elected to a full term in his own right before running on the Bull Moose ticket in 1912. In short, though Jim Farley's "unwritten law" was a barrier, it was not an insurmountable one if sufficient grounds could be found. In fact long before the start of the war in Europe Roosevelt's partisans had urged him to seek reelection, believing that only he could effectively pursue the New Deal's unfinished domestic agenda. "Between the third term precedent and the welfare of the country, can any patriotic citizen hesitate as to which course he will take?" Democratic Governor George Earle of Pennsylvania asked rhetorically in June of 1937.

For some, the failure of the 1938 purge of Democratic conservatives and the Republican victories that November illustrated Roosevelt's weaknesses as a lame duck, compelling reason that he run again. Tom Corcoran, one of the New Deal's brightest young legal lights, argued to Roosevelt that if he closed off the possibility of a third term, he would handicap himself in dealing with Democratic Party bosses around the country. Armed with what he described as Roosevelt's "non-dissent," Corcoran set out "subterraneously" to stir up support for a potential third term. He need not have bothered. The President was fully in charge of his own non-candidacy.

One favored tactic kept potential rivals off balance by encouraging nearly all of them while generating uncertainty about his own intentions. Chatting with Harry Hopkins in May of 1938, Roosevelt mentioned his own "disinclination" to run again and said Eleanor Roosevelt opposed the idea. Among other drawbacks to staying in the White House, the president said, was the effect on his personal finances. His mother, the imperious Sara Delano Roosevelt, was being forced to use her own savings to maintain the family residence at Hyde Park, and private life would presumably offer an ex-president lucrative opportunities.

Reviewing the field of possible candidates, the President quickly disposed of those most prominently mentioned by the press and other politicians. Secretary of State Hull was too old; Secretary of the Interior Ickes too abrasive. Roosevelt viewed his postmaster general and erstwhile campaign manager James Farley, whom he considered to be a foe of the New Deal, as "clearly the most dangerous" of the prospects, presumably because of his wide-ranging friendships among party leaders. Without benefit of explanation he rejected a number of others, including his Secretary of Agriculture Henry Wallace, and three present or former governors, Paul V. McNutt of Indiana, Frank Murphy of Michigan, and Earle of Pennsylvania.

Roosevelt then turned his attention to Hopkins's own prospects for the White House, an outlandish idea on its face since many Democratic professionals detested the 48-year-old Hopkins, who had never held elective office. Yet Roosevelt himself relied on Hopkins and the peculiar blend of idealism and cynicism that he brought to public service, more than on any of his other advisers. A social worker by profession, Hopkins early on earned a reputation for slashing red tape and trampling on bureaucratic egos as he ramrodded the programs of the New Deal's controversial new relief agencies. His hard-boiled bluntness often plunged him into hot water, most notably with one particularly telling phrase with which he was reported to have summed up the philosophy of the New Deal: "We shall tax and tax, and spend and spend and elect and elect." Conservatives viewed him as a dangerous left winger. Liberals mistrusted him as a ruthless schemer, and were put off by his fondness for first-class travel, fancy restaurants, and the company of Hollywood celebrities. Stricken with stomach cancer in 1937, he underwent surgery, which arrested the cancer but left him vulnerable to a host of other ailments.

Yet Roosevelt believed, or so he said, that Hopkins could overcome these liabilities, which also included a messy divorce. Hopkins could be elected, Roosevelt assured him, and would fill his presidential shoes better than any of the rest. To broaden Hopkins's experience and expand his public visibility, Roosevelt promised to make him Secretary of Commerce.[*] For the time being, Roosevelt counseled him to "keep back a little" on his candidacy to avoid premature exposure. As a result of what the playwright Robert Sherwood, an intimate of both men, described as this "extraordinary private conversation," Hopkins now believed that Roosevelt had designated him as his political heir. Even more extraordinary, though, was the number of other private conversations Roosevelt had with other ambitious men, to each of whom he artfully conveyed, along with his admiration, his professed conviction that each was well suited to be his successor, or at least to be on the national ticket.

"You can do it," he told his then Attorney General Homer Cummings in July of 1938, two months after he had pledged his support to Hopkins. "You make the best speeches of anyone in the Administration."

Three months later, in October of 1938, when Cordell Hull mentioned to him that some foreign policy issue could not be resolved "for several years, until this term is over," FDR replied: "Why that's fine. At that time you'll be in my chair, if my efforts succeed, and will be in good position to deal with it."

To Fiorello LaGuardia, a political maverick and nominal Republican who had won the New York mayoralty by defying Tammany Hall, Roosevelt confided early in 1939 that since he believed the party leaders wanted "a middle-of-the-road man," Roosevelt was prepared to accept Hull as the candidate—but only if the convention picked a progressive for second place. Among those acceptable to him in that role would be LaGuardia. In the same conversation, Roosevelt advised LaGuardia that progressives should threaten to run a third party candidate if the Democratic Convention failed to nominate a ticket to their liking.[†]

As for himself, in public and private Roosevelt continued to do what

---

[*]The President kept his word, nominating Hopkins to the Commerce Department post in December 1938. Hopkins was subsequently confirmed by the Senate.

[†]Roosevelt's admiration for LaGuardia was genuine, if not always expressed in a way that would have pleased "the Little Flower." Recalling for Homer Cummings how impressed he was with LaGuardia's delivery of a speech, he said that the Mayor had the audience "eating out of his hand," adding: "That little wop has something."

he had been doing all along, expressing his disinterest in another White House term. "You know Jim, it's a great comfort to me to know that there is no campaign lying in wait for me the end of this four years," the President told Farley at a Democratic victory dinner three months after his 1936 landslide triumph. "Yes sir, nothing but a nice long rest at Hyde Park." In his speech to the dinner audience Roosevelt declared; "My great ambition on January 20, 1941, is to turn over this desk to my successor, whoever he may be."

Asked a few months later about Governor Earle's implied endorsement of a third term at a press conference, Roosevelt said: "Oh my God! This hot weather is very hot," and then told the reporter who had asked the question: "Go over there and put on the dunce cap and stand with your back to the crowd."

Some who knew the President well felt that he protested too much. They noticed that his denials of interest in a third term were usually accompanied by belittling of other possible pretenders to the throne. "They were either too old or too young," Farley observed, "too ambitious or too unknown, too conservative or too radical, or in too poor health or too lacking in personality."

Perhaps the earliest such conversation Roosevelt held was with Henry Morgenthau, aboard the White House yacht *Potomac*, on a beautiful moonlit night in May of 1937, only four months into his second term. "I cannot help but think who will carry on as my successor after 1940," he said, then brought up several possibilities, most of whom he found wanting for one reason or another. Thinking about it afterward, Morgenthau suspected that the President wanted him to say: "Well, of course, Franklin you are the only one who can succeed yourself." But as he told his diary, "If that was what he was after, I did not rise to the bait."

The presidency "is a killing job," Roosevelt told Cummings when they talked in July of 1938. The ailing Jesse Jones, the 65-year-old Texas banker and head of various New Deal credit agencies, who was often mentioned for the job, "could not stand it for a month." As for Vice President Garner, whose cantankerous conservatism Roosevelt seemed to resent more with each passing day, "he could stand it by not attending to it." Henry Wallace shared his philosophy, the President believed, but "could not make a speech."

Conspicuously, the President always stopped just short of absolutely and positively foreclosing his possible candidacy. In his talk with Hopkins, Roosevelt "left a very slight margin of doubt" about his non-candidacy, in the event of a war. And when Harold Ickes in May of 1938 told the President that it would be hard to find a suitable liberal candidate to replace him, FDR "admitted the difficulty."

The fact was, as he acknowledged to Farley during a long after-dinner conversation in July 1939, Roosevelt did not really want people to believe that he had decided against running. He held that meeting with Farley, who since the death of Louis Howe in 1936 had been the man most directly involved with Roosevelt's political destiny, at a crucial point in their relationship which went back nearly two decades.

The son of Irish immigrants, born in Rockland County, New York, not far from Hyde Park, Farley early on displayed a natural bent for politics. At 23 he was elected town clerk in a heavily Republican community and won reelection three times. Affable, ambitious, hard-working, Farley rose steadily in the party, attracting the attention of Howe who recruited him to organize Roosevelt's campaigns for governor. Following Roosevelt's landslide reelection in 1930, Howe and Farley, with their eyes on the White House, cooked up a statement over Farley's name in which he declared: "I do not see how Mr. Roosevelt can escape becoming the next presidential nominee of his party, even if no one should raise a finger to bring it about." When Farley explained to Roosevelt what had been done, the Governor said only: "Whatever you said Jim, is all right with me."

That settled Farley's future. As manager and front man of Roosevelt's as yet undeclared candidacy, he roamed the country gaining allies and undercutting rivals. With Roosevelt's election Farley filled the dual role of national party chairman and Postmaster General, using the rewards of patronage to bolster the President's political stock. A celebrity in his own right, he gained sufficient fame to collect an endorsement fee from Lucky Strike cigarettes, though he did not in fact smoke or drink.

With his conservative political outlook, reflecting his Irish Catholic upbringing and his experience as successful purveyor of building supplies, Farley remained aloof from the great battles over policies and programs that absorbed most New Dealers. "I just want you to know that I'm interested in getting him the votes, nothing else," Farley once told Raymond Moley. "Issues aren't my business." To get votes, Farley put his faith in party organization and his own personal contacts. It was said that he never forgot a name or a face. A diligent correspondent, he penned a steady stream of brief but personal greetings, all signed with a flourish in green ink. Roosevelt's landslide reelection in 1936 crowned his career. Farley's grasp of the currents of the campaign allowed him to predict beforehand that the President would carry every state except Maine and Vermont.

The success, though, drove Farley and Roosevelt apart. The President suspected his manager of harboring ambitions for the presidency himself, while Farley believed that Roosevelt envied his own popularity in the party. Farley also resented that he was invited to the White House only for political occasions and never once as an overnight guest. He attributed these snubs to an attitude reflected in a remark by Eleanor Roosevelt: "Franklin finds it hard to relax with people who are not his social equals."

To help heal this rift, or at least discourage public speculation about it, mutual friends had persuaded Roosevelt to invite Farley to Hyde Park. After dinner in the fieldstone cottage where the Roosevelts had only a few weeks before served hot dogs to the King and Queen of England, the two went off to a small study to talk politics. There, while a breeze wafted through the huge trees outside, the President turned to one of his favorite subjects, the paucity of Democratic presidential talent available for 1940. "To begin with there's Garner," he said between sips of Danziger Goldwasser. "He's just impossible." Quickly he also turned thumbs down on some of the prospects in the Senate: Harry Byrd of Virginia, Millard Tydings of Maryland, Burton Wheeler of Montana. Significantly, though, he made no mention of Farley's own prospects.

Finally Farley asked Roosevelt about his own intentions. "Jim, I am going to tell you something I have never told another living soul," the President replied in a conspiratorial whisper. *"Of course I will not run for a third term."** But then he added significantly: "Now I don't want you to pass this on to anyone, because it would make my role difficult."

Farley gave him his word, and the President explained his plan. He would simply let pass, without taking any action, the filing deadline for candidates in the North Dakota presidential primary, which would fall on February 1 of 1940. From this, it could be inferred that he was not a candidate. Farley suggested a more direct approach; Roosevelt could write the North Dakota chairman to declare he was not running, but that was too direct for Roosevelt. Leaving Hyde Park the next morning, Farley realized that the Democratic Party's choice for the presidency in 1940 would remain a riddle, until the President solved it. But by seeming to take Farley into his confidence and not rejecting outright Farley's own ambitions, Roosevelt had assured himself of Farley's silence on this subject for some time to come.

With a year remaining before the Democratic convention, party

*The emphasis is in the original.

leaders stamped the potential presidential contenders as either loyalists or insurgents. The loyalists included men identified with the New Deal philosophy and record, like Attorney General Jackson and Hopkins, or longtime retainers, like Hull. Since their chances of nomination depended almost entirely on FDR's blessing, they were reluctant to put themselves forward until he had announced that he was not running.

The insurgents, men who had become disillusioned both with Roosevelt and the New Deal, notably Farley and Garner, had some support of their own. But they also were wary of asserting themselves prematurely, lest they unite the Roosevelt loyalists against them. By refusing to declare himself, the President froze both groups in place. As a result other political leaders stayed where Roosevelt wanted them, on the fence.

The outbreak of war in Europe, two months after his Hyde Park meeting with Farley and Farley's subsequent audience with the Pope, gave Roosevelt more flexibility. Opposition to his seeking a third term, as measured by the Gallup Poll, which had included about 60 percent of the public, declined by six or seven points after Hitler's invasion of Poland. With the country more evenly divided about his political future, Roosevelt could afford to bide his time. "Jim, we are on a day-to-day basis now, at home and abroad," Roosevelt told Farley in mid-September of 1939. "Problems will have to be met as they come along, including politics." Because of the emergency, Roosevelt said, he would have to scrap his idea to announce his own political plans by the North Dakota February filing deadline. "Now it looks as if I could do nothing until the spring, March or April." When Farley suggested that politics should be adjourned because of the war, the President heartily agreed.

Still, Farley could detect hints that the President was more unwilling than ever to rule out a third term. Less than two months after the start of the war, Secretary Wallace delivered a speech declaring that Roosevelt's talents were needed "to steer the country . . . to safe harbor." From a conversation with Roosevelt afterwards, Farley concluded that the President had known of Wallace's speech in advance. Roosevelt provided a stronger indication in November of 1939, when he told Farley he preferred that the Democrats convene after the Republican convention, thus buying him more time to conceal his hand. A few weeks later the President made plain that he wanted the convention in Chicago, where he was nominated in 1932, and where his faithful servant Mayor Edward J. Kelly could control the galleries.

Even if the President himself sought to avoid partisan talk, he dispatched Robert Jackson, whom he had just nominated as Attorney

General, to address a party fundraiser in Cleveland, where he hailed
Roosevelt as "our Lincoln" and scoffed at criticism of the President's
ambiguity about a third term. "Why should Franklin Roosevelt be the
one man in all public life now committed to accept or not accept a nomination?" Jackson demanded. "We do not want to put the greatest asset
of the Democratic Party in hock."

Regardless of what others might say, John Nance Garner did not
believe that Franklin Roosevelt was indispensable, or that the war justified waiving the third term ban. "I don't foresee any possibility of our
national existence hanging by a horse's hair, but I do see a dangerous
precedent in this third term business," the vice president told Farley. In
December of 1939 Garner announced his candidacy, inspired, many
believed, more by hopes of stopping Roosevelt than his own ambition.
Soon thereafter, Farley followed suit, after first checking with FDR. "I
think it's a grand idea," Roosevelt told him. And when Farley, seated
between Garner and Roosevelt at the election year Jackson Day
Dinner, began his address: "Fellow candidates," Roosevelt's laugh
"rang above the rest."

But so far as Roosevelt was concerned, third term politics was no
laughing matter, as Farley soon discovered. No sooner had his former
campaign manager actually declared his candidacy than Roosevelt
undercut him. He chose a weapon much favored in the capital, the calculated leak to the press, in this case, an account by a *Washington Post*
columnist and Roosevelt biographer Ernest K. Lindley of a supposed
conversation between Roosevelt and "one of the elder stalwarts of the
Democratic Party" about the forthcoming presidential campaign. Asked
whom he considered the most likely prospects to succeed him,
Roosevelt did not even mention Farley's name. And when the visiting
"elder stalwart" remarked on this, the President explained that while
Farley was much "deserving of recognition," and "a wonderful fellow,"
he feared that if Farley was put on ticket, even merely as vice-presidential running mate for Cordell Hull, his Catholic faith would hurt the
party's chances of winning. As Roosevelt was reported to have indeli-
cately framed the problem, it might lead people to suspect that "we
were using Cordell Hull as a stalking horse for the Pope." Asked about
this story the next day at his press conference, Roosevelt, instead of
refuting it, merely said he had not read it.

Outraged, Farley described the story in his diary "as one of the most
despicable things that has been done in a long, long time anywhere." To
Roosevelt he said nothing directly, but two weeks later, in an address to
the Friendly Sons of St. Patrick, Farley declared over a nationwide

radio hookup: "We must never permit the ideals of this Republic to sink to a point where every American father and mother, regardless of race, color or creed, cannot look proudly into the cradle of their newborn babe and see a future President of the United States."

Soon after the President congratulated Farley on his remarks and disavowed the Lindley column, contending that it was "made completely out of whole cloth." Roosevelt could afford that gesture. He had already accomplished one campaign year goal, which was to wound the candidate whom he regarded as most threatening to his own prospects.

The Lindley story accomplished another and equally important objective, elevating Hull to the phantom position of the Democratic Party's crown prince. Asked who he favored as his successor if he himself did not run, the President had replied, according to Lindley:

> Well I think Hull would be a good man, don't you? . . . He's safe. He can be elected. He would keep us out of war. And he's a lot more liberal than a lot of people around here think.

The logic underlying Roosevelt's decision to openly advocate Hull's candidacy, which he had hitherto only promoted in private conversation, was analogous to the thinking behind his choice of Hull as his Secretary of State. At the State Department Roosevelt looked to Hull, aided by his prestige and personal influence acquired during a quarter of century of service on Capitol Hill, to shield foreign policy from potential adversaries, particularly in the Congress. By designating him as most-likely-to-succeed to the Presidency, Roosevelt calculated Hull would cast a long enough shadow to blight the chances of other potential candidates with more energy and ambition.

Possessed neither of great imagination nor the gift of inspiring others, Hull nevertheless had earned respect for his probity, his diligence, and perhaps most of all for his durability. Hull was a survivor, the product of sturdy stock and a rigorous upbringing in the Cumberland foothills of Tennessee. His father had been shot and left for dead by a gang of Yankee guerrillas during the Civil War, but recovered enough to search out and locate his chief tormentor, whom he then summarily executed. For that deed no one ever raised a hand against him.

Born six years after the war was over, Cordell, one of five brothers, grew up wearing homespun. At 14 he dazzled a countywide audience by arguing the case for George Washington in a debate over whether the first President or Christopher Columbus had contributed more to America's greatness. His delighted father thereupon dug into his savings to help the young debate star go on with his education. The young man applied all his energies first to school, then to reading for the law, and finally to launching his political career with a post on the local Democratic county committee. Arriving in the U.S. House of Representatives, he soon gained fame for his dedication to the reduction of tariffs. More than any other factor, this issue drew Hull, freshly elevated to the U.S. Senate, to Roosevelt's presidential banner in 1931. Convinced that if Al Smith, Roosevelt's old ally and his chief rival for the nomination, had his way, the Democratic Party would become a protectionist stronghold, Hull turned to Roosevelt whom he had first met during Roosevelt's Wilsonian years at the Navy Department. In FDR's quest for the nomination, Louis Howe used Hull's Senate office as his Washington headquarters, while Hull rallied support for the New Yorker throughout Dixie.

After the election when Roosevelt asked him to become his secretary of state, the "thunderstruck" Hull conditioned his acceptance upon being assigned a major role in shaping foreign policy. "We shall each function in the manner you've stated," Roosevelt assured him and Hull signed on. The reality was very different. Not only did Roosevelt, who considered Hull to be boring and indecisive, insist on acting as his own secretary of state, but he also portioned out much of the remaining responsibilities to men with whom he was closer personally, including Undersecretary Sumner Welles and Treasury Secretary Morgenthau. Hull meanwhile pleased the President by not complaining and continuing to boost the cause of freer trade and lower tariffs.

When Roosevelt had first broached the possibility of Hull seeking the presidency in October 1938, Hull told him: "I think the world is going straight to hell, and I can be of greater service in the State Department." In the following months, as Roosevelt continued to drop his name in connection with the presidency to enough other people, Hull prudently told his friends he had no interest in seeking the office, without slamming the door shut. Then in March of 1940, hard on the heels of the Lindley story, he learned that his name had emerged as "being the most available and the best equipped," in a conversation Roosevelt had with Homer Cummings. As Breckinridge Long recorded in his diary, "All pointed to the thought that the Chief was going to be for Hull and Jackson—at least for the time being—but that he was himself still in the picture."

Roosevelt himself fanned Hull's hopes. When Mrs Hull, seated next to the President at a White House dinner in April 1940, remarked that her husband did not like to give speeches, Roosevelt replied: "Well tell him he had better get used to it. He'll have a lot of it to do soon."

Soon such machinations were overshadowed by the thrust of Hitler's armies across Europe. The Germans realized that their victories were aiding Roosevelt, whom they regarded as their most potent American adversary. Following the Norwegian invasion, Hans Thomsen, the German Chargé d'Affaires, cabled Berlin that U.S. public opinion was "in a high state of tension by allusion to dangers threatening America from an Allied defeat." Thomsen, who had been Berlin's top envoy to the U.S. since the U.S. reaction to the Kristallnacht pogroms of November 1938 forced Hitler to recall his Ambassador, concluded that with Americans succumbing to a mood "of hysterical excitement," Roosevelt's reelection chances "have improved considerably."

The polls supported Thomsen's appraisal. In March only 47 percent told Gallup they would vote to reelect Roosevelt; in his May survey a healthy majority of 57 percent gave their backing to the President. A seasoned politician like John Nance Garner had no trouble reading the trends. As the Germans swept across France and Roosevelt soared in the polls, Cactus Jack gave up on his candidacy and conceded that Roosevelt would be the nominee, thanks in part to his adroit maneuvering. "Hell," Garner told Farley, "he's fixed it so nobody else can run now."

Having established firm control of his own party, the President sought to shield his forthcoming candidacy from partisan attack by cloaking his presidency in the aura of national unity. Actually he had nurtured that stratagem since the start of the war, suggesting to Farley the previous fall that persuading Republican leaders to attend the Democratic Party's Jackson Day dinner would benefit the defense program. Farley, who considered that notion as "a hollow subterfuge at best," dragged his feet and despite Roosevelt's continued persistence nothing came of the idea.

Republican leaders, suspecting that Roosevelt wanted to lure some members of their party into his Administration, tried to head him off. Following a White House meeting two weeks after Hitler assaulted France and the Low Countries, Alfred Landon, the GOP's 1936 standard-bearer, demanded that Roosevelt disavow any third-term ambitions as the price for getting Republicans on board. Doing so, Landon contended, would establish the President as "the leader of the nation, instead of the head of a party." The only response was a White House statement saying that the President had no time to waste on politics because "he is too busily engaged with problems of far greater importance."

By June, with all of Europe under Hitler's heel and his own country in a state of turmoil and distress, the national unity theme appealed more than ever to the President. His cabinet problems offered him an irresistible opportunity to sound that note dramatically by installing two prominent Republicans in his Administration. On June 20 he announced the resignation of Army Secretary Woodring, to be replaced by Herbert Hoover's Secretary of State, Henry Stimson, and the replacement of Navy Secretary Charles Edison, who had resigned two weeks earlier, by Alfred M. Landon's 1936 running mate, Frank Knox. "The reason for the move," the President said, "was the overwhelming sentiment of the nation for national solidarity in a time of world crisis and on behalf of national defense, and nothing else."

The effect Roosevelt sought was marred by Woodring's exit. Anticipating his fate, the Secretary of the Army, a native Kansan, had conveyed his objections to the President's policies to the Topeka *Capital* with the understanding that they would be disclosed when the axe fell. In the subsequent story, Woodring claimed that "a small clique of international financiers" who wanted to entangle the U.S. in "the European mess" had forced him out because of his opposition to "stripping our defenses to aid the Allies."

Immediately Gerald Nye demanded a full-scale investigation into the ouster, decrying Roosevelt's choice of two men "whose utterances have been so definitely and directly in support . . . of a policy that might most readily land us in the middle of the European War." Noting reports that Knox's appointment had been discussed two or three months earlier, Nye unleashed his heaviest sarcasm: "The appointment was delayed until the opening of the Republican National Convention to avoid there being any ground whatsoever for a charge that there was a political consideration involved."

In fact Roosevelt's move added significantly to the already considerable confusion prevailing among Republicans who were gathering in Philadelphia for the official opening of their convention, on June 24, only four days after his announcement of the cabinet changes. Not since their bitterly fought 1912 convention, which culminated in Theodore Roosevelt's bolting the party to contest the candidacy of President Taft, had the normally staid Republicans been in such a state of turmoil. The reasons for the turbulence were not hard to identify: the war in Europe and the surging presidential candidacy of Wendell Willkie.

The war created a wrenching dilemma for the GOP as its leaders tried to hold on to its isolationist base yet still not lose touch with other Americans, who were growing increasingly concerned about the threat to the U.S. security from abroad. The Knox and Stimson appointments dramatized this split, and Republicans struggled to find a common response. In his indignation, John D. M. Hamilton, national chairman, who had been urging the party to broaden its appeal, excommunicated the two defectors. "Having entered the cabinet," he said, "these men are no longer qualified to speak as Republicans for the Republican organization."

The reaction of the man of the hour was far more measured. Wendell L. Willkie said only: "Each conscientious individual has to measure such things according to the dictates of his own conscience," language carefully chosen to avoid diverting attention from his drive for the Presidency which rivaled in speed and boldness Hitler's thrust to the English Channel.

Willkie's candidacy challenged credulity. Not only had he never held elective office before, he had made his fortune and his reputation as a utility company tycoon, in an era when big corporations still bore much of the stigma for the Great Depression. An ex-Democrat, he made his start in politics by reaching for the Republican Party's highest prize. Moreover, the Indiana native championed an internationalist faith that totally repudiated the isolationism which was one of the defining beliefs of his adopted party.

Yet his stock had soared in opinion polls, placing him second only to the front-runner, Thomas E. Dewey, whose triumphs as a gang-busting prosecutor in New York had established him as a national hero. In a party whose leaders seemed stuffy and remote, typified by Herbert Hoover, Willkie's fresh, vigorous persona stirred excitement not seen since Teddy Roosevelt's heyday. He bore the aura of a political outsider, always attractive to Americans with their natural suspicion of politics. Finally, but certainly not least in importance, he had benefited from a brilliantly conceived and executed promotional effort, that for the first time applied Madison Avenue's mass persuasion techniques to market a political candidate. "The Willkie boom was one of the best engineered jobs in history," conceded one of its draftsmen, Fred Smith. And its greatest achievement was that it somehow managed to seem spontaneous, down to the point of packing the galleries with Willkie supporters whose chant of "We Want Willkie" echoed through the convention hall.

Also boosting Willkie's cause were the national magazines which then greatly shaped public opinion and whose fervor reached its peak as the convention approached. The Luce publications led the way for Willkie. In an eleven-page article in its May issue, *Life* hailed him as "by far the ablest man the Republicans could nominate." In its June 10 issue, *Time* observed that while Dewey "was fumbling with the topic of foreign affairs, while Taft appeared to be running toward the wrong goal posts, Willkie seized the ball," by declaring that England and France were the first line of defense for the U.S. against Hitler.

The tide continued to run in Willkie's direction at the start of the convention when cool heads prevailed at the platform committee about the Knox–Stimson defections, a potential trouble spot for Willkie. The platform writers had intended to reinforce the GOP's traditional isolationist themes in the platform, which would have embarrassed Willkie who had made no secret of his conviction that the U.S. needed to aid the British. Fortunately for him, Landon, who had picked Knox as his running mate in 1936, also believed isolationism had outlived its political usefulness. In charge of the foreign policy plank, Landon minimized the reaction to the defection.

Unbeknownst to most of the participants, Hitler's regime, which was closely monitoring the campaign in both parties, tried to influence the outcome of the argument. Working through a front man, George Sylvester Viereck, who had been the Kaiser's agent in the U.S. during World War I, the Germans contributed to the cost of full-page ads in major papers on June 25 that trumpeted the isolationist case. Whatever the Germans hoped to accomplish, as it turned out, the Republican's foreign policy plank, adopted without debate, amounted to nothing more than a mushy manifesto, blaming the New Deal for unpreparedness and vowing to give "peoples fighting for liberty such aid as shall not be in violation of international law or inconsistent with the requirements of our own national defense." This document, remarked the journalist H. L. Mencken, was "so written that it will fit both the triumph of Democracy and the collapse of Democracy, and approve both sending arms to England or sending only flowers."

Regardless of the platform language, the war shaped the contest for the nomination. It wrecked the candidacies of the two most isolationist contenders: Senators Vandenburg and Robert A. Taft of Ohio, son of the president, whose views suddenly seemed outdated. In the midst of the Dunkirk crisis, Taft declared: "This is no time for the people to be wholly absorbed in foreign battles." Two days later, he remarked that he preferred a German victory to U.S. involvement in the war. For his part, Vandenberg, unable to break loose from his isolationist legacy, tried to change the subject by accusing Roosevelt of manipulating the Democratic nominating contest. "The only smoke-filled room this year will be in Chicago," he predicted, "and the smoke will come from one long cigaret holder."

As for front-runner Dewey, he had tried early in the race to find a middle position between Willkie and the isolationists. Influenced by the theory of his foreign policy adviser, John Foster Dulles, that Hitler was "a passing phenomenon," Dewey contended that the U.S. should stand aside and "wait for a stalemate" before exercising its influence. After Hitler's May offensive, Dewey shifted his stand, endorsing FDR's call for vastly increased defense spending. But the upheaval abroad made his youth and unfamiliarity with foreign affairs a handicap. With the world collapsing in Europe, one of his advisers said, Republicans were not about to nominate "a 38-year-old kid," whose political reputation derived mainly from his record as racket-busting district attorney and whose major experience abroad came from a bicycle tour of Europe taken in 1925. A skit at the annual Gridiron club dinner in Washington underlined Dewey's problem. When the actor playing Dewey was asked how he proposed to deal with Hitler and Mussolini, the crimebuster replied "Indict them!"

Dewey tried last-minute maneuvers at the convention, striving to make his middle way work. He supported aid for the Allies, while staying out of the war. When asked about selling destroyers to the British, though, he balked; "We haven't half enough warships as it is," he said.

But the rush of events was sweeping Willkie forward. Overwhelmed by the Wehrmacht, France had left the war two days before the convention opened, and England now stood alone against Hitler. In London, Churchill vowed to "fight on unconquerable until the curse of Hitler is lifted from the brows of mankind," and called upon Britons to conduct themselves so "that, if the British Empire and its Commonwealth last for a thousand years, men will still say: 'This was their finest hour.' "

Britain's supporters in the U.S. asserted that this was a crisis the Republican party could not afford to ignore. "For eighteen months the Republican Party has been walking in its sleep," Walter Lippman wrote in the *Herald Tribune*. "The speeches of Messrs. Taft and Dewey during these critical months make Mr. Neville Chamberlain seem like a far-sighted and strong statesman."

In Philadelphia, shaken by Europe's seismic upheavals, the GOP roused itself from its prolonged slumber. The British took heart from the "anti-isolationist" tone of the keynote speech delivered by the youthful Minnesota Governor Harold Stassen, Willkie's floor manager. He claimed that Roosevelt's bringing Republicans Knox and Stimson into the cabinet amounted to "a confession of failure" to prepare the nation's defenses. More important from the British point of view, he did not accuse the President of trying to lead the country into war.

The British also viewed as significant that Stassen got a much more enthusiastic reception than confirmed isolationist Herbert Hoover received the next night. "Every whale that spouts is not a submarine," Hoover declared as he sought to touch off a boom for another run for the presidency. "Three thousand miles of ocean is still a protection." As for Hitler and Mussolini, Hoover said: "The day will come when we might be of service to humanity in dealing with these same men for peace," a suggestion he struggled to clarify at a press conference the next day when he was asked if he meant to advocate the appeasement of the aggressors.

In this environment, Willkie's unorthodoxy, which would have gotten him hooted out of most previous Republican conventions, served him well. This was after all a year in which the columnist Dorothy Thompson suggested that both parties suspend their regular conventions and agree instead on a joint ticket of Roosevelt for President and Willkie as his running mate.

The outcome in Philadelphia was almost that astounding. On the sixth ballot, with Willkie gaining in nearly every state, Chairman Joe Martin, the House Republican leader, found it hard to keep order in the din raised by galleries chanting, "We want Willkie."

"Well, if you'll be quiet long enough, maybe you'll get him," he snapped.

Sure enough, in a few minutes, the Pennsylvania delegation put Willkie over the top. In a brief speech of thanks the next day, the newly chosen standard-bearer said: "In America we all have a common purpose at this time, that this way of life shall not pass from this earth."

For Hitler's Germany, the news of Willkie's nomination was "unfortunate," Chargé d'Affaires Thomsen cabled Berlin. "He is not an isolationist," Thomsen said, adding that "his attitude in the past permits no doubt that he belongs to those Republicans who see America's best defense in supporting England by all means 'short of war.' In makers of foreign policy the present difference between Willkie and Roosevelt is at most one of methods and not of belief. . . ."

The German appraisal was one that few American politicians would quarrel with, and it meant that, for Roosevelt, Willkie's nomination was a mixed blessing. He knew that Willkie was not likely to attack him for aiding the British, because of Willkie's own beliefs. But he also knew that Willkie's willingness to respond to the world crisis, along with his aggressiveness and spontaneity, made him a far tougher challenger than any of the conventional Republican politicians. The President said as much to Jim Farley when the two met at Hyde Park on July 7, for one last council of war before the Democratic convention. "You know if the war should be over before the election and I am running against Willkie, he would be elected," he said.

Roosevelt's mother also seemed to be concerned about her son's chances. "I would hate to think of Franklin running for the Presidency if you were not around," she told Farley when she welcomed him to Hyde Park. "I want you to be sure to help my boy."

"Mrs. Roosevelt," Farley blandly replied, "you just have to let these things take their course."

After lunch, when the two men took their coats and ties off in the heat of the summer afternoon and sat down alone in the President's study, Farley tried for the umpteenth time to draw from Roosevelt the truth about his intentions.

"Jim, I don't want to run and I'm going to tell the convention so," Roosevelt said.

"If you make it specific, the convention will not nominate you," Farley told him, mustering all his hopes behind his words. But when Farley challenged the President to issue a statement modeled after General Sherman's famous declaration that he would not run if nominated and would not serve if elected, Roosevelt said "I could not in these times refuse to take the inaugural oath, even if I knew I would be dead within thirty days."

Farley now realized that the President "had sold himself the idea, that with the world in crisis, he was the only one qualified to serve." Farley told Roosevelt that his own name would go before the convention, to show his opposition to the third term, but he left no doubt that he knew who the convention would select.

By this time Cordell Hull had reached the same conclusion after a similar conversation with Roosevelt during which, Hull noted, the President's "whole tone and language" had represented "a complete reversal" from what it had been not long before. In the face of this turn-about, Hull politely and loyally repeated previous disclaimers of his own interest in the presidency. Even Hull's loyalty had its limits, though. He rejected Roosevelt's offer to make him his running mate. Roosevelt persisted, phoning Hull at his home and asking to speak to his wife, Frances. "I'll convince her and she can convince you," the President said.

"Mrs. Hull has gone to bed," Hull told the president while his wife stood by his side. "I can't call her to the phone."

"If you don't take it, I'll have to get Henry Wallace," Roosevelt warned.

"That's all right with me," Hull said.

Even if all the principals now knew what the convention's outcome would be, the public suspense was not yet over. Sustaining it was essential to Roosevelt's convention strategy. Assured of the nomination, but concerned about trespassing on the third term tradition, he needed to demonstrate until the last moment his reluctance to serve and the convention's spontaneous determination to draft him.

In the week before the convention, he summoned his favorite speechwriter, Sam Rosenman, to the White House to help him prepare his acceptance speech. Then he dispatched Harry Hopkins to Chicago, bearing a letter from him to Alabama Senator William Bankhead, the keynote speaker. Roosevelt asked Bankhead to report to the convention "the simple and sincere fact" that he did not want to serve a third term, thereby releasing Roosevelt's supporters to vote as they pleased. But the letter did not make the sort of Shermanesque renunciation that Farley had suggested.

Over the weekend, while Roosevelt and Rosenman hammered out Roosevelt's speech on board the *Potomac*, Hopkins tried to take command in Chicago. He set up headquarters in Suite 308–309 of the Blackstone Hotel—the smoke-filled room that gave Warren Harding the presidency in 1920—and kept in touch with the White House over a special phone installed in the bathroom.

He had a hard time. Though Roosevelt made Hopkins his personal representative, he gave him no instructions. To blur matters further, when asked not long before by some of his key supporters to whom they should turn to for guidance, he had suggested another longtime confidant, Senator James Byrnes of South Carolina. With no definitive word from the President on the eve of the convention, the delegates fussed and grumbled. Hopkins did not help matters. Delegates complained to Farley, who was certainly a sympathetic listener, that Hopkins was "arrogant" and "demanded blind obedience."

In these circumstances, Roosevelt's foes made hay, promoting the idea of an anti–third term platform plank. They recalled that in 1896, the convention, determined to squelch any possible thought of renominating incumbent President Grover Cleveland, had declared a prohibition on a presidential third term to be "the unwritten law of this Republic."

In great distress, Roosevelt's supporters in Chicago called Rosenman to warn that if Bankhead read the President's message, the delegates might take him at his word and turn to Farley. Roosevelt relented to the point of delaying the reading of the message until the convention's second night when it would be delivered by Senator Alben Barkley of Kentucky, presumed to be more favorably inclined to a third term than was Bankhead.

Meanwhile, with the President distracted by this internal debate over tactics, a full-scale battle erupted over the party platform's foreign policy plan, with the isolationists demanding a firm stand against U.S. intervention. Once again, Hitler's regime played a background role, building on what Thomsen claimed to be the success of the embassy's efforts at the Republican convention. This time, in addition to sponsoring newspaper ads, the embassy contributed $4,350 to help pay train fare to Chicago for various isolationists.

The isolationists' drive to influence the platform was a broad effort. On July 15, the convention's opening day, a full-page ad in the *Chicago Tribune*, over the name of the National Committee to Keep America Out of Foreign Wars, carried the headline: "Stop the March of War," then ticked off supporting quotations from five Democratic Senators: Burton Wheeler, Hiram Johnson, Bennett Clark, David Walsh, and West Virginia's Rush Holt. Also on hand were such pacifist organizations as the National Council for Prevention of War and the Women's International League for Peace and Freedom which had helped to instigate the Nye Committee hearings four years earlier. Wheeler, who served as field marshal for the isolationists at the convention, credited both these groups for the influence of isolationists on the platform at a convention supposedly under the control of an incumbent president.

Concerned that the platform that was emerging sounded too isolationist, Hull complained directly to Roosevelt, but the President said it was too late to do anything, and promised that no matter what the platform said, it would not change his foreign policy. Ultimately the platform battle boiled down to a struggle over a plank backed by isolationists pledging that the U.S. would not participate "in foreign wars" or send troops to fight "in foreign lands." The President's compromise solution was to insert the phrase "except in case of attack."

With that out of the way, the time came for Kentucky Senator Barkley, serving in Bankhead's stead, to deliver Roosevelt's message to the delegates. No sooner did Barkley finish, than Chicago Mayor Kelly took over. He had arranged for the voice of Thomas D. Garry, Chicago's superintendent of sewers, to boom out over the convention public address system, chanting over and over again:"We want Roosevelt. The party wants Roosevelt. Everybody wants Roosevelt." The delegates, some of whom were at first puzzled by Roosevelt's ambiguous declaration, responded to Garry, picked up their state standards, and paraded around the floor. The next night on the first and only ballot, Farley, Garner, and Tydings of Maryland drew a combined total of 150 protest votes, while Roosevelt had nearly 950. In one last gesture to Roosevelt, Farley then moved to have the nomination officially recorded as by "acclamation."

One final discordant note was provided by the President's surprise choice of Agriculture Secretary Wallace as his running mate, just as he had warned Hull he would do. Roosevelt reasoned that Wallace's unabashed liberalism would help keep the New Deal torch burning. Also, his strong agricultural background would help counteract the appeal of Willkie's running mate Charles McNary, a longtime advocate of farm relief measures. But the delegates were in a cranky mood anyway; they resented the fact that Wallace was a convert from Republicanism, and many viewed him, in Farley's words, as "a wild-eyed fellow." Only a reassuring speech by Eleanor Roosevelt and all the energy of Roosevelt's lieutenants on the scene avoided an outright rebellion and gained approval of Wallace's nomination, by a vote of only 627 out of 1,100. But the mood was sour, that the President's new running mate prudently did not even attempt an acceptance speech.

The President had won a stunning personal victory, triumphing over not just the ambitions of other individuals but a tradition that many regarded as an inviolable component of the political system. He had overcome this system, which had often foiled him in the past, by using artifice to exploit circumstance. It remained to be seen how well these tactics would serve him in the future.

In his acceptance speech, made after midnight on the convention's final session, the President reiterated his statement, read by Barkley, that he did not want to run but explained that "my conscience will not let me turn my back upon a call to service." As he neared the end of his address the President framed the campaign within the context of the world crisis which had made his nomination possible. "We face one of the great choices of history," he said. "It is the continuation of civilization as we know it versus the ultimate destruction of all that we have held dear . . . ." "The American people must decide whether these things are worth making sacrifices of money, of energy and of self."

But the people would not choose until November. Before then, the President faced decisions of his own and time was running out.

# "Somebody's Nose Is Out of Joint"

Few Americans traveled to Europe in the tumultuous summer of 1940. Not surprisingly, then, the rumpled middle-aged man who presented himself at the LaGuardia Field boarding gate for Pan American's Atlantic Clipper on Sunday, July 14, attracted attention. He told reporters merely that he had been called abroad on "private business" which would keep in him London only for a few days. William J. Donovan had not had time to think of a more convincing cover story. His assignment was of the greatest urgency, commissioned by the highest authority. In his briefcase, along with a special passport, was a sheaf of letters of introduction. Addressed to the most prominent names in British industry and government, they explained that Donovan's mission had "the full approval of the President of the United States."

The British had received first word of his impending trip the previous Wednesday, July 10. That night German bombers struck at British shipping in the English channel and at docks in South Wales, opening the first phase of the Battle of Britain. In his subterranean war room Churchill brooded over a report from the Admiralty which showed that on this night and the next, high tides and the dark of the moon offered the enemy the "best conditions" for invasions at Dover and Portsmouth. Under the circumstances no one in authority at the Foreign Office paid much attention to Lord Lothian's cable from Washington reporting the imminent arrival in Britain of Colonel "Bill" Donovan, an emissary of newly confirmed U.S. Navy Secretary Frank Knox. As Lothian explained it, Donovan, who was vaguely remembered by some Britons as a much decorated hero of World War I, and the journalist Edgar Ansel Mowrer had been assigned to investigate the supposed undermining of resistance to the Germans in the countries they had conquered by "Fifth Column" Nazi sympathizers. Knox want-

117

ed assurance that the British would provide "all reasonable facilities" for expediting the inquiries of Donovan and his cohort.

Foreign Office officials initially assumed that Knox was still acting as proprietor of the *Chicago Daily News*, since if Donovan was on an official government assignment they would ordinarily have been alerted directly by the State Department. But two days later another cable from Lothian hinted that Donovan's mission had to be taken seriously, suggesting that "it would be very worthwhile for the Prime Minister to see him when in London." Four days later Lothian elaborated. He cabled that he had received a letter from Knox, explaining that Donovan was bound for England as his personal representative, and with the blessing of both the President and Secretary of State. Secretary Knox was eager that Donovan meet not only the Prime Minister, but "other leading personalties." The British swung into action, hastening to arrange Donovan's itinerary, sparing no effort.

As Donovan boarded the Clipper, the central question under discussion in Washington was whether providing the fifty destroyers sought by Churchill, or any other amount of U.S. aid, for that matter, would be sufficient to keep Britain fighting, or simply waste arms that the U.S. itself might desperately need someday. Stripped down to its essentials, Donovan's assignment was to give the British a chance to disprove the defeatist argument.

This mission seemed cut to order for him. In a situation where the nation's security was at stake, he was a bona fide war hero. And since World War I, he had kept abreast of advances in military technology, knowledge gleaned from first-hand inspections of battlefronts around the world. At a time when national unity was uppermost with the President, Donovan was a Republican in good standing. Moreover, as an Irish Catholic he was a member of a group that had long resented Great Britain and resisted giving that country any sort of help, even against the menace of Hitler. This background would lend extra weight to anything Donovan said to promote Britain's cause.

As one admiring colleague put it, Donovan, then 53 years old, was possessed of "indefatigable energy and wide-ranging enthusiasm combined with great resourcefulness." But perhaps more important in taking on this unprecedented task, Donovan prided himself on defying convention. He had little patience with detail and paid scant heed to lines of authority. "I'd rather have a young lieutenant with guts enough to disobey an order, than a colonel too regimented to think and act for himself," he would tell his staff during World War II, when as head of the Office of Strategic Services, he served as his country's chief spy-master.

He was born in Buffalo, to parents who were as staunchly Republican as they were Catholic, and in the best tradition of the lower middle class raised their children to be strivers. Donovan, the eldest, had two brothers, one of whom became a priest, the other a doctor. All benefited from their father's determination to compensate for his own lack of education by creating a library for them at home, encouraging Donovan to be a voracious reader all his life.

After graduating from Buffalo's parochial schools, Donovan thought briefly about entering the priesthood. He decided instead on Columbia University, earning tuition for his B.A. degree while he rowed in the crew and quarterbacked the football team. "He always played quarter-back," his brother Vincent later pointed out. "He liked to manage things." Donovan stayed on at Morningside Heights to attend law school, graduating in 1905. He was by and large as undistinguished a scholar as was his much more affluent classmate, Franklin Delano Roosevelt. Later, stumping New York in his first presidential campaign, Roosevelt would refer to Donovan, then running on the Republican ticket to succeed FDR as governor, as "my old friend and classmate." Irked by Roosevelt's condescension, Donovan remarked: "I didn't know Franklin Roosevelt at college, I came from the other side of the tracks."

With his new law degree, Donovan returned to Buffalo, where the city's biggest law firm recruited him and eventually elevated him to name partner. At age thirty-one he married Ruth Rumsey, the offspring of one of Buffalo's wealthiest families, who soon provided him with two children. This hard-won status in life would have satisfied most men, yet Donovan's interests extended beyond his profession and his family. He enlisted in a cavalry troop in the New York National Guard, quickly rising to captain. In 1916, with war raging in Europe, Donovan went abroad with an American relief mission, working closely with Herbert Hoover who was then establishing a reputation as overseer of relief to the Belgians.

When trouble broke out closer to home, on the Mexican border, Donovan and his horse soldiers joined in the long and frustrating puni-tive expedition under the command of General John J. (Black Jack) Pershing against Pancho Villa. By some accounts it was at this time that he gained the "Wild Bill" sobriquet. "Look at me, I'm not even pant-ing," he was said to have told his weary troops after one particularly rig-orous drill session. "If I can take it, why can't you?"

"We ain't as wild as you, Bill," someone supposedly answered.*

At any rate, "Wild Bill," Major Donovan, commanded a battalion in France with New York's "Fighting Sixty-Ninth" regiment. Attaining the rank of Colonel, he was wounded three times and earned the Army's three highest decorations, the Distinguished Service Cross, the Distinguished Service Medal, and the Congressional Medal of Honor, this last awarded for his exploits during the Meuse Argonne offensive. At Landres et St. Georges, when his men suffered heavy casualties assaulting a German strongpoint, he reorganized them and led them forward again. His left leg shattered by machine gun bullets, Donovan refused to be evacuated, staying in command until he could find a safer position for his battalion. Helping to perpetuate Donovan's fame for a later generation, in January of 1940, with Europe once more at war, "The Fighting Sixty-Ninth" was celebrated in an eponymous film starring James Cagney. Pat O'Brien played the regiment's legendary Chaplain, Father Duffy, and George Brent portrayed "Wild Bill."

In the postwar years politics beckoned. Some thought he was destined for the top. In France, Father Duffy had advised him that if he survived the war, he would go far in public office. Certainly, no one doubted his ambition. "He won't be satisfied until he is first Catholic president," remarked a former law partner, John Lord O'Brian. But bad luck and poor timing denied him elective office. In his first attempt, in 1922, a Democratic ticket headed by immensely popular Al Smith overwhelmed his candidacy for lieutenant governor of New York. In 1932, the landslide for Roosevelt for President swamped the New York Republicans who had nominated Donovan for governor. It did not assist his career that he was somewhat unbending. As U.S. Attorney in Buffalo, a post he was appointed to after his 1922 defeat, he led a raid on his own exclusive social club for violating the Eighteenth Amendment, an action that stirred widespread animus against him.

Still, Donovan moved up the appointive ladder at the Justice Department, first heading the Criminal Division, then becoming first assistant to the Attorney General and assuming charge of the department's antitrust cases. True to the spirit of the Coolidge Administration, Donovan let corporate America know they had little to fear from him. Business, he said at the time, "needs a traffic policeman, not a detective"; its leaders "should not be treated as though they were narcotics peddlers."

*Another, simpler explanation for the nickname is that it was inspired by Wild Bill Donovan, a major league pitcher of some repute who also managed the New York Yankees for three years, starting in 1915.

Donovan did not wear military ribbons on his lapel, not even the rosette of the Medal of Honor. At least once, though, he evoked his military service when he was hard pressed, during Senate hearings into his decision as antitrust chief not to probe harder into the operations of the Aluminum Company of America. His chief inquisitor, Democratic Senator Thomas Walsh of Montana, whose inquiries exposed the Teapot Dome scandal, insinuated that Donovan's alleged leniency reflected the fact that Treasury Secretary Andrew Mellon had once been a large stockholder of the company. Donovan retorted: "I do not give a damn whether it is a Mellon concern or any other concern. I am charged with the responsibility of enforcing the law."

"That is the way I want to interpret your purpose, Colonel," said Walsh, "by your acts, rather than what you say about it."

"Senator," Donovan heatedly responded, "I have learned my duty to my country at other places than around this committee table."

As the 1928 election approached, Donovan's reputation for loyalty and efficiency at Justice persuaded Washington insiders that the heavily favored Republican presidential nominee, Herbert Hoover, would elevate his old friend Donovan by making him his attorney general. Donovan took it hard when the new president passed him by, many believed because of Donovan's Catholic faith. He bounced back quickly, though, moving to Wall Street where his practice flourished defending corporate clients against antitrust actions brought by his old division at Justice. Meanwhile he kept an eye on the trouble brewing abroad, and maintained his ties with his old comrades. In 1935, as Mussolini moved against Ethiopia, Donovan wrote Army Chief of Staff Douglas MacArthur, who had been his World War I division commander, that he suspected "this little adventure of Italy" could escalate into "something that could include us all."

Without official sanction but with plenty of encouragement from the top brass in Washington, Donovan paid his own way to Rome, where he toured the battlefront with Mussolini's approval. At the time the invading Italian forces seemed bogged down. And the British were hopeful that economic sanctions imposed by the League of Nations, toothless because they left Italy free to buy oil, would somehow produce a stalemate. Donovan learned that the Italians had completed preparations for a great offensive which he was convinced would lead to their swift conquest of Addis Abbaba. He tried to get word to Anthony Eden, then British Foreign Minister, but the death of King George V prevented Eden from keeping a scheduled appointment with the American. Within a few weeks the Italians attacked, and their subsequent victory demonstrated the failure of British policy. Frustrated, Donovan returned to the U.S. to report on the strength and weaknesses of the Italian military establishment, an assessment which, as the War Department gratefully informed him, it found "replete with pertinent and valuable information."

With that trip Donovan created a role for himself which he continued to play as Europe's march to war gained momentum. As the veteran U.S. diplomat Hugh Wilson later wrote: "Bill is not happy if there is a war on the face of the earth and he has not had a look at it." In 1937, as an observer at German maneuvers, Donovan paid special heed to Hitler's new tanks and artillery. The next year Donovan roamed across through Czechoslovakia, the Balkans, Italy, and Spain where he watched Franco's insurgent troops storm the Loyalist fortifications at the Ebro. In 1939, in the wake of the Munich fiasco, he inspected the forces on both sides of the Rhine, leaving the British with the warning that the German army was "set for a fight."

Back in the U.S., Donovan relished the pleasures that his thriving law practice and his wife's fortune provided. Despite his modest origins, Donovan early on developed a taste for life's finer amenities. Even in war-torn France his mess reputedly had incited envy and wonderment among fellow officers; he hosted intimate dinners just behind the lines, serving culinary luxuries on fine linen. Now he was in far better position to indulge his tastes. The Donovans entertained lavishly at their Washington home in Georgetown and in their New York duplex on Beekman Place. Their guest lists glittered with the names of the rich, the powerful, and the distinguished from many walks of life, Hull and Stimson, Eve Curie and Albert Lasker, Bernard Gimbel, Margaret Sanger, Greta Garbo, Irene Dunne. Donovan moved easily with celebrities; he was one himself. In New York, when he dined, as he often did, at "21," he always insisted on a choice table, the better from which to hobnob.

Donovan's demeanor belied his "Wild Bill" nickname and his battle-field record. Friends described him as "roly poly," "bland of eye," and "soft of voice." Women found his well-chiseled features hard to resist, even in his middle age. If they were worldly enough and attractive enough, Donovan added them to a long list of conquests. As a faithful Catholic, though, he backed away from any affair that showed signs of becoming more than a dalliance. Though not given to back slapping or wisecracking, Donovan was possessed of a sardonic wit. In a tight spot during World II, he turned to an OSS comrade and said: "We know too much. If we are going to get captured, I'll shoot you first, then myself. After all I'm the commanding officer."

With the outbreak of war Donovan, drawing on the lessons he had learned from his inspection trips abroad, was among the first to sound the alarm at home. Americans should not give the world the impression "that under no circumstances will we fight," he told the American Legion in November 1939 two months after the German invasion of Poland. "In an age of bullies, we cannot afford to be a sissy."

Around this time, Donovan's name was often mentioned in Washington amid talk that Roosevelt would form some type of national unity cabinet that would include Republicans. Future Navy Secretary Frank Knox referred to Donovan in the course of turning down an earlier offer from the President to join his cabinet. Knox, who like Donovan left the AEF after World War I as a Colonel, recommended that the President consider "his very dear friend" Donovan, to be Secretary of War, citing his "magnificent" war record. In reply Roosevelt also claimed Donovan as "an old friend," and reminded Knox of how the last Republican President had given short shrift to Donovan's candidacy for attorney general. He would like Donovan in the Cabinet, Roosevelt wrote, "not only for his own ability, but also to repair in a sense the very great injustice done him" by President Hoover. For the time being he turned down the idea, though, because "to put two Republicans in charge of the armed forces might be misunderstood in both parties."

Six months later when the President did decide to install Republicans at the War and Navy Departments, Navy Secretary–designate Knox stayed at Donovan's house during his confirmation proceedings. At one point Knox considered making Donovan his Undersecretary, but events intervened and Donovan emerged instead as an unofficial presidential troubleshooter instead.

Among those who helped bring this about was a Canadian-born scientist, aviation and broadcasting pioneer, and former amateur lightweight world boxing champion named William Stephenson. Operating under the code name Intrepid, he had been assigned by Churchill in May of 1940 to direct British intelligence in the U.S., in part to help persuade the Americans to step up war supplies to the British. Stephenson and Donovan had met in 1916, when Donovan served with the American relief mission in Europe and Stephenson, an officer in the Royal Canadian engineers, was recuperating from being gassed on the Western Front. Years later Donovan remembered the Canadian as a "skinny kid," who "combined compassion and shrewdness in assessing German military and psychological weakness." Donovan evidently impressed Stephenson, too; soon after his arrival in the U.S., the "burning urgency" of getting supplies for Britain impelled him to seek

Donovan's help. He knew Donovan believed that "granted sufficient aid from the U.S., Britain could and would survive," and that at that very moment the Secretary of the Navy enjoyed the hospitality of his Georgetown home. This relationship mattered greatly to Stephenson because among all the supplies Churchill wanted from the U.S., those fifty destroyers from Knox's and Roosevelt's Navy still headed the list.

At Donovan's urging, Knox got Stephenson invited to a meeting late in June at the White House that included not only Knox, but also Secretary of War Stimson and Secretary of State Hull. "The main subject of discussion," according to Stephenson, "was Britain's lack of destroyers." It must have been evident to Stephenson, even if tactfully left unspoken by the Americans, that they wondered whether Britain's chances of survival against the German onslaught were worth the risk of fifty American fighting ships. To help settle that question once and for all, Stephenson proposed that Donovan, the veteran of high-level reconnaissance, see for himself whether Britain could stand the gaff. Knox heartily seconded the motion and the idea was submitted to Roosevelt.

If the President had thought favorably of Donovan in the past, he had even more reason to feel that way now. Not long before, when the appointments of Knox and Stimson had stirred up a storm of protest at the Republican National Convention, Donovan had wired Republican National Chairman Hamilton, urging that the Republicans rally behind the Commander in Chief and endorse the selections. The need to strengthen the national defense, Donovan contended, "transcends all other questions." Roosevelt could hardly have put it better himself. Without hesitation, he told Wild Bill to pack his bags for London.

To help Donovan find his way around among the inner circles of British power and leadership, Knox had assigned the journalist Edgar Mowrer to accompany him and to help in preparing a series of articles on the Nazi Fifth-Column methods. U.S. officials were in fact concerned about the Fifth Column; according to Donovan, Hull feared Nazi efforts to subvert some of the shaky regimes in Latin America. But the Fifth Column inquiry was also in good part a cover story for what Mowrer called the "real assignment—finding out for President Roosevelt the thing he needed most to know: Would and could the British hold out against the Germans?"

But for all the qualities that commended Donovan to Knox and Roosevelt, his mission also had much to do with the nature of the man whose role he was preempting, his Excellency the U.S. Ambassador to the Court of St. James, Joseph P. Kennedy. Donovan's visit, about which Kennedy was summarily informed, though not consulted in advance, reinforced Kennedy's darkest suspicions, that the President who had given him the ambassadorship, the richest prize of his life, did not entirely trust him. For Kennedy, whose pride matched the ambition that had brought him wealth and power, this was a bitter pill to swallow. He had devoted much of his life to constructing elaborate defenses against such affronts.

The son of a Boston saloonkeeper who was also a Democratic ward boss, Joe Kennedy early on challenged the Boston blue bloods on their own grounds, leaving the Catholic parochial schools to get his secondary school education at Boston Latin, then going on to Harvard. At Cambridge he concentrated on history and economics and on promoting upper-crust friendships that would compensate for his Irish origins. When he graduated in 1912 he promised himself that he would earn a million dollars a year by the time he turned 36. His relentless energy and ambition channeled into banking, shipbuilding, and financial manipulation easily drove him to that goal and beyond it. By 1932, having the foresight to add to his fortune by selling short before the Great Crash of 1929, he was worth about $6 million. Then he broadened his horizons by entering the political world, and with a speculator's intuition decided early on to tie his hopes to Franklin Roosevelt's rising star.

Kennedy had met Roosevelt during World War I, when FDR as Assistant Secretary of the Navy settled disputes with shipbuilder Kennedy in a high-handed fashion. When Kennedy balked at delivering two battleships that the Argentine government had ordered but not paid for, Roosevelt, determined to avoid an international imbroglio, simply sent two Navy tugs to tow away the ships. "The hardest trader I'd ever run up against," Kennedy would later say of Roosevelt. "When I left his office, I was so disappointed and angry that I broke down and cried."

Nonetheless, Kennedy was impressed. It was just the way he would have behaved had he been in Roosevelt's position. And that first encounter certainly did not prevent him from signing on some fifteen years later aboard Roosevelt's presidential bandwagon just as it got under way. After heavy-duty service as a fundraiser, and playing a timely role in William Randolph Hearst's crucial switch at the Chicago convention, Kennedy hoped for appointment as Secretary of the Treasury. Instead he had to wait for a year after the inauguration and then settle for chairmanship of the new Security and Exchange Commission.

Whatever regrets he may have had, Kennedy made the most of his

opportunity. He won wide praise for the agency's strong start and for
reviving the Depression-battered capital market. With Roosevelt, who
sometimes showed up for a private dinner at Marwood, Kennedy's
rented estate in the Maryland countryside, he argued incessantly over
policy matters. But the President seemed to find Kennedy's bluntness
refreshing. Nor was he the only one who felt that way. "I want you to go
right on telling Franklin exactly what you think," Eleanor Roosevelt
once told Kennedy.

Much as he enjoyed the access to power, Kennedy grumbled that he
was losing $100,000 a year because his post prevented him from play-
ing the stock market and that his responsibilities kept him too much
from his family. After a year he left to return to private business. Still,
he remained on good terms with FDR and a valuable liaison for the
New Deal with the upper echelons of big business and the inner circles
of the Catholic Church.

After his triumph in 1936, Roosevelt brought Kennedy back into government at the head of yet another new agency, the Maritime
Commission, where Kennedy toiled with some success to improve the
sorry state of the nation's shipping industry. He still wanted a more
impressive portfolio from Roosevelt, however. For his part, Roosevelt,
much as he valued Kennedy's good offices with the business community and his willingness to take on burdensome tasks, realized that the
ambition which had carried Kennedy so far was also a weakness,
because he would do almost anything to advance himself, and the
President took advantage of that fact.

When FDR first heard that this bumptious son of a saloonkeeper
wanted to be Ambassador to London, his son James said, "he laughed
so hard he almost toppled from his wheelchair." The President got an
another laugh in the fall of 1937 when he summoned Kennedy to the
Oval Office: Before offering the diplomatic post Kennedy coveted,
Roosevelt insisted that he drop his trousers. After a long, appraising
look, Roosevelt contended that Kennedy was too bowlegged to wear
the knee breeches and silk stockings required for the Ambassador's formal presentation to the King. Unfazed, Kennedy used his contacts to
obtain an official letter of permission to wear a cutaway coat and striped
pants.

In the face of such treatment, Kennedy remained loyal to his patron.
"I can't go against the guy," he explained to a friendly reporter in
December 1939 on a trip home. "He's done more for me than my own
kind." Soon thereafter Kennedy formally endorsed Roosevelt for
reelection on the basis of his pledge to stay out of the war. "We know

from what we have seen and heard that President Roosevelt's policy is to keep us out of war," he declared, "and war at this time would bring to this country chaos beyond anybody's dreams."

Kennedy's limited knowledge of international affairs and of foreign cultures narrowed his understanding of the dramatic events unfolding in Europe. Roosevelt thought him naive. Soon after the outbreak of war, Roosevelt complained to Farley that after Kennedy had been to tea with the King and Queen, he sent Roosevelt "the silliest message," urging the President "to do this that and the other thing in a frantic sort of way. . . . You know," he remarked, "Joe has been taken in by the British government, the people and the Royal Family."

In addition, Kennedy's ingrained bigotry, particularly his anti-Semitism, caused him to minimize the evils of Nazism. After discussing with Kennedy the American reaction to Germany's "Jewish question," Germany's Ambassador to Great Britain, Herbert von Dirksen, reported to Berlin in June of 1938 that Kennedy believed "it was not so much the fact that we wanted to get rid of the Jews that was so harmful to us, but rather the loud clamor with which we accompanied this purpose." As for Kennedy himself, according to von Dirksen, he "understood our Jewish policy completely." In addition, Kennedy's natural pessimism and cynicism led him to underrate Britain's capacity to contend against a an outwardly superior foe.

All this contributed to his sympathy for Chamberlain's reliance on appeasement, which made him the subject of gibes at home—even though some of his views scarcely differed from FDR's own policies. At a White House stag dinner soon after the outbreak of war, Harold Ickes coined a wisecrack for the President's benefit. "Chamberlain has decided to increase his Cabinet so that he can give Joe Kennedy a place in it," he remarked, whereupon, "The President threw back his head and had a good laugh."

Kennedy, then, was an almost constant source of trouble. From the very start of the war, pessimism clouded his thinking. Writing to the President on September 30, 1939, he said he could not find any military expert who would give Britain "a Chinaman's chance." He was persuaded that "England would go down fighting," but he did not think this would do "the slightest bit of good." As the war ground on, the Ambassador's once warm relationship with Chamberlain cooled as Kennedy realized that the Prime Minister, embittered by the lessons of Munich, was determined to prosecute the war through to victory. Moreover, Kennedy's dim regard for Britain's prospects soured his relations with others in the government, notably Winston Churchill, then still First Lord of the Admiralty. In March of 1940 at a stag dinner given by Chamberlain for Sumner Welles, Churchill went on at great length about the fortitude of the average Briton. "His back is up," Churchill claimed. "He will stand for no pulling of punches against Germany. He's tough."

"Well," Kennedy retorted, "if you can show me one Englishman that's tougher than you are, Winston, I'll eat my hat."

Aside from their irritation with Kennedy's negativism, a bizarre episode that unfolded right after Churchill became Prime Minister gave the British reason for unease about the U.S. diplomatic mission in London. On the morning of May 20 two Scotland Yard detectives, along with a British military intelligence official and the second secretary of the American Embassy, burst into the London flat of Tyler Gatewood Kent, a clerk at the U.S. Embassy. Inside they found more than 1,500 confidential documents, including abundant material on the secret correspondence between Roosevelt and Churchill. Brought before Kennedy, Kent, the 29-year-old son of a career consular official, denied involvement in espionage or any ties to foreign agents. By his own later account Kent claimed instead that he considered the material "important historical documents" and that he was concerned with the right of Congress and the American people to know of their President's clandestine negotiations with the British.

Kennedy turned him over to the British authorities, waiving diplomatic immunity. This extraordinary action allowed Kent to be tried *in camera* instead of being deported to the U.S., where it would have been much more difficult to withhold from the public the circumstances surrounding his arrest.

In Washington, the potential implications of the case stunned officials. "It is appalling," Assistant Secretary of State Breckinridge Long wrote in his diary after reading the catalog of papers found in Kent's rooms, which amounted to a complete history of U.S.–British diplomatic correspondence since 1938. Long recalled that in March Berlin had released a series of "White Books" which purported to show that U.S. diplomats had urged the Poles to resist the Germans by implying that the U.S. would enter the war. Now he thought it possible that the Germans would publish another such book, timed for the U.S. election campaign, using material they would have obtained from Kent. The objective, Long feared "would be the defeat of Roosevelt and the election of a ticket opposed to him and presumably in sympathy with Hitler."

So concerned was the State Department about the damage that

might be done to Roosevelt that it was reluctant to grant a British request for release of the material for use against Kent in his trial. "We agreed to some but could not implicate the Chief by consenting to correspondence between him and Churchill. . . ." Long noted. Apparently, the department was particularly distressed about the last cable that Kent had decoded before his arrest. In that message, sent May 16, Churchill had renewed his initial plea for the destroyers and warned of the dire consequences if some future British government would have to negotiate a peace with Hitler "amid the ruins." "Churchill's letter was a plea and confession of defeat," Long wrote. "The President did *not* accede to his request, but the very correspondence might be hurtful. (Emphasis in the original.) So we withheld permission to see or to use on the theory they had enough to convict without them."*

That appraisal proved correct. Kent was not formally charged with sending secrets to the Germans, nor was there ever any clear proof that he had done so. But his recklessness, his associations with Axis sympathizers and virulent anti-Semites, and the clear and present danger then facing Great Britain led to his conviction of violating the Official Secrets Act and a seven-year prison sentence.

Because of the veil drawn over Kent's prosecution, the fears of the State Department, presumably shared by the White House, did not materialize. But it was a close call, and the episode served to remind the President of the precariousness of his secret negotiations with the British.

As for Kennedy, by yielding Kent to the British he had saved both the British and his own government a shattering scandal. He had also demonstrated his patriotism and his personal loyalty, even when protecting the confidentiality of dealings some of which he personally opposed. But the action did little to improve his relations with the British. While they always knew of Kennedy's gloomy view of their prospects, Kent's cache of documents gave them a fuller and more detailed appreciation of the ambassador's negativism and its impact on their relations with Washington.

---

*Details of the correspondence remained secret till after the war. But some information about Kent's case filtered back to the U.S. because of the long fight waged by his mother, Anne H. P. Kent, to gain her son's freedom and because of questions asked in the House of Commons about the prosecution. In 1944 this produced demands by Sen. Nye and other congressional isolationists for an inquiry into whether Roosevelt and Churchill had conspired in 1939 and 1940, behind the back of then Prime Minister Chamberlain, to get the U.S. into the war.

Not that Kennedy was shy about letting the world in on his view of what should be America's attitude toward the war. In March of 1940 he told reporters that isolationist sentiment had been growing in America, adding: "I think it is stronger because the people understand the war less and less as they go along." That drew a tart rejoinder from veteran British diplomat and Member of Parliament Harold Nicolson, who took note of Kennedy's closeness to the appeasement clique in Britain. "Were I to frequent only those circles in which Mr. Kennedy is so welcome a guest, I also should have long periods of gloom." Actually Kennedy's admiration of Britain's leaders, Chamberlain in particular, had lessened with the march of events, as evidenced by his advice to his son, Jack, who in the spring of 1940 was hard at work on his senior thesis at Harvard, "Appeasement at Munich." The future president argued that the sorry state of Britain's military establishment left Chamberlain no choice but to yield to the Führer's demands. Not satisfied with the *magna cum laude* grade "Appeasement at Munich" won, the ambassador encouraged his son to turn it into a book, but also advised him to that he had not been critical enough in assessing Chamberlain's performance. A political leader, the Ambassador explained, was "supposed to look after the national welfare and to attempt to educate the people." The younger Kennedy wrote his father's suggestions into the book's conclusion. Published in midsummer, *Why England Slept*, with a foreword by Henry Luce, soon found its way to the bestseller list. In his foreword Luce castigated both Roosevelt and Willkie for failing to give Americans a realistic understanding of the dangers that faced the country. "America will never be ready for any war . . . until she makes up her mind that there is going to be a war," Luce wrote.

Meanwhile, though, with the advent of Hitler's spring offensive against France's Low Countries, Kennedy's mood darkened and his tone with the British sharpened. Meeting with newly installed Prime Minister Churchill on May 14, as the extent of the Allied debacle in France was just becoming clear, Kennedy asked: "What the United States could do to help that would not leave the United States holding the bag for a war in which the Allies expect to be beaten." It seemed to him, Kennedy cabled Hull, "that if we had to fight to protect our lives we would do better fighting in our own backyard." On June 12, with the German offensive a month old and France already on the verge of collapse, Kennedy underlined his previous warnings against U.S. involvement.

The condition of British preparedness equals [sic] her ability to fight the kind of war Hitler wages still appears to be appallingly weak. . . . It is only fair to say that short of a miracle this country, after, and if and when France stops fighting will hold on in the hope that the United States will come in. A course of action that involves us in any respect that presupposes the Allies have much to fight with except courage is, as far as England goes, I think fallacious.

By this time Kennedy's attitude and British reaction to his public and private utterances had undermined his usefulness in Roosevelt's sensitive discussions with the British about their requests for destroyers and other help. The President of course could have replaced him. But doing so would inevitably have generated a messy public debate about Anglo-American relations.

Thus Kennedy was an obstacle whom for the time being Roosevelt could not remove. Instead the President used Donovan to go around the ambassador. Kennedy, who had been irritated earlier in the year by the arrival of Sumner Welles on his peace mission, was even angrier when told of the Donovan visit, and he let Washington know his feelings. "I will render any service I can to Col. Donovan, whom I know and like," he cabled Hull on July 11, when he was told of Donovan's imminent arrival. The Ambassador contended, though, that his own staff was already gathering all the available information about Britain's strength; sending in someone else "is the height of nonsense and a definite blow to good organization."

When the State Department relayed this complaint to Roosevelt he passed the buck to Donovan's sponsor, Secretary Knox. "Please take this up with Secretary Hull and try to straighten it out," FDR asked Knox. "Somebody's nose seems to be out of joint."

But at the moment Knox had a more urgent matter on his mind. On Saturday, July 13, as Roosevelt and Rosenman cruised aboard the presidential yacht, *Potomac*, planning strategy for the Democratic Convention that would commence Monday, Knox and Donovan were lunching on Knox's own official yacht, the *Sequoia*, deciding on the priorities for Donovan's tour. They agreed that even more important for Donovan to gauge than Britain's military resources, which they knew to be badly depleted, was her determination to fight on, or as Admiral John H. Godfrey, the British Director of Naval Intelligence later put it, to judge "if we were in earnest about the war."

That evening, after the *Sequoia* docked, Knox and Donovan dined at the British Embassy with Lothian, who told them of his request for a Churchill–Donovan interview. Meanwhile Donovan's old friend, William Stephenson, was also hard at work developing his itinerary. "I arranged that he should be afforded every opportunity to conduct his inquiries," the intelligence agent later wrote. "I endeavored to marshal my friends in high places to bare their breasts."

Among the letters in Donovan's briefcase when he left New York for Lisbon July 14 was a note from Secretary Knox to Lord Beaverbrook, Britain's Minster of Aircraft Production, whom Knox had previously met at a gathering at Donovan's house. Reminding Beaverbrook of that encounter, Knox added: "I hope you will be as frank in talking to him as you might be in talking to me."

Candor was not necessarily what the British stressed most. They were trying desperately to impress Donovan favorably. Shortly after Donovan arrived, Captain Allan Kirk, the U.S. Naval Attaché in London, warned Roosevelt's emissary that the British would certainly present "the best side of the picture." Such an admonition from Kirk would hardly have surprised the British who complained among themselves that the naval office often expressed "defeatist views," once offering to bet a high Foreign Office official that the British would be defeated by early August.

No sooner had Donovan arrived on July 19 than he was hurried off to Buckingham Palace, where he was warmly greeted by the King, who handed him an intercepted German battle order, dated just three days before, from Hitler to his field commanders. "I have decided to prepare a landing operation against England . . . to eliminate England as a base for the prosecution of the war against Germany," the Führer had declared, adding that as a precondition of the invasion, the Royal Air Force must be destroyed. His Majesty remarked that the palace itself was bound to be on the Luftwaffe target list, but passed that threat off with a joke.

To Donovan, the British ability to decode Hitler's order matched the significance of the message itself. The King did not offer any explanation, nor did Donovan ask for one. But based on this evidence and other indications of British foreknowledge of German plans, Donovan surmised that the British had broken Germany's most secret cipher, the "Enigma" code. Whatever he knew about Britain's access to this intelligence material, code-named "Ultra," Donovan kept to himself as one of the war's tightest secrets. Still, this knowledge buttressed the British case that they could defend themselves against Hitler.

The British arranged an equally dramatic visit for Donovan to the innermost sanctum of Britain's war effort, Churchill's personal command post, converted from a labyrinth of centuries-old tunnels beneath Whitehall. Here Donovan and Churchill wearing his zipper "siren suit"

that gave him the appearance of an overgrown teddy bear dined together on trays from the underground mess and discussed Britain's strategy.
In addition to gritting their teeth and bearing up under the German
bombardment, the British intended to mount a guerrilla campaign
against the conqueror of Europe. In shoebox file cabinets, Donovan
found one red-bordered card describing a new intelligence organization called "Special Operations Executive." Its stated purpose: to create
"a reign of terror conducted by specially trained agents and fortified by
espionage and intelligence so that the lives of German troops in
Occupied Europe will be made an intensive torment."

Donovan found it difficult to maintain perspective. "In those dun-
geons under Whitehall you step into a Shakespearean play with stage
directions like 'Army Heard in Distance, Sound of Trumpets,'" he later
wrote Stephenson. "You know there isn't an army, but it's hard to be
sure, down there in the theater."

But the British had more than imaginary resources to show Donovan.
They demonstrated their new type of floating mine designed to blow up
German invasion barges, their radar networks that were baffling the
Luftwaffe bomber pilots, their speedy new fighter planes, and their
expanding coast defenses. Then, too, British intelligence briefed Donovan
about the "double-cross" operation, run by the XX Committee, which
turned captured German spies into counter-agents against Hitler.

The British saw to it that his schedule was full and that his days were
long. On July 24, for example, Donovan lunched with the Second Sea
Lord, Vice Admiral B. A. Fraser, spent the afternoon with First Lord of
the Admiralty, W. V. Alexander, the Secretary of State for Air, Sir
Archibald Sinclair, and the Minister of Information, Alfred Duff
Cooper. His day ended just before midnight at a meeting with Captain
Charles Balfour, Parliamentary Secretary of State for Air. To most of the
sessions Donovan brought a specific list of questions to which the
British promptly sent him lengthy answers.

Not long after his arrival he met up with his assigned collaborator,
Edgar Mowrer, explained the mission to him, then sent the correspondent off on his own tour of inspections and meetings. Though he "shud-
dered" at the lack of preparedness at the defense centers he visited,
Mowrer thought this weakness less important than the confident determination of Churchill, who told him at lunch that he found Britain's isolation "rather exhilarating." At their final meeting Donovan and Mowrer
agreed on what Wild Bill would report to Roosevelt: "Britain under
Churchill would not surrender to ruthless air raids or to an invasion."

Not surprisingly, the U.S. Embassy staff had to prod Donovan to dine with the Ambassador. "Mr. Kennedy is rather particular about knowing whether you are coming Sunday night or not," Captain Kirk wrote to Donovan, after the visitor had failed to respond to an earlier invitation. Having little choice, Donovan accepted, but the dinner disrupted his social life, forcing him to cancel plans for an evening at the home of Information Minister Duff Cooper, whose wife Diane, a famous beauty, seemed to have been as captivated by Donovan's charms as were many American women. "Dear Wild Colonel," she wrote the next day, thanking him for the yellow roses he had sent by way of apology. "I was so disappointed that the interest of our two countries came between us." She added, "I hope you had a hideous evening with Joe and I hope too that you will lunch or dine another day."

Donovan found a more kindred spirit than Kennedy at the Embassy in General Raymond Lee, the U.S. military attaché, who sharply disagreed with Kennedy about the British ability to resist. Assigned as military attaché in London before the war, Lee had been brought home to help train the peacetime army, then sent back in the spring of 1940 because of his experience and his reputation for writing reports that even Roosevelt himself would read. To Lee, Donovan's visit represented a chance to offset Kennedy's defeatism. "I like him," he wrote in his journal. "My theory is that I welcome anyone who gets the intelligence and sends it home."

Two days before Donovan's return home, Lee came away from a long breakfast with Wild Bill at his favorite hotel, Claridge's, persuaded that Donovan, after talking "to an extraordinary list of well posted people from the King and Churchill down, agrees with all our conclusions and is not at all defeatist." Donovan reckoned the odds in favor of the British holding out against the Germans as 60–40, almost as optimistic as Lee, who thought the British were a two-to-one shot. Later Lee was relieved to learn that Donovan, on returning to the United States, had expressed the same confidence in Britain's ability to survive that he had shown in London. This was what Lee himself had been reporting. If Donovan had said otherwise, Lee noted in his diary, "I would have been in a corner."

Donovan's return to the U.S. on August 4, after three weeks abroad, necessarily attracted attention, particularly because he was the sole passenger on the first British plane to cross the Atlantic since war brought an end to such flights. Beyond divulging that he had been on a mission for Knox, instead of on "private business" as he had first claimed, Donovan had nothing more to say than when he departed. "I went abroad for the Secretary of the Navy and you'll have to ask him," he told reporters, then headed for Washington where he spent an hour with Knox the next morning.

Roosevelt was no more communicative at his press conference on August 6. "You will have to ask the Secretary of the Navy and Wild Bill," he told eight reporters. All the President would divulge about Donovan was that he was taking him on a cruise on the Potomac, "so he can tell me what he found when he went over." And when the cruise was over, Knox would only say, "He went over as my eyes and ears to see what he could find."

"Anything to say, sir?" a reporter asked Roosevelt.

"Well you see it is his mouth," the President replied archly.

"Your eyes and ears, and Col. Donovan's mouth?" a persistent reporter asked Knox. That produced only laughter and someone changed the subject to ask about Roosevelt's new grandchild. But if the American press and public were left mystified about Donovan's trip, the British government was not. "He was deeply impressed and grateful for the frankness and courtesy of everybody he saw," Lothian reported to London on August 7 after talking to Donovan.

> He told me what he was going to say to people here, which seemed to me sane and realistic. He is pressing everybody here vigorously to supply us with destroyers and other equipment asked for, immediately. He expressed the view that we should beat off any attack this autumn though the price might be severe, especially in loss of shipping and cargoes.

"This is pleasant news," T. North Whitehead minuted on Lothian's cable. Throughout Whitehall, one could almost hear a great sigh of relief.

In Washington, Donovan and Mowrer collaborated on a series of articles on the Fifth Column menace which garnered wide attention around the country. More importantly, Donovan kept his promise to Lothian to proselytize on Britain's behalf. His most important session was of course with Roosevelt, with whom he spent part of two days. As Donovan later recounted it, Roosevelt began their meeting by launching into a monologue. But Donovan determinedly interrupted him several times to stress Britain's "excellent prospects of pulling through."

Only three weeks had passed since Donovan's departure. But Britain's chances had improved. Her fighter output in July had exceeded the production target by 50 percent, which meant that the RAF could deploy new planes faster than the Luftwaffe. Meanwhile nearly every day's report from the air battle over England showed higher losses for the German attackers than the British defenders. At this point, with the third term nomination behind him, and the mounting evidence of Britain's determination, Roosevelt not only wanted to be convinced by Donovan that Britain would survive, he also wanted him to convince others.

Donovan lobbied Stimson and Morgenthau and argued Britain's case with members of Congress, among them Senate Majority Leader Barkley of Kentucky, Senator Tom Connolly of the Foreign Relations Committee, and Senator Ed Burke of Nebraska, co-sponsor of selective service legislation then before Congress. To everyone he emphasized the British need for arms, particularly destroyers. He described British morale as "very high," and predicted they would throw back any invasion attempt. He pointed out that as Hitler himself acknowledged in his intercepted order of July 16, Germany could not conquer Britain unless the Luftwaffe could first destroy the Royal Air Force. Fighter Command's wide dispersal of its planes on fields all over England made that goal difficult to achieve, Donovan pointed out. Less tangible, but at least as important was the state of British morale. From the start Donovan had considered the key question to be whether the British will to fight on was strong enough to justify U.S. support. The answer, he told Roosevelt and others in the inner circle, was yes.

The Colonel had completed his mission. The next move was up to his Commander in Chief.

# The Other Battle of Britain

"In this country, owing to the constitutional equality of the status of the Executive and the Legislature, it is public opinion itself which is continually decisive."

PHILLIP KERR, Lord Lothian, February 15, 1940

"Stop Hitler Now!" This was the headline over a full-page advertisement that appeared in major newspapers around the United States on June 11 and 12. "If Hitler wins in Europe . . . America will find itself alone in a barbaric world," warned the text, written by Pulitzer Prize–winning playwright Robert Sherwood, soon to become a Roosevelt adviser. In even starker terms, Sherwood added:

> The Monroe Doctrine is not an automatic safety catch. . . . We cannot ignore the fact that Trojan Horses are grazing in all the fertile fields of North and South America. . . . Will the Nazis considerately wait until we are ready to fight them? Anyone who argues that they will wait is either an imbecile or a traitor. . . .

All through the summer of 1940, while the RAF fought the Battle of Britain against the Luftwaffe in the skies over England, another Battle of Britain, bloodless but equally portentous, raged 3,000 miles away in the United States to determine the nation's response to the war in Europe.

The Donovan mission had been an important event in this contest, aimed mainly at a small circle of influential leaders in the Administration and the Congress. The "Stop Hitler Now!" advertisement addressed a much larger audience, encompassing the general public, seeking to resolve its doubts about Britain's survival and the wisdom of U.S. aid. And within that arena a number of powerful forces maneuvered, each determined to shape public opinion to match its own interests and beliefs.

Potentially, the President of the United States overshadowed all the other players, since he was positioned to dominate this battle much as Churchill commanded the defense of Britain. Unlike the Prime Minister, however, the President for the most part avoided bold rhetoric. Instead, though he had pledged unstinting U.S. aid in his June 10 "dagger-in-the back" speech, for weeks afterward he took a back seat, relying on private organizations to shoulder the main burden of Britain's cause. While these groups sought to influence Roosevelt, he managed for the most part to manipulate them to advance his own ends. By choosing this role, however, the President enlarged the opportunities for isolationists and German propagandists to shape public opinion, surrendered the chance to define the choices facing the country, and frustrated and confused the groups supporting aid to Britain.

The largest such organization, bearing the unwieldy name of the Committee to Defend America by Aiding the Allies, claimed nearly two million members, with a host of prominent names covering a spectrum from J. P. Morgan to David Dubinsky on its masthead. It was often referred to simply as the White Committee, after its national chairman, Roosevelt's erstwhile ally in the fight to repeal the Neutrality Act, Kansas editor William Allen White.

As its first major effort to influence public debate, the White Committee had sponsored the full-page ad written by Robert Sherwood, which because of its harsh hyperbole drew a flood of bitter protests. Among those outraged was Oswald Garrison Villard, editor of the *Nation*, who bitterly wrote White that he and millions of other Americans who were uncertain about the nature of the threat to the U.S. were nevertheless, "just as loyal, just as sincere and just as earnest Americans as Sherwood or anybody else."

Roosevelt's response to the ad marked a high point in his enthusiasm for rallying the public behind Britain's cause, a spirit that would soon ebb. He placed a copy in plain sight on his Oval Office desk when reporters were summoned to the regular biweekly press conference on the day after his militant June 10 speech. "It is a great piece of work, extremely educational," he remarked in response to the inevitable question. "And without going into a specific endorsement of every phrase," he added, "it is a mighty good thing that Bill White and his committee are getting things like that out for the education of the country."

During the next two months, while the Germans pounded Britain from the air and made plans to cross the English Channel, Roosevelt had little to say about the most pressing issue facing the country. In part this was because the presidential campaign preoccupied him. Yet even after he won renomination, Roosevelt remained cautious to the extreme. In his acceptance speech to the convention he expressed his support for Britain's cause in peculiarly negative terms. "I do not recant the sentiments of sympathy with all free peoples resisting such aggression, or begrudge the material aid that we have given them," the President told the delegates and the nation. But he made no commitment for the future.

This silence fell as the fortunes of war turned against Britain and the bewildered public tried to sort out conflicting claims and beliefs. When Roosevelt had delivered his most combative address of the war, his "dagger-in-the back" address on June 10, aiding the Allies had become, as the British Embassy reported to the Foreign Office, "the dominant sentiment of the country." For example, a few days before, on June 2 the *Philadelphia Inquirer* ran a front-page editorial recanting its longtime isolationism and demanding all-out support for Britain and France. Calling upon Americans "to reappraise their attitude toward the cataclysmic war in Europe," the *Inquirer* declared: "As the situation of the Allies grows daily more critical, it becomes crystal clear to those who face the facts unblinkingly that our self-protection no longer begins on our home shores."

But within the next three weeks, as the Germans seized Paris, knocked France out of the war, and seemed poised to finish off the British, one emotion dominated American thinking—fear. The pro-Allied feeling late in May had been fostered by the fear that Hitler would threaten the United States, the British Embassy's "Washington Letter" reported July 3, "But when Paris fell and France collapsed, the same fear meant keeping all armaments possible in the United States and getting ready to live in a world with Hitler dominant. Getting along with Hitler was felt to be better than having to fight him."

In truth, Americans did not know what to believe or what to fear most. A Gallup Poll released July 7 showed that they were equally divided over whether the British or the Axis powers would win the war. Responses varied significantly with how the question was framed. Asked what was the most important thing for the U.S. to do, another Gallup survey that month found 59 percent saying it was more important to keep out of war while only 37 percent said it was more important to help England win, even at the risk of getting into war. But when the wording of the question was changed slightly, 73 percent said the U.S. should do everything possible to help England, except go to war.

Passions ran high on both sides of the issue. In Chicago, a new national organization calling itself the "Roll Call of American Women" pledged to prevent "armed U.S. involvement in the European war." In Detroit, another new antiwar group, The Mothers of the U.S.A., vowed to publicly horsewhip any legislator who voted for a declaration of war. Among those favoring aid to the Allies, The *New York Times* published "There Are No Islands Any More," a brief poem by Edna St. Vincent Millay, who wrote: "Oh build, assemble, transport, give, That England, France and we may live." In Dallas a massive Flag Day rally cheered one speaker who urged that the U.S. send the Allies all they needed except troops, adding defiantly: "If that leads to war, then we will meet that issue. . . ." But, at the end, when 15,000 bowed their heads in prayer, the words the crowd chanted in unison were: "Lead us not into war, but peace." On the floor of the U.S. Senate, Roosevelt's old populist ally Burton Wheeler voted one day to legalize the President's scheme for trading in so-called surplus weapons to manufacturers for sale to the Allies, but rose the next day to oppose "steps to get us into war." Wheeler, who had been one of the first to back Franklin Roosevelt for president, warned he would not endorse any presidential candidate, "no matter who he may be, who is going to try to get us into this war."

In this unsettled environment, advocates of aid to Britain urged the President to speak out, arguing that the underlying sentiment for helping the British was stronger than he realized. On June 10, the day Italy declared war on France, William Allen White wired Roosevelt to report that letters to his committee were "heaping up" in support of aid to Britain. "As an old friend," White added, "let me warn you that maybe you will not be able to lead the American people unless you catch up with them. They are going fast." A few hours later, Roosevelt delivered his forceful pledge of aid to battle aggression, pleasing White mightily. In the following weeks, though, as the President held his tongue while the Luftwaffe pounded Britain, it seemed to White, as he told a friend, that FDR "had, as it were, lost his cud."

Meanwhile the Germans, too, schemed to influence the struggle. As well as the British, they realized that fear of Hitler was driving American opinion. As a result of "intensive propaganda," Hans Thomsen, Hitler's top diplomat in the U.S. warned Berlin, "many Americans are beginning to believe in the danger of a German attack on the Western Hemisphere, either direct or by infiltration through Latin America after a possible Anglo-French defeat." To refute this "biased and naive belief," Thomsen proposed "an official German declaration" that would proclaim Germany's lack of interest in English and French colonial positions in the Western Hemisphere and pledge "to always respect the sovereignty of the Latin American states."

The *Wilhelmstrasse* looked favorably on Thomsen's idea. Hans Dieckhoff, the recalled Ambassador to the U.S. who remained in limbo in Berlin on special assignment, thought such a statement would "take the wind out of the President's sails." As a vehicle, Dieckhoff proposed an interview with Foreign Minister Joachim von Ribbentrop. But Hitler thought so well of the idea that he upgraded the subject of the interview to himself. It did not take the Germans long to find the right reporter. He was Karl Wiegand, the chief foreign correspondent of Hearst newspapers, whom Berlin remembered not only for favorable articles he had written in the past but also for the friendly warning that among all the leaders of the democracies, Roosevelt was Hitler's most dangerous opponent. "Roosevelt fights for his democratic aims with the same fanatic ideals as does the Führer for National Socialism," Wiegand told the German Consul in San Francisco in April of 1939. Wiegand's story was based on eight questions and eight answers supposedly from an interview with the Führer. After the war U.S. investigators learned that the entire interview, questions as well as answers, had been concocted in the German foreign office and that Wiegand had never talked to Hitler. But at the time the story created a sensation.

It reached readers of the Hearst papers, the *Chicago Tribune* and the *New York Daily News*, and the *Washington Times Herald*, which carried Wiegand's account June 14, under a page one headline that declared : "First Interview of Campaign: Invasion of This Hemisphere 'Fantastic,' Führer Asserts." Wiegand reported that Hitler had never "in dream or thought" considered intervening in the Western Hemisphere. Indeed Hitler pledged to respect the Monroe Doctrine, provided it was interpreted on a reciprocal basis: "The Americas to Americans, Europe to Europeans." Hitler described American fears of him and of Germany as "flattering but grotesque," Wiegand wrote, adding that the dictator labeled the idea of a German invasion of the U.S. as "stupid and fantastic."

Adding to the impact of Wiegand's "scoop," the German Embassy's redoubtable agent, George Sylvester Viereck, persuaded a friendly Congressman, Jacob Thorkelson of Montana, to insert the story in the *Congressional Record*. Thorkelson added his own comment that newspapers which had passed up the story "are trying to lead this nation into another foolish war." Meanwhile the Embassy's own publication, *Facts in Review*, showcased the interview in a special edition of 100,000 copies.

Roosevelt's response was remarkably muted. Asked if would comment at his press conference on June 14, he replied coyly: "No, except that it brings up recollections." Off the record, the President added that his remark could be "enlarged on with dates and nations, et cetera and so on, going back for quite a period of years."* Later that day, talking with a group of business editors at the White House, FDR again discussed the Wiegand interview off the record, urging his guests to fight against "the tendency of some politicians" to strive for advantage by professing to believe the Wiegand story. "There a lot of gullible Americans who will say, 'You see, he says he won't do anything over here. Why shouldn't we go easy?' " Roosevelt also warned that if Hitler conquered all of Europe he would be in a position to dominate Latin American countries by controlling their trade and using other economic weapons. "In other words you can gain domination over a large portion of this continent without sending troops over, and that is something we have to watch out for." This was a cogent argument for U.S. aid to Britain. But by denying the editors the right to attribute it to him directly, the President diminished its practical effectiveness. Nor did the President himself ever make this point publicly about the economic threat against the United States from Hitler.

Whatever the impact of the purported interview with Hitler, the Germans themselves realized that their best chance of undercutting public support for Britain was offered not by the Fuhrer but rather by a genuine American hero, Charles Lindbergh. Though the isolationist cause had many advocates, in the view of both his friends and foes, the 38-year-old Lindbergh stood head and shoulders over all the others, by virtue of his celebrity, his claim to military expertise as a reserve Colonel in the U.S. Army Air Corps, and the simple fact that he was not a politician.

He had turned his back on a political career and chosen the path of aviation and science, even though his father had served five terms as a Congressman from Minnesota. While the elder Lindbergh had opposed U.S. involvement in World War I as vehemently as his son later argued against aid to the British, the son shared none of the social reforming zeal which imbued his father. Instead the younger Lindbergh's thinking combined a naive patriotism heavily overlaid with blatant racism.

In a *Reader's Digest* article urging Americans to stay out of the war that had just broken out in Europe, he depicted it as a struggle "in which the white race is bound to lose and the others bound to gain." The greatest danger, Lindbergh argued, was not from Berlin but from the East. "While we stand poised for battle, Oriental guns are turning

---

*Under the prevailing guidelines at the time, Roosevelt could not be quoted directly at a press conference unless he gave specific permission.

westward, Asia presses toward us on the Russian border," he wrote. "It is time to turn from our quarrels and build our White ramparts again."

Long before the start of the war, Lindbergh's life had been defined by two stunning events. His solo transatlantic flight to Paris in 1927 overnight transformed this obscure Midwesterner into an international celebrity and a national icon. Five years later, the kidnapping and murder of his 20-month-old son, Charles, Jr., left him tormented and withdrawn. To escape the aftermath of "the crime of the century," Lindbergh and his wife, Anne, the daughter of the diplomat and banker, Dwight Morrow, sought a new life abroad. On visits to Germany he was wined and dined by the Nazi leaders who proudly displayed the growing strength of their air force. By 1938 Lindbergh had acquired a medal from Herman Göring that was to provide ammunition for his enemies for years to come and the conviction, as he wrote to Ambassador Kennedy in 1938, "that German air strength is greater than that of all other European countries combined and that she is constantly increasing her margin of leadership."[*]

This grim and dubious assessment, delivered on the eve of Munich, bolstered the arguments of British and French officials eaager to appease Hitler. It was also weighed by the State Department and the White House in deciding whether to pressure the British and French into taking a firmer stand.[†] "This amiable and attractive man," former Prime Minister David Lloyd George later told the House of Commons, "was the agent and tool of much more astute and sinister men than himself."

With the failure of the Munich pact, and the imminent approach of war, Lindbergh returned to the United States, where the Army Air Corps called him up for five months' duty as an adviser on research and production. This led to a brief meeting with Roosevelt, who was his usual cordial self. Lindbergh found the President likeable, but "a little too suave, too pleasant, too easy." In sum, he wrote in his journal, "It is

---

[*]The award, a notably belated recognition of Lindbergh's 1927 transatlantic flight, was the *Verdienstkreuz der Deutscher Adler* (Service Cross of the German Eagle). As Lindbergh noted in his diary, it was one of the highest German decorations for a civilian and presented at Hitler's own order. His wife Anne needed only one glance at the medal to sum up its implications. "The Albatross," she said.

[†]The truth of the matter, which emerged as a result of postwar inquiries, was that far from being numerically inferior, the French and the British between them had more aircraft than the Germans. But the Allies did suffer in the air from the French reluctance to use the aircraft they had, perhaps because they were saving reserves for what they believed would be a long war.

better to work together as long as we can; yet somehow I have a feeling that it may not be long."

He was right about that. With the outbreak of war in Europe, Lindbergh prepared to speak out against U.S. involvement. Before his first broadcast, on September, 15, he received an offer from Roosevelt, worried about anything that might impede congressional repeal of the arms embargo. As the proposition was relayed to Lindbergh, the President was prepared to create a new cabinet-level position, Secretary of Air, and give it to Lindbergh if the aviator would call off his talk. Rejecting the offer, Lindbergh delivered his speech on "America and European Wars," as planned. "As long as we maintain an army, a navy and an air force worthy of the name, as long as America does not decay within," Lindbergh declared "we need fear no invasion of this country."

By the spring of 1940, Lindbergh had emerged as the President's chief adversary on foreign policy outside the Congress. In a radio speech on May 19 he disagreed sharply with Roosevelt's warning to the nation, issued a few days before, that new weaponry in the hands of aggressors could bring war home to North America. Not so, Lindbergh declared. The U.S. was in no danger from invasion, he claimed, "unless American peoples bring it on" by interfering in the affairs of other nations. Isolationists cheered. "Magnificent," proclaimed Missouri's Champ Clark. "Lindbergh supplied the demoralized isolationists with the point around which to rally which they had previously lacked," a British survey of the American press noted.

On the other side of the fence, the *New York Times* claimed that Lindbergh was "a blind young man if he really believes we can live on terms of equal peace and happiness 'regardless of which side wins this war' in Europe." House Majority Leader Sam Rayburn was disapproving but restrained. The aviator's speech brought to mind, he said, "the old saying that every workman should stick to his bench." Similarly, Senator Byrnes, chosen as the Administration's spokesman, argued that Lindbergh was no more qualified to speak on foreign policy than "wrong-way Corrigan" or any other aviator who may fly the Atlantic Ocean. Beyond that, playing on the public concern about "Fifth Columnists," Byrnes declared that "those who consciously or unconsciously retard the efforts of this government to provide for the defense of the American people are the Fifth Column's most effective fellow travelers."

But neither the President nor any member of his official family was willing themselves to take on Lindbergh directly. Publicly, Roosevelt had no comment. Privately, however, he was seething. "If I should die tomorrow, I want you to know this," he told Henry Morgenthau. "I am absolutely convinced that Lindbergh is a Nazi."

As for the Nazis themselves, they could hardly have been more pleased about Lindbergh's performance. "Freemasons and Jews are no longer the sole rulers in the executive branch of the United States," the German military attaché exulted to Berlin after Lindbergh's May 19 speech. "They tried by mean tricks and spitefulness to belittle Lindbergh, the spokesman for the real America, and have thus succeeded in getting his views discussed everywhere today."

Lindbergh took to the radio again on June 15 in the wake of the Allied setbacks in France, warning that by helping Britain and France Americans would risk bringing catastrophe upon their own country. The President made no response. Senator Pittman, selected by the Democratic National Committee to speak for the Administration, instead of directly countering Lindbergh's arguments, limited himself to defending the legality of weapons sales to the Allies and suggesting that Lindbergh fire his political advisers and sign up as a volunteer adviser to the U.S. defense effort.

The quandary facing Americans was summed up by the *Des Moines Register* on the day after Lindbergh's speech. The practical question that Lindbergh raised, the paper observed was whether the U.S. should back away from the Allies as a lost cause or deny the inevitability of the Axis triumph and back Britain. "Only Providence knows which course would prove the wiser," the paper concluded. With Roosevelt unwilling to address this dilemma directly, William Allen White assumed the role of point man for supporters of Britain. It was a part he had played before, in the battle to repeal the arms embargo in 1939. After that venture, when Roosevelt wrote to thank him for "a grand job," White modestly replied that "I was just the rooster on the cow catcher, who mistakes his crow for engine's steam."

In fact, as the President certainly knew, White represented a significant political asset, particularly to a cause that seemed dominated by Democrats and Eastern elitists. The self-styled progressive Republican from Emporia, Kansas brought to the Aid-to-Britain effort the appearance of bipartisanship, the flavor of middle America and the influence of his far-flung contacts among the high and mighty in national life. At age 72, this journalist, novelist, and political amateur had been all but certified as a national institution. He forged his own public image as a folk philosopher. His friend, the New York book critic Lewis Gannett, once accused him "of having invented himself, of creating his own character as the shrewd, kindly country editor," when he was really "a sophisticated city guy." Gannett added: "New York is full of small town boys trying their best to forget that they are small-town boys. Will White made a career out of remembering it . . ."

The development of White's views on public affairs mirrored the transformation of the American creed by the various inequities and upheavals that ultimately produced the Roosevelt presidency and the New Deal. White's initial thinking, as the liberal critic Vernon Parrington wrote, was "a product of middle-class Puritan Kansas." Sentimental to the core, he romanticized small-town life and feared its corruption by the advancing urban-industrial culture. In 1896, as William Jennings Bryan's unsettling populism captured people all around him, the *Gazette*'s alarmed editor sternly advised his fellow Kansans to simmer down. "Because we have become poorer and ornrier and meaner than a spavined distempered mule, we, the people of Kansas, propose to kick," he wrote in an editorial titled "What's the Matter With Kansas?" destined to give him a national reputation. "We don't care to build up, we wish to tear down."

To his credit, White was able to outgrow such simplistic boosterism. And though he remained loyal to the Grand Old Party, with the passing years White's intelligence led him to reject many of the tenets of orthodox Republicanism. An ardent admirer of Theodore Roosevelt, he followed TR out of the GOP in 1912 to manage his campaign in Kansas, an activity that he somehow did not allow to interfere with his regular coverage of the campaign as a journalist. "No man has waged a gamer and more efficient fight for the Progressive Cause than you have," the grateful TR wrote White after his defeat.

Other Republican Presidents, White found, did not measure up to TR. Harding, he observed, "was almost unbelievably ill-informed." He described Coolidge as "looking down his nose to locate that evil smell which seemed forever to affront him." And White lost patience with Hoover's inaction in the midst of the Depression. "For a man who has high intentions and a noble purpose," White wrote in 1930 to a fellow Republican, "our beloved President has a greater capacity for doing exactly the wrong thing at a nicely appointed right time than any man who ever polished his pants in the big chair at the White House." Though he never voted for Roosevelt, White found it easy to accept much of the Democrat's domestic program, which he saw as similar to TR's Square Deal. "On the whole by and large I am for the New Deal," he declared in 1934.

White loved nothing better than to give advice. Understanding that, and eager to be on good terms with this paragon of middle America,

Roosevelt made a point of seeking his counsel whenever he could find an opportunity. In June of 1938, as the midterm elections approached, he wrote White asking about the possibility that an extremist cleric named Gerald Winrod, known as the "Kansas Nazi," might beat out the state's former governor, Clyde Reed, for the Republican Senate nomination. "Needless to say," Roosevelt promised the editor, "anything you tell me I will keep (cross my heart) between your honorable self and my honorable self." White promptly informed Roosevelt that Winrod was an erstwhile tent evangelist who knew the "tricks of Father Coughlin, Billy Sunday and Huey Long" and who until recently had been a purveyor of anti-Semitic pamphlets. "Unless we can change the Republican situation, he will win in the primary." As it turned out, though, Reed prevailed, and went on to easily win election in November.

White also felt free to make recommendations that went beyond politics. "Watch out for your health," he urged the President in the winter of 1938. "Politics will take care of itself if you keep your dauber up. . . . Specifically you are coming into the prostate zone. Don't dally with it. It whittles you down and gets your everlasting spiritual goat without you realizing it." White claimed that he himself had recently solved the problem, by undergoing "a bloodless operation done by an electrical gadget" at the Mayo Clinic. Though he adopted a joshing tone in this discussion, White closed with a sober note: "I am dead serious about this warning as you walk into the danger zone of the years," he wrote the President who was fourteen years White's junior.

"You are dead right to make that suggestion," Roosevelt wrote back. Then he quickly changed the subject to the Supreme Court.

It was neither the travails of advancing age nor the vagaries of domestic politics that brought White and Roosevelt together but rather the continuing crisis in Europe. Here again White's views had evolved as the world had changed. Despite his admiration for Theodore Roosevelt's trust-busting stance, he rebelled against TR's expansionist view of America's role in the world. When Roosevelt tried to settle the dispute between Germany and Britain and Venezuela in 1903, White wrote that "everyone in this town . . . is engaged in honest work and is looking after his own family. The *Gazette* contends that this is better than bothering with Venezuela."

World War I converted him to internationalism. "We may think we can stand aloof, but we tried that once and it didn't work," White wrote in 1921, criticizing the U.S. repudiation of the League of Nations. Throughout the 1920s he advocated international agreements on arms limits, became a leader in the League of Nations Association, and promoted other efforts at international understanding.

In the 1930s, like most of his countrymen, White was ambivalent and confused about how the United States should respond to the growing threat of aggression. He desperately wanted peace. "War is the devil's joke on humanity," he declared on Armistice Day in 1933. But with the outbreak of war in 1939, he argued vigorously that the U.S. needed to help the Allies in order to protect its own interests. And when Clark Eichelberger, head of the League of Nations Association, approached him, apparently at the President's behest, White took on the task of organizing support for repeal of the arms embargo.

The completion of that job, however, left much undone. In December of 1939 FDR wrote his "sage old friend," asking him to spend a night at the White House, to discuss ways to awaken Americans to the dangers facing them both in Europe and the Far East. In that letter, he outlined his own approach to the national dilemma over the war more frankly than he had anywhere else.

". . . My problem," the President explained to White, "is to get the American people to think of conceivable consequences without scaring the American people into thinking that they are going to be dragged into this war." If this seemed like an exercise in ambiguity, White did not object, perhaps because his own thinking was muddled. Unable to accept the invitation to come to Washington because of his wife's illness, he nevertheless said he shared the President's feelings. "I fear our involvement before the peace," White wrote, "and yet I fear to remain uninvolved letting the danger of a peace of tyranny approach too near."

By the following April, with the end of the phony war signaled by Hitler's invasion of Norway, White once again signed up with Eichelberger to spearhead a nonpartisan committee, this time to rally public support for aid to the British and French.

Their first move was to write, wire, and phone a vast array of prominent citizens an emergency appeal:

> The people of our country cannot avoid the consequences of Hitler's victory. The United States should throw its material and moral weight on the side of the nations of western Europe . . . that are struggling in battle for a civilized way of life.

By the time the Committee to Defend America by Aiding the Allies was formally organized on May 20, the luminaries on its board of directors included Henry Stimson, Columbia University President Nicholas Murray Butler, Frank Knox, and New York Governor Herbert Lehman.

President James Conant of Harvard and Mrs. Dwight Morrow, made nationwide radio addresses on the committee's behalf, with Mrs. Morrow's talk attracting particular attention because her views clashed with those of her son-in-law, Lindbergh. Sherwood's full page "Stop Hitler Now" advertisement, its impact magnified by Roosevelt's mention at his press conference, helped bring in 500 volunteers in 48 hours in New York alone.

Despite these endeavors, the British Embassy reported to London, the committee's leaders had a sense of being "all dressed up and nowhere to go." The committee needed a specific goal, besides increasing its own membership. White turned to the Oval Office. "I knew I had his private support," White said later about what he called his "morganatic relationship" with the President. "I never did anything the President didn't ask for and I always conferred with him on our program."

His first orders were to help the Senate fight to confirm the nominations of Knox and Stimson, both of whom were facing resistance because of their dedication to the British cause. Senator James Byrnes, Roosevelt's lieutenant in the Senate, turned over to White the names of doubtful Senators, who arranged for a flood of wires to the lawmakers from influential constituents urging confirmation. That task done, on June 29 White returned to the White House for further instructions. This time the President gave him what White had wanted all along: a specific goal on which he could focus the committee's efforts and resources. This was mobilizing public support to give Churchill the destroyers he wanted.

Intent on preserving the aura of nonpartisanship for his efforts, White waited until both political conventions were over and then forged ahead. On July 23 he wired an appeal to a long list of influential figures:

> Confidential information highest authority convinces me British government desperately short of destroyers. Successful defense of Great Britain may depend upon release through sale by the United States of fifty or sixty overage age but recently reconditioned destroyers. President already has authority or could secure Congressional authorization if necessary. Urge you wire President immediately advocating this action.

"If the President really wants to do this, it can be done," White declared in a follow up press release issued July 26, which showed him to be closely tuned to Roosevelt's own thinking. "But we must show him that the country will follow him on this matter."

To stir the public, the Committee placed large ads in the *New York Times* and other papers around the country on July 30. Under the heading: "Between us and Hitler stands the British fleet!" the copy declared that destroyers were Britain's most critical need, adding that the United States had plenty to spare. "What are we waiting for?" the ad demanded, imploring the public to write and wire Congress and the President, urging the transfer of the over-age warships to the embattled British— "before it is forever too late."

While White's committee worked on Britain's behalf in the open, another entity served the same cause, mainly behind the scenes. An informal aggregation of Eastern lawyers, journalists, and businessmen, they came to be known as the Century Group after the Manhattan club, a gathering place for the powerful and privileged, where they often met. Their driving force was a well-born, well-connected Virginian named Francis P. Miller, then on the staff of the Council on Foreign Relations. He had entered the debate over the U.S. role abroad in June when he rounded up more than a score of prominent citizens to sign a statement calling for an outright declaration of war against Germany. Released while France was still in the war, Miller's manifesto claimed "that the frontier of our national interest is now on the Somme," and contended that the U.S. could not get aid to the Allies fast enough unless it formally abandoned its neutrality. The statement, reported in the *New York Times* and other papers around the country, fell flat. If Americans agreed on anything it was that they did not want to go to fight: A Gallup poll at the end of May found 93 percent opposed to a declaration of war against Germany.

Miller decided to change his focus from declaring war to simply aiding Britain, with turning over the destroyers the British wanted as the first objective. His cohorts all were well positioned for pulling strings and twisting arms among the higher-ups in American society. They included Dean Acheson, then a Washington lawyer, Allen Dulles, at the time an attorney on Wall Street, Lewis Douglas, President of the Mutual Life Insurance company and previously Roosevelt's first budget director, Herbert Agar, editor of the *Louisville Courier Journal*, Will Clayton, Texas cotton broker and Vice President of the Export Import Bank, Dr. Henry Sloan Coffin, President of Union Theological Seminary, Henry W. Hobson, Episcopal Bishop of Ohio, Ernest M. Hopkins, President of Dartmouth College, Whitney Shepardson, Vice President of the International Railways of Central America, and Henry R. Luce, the founder of Time, Inc.

Of the twenty or so active members, most were of Anglo-Saxon origins and, like Miller himself, staunchly believed that most of what was good about their country derived from its British heritage. Miller had spent two years reading history at Oxford after World War I as a Rhodes scholar, then stayed on in England for two more years, working for the British Student Christian Movement and studying theology at Oxford. His Anglophile tendencies were reinforced by his wife, Helen, who was the Washington correspondent for *The Economist* of London. The British "practice our way of life," he asserted in a memorandum to other group members which argued that "the keystone of our foreign policy must be close collaboration with the British Commonwealth of Nations."

Impelled by his sense of civic obligation, in 1934 Miller and his wife had organized the National Policy Committee to promote what he regarded as "the general interest" against the goals of political parties and "special interests." To the financier and South Carolina native Bernard Baruch, Miller wrote about the new group's efforts to alleviate the desperate economic conditions in the South in the 1930s: "I, like you, feel that I have some personal responsibility in this matter since it was my cousin, Francis Pickens, who was Governor of South Carolina when that state seceded from the Union."

This same self-assurance colored Miller's outlook on foreign policy. Unlike his isolationist opponents, who claimed to reflect what the majority of Americans believed, Miller was convinced that Americans needed the Century Group to chart the nation's course for them. "The people do not yet realize the implications for our national freedom of an Atlantic Ocean controlled by hostile naval forces," Miller wrote William Allen White, informing him of the Century Group's plans in mid-July, "Under the circumstances we felt that it was the duty of each one of us to do everything in his individual capacity to arouse the country to the urgency of this situation."

While Miller pushed ahead with the task of organizing the group, he assigned a new recruit, Henry Pitt Van Dusen, to establish contact with the British through Ambassador Lothian. Van Dusen, like Miller, was not burdened by excessive humility. In a July 4 meeting at the Embassy, he told the ambassador that he and his friends would undertake to help Britain only if they could be assured that the British would promise "under no circumstance to surrender," and in case of invasion, to move the Royal Family, the Government, and, presumably most important of all, the Royal Navy to Canada.

If Lothian resented this presumption, Van Dusen did not notice. But when the Century Group assembled for the first time on July 11, he was able to report that the ambassador had informed him that Britain had no greater need from the United States than the destroyers for which Churchill had been asking. The group soon agreed that "the survival of the British fleet is a critical factor in U.S. defense," and that the "the period within which the United States can act to protect her interests . . . is a matter not of years, but possibly of only a few weeks more."

Lewis Douglas and Whitney Shepardson proposed massive U.S. aid to Britain, including U.S. Navy escorts for convoys and U.S. fleet protection for the British Isles, in return for which the British would promise to base their fleet in the U.S. if Hitler conquered England. All this was to be sealed by a treaty and ratified by the Senate. But Luce objected that this would amount to declaring war. He was unwilling to go that far. "There is a great deal still to be done which is not an act of war—repealing the Neutrality Act for example," the publisher wrote Miller.

Unable to agree on a specific course of action, they decided on more thought and legwork. Henry Sloan Coffin and Luce were assigned to visit Hull, Stimson, and, if possible, Roosevelt to press for destroyers for the British. Lewis Douglas, a member in good standing of the White Committee, was assigned to serve as liaison with that group, and also to make contact with Wendell Willkie's presidential campaign. Miller took leave from his job and set up an office in the Albee Theater Building on 42nd Street and Fifth Avenue in midtown Manhattan. This turned out to be next door to a German propaganda front called the American Fellowship Forum directed by one Friedrich Auhagen, who had ties to American fascist leader Laurence Dennis, ultimately charged with sedition. Miller fed the FBI information on Auhagen, who eventually fled the country to avoid deportation.

Meanwhile, in Washington the Century Group's emissaries were not finding much enthusiasm for giving the British destroyers at the upper levels of the Administration. After a session with Cordell Hull, who like most of his colleagues was discouraged about the prospects for getting congressional approval for the idea, Luce wrote to Lewis Douglas: "The noble old soldier has been working so long in an atmosphere of frustration and defeat that he has perhaps lost the necessary faith in the possible victory of his cause."

But the biggest obstacle seemed to be the President himself. At a White House dinner, Luce attempted to sound him out on the destroyer issue. Roosevelt's calculated ambiguity, compounded by Luce's own poor hearing, stood in his way. After dinner Roosevelt brought Luce back to his study, doffed his jacket in the midsummer heat, and sat back in his wheel chair ready to chat. Luce asked the President point blank about the destroyer proposal and understood him to reply: "It's out." But then Roosevelt mentioned that he planned to take Sen. Walsh, chairman of the Senate Naval Affairs Committee and his House counterpart, Congressman Carl Vinson of Georgia, on a weekend trip on the Presidential yacht in the hope that "he can bring them around to the idea."

Just as Luce took hope from that information, Roosevelt went off on another tack. He likened the request from Churchill to France's plea just before its final collapse in June for more RAF fighter planes to help beat back the German assault. Churchill had to consider the "probabilities" of France holding out against Britain's need for the planes for her own defense, Roosevelt said, and he pointed out, decided against the French. Luce did not think much of the analogy, but chose not to pursue it. Instead, he argued that the American public would approve of the transfer if they understood the danger of Hitler. "Harry," Roosevelt replied, "I can't come out in favor of such a deal without the support of the entire *Time-Life* organization for my foreign policy." It was a modified version of the President's message to William Allen White : Let Luce sell the idea to the people first, then he would act.

To offset Luce's lack of progress at the White House, the Century Group gained enthusiasm and information from a new journalistic recruit, columnist Joseph Alsop. For Alsop, the Group represented another opportunity to take advantage of his membership in what he later called "the Wasp ascendancy." Members of the WASP ascendancy, Alsop noted, tended to resemble each other in many ways and frequently knew each other as friends or at least acquaintances. Moreover, as he acknowledged, their connections with the hierarchy of the worlds of government and business added to their wealth and other advantages, and gave them "substantially more leverage than other Americans."

Alsop's own most impressive connection was his blood tie to the President's family; his mother was a first cousin and close friend of First Lady Eleanor Roosevelt. Thus on election night in 1936, when Alsop was among the reporters gathered in Hyde Park where the President received word of his victory, Roosevelt took him aside and handed him a slip of paper on which were scribbled some figures. They showed that Alsop's hometown in Avon, a longtime Republican stronghold where Alsop's mother, Corrine, was active in the GOP, had voted for FDR.

"How will Corrine like that?" Roosevelt teased. Alsop brought back word from his mother that she had managed to find enough Democrats to support the local Republican candidate for the state legislature to send him to the chamber in Hartford, "by just as good a majority as Franklin got for the Presidency." The President "roared with laughter" and told his cousin-in-law, "I knew Corrine was a professional."

So, too, was her son, at whatever task he undertook. In this case he had commissioned himself to prod his government into filling the British needs for destroyers. First, he passed on to the Century Group what he had learned from a friend at the British Embassy of the substance of the exchange of telegrams between Churchill and Roosevelt over the destroyer issue. Then he unearthed further information about Britain's predicament. "The Naval situation is more desperate than anyone realizes," Alsop reported, warning that the destruction Hitler's naval mines were wreaking against British destroyers might allow the Germans to "drive the English Navy out of the straits of Dover and therefore be able to storm across the English Channel. Unless the British are given immediate additional destroyers odds are absolutely against defending the British Isles." To back up Alsop's disclosure, Ambassador Lothian provided Miller with a firsthand accounting. Compared with the 433 destroyers that flew the Union Jack in 1918, Britain now had only 70 fit for service, Lothian estimated. "Since destroyers and torpedo boats are the only naval craft that can be used effectively in the Channel to repel an invasion," he added, "the British government views this situation with utmost gravity."

Armed with these somber assessments from Alsop and Lothian, the Century Group members concluded that the urgency of Britain's need for destroyers meant that the President should not spend the time it would take to gain congressional approval. Instead, they concentrated on convincing the President to act on his own.

Editor Herbert Agar summed up the thinking of the Century Group as their leaders waited for the President to meet with them:

> We war mongers knew that the enemy was at the gate, that the threat to our life was immediate, and that time was running out; but most of our fellow citizens did not agree. So all we could do in our frustration was to use our several influences whenever the chance came, to push the country toward war. The British plea for destroyers was such a chance.

But when Agar and two other Century Group members called on Roosevelt on August 1, they found him noncommittal at best, seemingly concerned that giving the British destroyers could damage his chances of reelection. Nor was the President greatly impressed with the scheme they outlined to him to get a number of prominent columnists, including Alsop, Lippmann, and Frank Kent to influence public attitudes by publishing a weekly newsletter for newspaper editors and the like.

Was there anything they could do that would make a difference? Agar asked. Roosevelt had a ready answer. He wanted the country's most celebrated living war hero, General John "Black Jack" Pershing, the commander of the AEF, to make a radio speech advocating the destroyer deal. If he himself asked Pershing, Roosevelt told them, he feared that word would leak out and he would be accused of exploiting a national hero to promote a controversial cause.

"If one of you asks, it probably won't leak," he said, as Agar later recalled the conversation. "If it does, and you say the idea came from me, I shall call you a liar, and all would be peaceful in Congress."

Actually the Century Group had been trying for some time to ask for Pershing's help. But the old soldier, now 80, who had waged his first campaigns against Geronimo's Apache warriors, was leading a reclusive existence, domiciled in Washington's Carlton Hotel. For all his far-flung contacts, Miller knew no one who knew Pershing. Finally he was told of a longtime friend of the General's by the name of George A. C. Christiancy, who now spent his days as a permanent resident of a New York hospital suite. Invited to lunch at the Yale Club with Miller, Christiancy agreed to pave the way for a meeting with Pershing.

This turned out to be no simple task. Despite his enduring relationship with Pershing, Christiancy did not want to ask the General directly for an appointment for himself. Instead he asked Miller to seek out another Pershing friend, former General James Harbord, an executive with RCA. Once the situation had been explained to him, Harbord rang Pershing up and got through immediately. After a few minutes of conversation, impeded by the fact that both former generals were hard of hearing, Harbord persuaded Pershing to agree to see Christiancy two days hence on July 31.

With this threshold cleared, Christiancy arrived from New York and, escorted by Miller, called upon Pershing. Christiancy's visit with the general lasted long enough for him to get Pershing to agree to receive Herbert Agar. Now that the stage had been set, Agar came to Pershing's hotel on the very next day, fresh from the White House and bearing the President's request for him to speak. Eager to help out the Commander-in-Chief, Pershing agreed to make a radio address the following Sunday night, August 4, endorsing the idea of sending destroyers to Britain. Before Agar left, Pershing told him that he had written Roosevelt right after the war started in 1939 to tell him that "we Americans would be in a sad way if Germany conquered Europe. I said

I knew nothing about politics or of what was politically possible; but I believed that as his senior General I should tell him what I thought."

An all-star cast prepared for Pershing's big moment. Alsop worked out arrangements with the radio networks and Agar and Lippmann drafted the speech, making a case that Churchill himself could hardly have improved upon. "I am telling you tonight before it is too late that the British Navy needs destroyers to convoy merchant ships, hunt submarines, and repel invasion," Americans around the country heard Pershing warn that Sunday night.

> We have an immense reserve of destroyers left over from the other war, and in a few months the British will be completing a large number of destroyers of their own. The most critical time, therefore, is the next few weeks and months. If there is anything we can do to help save the British fleet during that time, we shall be failing in our duty to America if we do not do it. If a proper method can be found, America will safeguard her freedom and security by making available to the British or Canadian governments at least fifty of the over-age destroyers which are left from the days of the World War.

The speech touched off an avalanche of favorable publicity, dominating the news. The *New York Times* led its Monday editions with the story under a three-column headline that underlined the thrust of Pershing's argument: "Pershing Would Let Britain Have 50 Old U.S. Destroyers To Guard Our Own Liberty." All the better from the point of view of the British and their supporters was that the response to Pershing's address overshadowed a speech given that same Sunday night by Colonel Lindbergh entitled "Keeping America Out of War." Addressing a crowd of 40,000 in Chicago's Soldier Field and a nationwide radio audience, Lindbergh called for "cooperation" with Germany if Hitler won the war, as a way of maintaining peace and civilization around the world.

As for Roosevelt, Agar and the Century Group had delivered to him just what he wanted. Yet it was difficult for them or any one else to guess where the President stood. A page one photo of Hull congratulating Pershing seemed to imply Administration approval of the address, but said nothing definite about whether Roosevelt was prepared to move ahead on the destroyers.

The President appeared to be balancing the impact of the destroyers on his chances for reelection on one hand, and on the other hand, Britain's prospects for survival. This was a delicate and dangerous calculation. A reminder of how high the stakes were had been provided to him from embattled Britain a few days before in a message from

Churchill. The Prime Minister's decision to break his long silence was prompted by a cable from Lothian, who through his contacts with the Century Group knew of their efforts to prod Roosevelt into acting.

"Strong pressure is being brought on the President to reconsider possibility of supplying us with destroyers," he advised the Prime Minister. "Now is the moment to send him most moving statement of our needs and dangers. . . ."

The former Naval Person was quick to respond. On July 31, the day after hearing from his ambassador, he renewed his request for destroyers, citing the heavy losses the British had suffered, ticking off the names of eleven destroyers sunk in the past ten days, and warning that worse was yet to come. "We could not keep up the present rate of casualties for long and if we cannot get a substantial reinforcement, the whole fate of the war may be decided by this minor and easily remediable factor," he told Roosevelt. "Mr. President, with great respect," the Prime Minster added, "I must tell you that in the long history of the world, this is a thing to do now."

# Belling the Cat

Churchill's impatience with Roosevelt echoed in the U.S., in private conversations and public declarations, by those who believed the President to be dawdling in the face of Britain's need. The tide of public opinion, which as August began once again shifted, this time in Britain's favor, added weight to these complaints. Nevertheless, Roosevelt moved at his own pace, his actions largely guided by his campaign year concerns. By the time of Pershing's speech he had let eleven weeks pass since Churchill's first plea for destroyers. Churchill had made his request in the full blush of spring. Now in the swelter of midsummer Washington, Roosevelt, hating air conditioning, working at his Oval Office desk in his shirtsleeves, at last appeared to be moving toward a decision. Still, he hedged every step with one objective always in mind, safeguarding his candidacy for reelection.

Influencing his calculations was the course of the war, which, for the moment at least, energized the forces demanding more U.S. aid for Britain. Most significant during the six weeks immediately following the fall of France was what did not happen. Despite expectations to the contrary, Britain had not collapsed. In fact she was striking back.

For the United States, the Royal Navy's assault on ships of the French fleet in the harbor at Oran, Algeria on July 3, preventing them from falling into Hitler's hands, provided the most important evidence of British resolve. Churchill used the attack, which knocked out three French battleships and outraged Britain's erstwhile ally, to drive home a point to an American public dubious about Britain's will to fight. Taking note of "the lies and rumors so industriously spread" by German propagandists that Britain was contemplating ending her struggle against Hitler, the Prime Minister told Parliament: "All idea of that should be completely swept out of the way by the drastic and grievous action we have felt ourselves compelled to take."

The American press's ability to find some strand of silver even in the darkest gloom also boosted the British cause. The British Embassy

159

reported to London that wishful editorials were filled with references to previous British triumphs over supposedly superior foes dating back to the Spanish Armada. Even papers like the *Tulsa World*, normally sharing in the Southwest's suspicions of perfidious Albion, spoke of "the valiant spirit of Britain" meeting its supreme test. The longer the British hung on, and fought back, the more confident and approving Americans felt. At the Foreign Office's American Department, T. North Whitehead studied summaries of U.S. press reports for the last two weeks of July and concluded: "The United States have never been so little critical of Britain or so sincerely concerned for her survival." Supplanting the "deep depression" produced by the French collapse, Whitehead believed, was "a more reasonable hope" for British survival.

The findings of the Gallup Poll lent credence to this evaluation. In early summer most Americans thought the Germans would win the war; on July 7, opinion was equally divided about the war's outcome; two weeks later the same question showed that a significant plurality of those interviewed, 43 percent, believed Britain would win, compared to only 24 percent who foresaw a German victory. Americans felt they had an important stake in the war's outcome. Seven out of ten said they would be personally affected if Germany won the war and also said they believed that a victorious Germany would try to gain control of South American countries. Asked if the U.S. should send food and arms shipments to Britain if her defeat appeared certain, 85 percent said yes. In April of 1940, nearly 60 percent objected to the suggestion that the U.S. should delay enlarging its own air force to ship planes to the Allies. But in July, nearly 50 percent were willing to send more planes to England, even at the cost of delaying America's own defense program, while only 44 percent disagreed.

This evidence of public willingness to aid Britain, apparent even before Pershing's speech, exacerbated the impatience of Roosevelt's critics. "There are risks in any policy we adopt," the *New York Times* argued at the end of July, but in the long run ignoring Britain might be the riskiest and costliest of policies. The basic problem "is that our foreign policy is not being publicly discussed by our politicians in these or any other realistic terms," the paper complained. Despite all the earnest expressions of good wishes for the British cause, the *Times* pointed out that help to Britain consisted mostly of whatever the British could pay for and carry home in their own ships.

If that's all we mean by "full help" we should say so candidly. If we mean more than that, we should decide quickly how much more we do mean.

In an open letter to the President on the destroyer issue, the Dallas *News* also urged candor:

> Aid—the most effective aid that the U.S. can render without impair-
> ing our own necessary defense—may be unpopular at the moment
> because men and women do not understand the dire necessity. But if
> they were told, sir, their support and their conviction would be immedi-
> ate in response.

*Time*, another proponent of backing the British, echoed these complaints about the lack of public discussion and worried that the
President might already have decided against giving the British the
destroyers. If such indeed was the case, *Time* charged that "a decision
that might be crucial had been taken without public debate, without a
presentation of the alternatives, without a common awareness that the
decision had been made."

A public debate on destroyers for Britain had no place on Franklin
Roosevelt's agenda. But on August 2, two days before Pershing's radio
address, discussion of the issue finally did begin within the President's
official family at Roosevelt's regular Friday cabinet meeting. The cata-
lyst was the British Ambassador. Lord Lothian's family motto was *Sero
Sed Serio*, "late but in earnest." Like his country, slow to sense the
threat from Hitler, Lothian now fought against time.

Taking his cue from his Prime Minister, the Ambassador had held his
tongue while partisan feelings ran high during that political summer.
Instead he busied himself behind the scenes, providing the Century
Group and other allies with evidence of Britain's desperate need for the
warships she sought. With the conclusion of the political conventions,
however, Lothian abandoned his self-imposed restrictions. On July 22,
just three days after the President had accepted renomination, in his first
first public appearance, Lothian told columnists Drew Pearson and
Robert S. Allen on their widely heard radio show that Britain needed the
destroyers "most urgently" to prevent invasion and fight submarines.

What if Britain were conquered that summer, Lothian was asked.

"Then both your prospects and ours are very bad," he replied. "You
have not today got any army or an air force of modern size, and you
have only one navy for two oceans."

This was far blunter talk than he felt he could have gotten away with
even four weeks before, Lothian wrote to a friend. "Today not a mur-
mur," he pointed out. In fact the British Embassy counted half a dozen
favorable editorials around the country.

Emboldened, Lothian now sought to exert more direct pressure on

Roosevelt. In search of a surrogate, he found the Secretary of the Navy, Frank Knox, an eminently logical choice. Apart from his longtime commitment to aiding Britain, Knox's Republican ties assured Roosevelt's attention to his views on politically sensitive issues. At age 66, the secretary retained much of the fire that had inspired him more than forty years before to join Theodore Roosevelt's Rough Riders. For TR's sake Knox bolted the GOP in 1912 to join the Bull Moose insurgency. At the no longer tender age of 43, Knox enlisted in the Army as a private soldier and emerged as a colonel, a title he still clung to at the head of the Navy. Starting as a newspaper publisher in Michigan, he had ultimately become owner of the *Chicago Daily News*, whose distinguished staff of foreign correspondents belied the Midwest's isolationist reputation.

Neither as mean nor as narrow as he sometimes made himself sound, Knox had earned the respect of his fellow former Bull Mooser, Harold Ickes, and those Democrats who regarded him as a man of reason and decency. Now he was determined to use his position to advance what he firmly believed to be his country's interest.

Lothian had presented him with an opportunity to do just that on the night before the cabinet meeting when he phoned Knox at home, reaching him at dinner, and told him that he had "a very important matter to discuss." He hurried to the Embassy, to hear Lothian plea for the destroyers with the full force of his emotions. Indeed, as Knox later told Ickes, Lothian was "almost tearful," when he claimed that he did not know what would happen to Great Britain if she did not receive the ships. He begged Knox to try every available means to help him.

Knox had an idea of his own, which would ultimately transform the destroyer issue from a British appeal for help from the U.S. into a far-reaching bargain between the two countries. "We want to help," Knox told Lothian. But the Administration's hands were tied, unless it could get congressional sanction. Would the British consider transferring some of their islands in the West Indies to pave the way for approval on Capitol Hill? The British should understand, Knox pointed out, that whether or not the islands were under the Stars and Stripes or the Union Jack, the U.S., not Great Britain, would bear the burden of defending them against any aggressor.

This was not the first time Knox and Lothian had talked about Britain's island possessions. Three weeks earlier, shortly after Knox was sworn in, the new Secretary asked Lothian about yielding the islands in return for cancellation of war debts. This was an idea which Knox had been pushing in his editorials at the *Daily News*. Lothian had warily suggested to Knox "unofficially" that the future of the Caribbean

Islands should be considered in the context of the naval problems which might soon face both countries.

Now Knox had taken up Lothian's suggestion, linking Britain's cherished island possessions to the destroyers she wanted. For the moment Lothian, playing the role of the discreet diplomat, would only say to Knox that he would take up his idea with London. Dealing with more immediate concerns, Knox asked if Britain would be hurt if details of her predicament were divulged in order to build support for her cause. This was a chance Britain would have to take, said Lothian.

Knox began planning his presentation for next day's cabinet meeting, trying to calculate the reaction of those among his colleagues likely to take the greatest interest in the issue. First to consider was Cordell Hull. Rigid and cautious, the Secretary of State could be expected to straddle the issue and to counsel delay. Next in importance was Knox's fellow Republican, Henry Stimson. A quick phone call confirmed what Knox had expected, that the Secretary of War would come down strongly on the British side. So, presumably, would Treasury Secretary Morgenthau, but other matters called him away that day and Knox would miss his voice.

Before the cabinet assembled, though, Knox heard from another committed backer of aid to Britain, Interior Secretary Ickes. The Interior Department would seem far removed from the issue of aid to Britain. But Harold Ickes was no respecter of protocol. His stilettolike tongue made him an obnoxious antagonist and a potent ally. When young Tom Dewey announced for the presidency, Ickes claimed he had "thrown his diaper in the ring"; he would later mock Wendell Willkie as a "simple, barefoot, Wall Street lawyer." At 66, he was the same age as his former Bull Moose comrade Knox. Unlike Knox, though, Ickes had deserted the Republican fold in 1932 to join Roosevelt's campaign and then his cabinet. There he had fiercely advocated conservation, resolutely opposed the forces of privilege, in the process trying the patience of the President. Roosevelt, though, valued his Interior Secretary's integrity and dedication enough to humor him during his intermittent sulks and tirades and to shrug off his occasional threats to resign.

Ickes was a man of many passions, petty and grand. A self-styled curmudgeon, his irascibility was rivaled by his ambition to expand Interior's bureaucratic frontiers, his self-righteousness, and, most significantly for this occasion, his intense hatred of Adolf Hitler. In 1937, after the helium-filled German dirigible *Hindenburg* exploded in mid-air, legislation was passed permitting the Secretary of Interior to sell helium to foreign countries to use in airships as a substitute for hydrogen, provided it was not used for military purposes. But when Germany subsequently contracted for the purchase of a huge amount of helium, Ickes, defying the President who approved of the deal, refused to go along. He insisted that given the helium, the Germans would certainly find a way to make military use out of it. "Who would take Hitler's word?" he asked Roosevelt. The deal died.

Now in a way the situation was reversed, as the British, like the Germans, sought to make a deal with the U.S. while Roosevelt resisted and Ickes pressured him to change his mind. Ickes had first taken up Britain's cause early in July, prompted by Ben Cohen, the brilliant New Deal lawyer, who was then General Counsel to the National Power Policy Committee, part of Ickes's Interior Department. Cohen had been approached by the columnist, Joseph Alsop, who had given him much the same information from his contacts at the British Embassy about Britain's dire need for destroyers that he had relayed to members of the Century Group.

Invited to the White House, Ickes argued at length with Roosevelt that "by hook or by crook we ought to accede to England's request." But the President said that in view of the Walsh amendment's restrictions, none of the World War I vintage destroyers could be sent to the British unless the Navy could certify they were "useless" for defense purposes. This would be difficult to do, Roosevelt pointed out, since the Navy was currently reconditioning more than one hundred of them for its own use. That had not stopped Ickes. Following their conversation at the White House, he sent the President a memorandum in July urging him to put forward an amendment to the Neutrality Act allowing him to send armaments to the British at his discretion, an idea Roosevelt rejected as impractical.

It was to relay yet another appeal on Britain's behalf, initiated by the poet Archibald MacLeish whom FDR had made Librarian of Congress, that Ickes had called Knox on the morning of the cabinet meeting. MacLeish, through friends who were members of the Century Group, had been told of Lothian's memorandum reckoning Britain's destroyer strength at no more than seventy. "The British were well-nigh desperate about holding the Channel in the event of a real push by the Germans," he told Ickes, urging him to pass the word to Knox.

Knox, of course, needed no urging from Ickes; it was he who urged Ickes to attend the cabinet meeting to back the British cause. Ickes's presence there would involve a measure of personal sacrifice. He had planned not to attend to demonstrate his pique with the President for not asking his advice during the Chicago convention. Looking back on that convention, Ickes had concluded : "If the President can retrieve this campaign after all the glaring blunders that he has made or been responsible for then the God of elections is indeed on his side." But Ickes decided, as he told his diary, that "If I could be of help in this desperate English situation, I was willing to waive any personal consideration."

From a portrait on the cabinet room's north wall, above the fireplace, Woodrow Wilson, the nation's World War I Commander in Chief looked down on Ickes and his colleagues as they gathered later that day to grapple with the challenge of World War II. About the length of a Pullman car, and several times wider, the cabinet room was spare and simple, dominated by a massive mahogany table around which the cabinet secretaries took their assigned places. The white walls were bare, except for the Wilson portrait and the paintings of Jefferson and Jackson, the Democratic Party's nineteenth-century patron saints, which Roosevelt had chosen for the west wall. On the east wall French windows opened on to the Rose Garden and, beyond that, a view of the stairs winding up to the south entrance of the White House. At morning meetings, cabinet members often could see FDR speeding down the covered path in his armless wheelchair, his Scottie, Falla, running alongside, his cigarette holder in his mouth, clutching some document he had been working on in his bedroom the night before. At other times, Roosevelt arrived less dramatically, through the tiny secretary's office that connected the Oval Office to the cabinet room, and wheeled himself to his customary place at the center of the table, a position that allowed him a clear view of everyone.

Knox bided his time after the meeting opened at 2 p.m., waiting while other matters were brought up and hashed over. Then he took the floor, recounted his conversation the night before with Lothian, and urged the President to give Britain the destroyers. While the chimes on the mantle clock measured the passage of every quarter of an hour, the President and his ranking advisers debated the pros and cons. True to form, Hull found problems, particularly with Knox's plan to trade the ships for the British West Indian islands. Earlier that very week a Pan American conference in Havana had agreed to set up joint machinery for protecting British possessions that appeared threatened by Germany. For the U.S. to take over the islands for itself, the Secretary of State thought, might violate the spirit of that agreement. Roosevelt himself suggested vaguely that some way might be found to lease a portion of the territory, as the U.S. had secretly done in 1939 to acquire the land for naval bases in Trinidad, St. Lucia, and Bermuda.

With that issue unresolved, Hull turned to another problem, the British fleet. Everyone assumed that any arrangement with the British would require action of some sort by Congress. And as Ickes noted in his diary, "The feeling was that the one preoccupying thought on the

Hill is what may happen to the British Navy." But Hull pointed out that even if Churchill promised to send the fleet to the U.S. in the event Hitler conquered England, another regime, friendlier to the Germans, might replace Churchill's government and violate that pledge. No one saw any way to guarantee against that risk. Still, they agreed that Lothian should be asked for whatever assurances he could provide.

For all of the concerns expressed, Ickes felt that the President and others were "more sympathetic" to the destroyer idea than they had been in the past. "Even Hull was in favor of doing something," Ickes noted. But they had yet to discuss the President's biggest worry, which he now raised. This was the threat from congressional Republicans, who Roosevelt feared might fight any legislation proposed to implement the transaction, perhaps defeating such a measure, certainly delaying it. Yet he also saw a way to safeguard against this risk: Get the Republican presidential candidate Wendell Willkie not only to agree himself to support the destroyer deal, but also to convince Republican congressional leader to give their endorsement, too.

When should this be done? Hull and the two Republican secretaries, Knox and Stimson, favored nailing down Willkie's endorsement in advance. Disagreeing, three highly partisan Democrats present—Henry Wallace, Roosevelt's vice-presidential running mate, his attorney general, Robert Jackson, and Interior Secretary Ickes—called consulting Willkie first "poor politics"; they urged that instead Roosevelt go ahead on his own, and as Ickes put it, "force Willkie's hand."

Then Jim Farley, Roosevelt's erstwhile campaign manager and the most seasoned politician present, save for Roosevelt himself, sided with Hull and the Republicans. Farley, who only the day before had stepped down as Democratic national chairman and would leave his cabinet post as Postmaster General at month's end, claimed that approaching Willkie beforehand would be "for the good of the country," adding "what was for the good of the country, was good politics." Stimson, equating this sanctimony with statesmanship, was impressed. "He showed himself really a big man," the Secretary of War observed later.

Getting Willkie's support before Roosevelt acted would also serve to lessen the risk for Roosevelt, a point that surely did not escape FDR. When the discussion ended, his was the only vote that counted and he wanted Willkie's endorsement in advance.

The next question was who would bell the cat? The answer occurring to nearly everyone in the room was William Allen White, long a Roosevelt confidant, more recent chum of Willkie's, and of course a zealous proponent of giving the destroyers to the British. "Many of us know him intimately and all have confidence in his character and integrity," Ickes observed.

To Secretary of War Stimson, who had served in that same post under President Taft and for four years as Secretary of State under Hoover, this meeting, as he later wrote in his diary, was "one of the most serious and important debates that I have ever had in a cabinet meeting." Indeed, he considered the situation so grave that he decided not to report on it in any detail even in his own journal.

By contrast, the President, who usually studiously avoided keeping track of cabinet discussions or any other meetings he attended, wrote a concise memo summarizing the long discussion at the August 2 session. His account revealed that after nearly three months of pleading, the British had finally convinced him and his advisers of the importance of the destroyers. "It was the general opinion without any dissenting voice," Roosevelt wrote, "that the survival of the British Isles under German attack might very possibly depend on their getting these destroyers." It had been agreed, Roosevelt wrote, that any attempt by him to get the necessary support, "without any preliminaries would meet with defeat or interminable delay." One preliminary was getting assurance from the British that their fleet "would not under any conceivable circumstances" fall into German hands. The other was getting Willkie and the Republicans behind the plan, and this depended heavily on William Allen White.

Before writing the memo, Roosevelt had phoned White and given the editor his marching orders. Getting Willkie's endorsement for the destroyer deal was only one part of the assignment. Just as important, Roosevelt wanted Willkie to enlist Joe Martin, the Republican leader of the House of Representatives, and Charles McNary, the top Republican in the Senate and also Willkie's running mate, in the cause. If White filled this large order, FDR promised him, "I would at once send a definite request to the Congress for the necessary legislation." Meanwhile, he stressed to White "the importance of having the issue acted on without regard to party politics in any way," an oxymoronic challenge in the midst of a presidential election campaign.

Never lacking in self-confidence, White reassured the President that Willkie supported the idea of destroyers-for-Britain as much as Roosevelt did himself. Unimpressed, Roosevelt explained that "Willkie's attitude was not what counted," rather it was the opinion of the congressional Republicans that he considered "the one essential."

Roosevelt had reason to feel pleased with himself. More than ten weeks after Churchill's initial plea for help, he had finally made a start toward getting him the ships he wanted. He had mollified the two cabinet members he most wanted to satisfy, the new Republican arrivals, Knox and Stimson, along with other advocates of the destroyer deal. "I think you will feel with me we made real progress," Roosevelt said in a note to Ickes dashed off a few hours after the cabinet meeting.

Moreover, by enlisting the country's most prominent lay Republican to get promises from the Republican presidential candidate and the party's congressional leadership, the President had taken another step toward his goal of avoiding political debate over his policies toward Britain. Perhaps best of all, at least for the time being, he had shifted responsibility for success or failure of the destroyer scheme to Willkie and his Republicans.

Meanwhile White soon discovered the difficulties of his assignment, as a result of the efforts of Archibald MacLeish to promote the destroyer deal. MacLeish had asked his friend, *Fortune* managing editor and Willkie adviser Russell Davenport to persuade Willkie not to speak against the destroyer deal. Willkie had rejected the idea out of hand, according to unnamed "friends of Mr. Willkie" quoted in an exclusive story in the *New York Times*. Although the story carried no byline, it was generally believed to have been written by the *Times*'s influential chief Washington correspondent Arthur Krock, a confidant of Willkie's.

Willkie's reasoning, as explained by Krock and Willkie's "friends," was that he did not have the information he would need to make such a commitment. Moreover, Willkie was said to feel that he should do nothing to hinder the responsibility of members of Congress to meet their obligation to their constituents and the country. The story caused consternation among the ranks of the Century Group whose members concluded that Krock had turned Willkie against the deal. "Sinister have been the meanderings of Arthur Krock's mind," the resentful Francis Miller wrote to one of his Century Group comrades. "He has really done us dirt."

As White was finding out, the problem was not just Krock. More fundamental was Willkie's understandable distaste for the contrived role that Roosevelt had scripted for him to play. White later described the candidate's reaction in understated terms: "I told him what was up and he didn't blow up very hard, considering." Still White pressed on. On August 3, the day after he had received his assignment from Roosevelt, he talked at length to Hull on the phone, told him that Willkie agreed "in principle" on the importance of aiding Britain. He wanted, though, to see a draft of any legislation the Administration proposed to submit to Congress to clear the way for the destroyer transfer.

The anticipated legislation was only one of the problems that Willkie faced because of Roosevelt's request. Simply by focusing attention on the destroyers, Roosevelt had put Willkie at a disadvantage. Concern over the war was perhaps the biggest single factor helping Roosevelt's candidacy, as the polls suggested. By a two-to-one majority Americans thought FDR would handle foreign affairs better than Willkie. And by a margin almost that great, they believed Roosevelt would do a better job of strengthening the nation's defenses than his Republican challenger.

More vivid than the polling numbers were the cheering crowds that lined the streets for miles as the Commander in Chief toured the naval base and shipyards at Norfolk, Virginia, on the Monday before the cabinet's destroyer debate. After a first-hand inspection of warships, aircraft, and coastal guns, products of the arms expansion he had set in motion, Roosevelt called what he had seen "a good demonstration of what we have been doing for national defense." Asked if he thought Washington could be invaded again, as it had been in the War of 1812, the President enigmatically replied: "That would depend entirely on where it came from and who it was." Then he added reassuringly: "A year from now we can feel a lot better." He scarcely needed to say who he expected to be in the White House at that time.

In dealing with the war Willkie theoretically had two options. He had already rejected one, attacking the idea of aiding Britain. Since he supported aid, the only gains he could make on the war issue would be to criticize FDR's management of support for the British. But the destroyer deal was by far the most important aspect of U.S. help for the British. By endorsing it sight unseen, he would throw away his chances of making a convincing case against Roosevelt.

On the other hand, Willkie could not simply dismiss Roosevelt's scheme. The Republican standard-bearer counted some Century Group members who backed the destroyer deal as his own supporters, among them Henry Luce. If he flatly opposed the idea, Willkie would risk alienating them, not to mention the many independent voters who favored help for the British.

On top of all that, if Willkie were actually to try to rally the GOP behind the destroyer idea, he was certain to aggravate the strains that already existed between himself and his party. To Roosevelt and other Democrats, Willkie was the strongest challenger the GOP had yet put up against FDR. "He's grass roots stuff," Roosevelt acknowledged to an interviewer. "The people believe every word he says. We are going to have a heck of a fight on our hands with him."

However, Willkie's free-wheeling style and nonpolitical background, the very qualities that appealed to voters, disturbed Republican politicians. They realized that his victory at the convention had been a personal success, rather than a triumph for orthodox Republicanism, and that his nomination enhanced his personal standing at their expense. In the wake of the convention, sophisticated New York, crucible of the New Deal, acclaimed the upstart Hoosier politician as an instant hero. When he took in a movie at the Radio City Music Hall, the crowd chanted "We Want Willkie," until he acknowledged the ovation. A few nights later, at Broadway's biggest hit, *Life With Father*, the theater-loving Willkie stopped the show. After taking a bow, he then led the applause at one of the show's top punch lines. "God!" the character playing Father complains, "Why does God make so many fools and Democrats?"

Veteran politicians, like his running mate McNary, viewed him with admiration mixed with unease. "I like Mr. Willkie very much," McNary, who had spent twenty-four of his sixty-six years in the U.S. Senate, wrote his wife after an early meeting with Willkie. "He is open and forthright and able." But, he added: "There are some traits he has that I would modify." Many Republicans would have found Willkie easier to take if his bounciness had been tempered with modesty and caution. Asked at a press conference early in the campaign about criticism of his bluntness, he snapped, "I don't know about that. But I do know that I am going to be just myself during the campaign."

Another measure of Willkie's unorthodox outlook and values was his refusal to break off a long time extramarital affair with Irita Van Doren, the 49-year-old ex-wife of the literary critic and Pulitzer Prize–winning historian Carl Van Doren. As the book editor of the *New York Herald Tribune*, she was an important figure in New York literary circles in her own right; her friends included the likes of Carl Sandburg, Sinclair Lewis, Rebecca West, and Virginia Woolf. Challenged by her intellect and captivated by her wit and Southern charm, Willkie fell deeply in love. He often spent weekends at Van Doren's Connecticut farm, commuting from his Wall Street office, but he was unwilling to ask his wife, Edith, for a divorce.

Van Doren nurtured Willkie's political ambitions and encouraged him to seek the presidency, even though she knew they would see less of each other. Once the campaign got under way in earnest, Willkie's wife of twenty years, Edith, was at his side for public appearances, filling her role with grace and even humor. "Politics makes strange bedfellows," she once remarked to her errant husband. But Willkie and Van Doren kept in constant touch through telegrams and letters. She cheered him up at times of strain. "You have pulled off triumphantly much worse situations than this," Van Doren wired him during one trying point in his candidacy on April 19, 1940, "and don't forget what I told you last night. There is no change of mind and won't be. Here's to a long and vivid sunset."

For his part, Willkie rebelled at what he regarded as hypocrisy. During the campaign, he even scheduled a press conference in Van Doren's apartment. When friends protested, he said, "Everybody knows about us—all the newspapermen in New York. If someone tried to cause embarrassment, he said, "I would say, go right ahead."

Whether Willkie was worried or not about the political impact of the affair, others saw his relationship to Van Doren as a potentially damaging issue, among them his opponent, Franklin Roosevelt. During the campaign the Democrats had stumbled on to of some of Willkie's letters to Van Doren, which they archly designated as the "dolly letters." About the same time, the Democrats learned that Republicans had laid their hands on another set of potentially damaging letters, these purportedly written by Roosevelt's running mate, Henry Wallace, to a White Russian mystic named Nicholas Roerich, whom he sometimes addressed as "Dear Guru." Wallace and Roerich conducted their correspondence, inevitably dubbed the "Guru letters," in a murky jargon, referring to Roosevelt as "The Great One" and "The Flaming One," Cordell Hull as "The Sour One," and Churchill as "The Roaring Lion."

Roosevelt was "sick at heart," according to Supreme Court Justice William O. Douglas, in whom he confided and who thought Wallace should resign. "My God," was all Roosevelt could say in response. Also deeply distressed about the potential damage to Roosevelt's candidacy, Harry Hopkins told Douglas: "This may kill the old man." Among countermeasures designed to head off disaster, Hopkins apparently proposed to counter the impact of the "Guru letters" with the release of the "dolly letters," a notion which appealed to Roosevelt himself.

"We can't have any of our principal speakers refer to it, but the people down the line can get it out," Roosevelt told one of his political troubleshooters, Lowell Mellett. "I mean the Congress speakers, the state speakers and so forth. They can use the raw material."*

Perhaps recalling his own long-ago and still secret dalliance with

---

*This conversation was one of a number of presidential conversations secretly recorded during 1940 on a microphone specially developed for Roosevelt by the Radio Corporation of America and installed in a booth in the White House basement. This surveillance, anticipating the much more elaborate system installed three decades later by Richard Nixon, was a result of the furor created by published reports of Roosevelt's secret meeting with the senate Military Affairs Committee in 1939, in which he was quoted as saying that the U.S. frontier was "on the Rhine." Roosevelt wanted the recordings to help refute what he regarded as erroneous leaks. The President did not always know when the microphone was on, and some conversations apparently were recorded unintentionally. The device was removed after the 1940 election.

Lucy Mercer, Roosevelt spoke kindly of Van Doren. "Awful nice gal," he said. "Writes for the magazines, and so forth and so on, a book reviewer. But nevertheless there is the fact."

As it turned out, the Republicans never found a publisher for the "Guru letters," so the Democrats never disclosed the "dolly letters." But Willkie's extramarital liaison was only one of the reasons for Republican uneasiness about their nominee. A more fundamental problem was his seeming remoteness from the party which had nominated him. A longtime Democrat, Willkie had been active at that party's past conventions including the 1932 gathering in Chicago, which nominated Roosevelt and at which Willkie had supported Newton Baker and the League of Nations to the bitter end.

And in case anybody needed to be reminded of his past allegiance to the other side, Willkie did that himself with his brief remarks at his moment of triumph at the convention. Breaking with tradition, he went to the convention hall on the day after he was nominated, becoming the first party standard-bearer to address the delegates who had chosen him. "I expect to conduct a crusading, vigorous fighting campaign, to bring unity to America . . . that this way of life shall not pass from the earth," he declared. Then he added a phrase that rankled many in the hall and lived on long after the rest of the speech was forgotten: "And so you Republicans, I call upon you to join me."

A few days later on a visit to Washington, the ex-Democrat finally got around to formally joining up with "you Republicans," enrolling as a member in the National Republican Club. While it was intended as a goodwill gesture, for many Republicans Willkie's enrollment served mainly as a reminder of all the years he had not belonged. The distance Willkie put between himself and his new party stemmed from more than rhetoric and symbolism. It also reflected the campaign's early strategy. Mindful that Roosevelt had beaten Landon by 11 million votes in 1936, Willkie calculated that even if he won the vote of every single Republican he would still lose the election. His chances depended on converting more than 5 million of the independents and Democrats who had voted for Roosevelt, and he bid for them openly. "I do not know of any reason why any Democrat who subscribed to and believed in the 1932 Democratic platform or believes in the historic principles of the Democratic Party or who was a Woodrow Wilson Democrat should not vote for me in preference to the President," he told reporters as he crafted his acceptance speech.

To many Republicans that sort of talk was like scratching chalk on a blackboard. Nor did it help Willkie's relations with the party regulars that along with his independent rhetoric, Willkie brought with him his own organization, the Associated Willkie Clubs of America. Willkie boosters around the country had organized this network of clubs to exploit grass-roots enthusiasm for their hero's quest for the nomination. To the dismay of party regulars, Willkie saw no reason why these clubs should pass into history, nor why other outsiders who had managed his campaign should give up their authority. "The amateurs won the nomination and they can win the election," he told one critic.

Tensions between Willkie and the regulars came to a head during the midsummer stretch, when he was under pressure to respond to FDR on the destroyer issue. The nominee was taking his ease under the red-tiled roofs of the Broadmoor Hotel, a sprawling Italian Renaissance resort in Colorado Springs, nestled in the shadow of Pike's Peak. Along with hiking in the Rockies, swimming in the Olympic pool, and browsing through a selection of books recommended by Irita Van Doren, Willkie talked politics with a range of visitors, often seeming more receptive to Democrats and independents than regular Republicans. And when the party's last President, Herbert Hoover, visited the Broadmoor he treated him with minimal civility. In the midst of a meeting with his party's last president and surrounded by reporters, Willkie heard that Roosevelt's second eldest son, Elliot, happened to be staying at the hotel. He promptly decided to invite young Roosevelt to join himself and Hoover for drinks and dinner.

"I wouldn't urge that too strongly," Hoover snapped while Willkie waited for the call to go through.

"Why not? why not?" the exuberant Willkie replied. "He's the President's son, isn't he? In my campaign I intend to discuss the issues, not personalities. I've never met him. Let's have him come up."

When Willkie finally did reach young Roosevelt, caution overcame him; he settled for a brief chat in his suite while Hoover sulked next door. Later Hoover wrote a friend that Willkie's behavior was "absurd," and that he did not think Willkie "had done himself any good" by his treatment of the former president. Still, Hoover loyally maintained, this was not important, "the big thing was to elect Willkie."

Equally committed to the cause was House Republican leader and fellow Hoosier Joe Martin, whom Willkie had persuaded to serve as Republican national chairman. Visiting Willkie at the Broadmoor, Martin suggested that the candidate restrain his natural tendency to speak his mind on touchy subjects. "Don't voluntarily assume positions unless you have to," he cautioned the candidate. "Let's avoid these unnecessary conflicts as much as possible."

In no area was the potential for conflict greater than in foreign policy, where Willkie's internationalist beliefs cut against the GOP's isolationist grain. If Willkie needed a reminder, the *Chicago Tribune* provided it by turning thumbs down on the idea of the destroyer transfer to Britain. "The sale of the Navy's ships to a nation at war would be an action of war," Col. Robert McCormick's paper intoned on August 6. "If we want to get into war, the destroyers offer as good a way as any of accomplishing the purpose."

Roosevelt had put Willkie in an impossible position, forcing him to make a choice that would cost him no matter what his decision. With William Allen White breathing down his neck, Willkie stalled for time. Searching for a convenient precedent, he reached back to 1932 when the world had also been gripped by crisis, this time over economics. Roosevelt had just defeated Hoover but had not yet been sworn in. The United States' hard-pressed World War I allies were appealing for postponement of their war debt payments. Having granted one moratorium, Hoover resisted authorizing another. At a White House meeting, he asked President-elect Roosevelt to back his demand that the Europeans pay their debts and also to help prepare the U.S. position in the forthcoming world economic conference.

Roosevelt would have none of it. After a two-hour session with Hoover, he reminded reporters that he was not yet president. "It's not my baby," he said.

Now it was Willkie's turn to revenge Hoover. On August 9, a week after the cabinet meeting at which Roosevelt had made his approval a requirement for going ahead with the destroyer deal, Willkie made public his refusal to go along. It had been suggested to him by various persons, Willkie said, that "I enter into certain commitments on specific proposals concerned with the foreign policy of the United States, provided the Administration would take certain positions with reference thereto." But, Willkie said: "I do not think it appropriate for me to enter into advance commitments and understandings."

Then he backed up his rejection by throwing FDR's words to Hoover back in his face:

> President-elect Franklin D. Roosevelt said to President Herbert Hoover in November 1932: The immediate questions raised create a responsibility which sets upon those now vested with executive and legislative authority. Much doubt was expressed as to the wisdom of that statement by a President-elect. None can doubt its correctness when taken by a candidate for President.

Willkie's riposte alleviated some of the public pressure and served to remind the electorate of Roosevelt's habitual evasiveness. But in the long run Willkie's effort to cast himself in Roosevelt's 1932 role was doomed by political reality. In point of fact, Willkie's position now was closer to Hoover's in 1932 than it was to Roosevelt's then. Like Hoover in 1932, Willkie in 1940 was not free to act on his own; while Roosevelt for his part knew in 1940 what he had known in 1932, that time was on his side. Neither the destroyer issue nor the war would evaporate and Willkie's demurral had left the President still in control.

While Willkie struggled to find a better answer to his dilemma, William Allen White attempted to smooth over matters. On Thursday, the day before Willkie issued his statement, White told Secretary of War Stimson that he had seen a draft of the acceptance speech Willkie would give on August 7, and found it "highly satisfactory" on foreign policy. In fact, while it did not mention the destroyer issue specifically, "the attitude which it took would justify it."

White had offered no hint to Stimson of Willkie's statement the next day, which certainly seemed to contravene the optimism the editor had expressed. Somewhat abashed, Roosevelt's emissary sent off a reassuring telegram to the President in Hyde Park. "It's not as bad as it seems," claimed White, who as usual relished playing his insider's role:

> I have talked with both of you on this subject during the last ten days.
> I know there is not two bits difference between you on the issue pend-
> ing. But I can't guarantee either of you to the other which is funny for I
> admire and respect you both. I realize you in your position don't want
> statements, but Congressional votes. Which by all the rules of the game
> you should have. But I've not quit.

From Roosevelt's point of view, White's effort during the past ten days since the August 2 cabinet meeting had produced a mixed bag. If White was to be given any credence, Willkie would not publicly attack the destroyer proposal. And by focusing public attention on his handling of the issue, Roosevelt had succeeded in aggravating the differences between his opponent and his party.

That was all to the good. On the debit side , it seemed clear to Roosevelt now, if it had not been clear all along, that Willkie was in no position to deliver the congressional Republicans in favor of the destroyer deal. And this was not to mention Senators Walsh and Wheeler and the other Democrats who could be expected to align themselves in opposition. If Roosevelt's problem with Willkie had been avoided, the problem with Congress still begged a solution.

# Getting Around the Law

"Ambition must be made to counter-act ambition," James Madison wrote of the relationship between the Congress and the President. "The interest of the man must be connected with the Constitutional rights of the place." Underlying the difficulties that loomed for the destroyer deal on Capitol Hill was Madison's grand design of the American political system, a blueprint informed by mistrust of government and of human nature itself. His genius produced a structure that converted self-interest into a self-generated restraint on power. The President, guided by his beliefs and his political interests, might propose; but Congress, with its own, often contradictory imperatives, would dispose. Madison's system worked so well that even when, as in the summer of 1940, the same party controlled both the Congress and the White House, the two branches of government treated each other as hostile forces.

In Roosevelt's case the resentment between the Chief Executive and the legislature had mounted steadily in his second term as the lawmakers rebelled against the President's continuing quest for new ways to cure the stubborn Depression. "For God sakes, don't send us any more controversial legislation," Rep. Martin Dies of Texas, speaking for a group of his House colleagues, admonished the White House in the spring of 1938 as Congress resentment of Roosevelt's ambitions mounted on Capitol Hill. By 1940 the focus of controversy in Congress had shifted from the economy at home, now showing signs of vigor as defense spending climbed, to aggression abroad, but anxiety and resentment persisted. No only the hard-line isolationists gave Roosevelt cause for concern; a good many other lawmakers viewed with misgivings any U.S. involvement abroad. All they knew for sure, as they looked ahead apprehensively to election day, was that they did not want to be put on the spot.

Given this atmosphere, if Roosevelt wanted to pursue the destroyer deal he had two choices. He could heed the urging of his pro-British critics in the press, speak directly to the public, and forcefully demonstrate that Britain's need for the destroyers conjoined with the need of the United States to protect its own security, in this way bringing pressure on Congress to give the destroyer proposal a green light. But this course would have required Roosevelt to risk his personal prestige, a gamble he regarded as politically unacceptable. The President's only other option was to go behind Congress's back by circumventing the substantial legal obstacles, a choice which he at first considered out of the question. But as the summer wore on, the more Roosevelt pondered the difficulties of gaining congressional approval, the more the idea of bypassing Congress tempted him.

Additional incentive came from Senator McNary, Willkie's running mate and, more important from Roosevelt's point of view, the Republican Senate leader. Through an intermediary, McNary sent word that he could not support the destroyer transfer if it required formal Senate approval before the election. McNary let Roosevelt know, though, that he would not object if Roosevelt could justify striking the deal without asking the Congress to act.

Several men, all part of the New Deal or closely linked to it, helped Roosevelt to find a way around Congress. All were highly esteemed not only for their talent and accomplishments but also for their integrity. Yet all were members of a network, who owed some measure of their standing to their adroitness at evading the strictures and conventions of the political and governing system to which all paid allegiance. They compromised principles, bent the rules of propriety, poked loopholes in the law. They rarely got into difficulty because, above all else, they were always willing to help each other out. At times ambition drove them. On on other occasions larger causes engaged them and it was this spirit that gave birth to the first rough blueprint for dodging Congress's presumed authority, authored by Ben Cohen, one of the foremost legislative architects of the early New Deal.

Domestic affairs had dominated Cohen's entire experience in the Roosevelt Administration up to that point. His involvement with the destroyer deal could be traced to the ubiquitous Joseph Alsop, acting as the British Embassy's unofficial liaison with the Roosevelt Administration. Alsop realized that Cohen's position at Interior gave him ready access to Harold Ickes, who was known to favor the British cause. The sheer power of intellect had thrust the shy and bookish Cohen from his middle-class Jewish origins in Muncie, Indiana, to the uppermost echelons of business and government. After first training at the University of Chicago Law School, which awarded him the highest grades in its histo-

ry, he went on to Harvard, catching the ever-watchful eye of Felix
Frankfurter, one of the stars of its faculty. A Federal Court clerkship
taught him the intricacies of corporate law and prepared him for his
World War I job as an attorney for the Washington Shipping Board.

In wartime Washington, he met Frankfurter's mentor, Supreme
Court Justice Brandeis, an ardent Zionist, leading to Cohen's first
involvement in foreign policy. As counsel for the American Zionists he
helped to negotiate Great Britain's Palestine Mandate at the Paris Peace
Conference. Though he was not a practicing Jew, the experience made
Cohen a Zionist and also fostered warm feelings for Britain, where he
had formed a host of friendships. On his return to the U.S. to enter private practice, Cohen soon established his expertise in corporate law
and the stock market. Plunging in with the boldest of the bulls he
scored heavily; he profited so handsomely from Chrysler's stock that it
was said he liked to call attention to the company's products each time
one rolled by on the street. In the midst of wealth he maintained a
social conscience; his *pro bono* services included assisting Frankfurter
in drafting model minimum wage legislation for women and advice to
the National Consumers' League.

When Roosevelt launched the New Deal, Frankfurter sent Cohen
along with others, known as "the little hot dogs," to join the ranks of
reform. In Washington, the introverted Cohen found the perfect partner in another Frankfurter protégé, the flamboyant Thomas Corcoran.
The two men labored together so closely that their names were often
pronounced as if they made up one word, "corcorandcone." Their first
joint accomplishment, the Truth in Securities Act, centerpiece of the
New Deal's reforms of the financial industry, set their pattern. Dubbed
the "Gold Dust Twins," after an advertising slogan for powdered soap,
they cleaned up the Augean stables of capitalism with landmark legislation regulating stock trading, public utilities manipulation, and wages
and hours. One favorite gambit: ramrodding an excessively rigorous bill
through one house of Congress, and then trading off its toughest provisions in the other house. "When you want one loaf of bread you've got
to ask for two," Corcoran maintained. Overused, however, this tactic
ultimately eroded the President's credibility, and contributed to his difficulties on Capitol Hill.

Both Corcoran and Cohen worked endless hours which left them little time for anything else, even sleep. To relax, Cohen went to the
movies, but almost invariably dozed off in his seat. His frantic schedule
and his shyness discouraged friendships with women from ripening
into romance. "The only way you are ever going to sleep with Ben," the

young New Deal lawyer Joe Rauh told one frustrated young woman, "is to go to the movies with him."

As the New Deal's foremost legal troubleshooter, Cohen defended the constitutionality of the Federal Public Utility Holding Company Act. The law, which Cohen had drafted, cracked down on those electric power empires which cheated consumers and milked their own stock-holders. Realizing it would almost certainly be held unconstitutional by the conservative 1935 Supreme Court, Cohen decided not to ask the high court to overturn adverse decisions on the law from two lower courts. Instead he played for time. He spent spent three sleepless nights writing a brief urging the high court *not* to review the case; heeding Cohen's arguments the court allowed the law to stand pending further appeal. Two years later, after Roosevelt's appointments had moved the Court to the left, Cohen filed his appeal and won a decision reversing the lower courts and upholding the constitutionality of the act.

In a government brimming over with ambition, Cohen and Corcoran naturally inspired jealousy. Henry Morgenthau complained to Eleanor Roosevelt that Cohen and Corcoran "were wielding the greatest influ-ence" on the President, which he feared would somehow lead to his being forced out of government. The passage of time eased Morgenthau's anxieties. With Roosevelt's activist agenda exhausted, the team broke up and Corcoran and Cohen lost their major roles in the New Deal drama. Corcoran tried to drum up enthusiasm for a third term for Roosevelt, but his aggressiveness left lasting resentments among conservatives and made him a political liability. Cohen, while maintaining the respect of insiders, faded into the background, with lit-tle in the way of recognition or reward. His friends had put his name forward for promotion to more prestigious positions than his relatively obscure job at Interior, but Roosevelt invariably passed him over, some-times giving the excuse that it might provoke an anti-Semitic reaction.

Meanwhile, with Hitler on the march in Europe, the threat to European Jewry worried Cohen more and more. His concern prompt-ed his meeting with Joseph Alsop, whose information about Britain's destroyer needs he had passed on to Ickes. After Roosevelt turned down Ickes's appeal on Britain's behalf, Cohen decided to approach the President on his own. He spent the next few days polishing a legal memorandum which he titled, "Sending Effective Material Aid to Great Britain with Particular References to the Sending of Destroyers."

Cohen analyzed the destroyer issue much as he did the New Deal legislation he had drafted and sustained in the courts, drawing on his political acumen as well as his legal training. In successfully defending the Holding Companies Act, when everyone believed he would be defeated by the unfriendly Supreme Court, Cohen had stalled, counting on the court ultimately changing with the election returns. Trying to justify the transfer of destroyers to Britain, when everyone believed this was prohibited by law, Cohen relied on hairsplitting technicalities and unprovable assertions about national defense. His memorandum stretched the law, creating a loophole wide enough for the warships to steam through on their way to join the Royal Navy.

Cohen drove to the heart of his case in his covering letter to the President. The legal barriers to the destroyer transfer would disappear, Cohen maintained, if the transaction "would, as at least some naval authorities believe, strengthen rather than weaken the defense position of the United States." Elaborating, Cohen first pointed out "that in the present state of the world the maintenance of British sea power is of inestimable advantage to us, in terms of our own national defense." He acknowledged that the Walsh Amendment, on which the ink was still fresh, ruled out releasing destroyers unless the Chief of Naval Operations first certified that the ships were "not essential to the defense of the United States." He contended, though, that "it would seem the most specious sort of legal argument" to insist that these old ships were essential to the national defense, if in fact "the present requirements of national defense would be best served by their release." That sort of narrow thinking, Cohen insisted, while technically seeming to be in compliance with the law, would, in actuality, undermine its fundamental purpose, and he cited three Supreme Court decisions to buttress his reasoning.

Cohen then turned to another apparent bar to the sale—a 1794 statute that ruled out "the arming of any vessel with intent that such vessel shall be employed in the service of any foreign prince or state." This restriction, Cohen pointed out, was initially designed to prevent French privateers from being equipped in U.S. harbors to raid British shipping, but "was in no way aimed at the *sale* of ships to belligerents," backing up his argument with another Supreme Court decision.

With similar logic Cohen disposed of a more recent statute, the Espionage Law of 1917 which declared it a crime "to send out of the jurisdiction of the United States any vessel built, armed or equipped as a vessel of war . . . with any intent or under any agreement or contract . . . that such vessel shall be delivered to a belligerent nation." On its face, this language would seem to be an airtight prohibition against the destroyer deal. Not so, Cohen argued, pointing to the phrase: "with any intent or under any agreement or contract." Those words, Cohen insisted, restricted the ban to apply only to vessels which had been initially built or equipped for delivery to a belligerent nation, in this case the British.

Thus the ban *did* cover the abortive torpedo boat transaction, which had set off Walsh's tirade on the floor of the Senate, leading to the Walsh amendment, and which Attorney General Jackson had ruled illegal. The key difference was that the torpedo boats were supposed to have been turned back to the Electric Boat Co., which would refit them to suit the needs of the British. The destroyers, on the other hand, were not covered by the law's prohibition because they had been built to fly the Stars and Stripes, not the Union Jack.

Just as the laws of the United States did not bar the transfer of destroyers to the British, Cohen contended, neither did international law. To be sure, Cohen mentioned in a footnote, his arguments were based on the assumption that the destroyers would be turned over to private U.S. companies, the procedure used to send "surplus" aircraft to the British. For the U. S. government to deal directly with the British, he conceded, might raise questions of international law about "the government itself committing an unneutral act." Against that prospect Cohen argued that Hitler's Germany, having committed various acts of aggression against neutral countries, was hardly in a position to complain about international law.

On July 19, while Cohen's boss, Ickes, was in Chicago for the Democratic convention and while Roosevelt himself was touching up his acceptance speech, Cohen sent his handiwork to the Oval Office. "Dear Missy," he wrote in a brief covering note to Roosevelt's secretary Marguerite LeHand, "Could I trouble you to give the President the enclosed letter with attached."

At first Cohen's imaginative contrivance fell on deaf ears. His old collaborator, Tom Corcoran, told him he was off base. So did his boss, Ickes. Unimpressed by Cohen's attempt to distinguish the destroyer deal from the ill-fated torpedo boat transaction, Ickes reminded Cohen of the President's retreat on that issue. "The President could not now reverse himself," Ickes told Cohen. "He couldn't get away with it in public opinion."

As for the President himself, though in his younger days he had been a practicing attorney in New York for a few years, he harbored no pretensions to legal scholarship. He had flunked two courses during his freshman year at Columbia Law, and when word reached him on his honeymoon in Europe that he would have to take make-up exams he broke out in hives, which seemed to plague him at times of tension. Young Roosevelt persevered and conquered the make-up tests, but after his second year at Columbia he passed the New York State bar examination and decided that was all the legal education he needed or wanted.

In the President's view, Cohen's ingenious arguments lacked the force required to override political reality. He passed the memo on to Secretary Knox with a note that described it as "worth reading." In light of the Walsh amendment which he had just signed into law, he added: "I frankly doubt that Cohen's memorandum would stand up." Without reference to the legal merits of Cohen's case, Roosevelt simply said: "I fear Congress is in no mood at the present time to allow any form of sale."

The only proposal of Cohen's that interested the President concerned politics, rather than law. "I appreciate that even if Congressional approval is not required," Cohen had noted in his covering letter, "Congressional opinion would have to be taken into account." To avoid congressional indignation, Cohen had suggested that the destroyers might be placed under Canadian control, ready to defend the U.S. coast even if Britain lost the war. This gambit might be worth pursuing, Roosevelt thought, but only if Congress could be brought into line. In his memorandum to Knox, Roosevelt urged the Secretary to consider the possibility "at a later date" of prodding Congress into approving sale of the ships to Canada, on the condition their use would be limited to the Western Hemisphere. If nothing else, the President pointed out, that would release other Canadian ships for duty elsewhere, and ease part of the burden of maintaining the American neutrality patrol.

Roosevelt's reluctance to bypass Congress was soon reinforced by another memo from another government lawyer, State Department General Counsel Green H. Hackworth, passed on to the President by Secretary Hull. Traversing the same statutory minefield that Cohen had covered, Hackworth found no such legal openings. Instead, he proposed a new law to permit the President to sell the destroyers to Britain, provided Britain laid official claim to them before they left port here. But that idea still left the President with the task he did not want to undertake—convincing Congress to part with the destroyers. Hull and Roosevelt agreed that the mere act of sending legislation to approve the destroyer deal would, as Hull put it, "stir up considerable isolationist antagonism," Then, too, the legislation would face "many weeks of discussion before it could be enacted."

While the President and Hull deliberated, Britain's plight worsened. On August 4, the same day he talked with Roosevelt, Hull learned from Lothian that the Royal Navy had lost five more destroyers in the previous week, sapping its ability to stand off the German invasion flotilla whose arrival in the English Channel was expected at any moment. On

August 1 Hitler had issued a new directive decreeing that all invasion plans should be completed by September 15 in time for landings to take place during the following week. In Africa, heightening the pressure against the British, the Italians invaded British Somaliland with an army seven times larger than the defending force of 25,000.

In the United States, Roosevelt continued to tread a narrow line. At his August 2 press conference, he had favored enactment of the first peacetime draft in the nation's history, calling it "essential to national defense." The President allowed reporters to quote only one sentence from his remarks, however, as, following his past behavior, he tried to distance himself from the emotional battle over conscription raging on Capitol Hill. Other concerns distracted Roosevelt; his presidential candidacy was off to a slow start. A Gallup poll published on the day he and Hull had discussed Hackworth's memorandum on the destroyer issue showed Republican Willkie leading in twenty-four states with a majority of votes in the electoral college. Yet it was difficult for Roosevelt to forget about the war which for him had now taken on personal meaning. His son, Franklin, Jr., an Ensign in the Naval Reserve, had just reported for two weeks of training to the destroyer U.S.S. *Lawrence*, part of the Navy's neutrality patrol in the North Atlantic.

With the world in turmoil, Secretary Hull nevertheless went ahead with his long-planned three-week rest in White Sulphur Springs. Out of deference to the crisis, he had a phone line installed in his vacation apartment, and arranged for daily pouches from the State Department. As for the destroyer deal, despite all the earnest debate at Roosevelt's Cabinet meeting, for the moment it seemed as dead in the water as if it had been struck by a U-boat torpedo.

It might have sunk without a trace except for Cohen's determination and the restless mind of his longtime friend and advisor Felix Frankfurter, to whom he now turned for help. One of the fundamental principles of the American system of government holds that members of the nation's highest court should stand apart from politics, out of respect for the Constitution's insistence on separation of powers and the Supreme Court's special need to maintain its independence and the confidence of the public. Cohen of course knew that. But he also knew that some justices had made exceptions to the rule and that, since Frankfurter's appointment to the High Court the year before, he had behaved almost as if the stricture did not exist.

Frankfurter was following the example of his own mentor, Justice Brandeis, who had been eager to advise both the President who appointed him, Woodrow Wilson, and Franklin Roosevelt, whose policies represented the fruition of many of Brandeis's strongest beliefs. Until he left the Court in 1939 a few weeks after Frankfurter was sworn in, Brandeis found ways to take part in the furious internal debate over the New Deal's goals and policies, opposing some measures, such as the National Industrial Recovery Act, while helping in the detailed drafting of others, such as the Social Security Act. Sometimes his involvement was direct, but often he relied on intermediaries of whom none was more trusted and effective than Frankfurter. Years later, it was revealed that Frankfurter received significant sums of money from Brandeis to promote the causes both men believed in, and in order to supplement his modest finances.

The Roosevelt presidency opened the way for Frankfurter to play an even larger role in public affairs, not only as a conduit for Brandeis but as a force on his own. Along with another liberal lawyer, Jerome Frank, a product of the University of Chicago Law School, Frankfurter gained a large measure of influence by placing his young protégés in the burgeoning Federal government. "A plague of young lawyers settled on Washington," Jerome Peek, the first Director of the Agricultural Adjustment Administration, later grumbled. "They all claimed to be friends of somebody or other and mostly of Felix Frankfurter and Jerome Frank." Professor Frankfurter's commitment to reform, his forceful personality, and his intellectual prowess had made an indelible impression on his students at Harvard, and many continued to look to him for guidance in Washington.

"If it weren't for him I would be a fat corporate lawyer in Cincinnati, Ohio," recalled Joe Rauh who went from Frankfurter's classroom to become an assistant to Cohen and Corcoran. For those two Frankfurter recruits, it seemed to Raymond Moley that, "Felix was a patriarchal sorcerer to their apprenticeship, forever renewing their zeal for reform and their pride in fine workmanship."

Meanwhile, Frankfurter's contributions as a policy adviser won him friends in high places, including Ickes, Hopkins, and Robert Jackson, all of whom lobbied hard for his nomination to the Court after Justice Cardozo's death in 1938. Frankfurter would later refer to his being chosen by Roosevelt as "a bombshell," which led Cohen later to observe: "I don't know why Felix was so surprised." Cohen pointed out that Corcoran lobbied vigorously for Frankfurter's selection "and would call him every night to report what had been done."

Despite all these behind-the-scenes efforts, Roosevelt had been reluctant to nominate Frankfurter, because of his liberalism and also because of his religion. Cardozo's resignation still left one Jewish justice on the court in Brandeis, which some thought was one Jew too many. A group of prominent Jews, among them Arthur Hays Sulzberger, publisher of the *New York Times*, called on Roosevelt to urge him not to nominate Frankfurter because, they maintained, doing so would foster anti-Semitism. Frankfurter was saved from the anxiety of his coreligionists by the endorsement of Senator George Norris of Nebraska, with whom he had worked on labor legislation, who had the advantage of being both a Protestant and a Republican.

Once on the Court, having begun advising the Roosevelt Presidency as a Brandeis collaborator, Frankfurter saw no reason to abandon that role. In the spring of 1940 when he met with Roosevelt to discuss replacements for Secretary of War Woodring, he gave his blessing to Stimson, who at age 73 might seem unduly old for the job, particularly to those who remembered Roosevelt's complaint about the inefficiency of elderly Supreme Court justices. Frankfurter solved that problem by linking Stimson's appointment to the nomination as his first assistant of the young and vigorous Robert P. Patterson, then a Federal Judge and, inevitably, a former Frankfurter student. Once Roosevelt accepted Frankfurther's advice and announced the two nominations, no surge of modesty prevented Frankfurter from wiring his congratulations to the President.

On no issue was Frankfurter more committed than on the need to confront the threat of Nazi Germany. In addition to his contempt for Hitler and his outrage at persecution of the Jews, his heart belonged to Great Britain. An academic year at Oxford had given him many British friends, among them scholars such as Harold Laski and John Maynard Keynes who called on him on their visits to the United States. And he had opened his home to three children of a British lawyer and former student, furnishing them with a refuge from the Luftwaffe's assaults.

Asked by Roosevelt shortly before that summer's Democratic Convention to create a rationale for seeking a third term, Frankfurter's response reflected his own view of the U.S. role in the world crisis. Depicting FDR as Frankfurter would like him to behave, and as Roosevelt surely would like others to see him, Frankfurter wrote:

> . . . In these last few months and years you pursued your campaign against the aggressors and pursued your campaign to preserve the world's endangered peace against the opposition of powerful newspapers and leading public men who charged you with being guilty of hysteria and war-mongering. But you have no apologies to offer, no excuses to make. History will judge your actions, and every day your motives are becoming clearer for all to see and understand.

Eleven months after they closed the destroyer deal, Roosevelt and Churchill meet
aboard HMS *Prince of Wales* to promulgate the Atlantic Charter.
(Courtesy Franklin D. Roosevelt Library)

General John J. Pershing, Armistice Day ceremonies, November 11, 1942.
His voice drowned out Lindbergh's. (Courtesy Franklin D. Roosevelt Library)

Ambassador Joseph P. Kennedy:
"I do not enjoy being a dummy."
(Courtesy John F. Kennedy Library)

"Wild Bill" Donovan in AEF
battle dress. (Courtesy U.S. Army
Military History Institute)

Donovan: the Hero between
World Wars. (Courtesy U.S. Army
Military History Institute)

In the wake of Hitler's blitzkreig, Roosevelt asks a joint session of Congress on May 16, 1940, for a massive increase in defense spending.
(Courtesy Library of Congress)

Relaxing for the weekend at Hyde Park, August, 1940, FDR picnics with Henry Morgenthau, left foreground, and Harry Hopkins, left background.

High Command. From left to right: Chief of Staff Marshall, Secretary of War Stimson, and Admiral Stark. (Courtesy Franklin D. Roosevelt Library)

Churchill inspects coastal defenses as Britain girded against Hitler's expected invasion in July of 1940. (Courtesy Imperial War Museum)

While Churchill and Roosevelt haggled, the Luftwaffe darkened the skies over Britain.
(Courtesy Imperial War Museum)

The Royal Navy set the French battleship *Provence* ablaze in Oran harbor in the
summer of 1940 during the assault to keep the French fleet from falling into Hitler's
hands. Soon after this photo was taken, *Provence* exploded.
(Courtesy Imperial War Museum)

FDR signs repeal of the arms embargo in November, 1939. Pictured from left are Senator Key Pittman, Representative Sol Bloom (Chairman of the House Foreign Affairs Committee), House Speaker William Bankhead, Secretary of State Hull, Vice President Garner, Senator McNary, and Kentucky Senator Alben Barkley.
(Courtesy Franklin D. Roosevelt Library)

This advice evidently struck a chord with FDR, because the speech he actually delivered had lines strikingly similar to Frankfurter's suggestions. "I would not undo if I could the efforts I made to prevent war from the moment it was threatened," the President declared. "I do not regret my consistent endeavor to awaken this country to the menace for us and for all we hold dear."

Whether Roosevelt was nearly as forthright in dealing with aggression as Frankfurter made him out to be was certainly open to question. But Frankfurter himself had no question about what course the President should follow. Thus, when Cohen sought his help on promoting the destroyer deal, he readily agreed.

The Justice realized that the key to convincing Roosevelt to accept Cohen's argument had little to do with the law and a great deal to do with politics and public opinion. In legal terms Frankfurter could easily see that some court of law might find Cohen's artful argument to be as flimsy as the paper on which it was typed. What counted, though, was whether Cohen's argument could win backing in the political arena. Cohen himself could not advocate his cause because of his post in the Roosevelt Administration. Beyond that, Cohen's own background as a liberal reformer would inject additional controversy into the destroyer debate, as would his Jewish faith.

With a provocative cause, as Frankfurter recalled from his own nomination, the proper sponsor was crucial, someone who could lend Cohen's argument added credibility and help it command public attention. He found the right man in Dean Acheson, an old friend who, at the time of Frankfurter's nomination, had been in his way as helpful as Senator Norris.

Tall, elegant, self-assured, the 47-year-old Acheson looked every inch the pillar of the Washington legal establishment that he was. Like Frankfurter a Harvard law graduate, he had clerked for Justice Brandeis and served briefly as Undersecretary of the Treasury in the Roosevelt Administration before embarking on a career as a private attorney in the capital. His prestige was such that he had been retained to represent the New York Stock Exchange in 1938 during Federal hearings stemming from the disclosure of embezzlements on a monumental scale by the Exchange's former president, stockbroker Richard Whitney. After laboring each day at the hearings in New York City, Acheson unwound on the train back to Washington, sipping a drink in the club car and writing limericks lampooning the proceedings.

Acheson demonstrated his poise and coolness at the start of Frankfurter's hearings. Misgivings were so widespread that on the day the nomination was announced, Frankfurter received an ominous telegram from his friend, Groucho Marx: "Congratulations. If confirmed please send autographed photo." When the nominee's supporters urged Acheson to insist on the right to cross-examine an anticipated flood of hostile witnesses, Acheson rejected that idea. "Fools and bigots would show themselves up and friends on the committee, with help where necessary, could correct downright falsehood," he reasoned. His own role, he explained, was not to wage a battle, but simply expedite Frankfurter's confirmation.

Asked if Frankfurter would testify, Acheson agreed, but made sure that his client would not be required to answer questions touching on cases before the Court. Once sworn in as a witness, Frankfurter sought to extend that prohibition to cover any questions about his basic beliefs. Hectored mercilessly by Nevada Senator Pat McCarran about his views on Marxism, Frankfurter finally replied:

> Senator I do not believe you have ever taken an oath to support the Constitution of the U.S. with fewer reservations than I have or would now, nor do I believe you are more attached to the theories and practices of Americanism than I am. I rest my answer on that statement.

This classic defense of free speech and free thought drew a burst of applause from the crowded hearing room, lasting more than two minutes. But Acheson was reluctant to let that utterance stand as the nominee's last words on the subject, leaving the impression that "Frankfurter was a dangerous radical, or even a communist." After a few whispered words of advice from his lawyer, Frankfurter modified his tactics. Asked point blank if he was a communist he said no, and then elaborated on that in response to a followup question. "I mean that I have never been enrolled and have never been qualified to be enrolled, because that does not represent my view of life, nor my view of government." While that answer may have undercut the principles of the First Amendment, Acheson believed it assured Frankfurter's nomination, which was then swiftly approved by Judiciary Committee and the full Senate without a dissenting vote.

Along with Acheson's demonstrated political and legal acumen, his previous relationship with FDR made him particularly well qualified for the role Frankfurter and Cohen wanted him to play. Selected by Roosevelt to be his Under Secretary of the Treasury, Acheson quit after a bitter dispute over monetary policy that brought the President's wrath down on his head.

True to his gentleman's code, Acheson wrote a gracious letter of resignation, and even showed up at the Treasury for the swearing in of Henry Morgenthau as his successor. When that ceremony was over, Roosevelt motioned Acheson over to his desk; "I have been awfully angry with you," he said in a stage whisper. "But you are a real sportsman." Several months later when another Treasury official quit in anger, publicly denouncing Roosevelt's fiscal policies, the President suggested that the malcontent should "read Dean Acheson's letter of resignation and learn how a gentleman resigns." Acheson thus emerged from his brief tour of duty with the New Deal with both the respect of the public for his independence and of the President for his good breeding

Just as Acheson's background was tailored to the role of Cohen's collaborator, his beliefs were equally well suited. A Century Group member, he shared Cohen's and Frankfurter's feelings about the need to aid the British. Once Acheson signed on as Cohen's partner, the two men closeted themselves in Cohen's New York apartment, where they produced a hodgepodge of lawyerly precedents and military theories which closely tracked Cohen's prior thesis that the President had the authority in his own right to sell the destroyers without congressional approval. In addition, the letter attempted to capitalize on the powerful positive response to General Pershing's August 4 speech, delivered after Cohen wrote his original memorandum, citing his words to back the claim that the release of destroyers to Britain "is not only compatible with, but is vitally important to, the safeguarding our national defense."

Also, hoping to shield the President against criticism that he was disregarding Congress, Acheson and Cohen declared that they would not advocate action without congressional approval if they thought that a majority in Congress was opposed to such a transaction. "But believing as we do, that the preponderating opinion both in and out of Congress favor such action," the letter said, "we are loath to see time lost to secure authority which already exists when time may be vital to the preservation of our own liberties." Acheson and Cohen would have been hard pressed, though, to support that claim. According to one survey of the Senate in early August, to which Cohen was privy, 23 Senators, 12 of them members of the President's party, opposed the sale of destroyers to Britain, only seven were "probably" in favor, with the remaining 63 undecided. As to the general public, while general sentiment favored aid to Britain, no one yet had any basis for measuring attitudes on the specific proposition of a destroyer sale.

Untroubled by such fine points, Acheson now set out to recruit additional signatories with prestige comparable to his own. His first choices indicated the impression of bipartisan prominence he sought to create:

John Davis, the Democratic presidential standard-bearer in 1924 and
presently the head of his own Wall Street Law firm, and John Foster
Dulles, another Wall Street lawyer, who had been foreign policy adviser
to Republican presidential aspirant Tom Dewey. Both turned him down,
pleading a potential conflict of interest with their clients. Ultimately
Acheson settled on three other men of considerable distinction: Charles
Burlingham, known as "C.C.," a patriarchal figure in the New York Bar
and the reform movement in New York politics; Thomas D. Thacher, a
former U.S. District Court Judge and a good enough Republican to have
served as Hoover's Solicitor General; and Acheson's own law partner,
George Rublee, a progressive Republican in the Knox-Stimson mold,
who had served in the Wilson Administration and championed the
League of Nations.

"I have very rarely joined in a letter which I had no part preparing and
with so little consideration as I gave yours this time," Burlingham later
wrote to Cohen, underlying the limited nature of the role played by him
and the other signatories. "I feel rather embarrassed, but having
embarked on this voyage, I rely on you to carry me through." Burlingham's embarrassment set him apart from the other signatories, whose
conviction in the righteousness of their cause encouraged them to ignore
the scruples that ordinarily would have restrained their conduct.

With his prestigious cosigners on board, Acheson now had to find a
vehicle for publication. The *New York Times* was the obvious choice,
and making use of yet another contact he called Charles Merz, its editor,
whom he had known since they were undergraduate classmates at Yale.

Would Charles find room in his newspaper for a letter that Dean
thought to be of overriding importance?

Of course, he would.

The letter ran on Sunday, August 11, under a three-column headline
which would have given the casual reader the impression that the
Cohen–Acheson brief had the *Times*'s own endorsement: "No Legal
Bar Seen to Transfer of Destroyers. Ample Authority for Sale of Over-
Age Naval Vessels to Great Britain Exists in Present Laws, According to
Opinion by Legal Experts."

Given its prominent display, occupying nearly one half of a page in
the Sunday *Times*, the letter obviously attracted widespread public
attention. "But that was not the purpose of the exercise," as Acheson
said later. He and Cohen had aimed their missive mainly at two men,
and they did not want to depend on either of them reading it in the
newspaper.

The first target was Attorney General Jackson who was camping out in the Pocono Mountains of Pennsylvania with his daughter. Since the camp site had no phones, a messenger was dispatched to ask Jackson to call Acheson on a matter of urgency. Within a few hours, the Attorney General was on the line. "To say that he was in a happy state of mind would not be truthful," Acheson acknowledged, "but friendship helped him control annoyance and listen." Acheson pleaded "the dreadful urgency of the President's knowing that he had the power, and with it the responsibility to act," and outlining the legal argument. Jackson said he would take it under consideration.

The other target for the letter was of course the President. Ben Cohen took on that assignment himself. On August 12, the day after the letter ran in the *Times*, and little more than three weeks after his initial memorandum, Cohen sent a copy of the letter to Missy LeHand with a one-sentence covering note suggesting that the President "might be interested to glance" at the letter he was enclosing.

At this point advocates of the destroyer deal were fighting against despair. "The whole destroyer business now seems to be suspended like Mohammed's coffin, somewhere in midair," Joseph Alsop wrote to Helen Reid, wife of *New York Herald Tribune* publisher Ogden Reid, on August 13, two days after the publication of the Cohen–Acheson letter, "As it already looks too late for effective action I suppose there is nothing further to do about it except remember it against the politicians who are responsible."

The apparent impasse left Secretary Stimson "filled with foreboding and anxiety." To offset the depressing news from the battlefronts, Stimson hoped for good news from Willkie, but heard nothing. Lunching together at Stimson's apartment at the Woodley Hotel, about three miles from the White House, he and Knox did nothing to cheer each other up. "Both of us were in a very serious mood because we thought it was a crisis," Stimson wrote later. Both believed that giving the destroyers to Britain was a step that now should be taken, but also were haunted by the thought that "it may be too late."

But it was on that very afternoon of August 13 that Roosevelt summoned them both to the White House along with Morgenthau and Sumner Welles, in place of the vacationing Hull. They entered by the side door on East Executive Avenue, avoiding the prying eyes of the press. As soon became clear to the President's advisers, he had only one item on the agenda: destroyers for Britain.

The publication of the Acheson letter followed several other developments that encouraged Roosevelt to move ahead on the destroyer deal. The efforts of Donovan, William Allen White and the Century

Group, and perhaps most importantly, the RAF's ability to challenge the Luftwaffe in the skies over England had all endowed the enterprise with plausibility.

Now, although the President made no direct reference to the letter in the *Times*, its influence on his thinking could be readily inferred from the way he framed the all-important question of how to deal with Congress: Should he make the deal with Churchill first and then tell Congress, or vice versa?

This was a dramatic turnabout. For three months, in every discussion of the destroyer issue, Roosevelt had invariably referred to the difficulty of getting Congressional approval before he could act. Now for the first time he had indicated, as Cohen and Acheson had contended, that this was a problem he might not need to solve.

In answering the President's query at the White House meeting, Morgenthau suggested that the President should "tell Congress first," but the others adopted the more practical view and argued for the opposite course. That seemed to be exactly what the President wanted to hear. At any rate he said he would now ask Attorney General Jackson for a formal opinion on the transfer, and the relevance of the Cohen-Acheson arguments.

"For the first time that I discussed the destroyers with the President," Morgenthau jubilantly reported in his diary, "he seemed to have made up his mind." In the ten days since the August 2 Cabinet meeting when the President had conceded that the destroyers could make the difference between life and death for the British, his behind-the-scenes maneuvers had overcome potential obstacles to the destroyer deal. Donovan had circumvented Joe Kennedy, Pershing had overshadowed Lindbergh, William Allen White had been assigned to neutralize Willkie, and Cohen and Acheson had found a way to bypass the Congress.

But during this period, while he labored to disarm the opposition to the transaction, the President was running into difficulty with its intended beneficiaries, the British. Ten days of trying to negotiate the terms and conditions under which the U.S. would turn over the destroyers to Great Britain had produced confusion and disagreement, leaving the President and his friend and collaborator, the Prime Minister, each stubbornly headed in different directions.

# "A Rather Hard Bargain"

Franklin Roosevelt's previous experiences negotiating with the British had left him with a sour impression. "When you sit around the table with a Britisher he usually gets 80 percent of the deal and you get what's left," he once told Henry Morgenthau. During a later imbroglio over the sovereignty of two obscure Pacific islets, Roosevelt increased that estimate, complaining that the British in the past had "invariably demanded 90 percent," while in the current dispute, "Great Britain does not even seem to be offering the United States 10 percent." Whatever the exact figure, when it came to parting with fifty U.S. Navy destroyers, the President was determined that he would not come out behind.

As in his negotiations with Willkie, the concessions Roosevelt sought, which he insisted were needed to get congressional approval, were designed to give him maximum political advantage. In his vigorous pursuit of his election year objectives, however, Roosevelt paid no heed to Churchill's own political problems. As a result the President's demands on the Prime Minister delayed the already prolonged negotiations and almost derailed them completely.

Caught in the middle between these two powerful personalities was the British Ambassador, Lord Lothian. Overworked and overwrought, miserable from rheumatism and from Washington's hot and soggy summer, the 58-year-old Lothian created confusion and antagonism on both sides of the Atlantic. On July 22, after Hitler's speech presenting Britain with the choice of peace or "unending suffering and misery," Lothian phoned Foreign Secretary Halifax beseeching him not to close the door. He claimed that German diplomats had told him that Hitler's terms were "entirely satisfactory."

When Halifax rejected his advice and Hitler's offer, Lothian turned back to the U.S. and the hope of obtaining destroyers. On August 1, only hours after his emotional plea to Secretary Knox for the warships, he cabled a warning to Churchill that he might well be "confronted almost immediately" with the question of a trade: destroyers for naval bases on British possessions. Lothian's cable referred to Newfoundland, Bermuda, Trinidad, "and possibly one or two minor islands." Whatever the Americans wanted, Lothian contended: "We cannot afford to haggle." Both Britain and Canada stood to benefit from the U.S. establishing such bases, he said. "I believe in the long run we . . . have everything to gain by treating the defence of the Atlantic Coast of America as a joint Anglo American co-operative interest."

But the air and sea bases were only one of the conditions Roosevelt had in mind, as Lothian learned on August 3, the day after Knox had reported the Ambassador's appeal to the cabinet, when the President summoned him to the White House. Sitting behind his mahogany Oval Office desk, which the furniture manufacturers of Grand Rapids had bestowed on Herbert Hoover, Roosevelt once again told Lothian what the Ambassador surely must have understood by then, that only with congressional approval could he provide Churchill with the destroyers. The threat of a Senate filibuster by "15 or 20 determined isolationists" stood in the path of the necessary legislation. That "would wreck the project until after the election." Roosevelt could see no way to avoid such a disaster, he told his visitor, except by feeding Congress "molasses"—concessions from Britain that would allow the Administration to argue that the nation's security would not be weakened by yielding up the destroyers.

Roosevelt wanted two kinds of molasses. One was an assurance that "if things went badly" for the British cause, the fleet, or whatever remained of it, would carry on the fight overseas. The second was an agreement to furnish air and naval facilities to the U.S. for hemispheric defense, along the lines Lothian and Knox had discussed two days earlier. Even with these concessions in hand, Roosevelt warned Lothian, convincing Congress to do what he wanted it to do would take another three weeks to a month.

Lothian was by now on tenterhooks. Eager to speed the process along, he promised the President that Britain would provide the U.S. with the "naval and air facilities in question" as soon as the destroyers flew the British flag. That was the first in a series of errors for Lothian. The Ambassador had no commitment from his government to turn over the facilities "in question," whatever that hazy term meant. All he had was an offer, freshly approved in London, to grant the U.S. facilities far more limited than it now wanted. Moreover, the British had made this tender as a gesture of good will, not as a quid pro quo for destroyers. If anyone should have understood this distinction it was Lothian.

Modest as London's offer was, the Ambassador had labored for weeks to convince his government to put it forward. He had been caught up in this issue since Hitler's victories in Europe had vastly enhanced the importance of European possessions in the Americas. Until then the idea of foreign bases for the U.S. was, as an official Army historian put it, nothing more than "a favorite political tom-tom for Anglophobes and isolationists." Most of the public attention that notion had received resulted from the efforts of the tireless German agent, George Sylvester Viereck, who in December 1939 set up the Make Europe Pay War Debts Committee. To stir trouble between the U.S. and Britain and France, Viereck's group promoted the idea of the U.S. acquiring British and French possessions in the Western Hemisphere and charging off their value against their still unpaid World War I debts. Its high water-mark came in March of 1940, when two Democrats, Senator Robert Reynolds of North Carolina and Representative Jennings Randolph of West Virginia, introduced a joint congressional resolution calling for the acquisition of British possessions in the Caribbean.

The British themselves had considered this concept a year earlier, before the start of the war. But the Royal Navy was reluctant to do anything that would strengthen America's sense of security about its defenses. As one high naval officer said at the time: "We want to make it difficult, not easy, for the U.S. to remain neutral" in the event of war. Furthermore, Prime Minister Chamberlain described the notion of surrendering Britain's possessions "outside the realm of practical politics."

For their part, U.S. strategists had seen little military value in these outposts. With the German blitz in the spring of 1940, however, the U.S. suddenly faced the danger that Germany would seize British, French, and Dutch possessions along with the need to shore up its own ramparts in the Western Hemisphere. Now Washington began updating a contingency plan called "Rainbow 4," long one of five major options for U.S. strategy, which previously had been given the lowest priority. By the end of May Rainbow 4 had been revised to cope with a scenario in which Britain and France were both defeated and the U.S. had to contend against efforts by Germany and Japan to make inroads in its own backyard. If that happened, the plan stipulated that U.S. forces would occupy the British and French possessions.

Washington's alarm heightened in late May with the British report that transports carrying some 6,000 German troops were headed toward its side of the Atlantic, perhaps destined for the Guianas or Brazil. Though nothing more was ever heard of this expedition, the report galvanized Congress into adopting a joint resolution declaring that the U.S. would not recognize the transfer of possessions from one European power to another. If any such move was attempted, the U.S. would act together with other countries in the Americas "to safeguard common interests."

Meanwhile the idea of using the British possessions as part of a trade gained influential adherents. Roosevelt's old friend, Joseph Davies, formerly ambassador to Moscow, then a Special Assistant to the Secretary of State, wrote the President, urging an effort to coax the British and French to yield possessions "vital to our defense in consideration of the relinquishment of their obligations to us." In London, George Paish, a former economic adviser to the Chancellor of the Exchequer, suggested bartering the West Indies for American planes and pilots. Americans dismissed the part about pilots but several newspapers supported the notion of swapping planes for the islands.

Public concern about the European possessions was also spreading. The Wilmington, Norht Carolina *Morning Star*, declared that it would be a "gracious thing" for France and Britain to cede their colonies "without delay." The more sophisticated *New Republic* recommended that the U.S. purchase the British and French possessions under a contract "permitting the re-purchase by the original owners after the war but not by a state that had conquered them." In New York, members of the National Council of the Steuben Society of America, weary of feeling defensive about their forebears' roots in Germany, adopted a resolution calling for the takeover from Britain of Bermuda, a focal point of resentment because the British used the island as a base for mail censorship. This move would not only help protect U.S. "peace and safety" but also help end "the indignity of search and seizure of our mail by a foreign power."

In light of this mounting American anxiety, Lothian had suggested to Whitehall that instead of waiting for the U.S. to act, the British take the initiative by volunteering to lease land for air and naval facilities on British territory. As possibilities he mentioned Trinidad, from where the U.S. could monitor feared Axis incursions into Brazil, and Newfoundland where a base would help protect undefended Iceland. Such a demonstration of British willingness to contribute to reinforcing U.S. defenses, would, Lothian contended, "make a deep impression" on Americans, strengthen Britain's own military position in the hemisphere, and encourage cooperation between the U.S. and Britain. "If you act now you will have all the advantage of spontaneity," he urged.

But the proposal ran into stiff resistance in London, where it could hardly have arrived at a darker hour. The British Army was just beginning the Dunkirk evacuation when Lothian's idea came before the war cabinet, in its basement meeting room in the New Public Offices on Great George Street, facing St. James Park. Still smarting from Roosevelt's rebuff of his request for destroyers, Churchill opposed relinquishing any territory to the U.S. "except as part of a deal," for some asset from the U.S., such as destroyers. "The United States had given us practically no help in the war," he pointed out. "And now that they saw how great was the danger, the attitude was that they wanted to keep everything which would help us for their own defense."

A. V. Alexander, Churchill's replacement as First Lord of the Admiralty, agreed. "We must not bargain away facilities essential for the defense of the Empire," said Alexander, who had fought in World War I, first in the ranks and then as an officer. Former Prime Minister Chamberlain, now bearing the title of Lord President of the Council, thought the idea would be more promising if the U.S. had first asked for the facilities itself. An opening move from Britain would only arouse suspicions as to her intentions and would be "playing straight into the hands of the isolationists."

Others had more specific complaints. The Secretary of State for the Colonies maintained that leases on a large scale in the oilfields of Trinidad would amount to a virtual cession of sovereignty. The Secretary of State for Dominion Affairs observed that the airfield at Newfoundland had only just been completed after three years' work and granting facilities there to the U.S. would be "bitterly resented" on Newfoundland, to say nothing of the anger it would create in Canada, whose government was supposed to assume responsibility for it.

If anything else was required to kill his plan, Lothian provided that himself, by referring to his proposal as an extension of the leases negotiated only a few months before with the U.S. for bases on Trinidad, St. Lucia, and Bermuda. This agreement, Lothian said, was "never carried out." In fact, as John Balfour, head of the Foreign Office's American department, noted in a memorandum following the war cabinet discussion, the agreement had indeed been completed, but the U.S. had left the leased areas untouched. If the U.S. wanted to construct bases in the Caribbean, Balfour pointed out, it could do so without any further offer from the British. "The fact that they have not moved suggests that at present they do not wish to do so." Under the circumstances, Balfour concluded that the prospects for some sort of deal with the U.S. for island bases, as Churchill had mentioned, "are not very favorable." And he reasoned that a unilateral offer from Britain "would inevitably appear as a sign of desperation." Lothian was duly informed that, as

Halifax put it, his idea faced "serious political difficulties" and that such a move could be considered only if, after talking to the President, "he could produce convincing reasons for expecting concrete results."

Three weeks later, Lothian revived his idea, on a much more modest scale. Instead of long-term leases, this time he mentioned only landing rights for U.S. military aircraft on three British Islands, Jamaica, British Guiana, and Trinidad, along with the right for the Army to send "occasional training flights" to Newfoundland. As part of the deal, which Lothian described as based on information from the U.S. military gained through "informal channels," Pan American Airways, acting as agent for the United States government, would construct a warehouse on British Guiana and an airfield on Jamaica.

This arrangement, according to Lothian, would expedite U.S. defense of the Panama Canal and allow speedy reinforcement of South American republics in case of "Nazi-inspired trouble." In political terms, the agreement would "cut away part of the ground from under a growing demand in popular press for the U.S. to take over the islands to improve defense and forestall their seizure by Germans."

London's reaction was mixed. The Air Ministry favored the idea, and the War Office had no objection. The Admiralty, however, once again demanded a *quid pro quo*, insisting that aiding the U.S. to provide for her own defense would reduce her self-interest in Britain's fate. The Colonial Office also protested, principally because of the role of Pan American Airways, which it complained had in the past often been "hostile" to British interests. These objections prolonged the debate over Lothian's proposal for six weeks, an interval that might seem unreasonable in view of Britain's critical predicament. But these matters were as important in London as similarly parochial preoccupations of Franklin Roosevelt and the Congress were in Washington.

Whitehall's final judgment was based on a combination of short-term pragmatism and concern with broader and longer-range considerations, summed up by Lord Halifax. He conceded Lothian's point that by making this offer, "it will prove possible to stave off wider demands" from Washington. But a more important reason for approving the arrangement, the Foreign Secretary said, was the hope that it would set a pattern for future relations between the two countries. "Our aim," Halifax counseled his cabinet colleagues in a deft and farsighted phrase, "should surely be to assist America in the tasks of assuming a new and heavy responsibility for which so little in her tradition and history has prepared her."

But Lothian had more immediate problems, some of his own creation. Not until August 2 had London informed him that the cabinet had finally approved his recommendation for U.S. aircraft landing privileges on the three Caribbean possessions and Newfoundland. This was the day after he had cabled London the outlines of a far more extensive grant now sought by the U.S., including naval facilities. Lothian may have interpreted the August 2 cable as an a response to his August 1 appeal, rather than to his earlier proposal, or he may have anticipated a favorable answer. At any rate, as we have seen, in his August 3 meeting with Roosevelt, Lothian had assured the President, incorrectly, that he already had approval to give the U.S. the bases it wanted, once Britain got the destroyers. The next morning, on August 4, Lothian finally had in hand Churchill's response to his August 2 cable, in which the Prime Minister, agreed "in principle," to the idea of a destroyers-for-bases trade. The Ambassador soon realized, however, that his government was not ready to offer the U.S. more than the three base sites already leased in 1939, on Trinidad, Bermuda, and St. Lucia, along with the aircraft landing rights he had himself proposed. Another distinction, which would produce even more consequential difficulties, was that the British offer, as Lothian had recommended, had no strings attached, while the U.S. wanted the bases as a *quid pro quo* for the destroyers. Now Lothian would have to explain the significant discrepancy between what the U.S. wanted and what Britain was prepared to give.

The issue of gaining assurances about the disposition of the British fleet, Roosevelt's other serving of molasses, also created a muddle. Much of this could be blamed on no one else but Churchill, who seemed continually torn between conflicting impulses. In his initial dealings with the Americans, the Prime Minister had followed his natural inclination to put up a bold front, the posture he adopted when he met with Ambassador Kennedy while the Allies were staggering from the first shock of the great German offensive. Churchill, who had been named Prime Minister only four days before, out of deference to his predecessor Neville Chamberlain and his family was doing his night work at his former headquarters at Admiralty House, rearranging its ground floor to suit his purpose. The new PM had converted the dining room into office space for his private secretary and one of his specially trained typists, and turned the drawing room into a reception hall, setting aside an inner chamber for his private office. His desk top served as repository for a wide assortment of odds and ends, among them toothpicks, gold medals serving as paperweights, various pills and powders, and special cuffs to guard his jacket sleeves from the dust. Alongside, he kept a table laden with bottles of liquor and assorted accompaniments.

Here, just after midnight on May 15, the Prime Minister received Kennedy, whose dim assessment of British prospects he knew all too well. By his own account the Ambassador scarcely tried to soften his belief that if Americans "had to fight to protect our lives we would do better fighting in our own backyard." Of the Prime Minister, he inquired what help the U.S. could offer "that would not leave the United States holding the bag in a war in which the Allies expected to be beaten."

Stung, Churchill replied that "regardless of what Germany does to England and France, England will never give up as long as he remains a power in public life even if England is burnt to the ground. Why, said he," Kennedy reported to Hull, "the Government will move to Canada and take the fleet and fight on." With notable prescience, Kennedy commented: "I think this is something I should follow up."

But anyone trying to follow up would have stumbled into a tangle of contradiction. Alerted by Lothian that Roosevelt, apparently reacting to Kennedy's report, had raised the possibility of the fleet seeking refuge in Canada, the Prime Minister had delivered his blunt warning to the President that if some successor government to his own "came to parley amid the ruins," Britain might bargain away its fleet to Hitler.

Unhappy with that response, Roosevelt broached the subject with Lothian again a few days later, stressing that "if things came to the worst," the British government should regard the Royal Navy not as England's alone, but as a possession of the British Empire, to be transferred to Canada or even if necessary to Australia.

Lothian told him any decision made about the fleet in such dire circumstances would depend on whether or not the U.S. had entered the war on Britain's side. That, Roosevelt countered, depended on Congress. He added, though, that he himself thought it "probable" that America would fight, an assessment strikingly different from his publicly expressed views. For this to happen would require "a German challenge to some vital American interest," but he noted that public opinion was rapidly changing "as to what the vital interests of the United States were."

The British tactics, as one of the Foreign Office's American specialists remarked in a memorandum, were "rather like blackmail, and not very good blackmail at that." This approach entailed considerable risk. Instead of encouraging the U.S. to rally to Britain's side, it could foster defeatism and withdrawal. Referring to invitations from the British to "move into the war now," Assistant Secretary of State Adolph A. Berle, a longtime Roosevelt adviser, wrote in his diary:

If their fright is justified, nothing we could do could get there in time, even if we wished to do that. Instead, it seems plain that our job is to collect the strongest and solidest defense force we can and not to fritter away small detachments to the other side of the Atlantic.

Moreover, the Americans could also play the blackmail game. Upon receipt of Churchill's blunt cable of May 20, FDR prepared a reply "in terms as blunt as those contained in your message." "If worst came to worst, I regard the retention of the British fleet as a force in being as vital to the reconstitution of the British Empire and British Isles themselves." Although Roosevelt never sent that message, Churchill scarcely needed to be reminded that Britain's chances of retaining her Empire depended on retaining her fleet.

The other problem with Britain's blackmail strategy was that Churchill found it difficult to implement; instead he went off first in one direction, then in the opposite. Following his display of bravado at his midnight meeting with Kennedy, he and Lothian had spent the next three weeks trying to disabuse the Americans of the notion that the fleet would, so to speak, fall into their laps. Then Churchill contradicted himself massively and dramatically in his June 4 address recounting the success of the Dunkirk evacuation, when he pledged that even if England itself were conquered, "our Empire across the seas, *armed and guarded by the British fleet*, will carry on the struggle." (Emphasis added.)

Listening to that speech in the embassy in Washington, Lothian could scarcely contain his distress. Churchill's words, the Ambassador warned the Foreign Office on June 7, "have given courage to those who believe that even though Great Britain goes, the fleet will somehow cross the Atlantic to them." This impression needed to be countered by "constant private explanations in important and influential quarters," Lothian said, citing a talk he himself had given a few days before in which he told Americans: "It is not for us to offer you any advice as to what you should do any more than it is for you to offer us advice on what to do with our navy if and when that tragic crisis comes."

In explanation, Churchill cabled Lothian that "of course" he had addressed his peroration "primarily to Germany and Italy to whom the idea of a war of continents and of a long war are at present obnoxious." He had always had Lothian's point in mind, he said, and he urged the Ambassador to continue to drive it home, by reminding FDR of what might happen to the fleet if some "Quisling government" should take charge at Whitehall.

Against this confused and enigmatic background, Lothian sought to represent his country's interests as the serious bargaining over the destroyers commenced in the first week of August. His first obstacle was the Secretary of State, about to leave on vacation, whom he visited at Roosevelt's suggestion on Sunday morning, August 4. Typically sententious, Hull reminded Lothian that selling warships to a belligerent would normally be construed as an act of war and that the isolationists would certainly capitalize on this point. Providing assurance that the Royal Navy would fight on, no matter what happened to England's fortunes, seemed to Hull to be a useful idea, but probably not useful enough. After citing the various statutory obstacles to the deal, Hull remarked: "An amendment to these provisions of law may be necessary and you well know that such procedures move slowly." In what Lothian described as a "somber moment," the Secretary of State even went so far as to reckon the odds on legislation passing as "four to one" against.

For Lothian this was like a kick in the stomach. To Henry Van Dusen of the Century Club, with whom he lunched later that day, he appeared haggard and worn. "It's no use," Lothian said of his talk with Hull. "He says nothing can be done about the destroyers until after the election."

His meeting the next day with Hull's deputy, Undersecretary Welles, who in the absence of the vacationing Hull presided over the State Department, did nothing to cheer him up. In Welles, Lothian was confronted with an American diplomat who fit the American stereotype of what British diplomats were like. Like Roosevelt, with whom he was linked by family connections, and at whose wedding the 13-year-old Welles had been a page, Welles possessed the breeding and background of an aristocrat. He notably lacked, though, the President's leavening humor and bonhomie. The grandnephew of the abolitionist senator Charles Sumner, he had been educated at Groton and at Harvard, where he was a classmate of Eleanor Roosevelt's brother Hall. Encouraged by Roosevelt himself to enter the foreign service, Welles was assigned to Buenos Aires, where he soon made his mark as an authority on Latin American affairs. Serving as Assistant Secretary of State under Roosevelt and Hull, he concentrated on Latin-American relations and was said to have coined the phrase, Good Neighbor Policy. As war loomed abroad, Roosevelt promoted Welles to undersecretary, in which role, aided by his relationship with the President, and despite the growing resentment of Hull, his views gained influence on a wide range of issues.

Tall, dignified, and aloof, he was a man "of almost preternatural solemnity and great dignity," Harold Ickes observed. "Just to look at him, one can tell that the world would dissolve into its component parts if only a portion of the weighty secrets of state that he carries about with him were divulged." A British diplomat put it more succinctly when he remarked: "It's a pity that he swallowed a ramrod in his youth."[*]

On the occasion of his August 5 meeting with Lothian, Welles treated the ambassador as if he were a wayward schoolboy. After hearing Lothian outline the British position on the bases and the fleet, Welles lectured him that "it's most important that nothing should be said in England or allowed to leak into the press about arrangements which his Majesty's Government were prepared to enter into if destroyers were forthcoming." In similar vein he added that, as Lothian reported to London, "the matter must be left to the President who would inform me if he wanted action taken from London."

All this was offensive enough in its imperious tone. But then Lothian's own carelessness reexhibited itself and turned the Welles interview from a minor irritant into a major obstacle. Lothian began the last sentence of his next message to London by explaining that the U.S. wanted the British government "to make a declaration to the effect that His Majesty's government is determined that the British Fleet will go on fighting for the Empire even if it is compelled to evacuate Great Britain." He then concluded it with this phrase, "if and when the President asks for it." Even placed where it properly belonged, after the word "declaration," this language would have seemed high-handed. But when Lothian dangled it at the end, the words sounded inexcusably arrogant to officials in London, particularly to the Prime Minister.

Churchill interpreted Lothian's message to mean that not only did the United States want a public promise that Britain would evacuate its fleet, but it also wanted the fleet evacuated whenever the President of the United States was pleased to order it. This was too much for him. "For the sake of giving the President what he called 'molasses' for a Congress whose attitude was in any case uncertain," he fumed, "we were now for the sole sake of getting a number of second-hand destroyers to barter a way our freedom of action in regard to the future of the fleet." Accordingly Churchill instructed the Foreign Secretary to draft a reply that made clear that only His Majesty's Government would decide when, if at all, to evacuate the fleet. But he was dissatisfied with

---

[*]Despite Welles's elegant demeanor, many in his circle in Washington knew of allegations, supported by an FBI investigation, that indicated Welles was an alcoholic with homosexual tendencies, charges which ultimately led to his resignation in 1943. The official reason given at the time was the illness of his wife.

Halifax's effort to reply to Lothian's telegram, which he referred to as "ambiguous and ill drafted."

Still furious over the Foreign Office's effort, Churchill sent for John Balfour. Arriving at 10 Downing Street, the head of the Foreign Office's American department found Churchill with the First Lord of the Admiralty, A. V. Alexander, and the First Sea Lord, Sir Dudley Pound. In this nautical company Churchill had grown even more outraged about the American demands. After complaining to Balfour about the lack of "feeling" in the Foreign Office draft, Churchill dictated his own message, marching back and forth across the room, while thrusting at the air with his cigar. "It doesn't do to give way like this to the Americans," he admonished Balfour. "One must strike a balance with them," he insisted, illustrating his remark by stretching his arms and waving them up and down.

"I have already several weeks ago told you there is no warrant for discussing any question of the transference of the fleet to American or Canadian shores," Churchill reminded Lothian in the Balfour draft.

> I should refuse to allow the subject even to be mentioned in any staff conversations, still less that any technical preparations should be made or even planned. . . . Pray make it clear at once that we could never agree to the slightest compromising of our full liberty of action, nor to tolerating any such defeatist announcement, the effect of which would be disastrous.

But before that message could be dispatched, another cable from Lothian arrived in the Foreign Office, prompted by a conversation with yet another cabinet officer, Secretary Stimson.[*] He advised the ambassador that the President "is anxious for an immediate reply in regard to the future of the fleet." According to the Secretary of War, Roosevelt wanted a pledge that if Hitler conquered England itself, the fleet would not be scuttled or surrendered but instead steam off to fight another day. "It is evident that this argument is one which has the most effect on Congress in the matter of destroyers," Lothian said.

At this point Churchill threw up his hands and turned the matter over to Halifax, after admonishing him to reject Stimson's plea for a declaration about the fleet. "We must never get into a position where

*Though the message was ultimately scrapped, its text appears in Churchill's chronicle of the period as if it had been transmitted. According to the explanation later offered to James R. Leutze, Churchill thought the message "so stirring and patriotic" that he "couldn't bring himself to leave it out."

the United States government might say, 'We think the time has come for you to send your fleet across the Atlantic."

Following orders, Halifax cabled Lothian warning him of the "very great difficulties" Britain faced in providing the guarantees on the fleet the U.S. wanted. Not only was the fleet a problem, so also was the haziness surrounding just what sites the U.S. wanted for bases, as Halifax stressed in another telegram to Lothian. Since the consent of the local governments would be required, London needed to know "exactly what is wanted." And as still another complication, Halifax mentioned other war material the British had targeted—specifically motor torpedo boats and flying boats which they expected to receive, along with the destroyers, in return for the leases.

Meeting with Welles August 8, Lothian handed him a list of the base sites the British were prepared to offer. As to the fleet, he said that the Churchill government could not make any public commitment beyond what Churchill had already said in his June 4 speech. He also passed on a list of what he described as "British desiderata"—twelve flotillas of eight destroyers each, twenty motor torpedo boats, fifty airplanes, five flying boats and 250,000 Enfield rifles.

Welles was unmoved. He noted that the British position on the fleet was merely a reiteration of what Churchill had said on June 4, which was of course all that Lothian had claimed it to be. "This statement implied no commitment whatever except so far as his own government was concerned," Welles complained in a letter to FDR, although Churchill had pointed out all along the obvious fact that he could make no pledge that would be binding on any other government. Later, in a note to Ambassador Kennedy, Welles described the British offer of bases as "restricted and entirely unsatisfactory" and referred to Lothian's desiderata as "a very ample statement . . . far greater both in scope and in kind than would be possible to consider."

On the day following his bleak audience with Welles, Lothian encountered Roosevelt, headed for the *Potomac* and a weekend cruise with his returned emissary Wild Bill Donovan as special guest. Asked about the progress of negotiations, Roosevelt told the ambassador he was still waiting to hear from Willkie about where he and the Republicans stood on the destroyer deal. If he had no word from the Republican nominee by his return, the President promised, he would act on his own.

It was on the following Tuesday, August 13, that Roosevelt met at the White House with Knox, Stimson, Morgenthau, and Welles and mapped U.S. strategy for the destroyer deal. Before that session adjourned, Roosevelt shared with his visitors the rough outline of the offer he would send to the British. Though "drafted very hastily," Stimson thought what the President presented to be in "admirable shape." In contrast with the British request submitted by Lothian, Stimson felt, the President's draft "went to the very teeth of the matter."

When it was finally cabled to Churchill early that evening, Roosevelt's proposal closely resembled what Roosevelt had told Lothian ten days earlier. While he was ready to give Britain the ships and planes it wanted, the President wrote, he could only provide such assistance if he could persuade Congress and the public that the transaction would strengthen their own country's national defense. To accomplish this, Roosevelt still needed, though he did not use the word, molasses of two kinds. Regarding the fleet, the President would settle for Churchill's personal pledge rather than insist on a public statement. Beyond that he asked for the right to buy or lease, for ninety-nine years, sites for air and naval bases on seven British possessions in North American waters, from Newfoundland to British Guiana, considerably more territory than the British had previously agreed to grant. In contrast with the initial British offer of landing rights on three colonies, the U.S. now asked for a century-long hold on air and naval bases on seven colonies.

An accompanying cable from Lord Lothian explained that Roosevelt had found the previous British offer of bases, "too complicated and restricted." London should bear in mind, Lothian stressed, that the President's offer linked the destinies of the U.S. and Great Britain more closely than ever. Washington now accepted the British fleet as its outer line of defense, and considered the British islands off the North American continent its inner defense line.

The conditions set by the President provoked some resentment in London. "This rather smacks of Russia's demands on Finland," John Colville, one of Churchill's private secretaries, noted in his diary. For the moment, though, Churchill raised no objections. Indeed, he saw even greater significance to the proposed agreement than did Lothian. The closing of the deal, he told the War Cabinet in its basement chamber, would mean that "the United States would have made a long step toward coming into the war on our side." Seated on a large wooden chair with a huge wall map of the world behind him, the Prime Minister looked straight across a hollow square formed by the room's four conference tables at the military chiefs of staff, Admiral of the Fleet Sir Dudley Pound, General Sir John Dill, and Air Chief Marshal Sir Cyril Newall. Selling destroyers to a warring power, Churchill pointed out to the masters of Britain's military, "was certainly not a neutral action." The ships themselves would be "of enormous value to the Admiralty," and the impact of the proposal on Germany would be, he said, "immense."

The Prime Minister's comments cued the debate toward a broad view of the issue. As the official minutes noted:

> the present proposal could not be looked at merely from the point of view of the exchange of destroyers, motor torpedo boats and flying boats for certain facilities by way of naval and air bases. It might well prove to be the first step in constituting an Anglo-Saxon block or indeed a decisive point in history.

With history beckoning, Churchill did not hesitate. "I need not tell you how cheered I am by your message or how grateful I feel for your untiring efforts to give us all possible help," he cabled the President only a few hours after the War Cabinet meeting concluded. The Prime Minister took pains to make clear just how much help the British were expecting. In addition to the motor torpedo boats mentioned by Lothian, and the destroyers whose value, he said "is measured in rubies," Churchill asked for "as many flying boats and rifles as you can let us have." He added: "We have a million men waiting for rifles."

In return, Churchill accepted Roosevelt's conditions. As to the fleet, he was ready to repeat to FDR his public pledge of June 4—but counted on the President's discretion in using that promise with restraint, out of consideration for British morale. Nor did the naval and air bases pose much of an obstacle to the Prime Minster, who suggested that details of the leasing could be worked out "at leisure," and asked only time to consult the governments of Newfoundland and Canada about the Newfoundland base.

Meanwhile word of the negotiations had reached the press. On August 16 the *New York Times* in a front-page story attributed to "well-authenticated advices" from London, reported that Roosevelt was considering a proposal from Churchill to trade fifty or more destroyers in exchange for bases on British possessions in the Western Hemisphere. Knowing that he would be asked to confirm the report at his regular press conference that day, the President tried to create an aura of nonchalance.

"Why, there he is," he greeted Earl Godwin, the veteran broadcaster and a favorite target for Roosevelt's often heavy-handed humor. "Who let him out?"

Another reporter asked if the Georgia peaches ripening on his desk were from his own land in Warm Springs.

"They are not unfortunately," the President responded. "I cut all mine down."

Having exhausted his store of trivia, the President got down to the business of presenting his version of the *New York Times* story, determined to focus attention on what the U.S. was getting, not what it was giving up. "This has got nothing to do with destroyers," he first of all declared, before announcing that he was negotiating with the British for air and sea bases in North American waters. For good measure, he added that the U.S. and Canada would soon commence discussions dealing with North American defense.

If the negotiations had nothing to do with destroyers, a reporter asked, why had he raised the subject in the first place. "Because some one over here was going to ask about destroyers, that is all," the President replied lamely. "In other words the emphasis is on the acquisition of the bases—that is the main point—for the protection of this hemisphere, and I think that is all there is to say."

At the very same time that the President was denying any connection between the bases and the destroyers, his attorney general was developing a legal rationale for giving the destroyers to the British founded on just that connection. As Roosevelt well knew, it was the *quid pro quo* between destroyers and the bases which made the transaction arguably permissible under the federal statutes, and feasible in political terms. In fact, it was the President's insistence on maintaining this connection that would nearly wreck this transaction.

For the time being, though, the President seemed to have everything under control as he set off on August 17 for Ogdensburg, a town in upstate New York, where he would combine a review of army maneuvers and defense discussions with Canada's Premier Mackenzie King. The opportunity for Roosevelt to act out his roles as Commander in Chief and world statesman could not have come on at a better time; on this same day his challenger, Wendell Willkie, would deliver his long-awaited speech accepting the Republican presidential nomination.

Indeed, as he chatted with King and Secretary Stimson, Roosevelt joked about "stealing half the show" from Willkie. At certain times, he confided, a politician was smarter not to campaign. As he reviewed the massed formations of the U.S. First Army, the President heard ten 21-gun salutes and also got an earful from Major Gen. Clifford Powell, commander of the 44th Division, about the shortages faced by the expanding military. "It is pretty good, what there is of it," Powell said of the available equipment. "But we are using broomsticks for machine guns and rain pipes for mortars." FDR laughed and offered the dubious comfort that the rest of the army was in the same boat. He preferred to dwell on more positive aspects. "I think the important thing is that this is the largest gathering of American troops since the Civil War," he told reporters.

Later, while he was meeting with King and Stimson in the privacy of his observation car, the President referred to a report that in his acceptance speech Willkie had challenged him to a debate. Roosevelt had no doubts about how that encounter would turn out. "If that is true," he said with conviction, "Willkie is lost."

For all his eagerness to see the full text of Willkie's talk, the President scarcely seemed concerned about its content. Wearing his favorite white summer suit, sipping a lemonade, he looked "exceedingly well," and seemed to his Canadian guest to be "in a very happy mood." At dinner with King and Stimson, the President polished off a huge steak. "Neither Stimson nor I could have taken one-eighth of it," King noted in his diary. Midway during dinner, Willkie's text arrived, and the President searched for the parts that dealt with foreign policy. Willkie had been under heavy pressure from both sides on the destroyer issue. Just as William Allen White and Century Group members had tried to persuade him to endorse the idea, isolationists had been arguing the opposite, among them his party's last President, Herbert Hoover.

Hunting for ammunition, Hoover called his old friend, John C. O'Laughlin, publisher of the *Army & Navy Journal*, who had been the former president's eyes and ears in Washington since he had left the White House. O'Laughlin in turn queried former Army Chief of Staff Malin Craig, George Marshall's predecessor, who advised him that Britain was too far gone for any rescue scheme. "If we turn the destroyers over to England we will lose them," he told O'Laughlin, "and if England is conquered we will need them not only against Germany but against Japan." By the time O'Laughlin relayed this to Hoover, the former President had already wangled a promise from Willkie not to mention destroyers in his speech. But Hoover said the old general's views would help him to keep Willkie from changing his mind.

Willkie kept his word to Hoover in addressing the 150,000 supporters who gathered in his hometown of Elwood, the largest political rally the nation had yet seen. He refrained from any specific reference to the proposed destroyer deal, but he did allude to the importance of the British fleet to U.S. defenses. And recalling Roosevelt's promise to support victims of aggression, he said: "I should like to say that I am in agreement with those principles as I understand them."

For Roosevelt, as he finished off his dinner, that language was as good as dessert. After reviewing Willkie's text, he and Stimson both "said at once it was all right," King noted. Stimson declared that Willkie's stance would fit into the discussions with the Canadians over destroyers and mutual defense "like a piece in a jigsaw puzzle."

After dinner when he and King turned to the destroyer issue, Roosevelt confided that up to a few days ago he had "almost despaired" of being able to give Churchill the ships he wanted. He claimed that he had been warned by friendly legislators, presumably referring to Sen. McNary: "For God's sake don't put this question to Congress or you will have a few months debate on it. Find some other way to deal with the matter." Now, the President said, only "legal technicalities" stood in the way of consummation.

Still, the President reminded King, all depended on the *quid pro quo* from the British in the form of bases. He could not understand why the British had been so hesitant about their end of the deal. If the British were worried about losing sovereignty over the islands, he could set their minds at ease; he would not want them, even as a gift. With their weak economies and restless populations, "they were a source of continued local trouble." To ease British concerns, the President said, he would be willing "to have the British have their guns trained on the U.S. sites to use at any moment." At any rate, Roosevelt told King, if the U.S. should go to war with Germany and he felt it necessary to seize the islands, he would not hesitate to do just that. He acknowledged though, "it was much better to have a friendly agreement in advance."

Instead of returning directly to the White House, Roosevelt departed Ogdensburg for Hyde Park, where on Monday, August 19, he approved the proposed agreement read to him over the phone by Sumner Welles. One part of the draft covered the British pledge on the fleet and the leases to the naval bases, while a second part dealt with the U.S. obligations. To fulfill its side of the bargain, in addition to the fifty destroyers, the U.S. agreed to deliver twenty motor torpedo boats, five Navy PBY patrol bombers, five Army B-17 Flying Fortresses, 250,000 Enfield rifles and 5 million rounds of ammunition.

Eager to push ahead with the deal, the Canadians next day sent Welles a memorandum, inquiring about such practical matters as the delivery time of the destroyers and their seaworthiness. Welles sent the note to Knox at the Navy Department and notified the President. All seemed in readiness.

But on the other side of the Atlantic, Churchill was undergoing a change of heart about the bargain he had struck with the Americans. The conditions which Roosevelt had tailored to fit his reelection year strategy were adding to Churchill's own political difficulties. These included anti-Americanism, heightened by the U.S.'s role as a spectator to Great Britain's struggle for survival, Churchill's still insecure leadership position in his own Conservative Party, and lingering interest, particularly among some of his fellow Tories, in a negotiated peace.

These pressures contributed to Churchill's initial outrage over the U.S. demands for guarantees about the fleet. And despite his cable to Roosevelt approving the broad outlines of the deal, haggling over the details soon caused new resentment. "Isn't it a rather hard bargain for you to drive?" one member of the War Cabinet pointedly asked Ambassador Kennedy, a complaint that encapsulated the attitude of many British officials, not excluding the Prime Minister.

Sumner Welles's letter of August 19 to Lord Lothian setting forth the specific terms for the agreement added fuel to the fires of British resentment. While the message followed the outline on which the President and the Prime Minister seemed to agree, Welles's high-handed tone in discussing arrangements for the leases was bound to grate on British sensibilities. The sites, Welles wrote, would be selected "as may be required in the judgment of the United States." Moreover, discussing the leases, Welles wrote that the British would grant to the U.S. all the "rights, power and authority" over the bases that it would exercise as if it were "the sovereign of the territory and waters."

These stipulations helped bring home to Churchill the extent of Roosevelt's determination to depict the deal to Congress and the electorate as what the Prime Minister later called "a highly advantageous bargain" for the United States. Britons, Churchill feared, would inevitably contrast the value of the "antiquated and inefficient" destroyers with the "immense" advantage gained by the United States and conclude that their country had come up short. "If the issue were presented to the British as a naked trading away of British possessions for the sake of the fifty destroyers," Churchill believed, "it would certainly encounter vehement opposition."

In May, when Lothian had proposed offering bases to the Americans as an outright gift, Churchill had balked, and demanded a *quid pro quo* arrangement. Now, nearly three months after balancing the *quid* against the *quo*, he decided he would be better off by adopting Lothian's initial scheme and offering the bases to the Americans free and clear of any obligation.

Churchill also had taken note of the President's denial at his press conference of any connection between the gift of destroyers and leasing of bases. If Roosevelt could make that claim, then Churchill reasoned, so could he.

The occasion was a major speech to Parliament on August 20, as the war neared its first anniversary. Churchill relegated the destroyers which he had been seeking for so long to only a brief mention. Boasting that the Royal Navy was stronger than at the war's outset, Churchill added: "We hope our friends across the ocean will send us a timely reinforcement to bridge the gap between the peace flotillas of 1939 and the war flotillas of 1941."

As to the bases, the Prime Minister explained that the British had concluded that U.S. and British interests would be well served by expanding U.S. facilities in the Western Hemisphere. As a result, Britain had decided, and here he chose his words carefully, "*spontaneously and without being asked or offered any inducement*" to offer such facilities to the U.S. in its trans-Atlantic possessions. (Emphasis added.)

With that phrase Churchill effectively demolished the concept of *quid pro quo* on which Roosevelt had based the entire legal and political argument for the trade. That was not Churchill's worry, not at the moment, anyway. The Prime Minister blithely continued his remarks to Parliament, pointing to the long-range meaning of this transaction. Britain and the U.S., he said,

> will have to be somewhat mixed up together in some of their affairs for mutual and general advantage. . . . I do not view the process with any misgivings. . . . No one can stop it. Like the Mississippi, it just keeps rolling along. Let it roll on—full flood, inexorable, irresistible to broader lands and better days.

Churchill was delighted with himself. He had given a rousing speech with a glorious peroration. Not only would he get the destroyers he wanted from the Americans, but he would give them the bases they wanted, on his own terms. Leaving the House of Commons in his car, he sang "Old Man River" all the way back to 10 Downing Street. Across the Atlantic, however, his hard-bargaining collaborator, the President of the United States, was calling a different tune.

# "Two Friends in Danger"

On August 21, the officials of the United States government charged with closing the destroyer deal assembled in Attorney General Jackson's fifth-floor office in the Justice Department's massive limestone headquarters, ten blocks from the White House. Only the day before, Churchill, in his speech to Parliament, had threatened to knock the underpinnings from under the transaction by contravening the idea of a *quid pro quo* arrangement between Britain and the U.S. Nevertheless they conducted their meeting as if nothing untoward had happened, behavior that testified to FDR's circuitous management of events.

The press, having been admonished only a few days before by the President to disbelieve reports of a connection between the bases and the destroyers, had little reason to remark on Churchill's description of the British offer of bases as "spontaneous." Another dog that did not bark was the U.S. Ambassador to the Court of St. James. From the visitors' gallery in the House of Commons, Joseph Kennedy listened closely as Churchill spoke. But since Roosevelt had gone to great lengths to keep him in the dark on the progress of the talks, he also had no basis to realize that matters now threatened to go awry.

Besides all this, no one in Washington had any reason to anticipate Churchill would reject the way the Americans had structured the deal. Only the week before he had appeared to give the plan his wholehearted support. Considering the stakes involved, most Americans told of his complaints would have dismissed them as quibbles and suspected the Prime Minister of only posturing.

Canadian Prime Minister Mackenzie King, whose aid Churchill had previously sought in lobbying the Americans on the destroyer deal, attributed the Prime Minister's shift in position to the RAF's victories in the Battle of Britain. "When matters were going badly Churchill had been ready enough to appeal urgently to the United States for help and to ask my cooperation in getting it," King complained to Sir Gerald

Campbell, the British High Commissioner for Canada. "When, however, it looked as if the British might still win because of immediate success of their air force, they were ready to pull away from United States cooperation."

But Churchill had not made his way in public life for more than four decades, or pulled Britain back from the abyss in the past three months, by giving ground in a fight. Most of the disagreement between himself and the President had to do with appearances, but appearances mattered greatly on both sides of the Atlantic. The Americans clearly held the advantage because Britain had begun the bargaining, but Churchill also controlled assets of his own.

Despite Churchill's deserved reputation for impetuosity, certain enduring convictions, a strange mixture of radicalism and traditionalism, guided his important decisions. He was only a half-hearted believer in the tenets of his Conservative Party, yet his wife, Clementine, once remarked that he was probably the last surviving adherent of the divine right of kings. He brought considerable insight and sensitivity to his dealings in domestic politics, but in foreign affairs he preferred to disregard change, particularly when it might undermine the Empire. "For him," his secretary Colville observed, "India, Egypt and Africa were and should remain as they had been at the time of Omdurman."[*]

In the midst of the dispute over the destroyers, he had invited General Raymond Lee, the U.S. military attaché, to dinner at 10 Downing Street. After the excellent food and fine wine, the Prime Minister, puffing on an "immense cigar," predicted that once the war was won, the U.S. would be confronted by a "United States of Europe," with Great Britain in a leading role. In his pocket diary Lee summed up his impressions of the evening: "10 Downing Street—powerhouse." Churchill would soon confirm this judgment by the tenacity and vigor with which he pressed his objections to the U.S. plans for the destroyer deal.

In the meanwhile the *quid pro quo* arrangement's importance was underlined around the walnut conference table in Jackson's spacious office. The red Oriental rug covering the floor and two striking murals at either end, Justice Triumphant and Justice Denied, reaching toward the cathedral ceiling, lent the room an air of elegance. Among Jackson's guests, who included Navy Secretary Knox, Army Secretary Stimson,

*At the legendary battle near the central Sudan city of Omdurman on the White Nile in 1898, Lord Kitchener's Anglo-Egyptian Army defeated the forces of Khalifa Addallah, the Muslim ruler, assuring British control of the Sudan.

Undersecretary of State Welles, Army Chief of Staff Marshall, and the Chief of Naval Operations Harold Stark, it was Stark whom the prospective transaction troubled most. As the nation's top admiral, he was being asked to approve the transfer of fifty destroyers not long after he had paid a number of visits to Capitol Hill to convince the Congress of the navy's need for these same ships. To make matters even more awkward the Commander in Chief who wanted to give the ships away was a friend of nearly thirty years' standing.

At the age of 60, with his white hair, pink cheeks, and reserved manner, Stark, as one naval historian observed, looked more like a cleric than a sailor. A cautious and reticent man, he was reluctant to challenge Roosevelt's sometimes far-fetched schemes, allowing the President to interpret his silence for assent.[*] Though he had been a serving naval officer since 1903, Stark still signed personal notes with his Annapolis nickname "Betty," after the wife of a Revolutionary War hero.[†] It was only natural that he looked at destroyers differently than the others gathered in Jackson's office. His first commands as a young officer were destroyers. And, according to a story bruited about in wardrooms, it was as captain of one of them, the U.S.S. *Patterson*, that Stark, with a boldness that he would later outgrow, refused to yield the conn to a bumptious young Assistant Secretary of the Navy named Franklin Roosevelt.

Despite, or perhaps because of, that first encounter, these two up-and-coming careerists became somewhat chummy, keeping up a correspondence over the years. By the time FDR reached the White House, Stark was aide to the secretary of the navy. "Do run over and see me late some afternoon," Roosevelt wrote him. And when Stark, after a tour of sea duty as commander of a cruiser division, returned to Washington in March of 1939 as chief of naval operations, the President warmly welcomed his old friend to his new post. ". . . You and I talk the same language," the President wrote. "My only objection is that if we get into a war you will be a desk Admiral—but cannot have you in two places at once!" But on this troublesome destroyer issue it appeared

---

[*]Early in the war, when Roosevelt broached the idea of expanding the neutrality zone the Navy had to patrol, Stark merely replied that this would require a large number of ships and planes. Roosevelt took that as a green light, and plunged ahead.

[†]At the battle of Bennington in 1777, John Stark rallied colonial troops defending a strongpoint against General Burgoyne's redcoats by shouting: "We'll hold this line or Betty Stark will be a widow tonight." Stark became a brigadier general and his wife's name became a household word.

that the President and the naval officer were talking a different language and that "Betty" Stark, for the first time since he commanded the *Patterson*, stood in Roosevelt's way.

At the heart of the problem was the Walsh amendment's ban on the transfer of any armaments unless they were first certified as not essential to the country's own defense by either of the service chiefs of staff.[*] For Stark this restriction created difficulties, which he had already outlined to Knox, in a lengthy letter filled with misgivings. In part his objections stemmed from a memorandum written for Jackson by Newman A. Townsend, the Acting Assistant Solicitor General, which suggested that the legal solution was to have the ships declared obsolete and then turned over to private firms for sale to the British. This resembled the procedure that had been followed earlier in the year to sell so-called surplus planes. Stark would not go along with that. To declare these ships obsolete would be false on its face, he stressed to Knox, "else the British would not be so anxious to get the same destroyers." Beyond that, Stark doubted that any board of naval officers could be found to make such a finding; even if one did, he, Stark, would personally veto it.

Townsend's memorandum had concluded that "after all is said, the question of the disposition of overage destroyers is probably more political than legal." If it came to politics, Stark had his own problems to think about, too. No one in his position had ever worked harder to ingratiate himself on Capitol Hill among the holders of the purse strings that determined the navy's destiny. When a member of the House Appropriations Committee asked Stark in November 1939 if he considered the navy or the army to be the nation's first line of defense, the Admiral looked up at the committee members and replied: "I think the first line is around this table."

"I think you have got something there, Admiral," responded Rep. Clifton Woodrum of Virginia.

Stark's main purpose on that occasion, less than a year ago, was to gain approval for $36 million in emergency appropriations, most of it to cover the cost of recommissioning 108 of the navy's old destroyers. "I believe the Navy should be ready," Stark told the committee. "I personally would strongly urge that we stay 100 percent manned."

---

*Army Chief of Staff Marshall thought the provision was probably unconstitutional, because it put him in the position of vetoing decisions made by his commander in chief. At any rate he had no difficulty submitting the required certification for the army bombers and rifles promised to the British.

Six months later, in May of 1940, when he was asking the Senate Appropriations Committee to endorse an additional $10 million for overhauling old destroyers, Stark stressed their value to the navy:

> The British are working their destroyers very hard. Ours will be in general service just as the rest of the fleet is in general service, ready in case of need. . . . They would be used for antisubmarine work; they would be used for scouting; they might be used for combat. They would be used for escort work. They would be used whenever we need them.

Now the question that Stark had to face was, how could the navy afford to give away such valuable ships after spending nearly $50 million to refurbish them? No easy answer suggested itself. As a naval officer, he had to take orders from his Commander in Chief. If Roosevelt directed him to sign a statement clearing the way for the destroyer transfer, he told Knox, of course he would comply. But as chief of naval operations he had his relations with Congress to consider and the welfare of the fleet. If he was obliged to do anything that "would jeopardize the good-will and the reputation for honest frank open dealings" that he had worked for months to foster, then "he might just as well be relieved."

Even though Stark had said he would give his assent to the destroyer trade if he was under orders, all present in Jackson's office knew that the President could not afford to force the deal down Stark's throat. If that happened, Roosevelt would never hear the end of it from Stark's friends on Capitol Hill. To effectively eliminate Stark's opposition, the President could not rely on the chain of command. He had to find a justification for the destroyer deal that could be reconciled with the law and not stir a furor in Congress and the country. This was the job assigned to the meeting's host, Attorney General Jackson.

Given his choice of someone to help him in a political crisis, Roosevelt could hardly have found anyone more dependable than Robert Houghwout Jackson. The President's relationship with Jackson went back as far as his friendship with Stark—to the Wilson presidency when Jackson was a young country lawyer breaking into Democratic politics in Roosevelt's home state, and FDR was Assistant Secretary of the Navy. After Roosevelt's inaugural, he brought Jackson into the New Deal, first in the Treasury Department, then the Securities and Exchange Commission, and finally the Justice Department, first as Solicitor General, now as Attorney General. During all this time Jackson had passed every test of loyalty to the President, including the most severe trial in 1937 when he forcefully backed Roosevelt's ill-starred court-packing proposal while many other allies deserted him.

"The President never, never told me he wanted me to write some particular opinion," Jackson would later say. "A man would not be a self-respecting lawyer" if he asked another lawyer to do that. "Roosevelt was not that kind of bird."

In reality, Jackson did not have to be told what to do. Ten days earlier he had been alerted at his mountain vacation retreat by Dean Acheson's phone call about the letter in the *Times* arguing the case for the destroyer transfer. After reading that letter and noting its signatories, Jackson could not help realizing that this was no casual enterprise. Weeks before, in dealing with a similar case, the navy's attempt to turn over torpedo boats to the British, he had held that transfer was illegal. Now it was evident that the President wanted his chief legal officer to reach a different conclusion about the impending destroyer transaction.

If Stark saw the destroyer deal from the perspective of a naval officer, Jackson looked at it from the viewpoint of a lawyer trying to solve a problem for a client. In this case the client was the President of the United States. "The Attorney General is the attorney for the Administration," he once said. "I don't think he should act as judge and foreclose the Administration from making reasonable contentions." On a close question, he said, he would give his client, "the benefit of a reasonable doubt as to the law."

That is exactly what Jackson had done for Roosevelt in a four-page brief he had submitted to Knox on August 17, and which he now explained to the group in his office. His opinion, relying on the same logic as the Cohen–Acheson letter, poked through the loophole the Senate had left in the Walsh amendment. In its original version, as the Attorney General pointed out to Stark and the others, Senator Walsh's amendment would have banned the transfer of the destroyers unless the Navy first certified that the ships were "not essential to and cannot be used in the defense of the United States." After Walsh's Senate colleagues complained this language would doom any kind of transaction, Walsh agreed to drop the words "and cannot be used" from the amendment. Thus the sole criterion for approving the deal was whether the destroyers were "essential" to U.S. defense.

In judging what was essential to national defense, Jackson followed the theory advanced in the Cohen–Acheson letter that the navy should be free to consider the net result of the deal. On these grounds he had a much easier case to make than Cohen and Acheson, who could only argue the advantage to the U.S. of strengthening the Royal Navy. Jackson, on the other hand, could point to the benefits that would come with the British bases. His conclusion:

> . . . The Chief of Naval Operations may, and should, certify . . . that
> such destroyers are not essential to the defense of the United States if in
> his judgment the exchange of such destroyers for strategic naval and air
> bases will strengthen rather than impair the total defense of the United
> States.

That was a crutch on which Stark could lean. Right after the meeting he
sent Roosevelt a memorandum assenting to the transfer of destroyers,
contingent on the U.S. getting long-term leases for bases in return. The
memo parroted Jackson's language, though a postscript signaled his
continued unease: "This is the time," he wrote, "when a 'feller' needs a
friend."

Jackson had done "a pretty good job," of dealing with the legal problems, Stimson noted later in his diary. The secretary of war had been
troubled by his own misgivings about the venture, but these had largely
been set aside the week before by Mr. Justice Frankfurter, whose advice
he had sought on the arguments set forth in the Acheson letter.
Frankfurter had known Stimson for more than thirty years, having been
his special assistant when Stimson was U.S. attorney for the Southern
District of New York and then when he was secretary of war.
Remarkably though, the Justice did not find it relevant when he called
Stimson in response to the letter to mention his active role in the legal
controversy over the destroyers. Frankfurter had after all encouraged
and helped arrange for publication of the document that had become
the principal vehicle for the argument to allow the transaction to pro-
ceed.

Instead, Frankfurter simply said that after "thinking it over hard for
two or three days," he had concluded that the issue over the destroyers
really turned on the question of national defense. From that point of
view, as a result of Britain's offer of bases as a *quid pro quo* for the
destroyers, the U.S. would be "tremendously strengthened" by the
transaction. Anyway, he told Stimson, this situation was entirely different from the cases to which the statutes under discussion were intended to cover. Stimson, assuming that his old friend was dealing with him
in good faith, was grateful. "It was very good of him to have taken all
this trouble to help me out in this way," he wrote in his diary. When he
called the President to share his good feelings, Roosevelt was "greatly
pleased" and Stimson judged was "about ready to push it ahead."

With the military and the Cabinet safely in line, Roosevelt now
sought to use the promised British bases, which had softened Stark's
resistance to the destroyer deal, to convert another formidable oppo-

nent, the chairman of the senate Naval Affairs Committee, David Walsh. At first, rather than confront the issue directly, the President had invited Walsh on a cruise on the *Potomac* two weeks earlier. Unswayed by the shipboard hospitality, Walsh wrote the President August 19 to tell him that "it would be a grave and great mistake" to sell the destroyers to the British. He emphasized the political fallout on the Democratic Party, and presumably Roosevelt's own candidacy. Voters feel, Walsh warned, that "we are either excessively war minded or at least pursing policies that will tend to involve us in the present war." He added a polite postscript: "I do not know when I have had three more pleasant days than when I was with you on the yacht *Potomac* and I want you to know I am most grateful."

Still, the President did not give up. On August 22, the day he returned to the White House from Hyde Park he wrote back, dismissing the political consequences about which Walsh had warned. As commander in chief, the President said, he had no right to think about "being a candidate or desiring votes." Then he offered Walsh what he called "the real meat in the coconut," adopting the folksy approach he often employed. In a rough approximation of rural dialect, Roosevelt relayed what he claimed to be the views of a Dutchess County farmer on the defense aspects of the deal. "Say ain't you the Commander-in-Chief?" this perceptive citizen supposedly asked. "If you are and own fifty muzzle loadin' rifles of the Civil War period, you would be a chump if you declined to exchange them for seven modern machine guns. . . ."

Roosevelt could see no point in worrying about German retaliation. If Germany wanted to go to war against the U.S., he wrote, " Germany will do so on any number of trumped up charges." And in what he may have thought to be his strongest argument, he appealed to Walsh's deep-rooted stinginess, claiming that the destroyers at issue were of the same type that were being sold for scrap for $4,000 or $5,000 apiece. Multiply that unit cost by the fifty destroyers in the deal, Roosevelt said, and that meant the cost of the island bases would set the Treasury back only $250,000. Roosevelt of course avoided mentioning the nearly $50 million that the U.S. had laid out to overhaul the ships.

Whatever the problems that Walsh might cause, they paled when compared to the difficulties that Roosevelt now faced with the British. In a fresh cable from Churchill, two days after his speech to Parliament, Churchill underlined his determination not to link the destroyers and the bases in a trade. "I had not contemplated anything in the way of a contract bargain or sale between us," he told the President. Insisting the British had offered the bases independently of the promise of destroyers, the Prime Minister said:

> Our view is that we are two friends in danger, helping each other as we can. We should like to give you the facilities mentioned without stipulating for any return and even if tomorrow you found it too difficult to transfer the destroyers, et cetera, our offer still remains open because we think it is in the general good.

The trouble with striking a bargain, Churchill explained, is that "people will contrast on each side what is given and received. The money value of the armaments would be computed and set against the facilities and some would think one thing about it and some another." Citing heavy merchant ship losses on the northwestern approaches to the British Isles, Churchill said: "Your fifty destroyers if they came along at once would be a precious help." He stressed, however, that their bestowal on the British would be regarded as "a separate spontaneous act on the part of the United States, arising out of their view of world struggle and how their own interests stand in relation to it."

It detracted something from the selfless tone of Churchill's message that, on the same day it arrived at the White House, Lothian submitted to Welles a new list of military desiderata. If the Americans could not turn over a substantial number of older PBY-4s patrol bombers, the British would like one out of every two new ones that rolled off the assembly line. And if the RAF was hard pressed in the next weeks, they wanted up to 200 fighters, "equipped and ready for action," in the next few weeks. Also on the list was an "immediate priority" request for 70 tanks, which the British would deploy against Italian forces in North Africa, thus providing the U.S. with the benefit, Lothian asserted, of combat testing.

Roosevelt could cope more easily with the British pleading for extra weapons than with their offering the bases as a gift with no strings attached. Summoning Welles, he instructed him to make clear to Lord Lothian that Churchill's gift-for-gift approach would not work on the American side of the Atlantic.

That meant Lothian had to take on the challenge of convincing the Prime Minister that the President meant what he said. Roosevelt could not make the deal without "molasses," Lothian reported to London after his meeting with Welles. Although Roosevelt now intended to bypass Congress, he still needed the bases to get the approval of the U.S. Navy. The British really had little choice, Lothian contended, except to go along with the American plan for an exchange of letters between Britain and the establishing the *quid pro quo* arrangement for the deal. "We are up against a deadlock caused by the American Constitution . . . which can only be solved by our acquiescing. . . ."

Far from being persuaded, Churchill grew angrier. "He (is) rather incensed and won't have an exchange of letters," Alexander Cadogan wrote in his diary after meeting with the Prime Minister. "Says he doesn't mind if we don't get destroyers." To the startled Cadogan, Churchill explained that Britain's need for destroyers was not as great as he had always proclaimed. He had been painting the picture "in rather vivid colors" to impress the Americans. In reality, the Prime Minister now asserted, given the anticipated arrival of new construction, England would have the ships she needed by year's end. It bothered Churchill that not only were the bases worth vastly more than the destroyers, but that the American gift was finite and specific, fifty warships, no more, no less, while the British part of the deal was open-ended. "Won't expose himself to a wrangle with Americans having made us definite gift, haggling over the extent of ours," Cadogan noted in his clipped prose. "Dare say he's right."

Instead, Churchill proposed to put together a very generous offer of bases for the Americans, but one that would be explicit as to its metes and bounds. The Prime Minister believed that as a result the Americans would be "shamed" into turning over the destroyers to England not as a trade but as a gift.

It was not shame Roosevelt was feeling, just impatience. Frustrated by the exchange of cables, the President tried a transatlantic phone call. He deputized his attorney general to explain the legal issues to Churchill. Jackson outlined the law as interpreted by Ben Cohen and Dean Acheson.: The President could not give the destroyers to the British because of the existing federal statutes but he could trade them in a deal in which the U.S. demonstrably came out ahead. The very part of the transaction that disturbed Churchill—the palpable U.S. advantage—was essential to its consummation.

"Empires just don't bargain," the exasperated Churchill replied.

"Well," Jackson countered, "Republics do."

Later Roosevelt, trying to soothe the Prime Minister, told him: "The trouble is I have an Attorney General and he says I have got to bargain."

"Maybe you ought to trade these destroyers for a new Attorney General," Churchill groused.

Discouraged, Roosevelt later in the day called in Knox, Hull, and Stimson for consultation. At the top of his old school form, Stimson entered a plea for understanding: "Each side had its own difficulties to surmount," he said, stressing the need "to avoid recriminations which will take the spirit—the high spirit of grand policy—out of the entire transaction."

Hull sounded a harsher note. In the backwoods of Tennessee where he was raised, men stood by their word and a deal was a deal. To him, he told the President, it appeared that the British were "crawfishing." This was the sort of response the President was looking for. "See what you can do," he told the secretary of state.

Before Hull could do anything, Churchill fired off yet another cable. This one, arriving on Sunday, August 25, presented the Americans with the same arguments the Prime Minister had rehearsed two days before with Cadogan. He pointed out that the British were asking for a "precise list" of desiderata while the U.S. in return was demanding what amounted to "undefined concessions" on the British possessions. That could lead to serious misunderstandings, Churchill warned, and charges that the British were breaking their contract.

As an alternative to the scheme outlined by Welles, Churchill proposed that the British would make an offer of bases which they would then be willing to negotiate with the U.S. If the U.S. government for its own reasons had to present this gift to its people as a *quid pro quo* for the destroyers, why did the British have to come into this at all, Churchill asked.

But the U.S. was in no position to allow for British pride, as Hull, now assuming his assigned role as Roosevelt's chief negotiator, emphasized to Lothian. "The President had no authority to give away government property," he told the ambassador as they both waited at the White House for a meeting with the President on August 25 to discuss Churchill's latest cable.

Lothian had dug in his heels, presenting Roosevelt and Hull with a letter from himself in which he argued that British public opinion would not support a bargain such as the Americans insisted on, and proposed instead a variation of Churchill's voluntary gift formula. Hull was unmoved. "I said for the third time to the Ambassador and for the first time to the President," he later wrote, "that the latter had no authority whatever to make a gift of public property to any government or individual." Roosevelt then left it to Hull to reach a solution with Lothian.

The answer was provided by Hull's own solicitor general, Green Hackworth, demonstrating a lawyerly flexibility. Asked only two weeks before to analyze the legal problems facing a destroyer deal, Hackworth had stomped on the idea unless Congress approved. Since then the winds of politics had blown in a different direction, toward a path around the legal obstacles that had seemed so insurmountable. Now a new barrier loomed that had more to do with politics than law, and with the politics of another country. Just as King Solomon had suggested cutting the baby in two to settle a dispute, Hackworth proposed dividing the British possessions into two parcels—one for giving and the other for trading. He recommended designating Newfoundland and Bermuda as gifts, and put on the trade list the other six bases clustered in the Caribbean nearer the Panama Canal and thus of more strategic importance.

No stroke of genius, like most successful compromises this scheme benefited from being offered to disputants who had been arguing at length without getting anywhere. The Americans eagerly accepted Hackworth's idea, which was tilted to their advantage. "I saw at once that this was the formula for which we had been looking," Hull declared. He quickly sent Hackworth to Roosevelt who just as quickly agreed. The next day, August 27, Hull, Knox, and Stimson went over the draft with the President who stamped his approval.

The British dragged their feet at first. Churchill was still adamant about holding his position, as he demonstrated in yet another cable, before he had been told of Hackworth's offer. Hoping to soften the U.S. position, he sweetened the British offer, adding the island of Antigua to the list of seven sites for U.S. bases. "Our settled policy is to make the United States safe on their Atlantic seaboard," Churchill said. If the Americans subsequently felt able to provide the British with the "instrumentalities which have been mentioned this could be expressed as an act not in payment . . . but in recognition of what we had done for the security of the United States."

Once again, Churchill warned of the urgency of his country's predicament. Mussolini, having conquered Albania in April of 1939, was massing troops on the Greek border. If the U.S. and Britain could conclude "this business" swiftly, the Prime Minister said, "it might even now save that small historic country from invasion and conquest. Even the next 48 hours are important."*

At this point Lord Lothian, following his encounter with Hull, now sought to get across to the head of his government that his own intransi-

*Churchill did not explain how the transfer of U.S. destroyers would discourage the Italians from attacking Greece. Two months later, in October of 1940, Mussolini did invade Greece but his troops were stymied by stiff Greek resistance.

gence was the chief impediment to completion of the deal. Moreover his stubbornness irritated the Americans all the more because they felt, as Hull had put it to Lothian, that for Britain's sake they were "putting their political life at stake." As Hull viewed it, the transaction was "of arguable legality." And if Hitler should "react violently," the Administration might be forced to face the charge in the midst of an election campaign, "that it was obviously leading the United States of America into war." To the British, struggling for survival as a nation these points might seem "of course fantastically small," Lothian conceded, but added that given the political condition facing FDR, "they loom large."

As if to help Lothian make his case to Churchill, Hull summoned the ambassador to the State Department offices on the following day and gave him a memorandum that bluntly expressed the matter. Weary of hearing the British claim that they were happy to give the U.S. the bases for nothing, Hull said:

> The fact is that the destroyers have been in the mind of the British government throughout and prior to the beginning of the discussions regarding bases. If the British government desires to drop the idea of acquiring the destroyers and to turn over the bases as an unqualified gift, a different situation would be presented.

That appeared finally to have done the trick. On that evening, August 29, Lothian showed up at Hull's Carlton Hotel apartment with a British counterproposal that upon close inspection differed only in "a few details" from what the Americans wanted. Within a few hours, both sides began drafting the documents needed to implement the transaction.

Just as all appeared on its way to resolution, Ambassador Kennedy sounded a last minute alarm. He had previously expressed to the White House his sense of injury over the Donovan visit, aggravated by the realization that he was being shut out of the climactic destroyer negotiations. "As far as I can see, I am not doing a damn thing here that amounts to anything," he cabled Roosevelt on August 27. "To be perfectly honest, I do not enjoy being a dummy."

Fearful of a public outburst from his ambassador at this delicate point in negotiations, the President hastily dispatched a conciliatory note from Hyde Park. The destroyer bargaining had been handled directly with Lothian, Roosevelt explained, because the pressure of daily developments required personal contact. After briefly describing the outlines of the transaction, Roosevelt added: "Don't forget that you are not only not a dummy but are essential to all of us both in the government and the nation."

Kennedy was in no way mollified. The next day he fired off a message to Hull which reflected both his frustration at being excluded from the negotiations about the deal, as well as the Anglophobia which had led to his exclusion. Kennedy accused the British of planning a blatant breach of faith: to disclose, when they announced the destroyer deal, that they were only presenting it as a trade to help Roosevelt avoid "legal and constitutional difficulties."

"Now of course as I told you I know nothing about the background in the United States for all these negotiations," Kennedy said. ". . . England never gets the impression they are licked and therefore they never understand why they should not get the best of a trade." He had seen this trouble brewing, Kennedy said, "but because I had no background I have not been able to do anything about it."

That querulous message went off from the Embassy at 5:40 P.M. on Saturday August 29. Less than two hours later that same night, while Hull and Lothian were crafting the final accord in Washington, Kennedy felt obliged to send a new cable, correcting himself. Having "just seen" Halifax and Churchill, Kennedy had learned that Churchill would not after all offend the government of the only country that stood between Britain and disaster. Churchill will "leave the matter open," Kennedy reported. "England will handle her politics in the manner she thinks best and the United States will of course handle hers in her own way."

Now that the deal was on the verge of completion, Kennedy was all for it. It put "a ring of steel" around the U.S., he said. "And no matter what criticism may be leveled at the giving of a few destroyers, the President can very properly say: 'At least I have conducted the affairs of this country in such a manner that it has been possible to obtain these important leases for 99 years with no real loss of anything worth while to America.' "

With Kennedy placated, the negotiating process moved toward its long-delayed consummation. On Friday, August 30, the President and the Prime Minister finally resolved the issue of the British fleet. In consideration of British pride, the U.S. had agreed to deal with this matter separately from the main agreement over bases and destroyers in a simple exchange of correspondence between Roosevelt and Churchill. Following the procedure worked out by Hull and Lothian, the President cabled the Prime Minister recalling his memorable pledge of June 4 that even if the British Isles were conquered, the British fleet would weigh anchor and sail overseas to fight on. Roosevelt then asked pointedly whether that statement "represents the settled policy of the British Government."

"It certainly does," the Prime Minister replied the very next day, according to plan. But concerned about British morale, he added a flourish intended to take some of the curse off this speculation about military defeat: "I must however observe that these hypothetical contingencies seem more likely to concern the German Fleet, or what is left of it, than our own."

The bargain was struck. All that remained was to break the news to the country.

# "Fait Accompli"

On August's final Saturday, Roosevelt revealed what he called "a perfectly tremendous secret." This disclosure, during a speech at Hyde Park, had nothing to do with the impending destroyer deal. Instead the President merely announced that he would nominate Frank Walker, the former treasurer of the Democratic National Committee, as postmaster general to replace "a very splendid old friend of mine," Jim Farley, "who has made such splendid record in that office."

At ease and confident, the President offered no hint that momentous international events were heading toward a climax. He did provide his assessment of the national condition more than ten years after the onset of the Great Depression and more than seven years after his inauguration. "We're getting on awfully well—on the whole, awfully well," he declared.

The occasion for these remarks was the annual meeting on his estate of the Franklin D. Roosevelt Home Club, an informal association of his Dutchess County neighbors. The entertainment had a Western motif. Shaded by maple trees, several thousand listened relaxed while the Buckaroos quartet strummed their guitars and banjos and Chief Lone Bear, decked out in feathered headdress and wampum, offered up a Pawnee tribal prayer asking divine guidance for the "Great White Father." Even in this bucolic setting, the presence on the platform of Crown Princess Martha of Norway, who like the rest of her country's Royal Family had fled the German invasion into exile, reminded of the war in Europe.

In his talk the "Great White Father" only briefly alluded to the fighting abroad, urging Americans to make sure "that nothing can happen to take away from us what we have accomplished in these later years." Noting that the sun was shining, despite an earlier forecast of rain, he remarked that he did not know whether to credit this to the prayers of the event's sponsors or to "just old-fashioned Roosevelt luck." Sure enough, soon after the President's speech was done and the crowd scattered, a heavy thunderstorm drenched the grounds.

On this day the President had clear reason to be grateful for
"Roosevelt luck." For nearly three months now, while Churchill had
pleaded for destroyers that he claimed Britain needed to survive,
Roosevelt had put him off. In the world crisis, time was of the essence.
Only six weeks passed from the launching of the blitz to the collapse of
France. Roosevelt let more time than that elapse between his June 10
speech at Charlottesville, pledging all-out aid to the Allies, and the
August 2 cabinet meeting when he first began to move in earnest on the
destroyers.[*]

So far as the public revelation of the destroyer deal was concerned,
Roosevelt was leaving nothing to chance. He had carefully arranged to
make this the climax to a two-day presidential trip that was already
laden with symbolism. Traveling to his party's stronghold in the South,
he would give his first public addresses since his renomination, thus
unofficially launching his campaign for a third term. And he would
leave on September 1, the first anniversary of the outbreak of the war,
and inevitably a time for reflection by politicians and the press on
America's changing role in the world.

Just the week before the Senate had passed a military conscription
bill, similar to a measure earlier adopted by the House. All that
remained was for the technical differences between the two bills to be
reconciled before the nation's young men would be drafted into military service in peacetime for the first time in history. In anticipation,
Roosevelt had authorized $25 million in emergency funds to go toward
construction of training camps.

On the same Saturday he spoke at Hyde Park, Roosevelt issued an
executive order calling four divisions of the National Guard to active
duty. The sense of crisis was also evident in the President's annual
Labor Day message. He pointed with pride to the gains made since the
dark Depression days of 1932—nine million more jobs, a $3 billion dol-
lar increase in farm income, burgeoning profits for the nation's biggest
corporations. He added, though, that this Labor Day, with the nation
embarked on a program of national defense, required more than ordinary observation. "It demands," the President said, "the dedication of

*As evidence of the risk Roosevelt took, in late May 1940 the British cabinet dis-
cussed possible peace with Hitler, with Halifax indicating that if Hitler would grant
terms that guaranteed British independence he would favor accepting them and avoiding further slaughter. Even Churchill, despite his fiery rhetoric, would not rule out a
negotiated peace if the terms were right. "If we could get out of this jam by giving up
Malta & Gibraltar & some African Colonies he would jump at it."

labor, management, farmers and government to a common purpose so that this great democracy, which is our heritage, shall be protected."

Some voices still resisted the new martial tone in national life, fearing the drift toward war. For them the proposed destroyer deal, now the subject of much speculation if not informed debate, was a prime target. That Sunday, as Roosevelt prepared to depart Hyde Park, Senator Gerald Nye declared that sending the ships to the British "would be a belligerent act making us a party to the war and would in addition weaken our own defense." The war, Nye maintained, was "nothing more than a continuation of the old European conflict of power politics, a fight to save an Empire." Although Nye and his fellow isolationists still had plenty of vocal adherents, their numbers were dwindling, particularly on the destroyer issue. Two weeks earlier, 62 percent of Americans interviewed said they approved of selling U.S. destroyers to Britain, while only 38 percent objected.

A less scientific survey by the *New York Times* published on September 1 suggested that the tide of public support for Britain's fate was rising around the country. "New England continues to favor overwhelmingly every possible aid for England short of an outright declaration of war and the sending of troops overseas," F. Lauriston Bullard reported from Boston. Even in the Farm Belt, the supposed bastion of isolationism, *Times* correspondent Roland Jones observed that on the destroyer issue, "many favor making the best deal possible and putting it through without delay." Sentiment in the Anglo-Saxon South is "so strongly behind measures to aid the British 'short of war' that any such steps by the National Administration would undoubtedly be popular here," Virginius Dabney wrote from Richmond. From San Francisco, Arthur Caylor reported that on the West Coast the idea of sending destroyers had majority backing. "It feels definitely that this country has gradually become so concerned in the Battle of Britain that it is nonsense to think a victorious Hitler would laugh off this country's record to date."

These attitudes, apparent for some time, had finally prodded the President into acting on the destroyers. Now he took the final steps to implement his decision. As he motored from Hyde Park to Weehawken, on the New Jersey side of the Hudson, where he would board the special train that would carry him South, he pored over the three documents implementing the destroyer deal that the State Department had sent him for review—an exchange of notes between Hull and Lothian, laying out the terms, and a presidential message to Congress announcing the transaction.

Lothian's note followed the Hackworth compromise. It offered the leases on two of the islands, on the Avalon Peninsula and southern coast of Newfoundland and on the east coast and Great Bay of Bermuda, "freely and without consideration," in view of His Majesty's Government "friendly and sympathetic interest" in the U.S. national security. The other facilities—in the Bahamas, Jamaica, St. Lucia, Trinidad, Antigua, and British Guiana—were provided "in exchange for naval and military equipment and material," which the U.S. would transfer to Britain.

As with the fleet guarantee, the arrangements outlined in Lothian's note paid some deference to British sensibilities. He deleted Welles's offending reference to the U.S. exercise of "sovereign" authority as well as his demand that Washington's "final judgment" should be the ultimate arbiter on the location of the bases. Instead, Lothian left it that the two governments would work out the exact locations "by common agreement."

In his letter Hull acknowledged "the generous action" of the British to enhance U.S. security. But he allowed no doubts about the *quid pro quo* aspect of the deal. "In consideration of the declarations above quoted," Hull wrote, referring to the offer of bases, "the Government of the United States will immediately transfer to his Majesty's government, fifty United States destroyers."

But when Lord Lothian inspected the final version of the documents, he was most disturbed not by what Hull said, but rather by what he left unsaid. The secretary of state had completely ignored the "military equipment and material," the motor torpedo boats, Navy and Air Corps bombers and rifles, that the earlier version of the agreement, drafted by Welles, had promised the British. In a striking oversight Welles had neglected to pass the list of desiderata on to Hull when the secretary returned to take charge of the negotiations. For all his abrasive insistence that the British meet their obligations, Welles had failed to ensure that his country live up to its end of the bargain.

Even though his country was being shortchanged, Lothian feared to jeopardize the main prize of fifty destroyers, the main prize sought through his prolonged bargaining, for the sake of the additional munitions. Under the circumstances, the ambassador went ahead and signed the documents, after raising enough of a protest to help him to pursue the matter later.

Actually, as Lothian would soon discover, while the omission of the bombers and rifles was simply due to oversight, the absence of the motor torpedo boats was deliberate, a consequence of Roosevelt's convoluted legal strategy. In effect the torpedo boats had to be sacrificed to legitimize the transfer of the destroyers.

Attorney General Jackson had reached this decision in his opinion which he had submitted to Roosevelt on August 27. Following closely the trail blazed by Ben Cohen and Dean Acheson, Jackson maintained that the 1917 Espionage Act's ban on sending warships to a belligerent applied only to warships still under construction. That clearly did not apply to the destroyers, all more than twenty years old, but it did pertain to the torpedo boats, still abuilding at the Electric Boat Co.

Jackson's case was bolstered by an alteration in the punctuation in the critical sentence of the statute, a small change nevertheless freighted with significance. By accident or by design, the attorney general added a comma after the words "any vessel" so that the language defining the unlawful act now read "to send out of the jurisdiction of the United States any vessel, built, armed or equipped as a vessel of war . . . with any intent or under any agreement or contract . . . that such vessel shall be delivered to a belligerent nation." With the additional punctuation Jackson could more readily argue that the phrase referring to building or equipping with the intent to deliver to a belligerent nation was essential to the definition of illegality.

Next, Jackson dealt with the Walsh amendment's prohibition on transferring essential war material, the same ground he had covered two weeks earlier in his brief for Knox which had eased Admiral Stark's qualms. Once again Jackson relied on the theory that in deciding whether military material to be traded was essential, it should be balanced against what would be gained in return; in other words the destroyer exchange was not illegal if the British bases strengthened the United States.

The most fundamental question Jackson addressed was whether, under the Constitution, the President had the right to acquire the island bases from the British by executive agreement, instead of being obliged to negotiate a treaty subject to senate ratification. Since Roosevelt had already done exactly this a year earlier to get bases in Trinidad, Santa Lucia, and Bermuda, Jackson would have gravely embarrassed his president if he now held that such action was unconstitutional.

A century and a half earlier, when the great debate over ratifying the Constitution raged in the infant Republic, John Jay had defended the treaty-making provision in the *Federalist Papers*. By allowing the President to negotiate treaties on his own but requiring the Senate's ratification, the system "offers every advantage that can be derived from talents, information, integrity and deliberate investigations on the one hand and from secrecy and despatch on the other," he wrote. In designing the destroyer agreement, Roosevelt certainly had relied heavily on the advantage of secrecy. The President had, however, sacrificed whatever benefits might have come from senate participation.

This substantial omission forced Jackson to search the Constitution and the statute books to find authority for Roosevelt's actions. First, as Commander in Chief, the President had not only the right but the obligation to enhance the nation's defenses, Jackson asserted. It seemed "beyond doubt," he argued, "that present world conditions forbid him to risk any delay that is constitutionally avoidable." In addition, Jackson also found justification for Roosevelt's actions in the President's constitutional authority to control foreign relations. "The President's power over foreign relations . . . is not unlimited," Jackson conceded, particularly in conducting negotiations which commit the U.S. to future action for which congressional approval would be required. But happily, Jackson advised the President, once the destroyers were transferred, the acquisition of the bases would not require any further commitment. "It is not necessary for the Senate to ratify an opportunity that entails no obligation," he concluded.

At the outset of his opinion Jackson stated that he was solely concerned with "questions of constitutional and statutory authority." He scarcely mentioned international law, for understandable reasons. In their brief, Cohen and Acheson had assumed that the destroyers would be transferred to Britain by private contractors whose actions, in their view, would not be restricted by international law. In reality, the U.S. government itself was carrying out the transfer; if a respectable argument existed to endorse that action under international law, Jackson could not find it to put in his opinion. In fact, the State Department itself privately conceded that the U.S. was out of bounds. "We agreed that the transfer of fifty destroyers to England would be a violation of international law and that Germany might take umbrage at it," Breckinridge Long recorded in his diary August 28, 1940, after discussing the transaction with Hull.

This was not an issue the President chose to address in his message announcing the deal to Congress. His fewer than 300 words included no reference to congressional approval; Roosevelt simply stated that he was informing Congress of action he had already taken, as explained by the Hull–Lothian exchange of notes, and as legally justified by Attorney General Jackson's opinion. The note emphasized that the transaction in no way modified the status of the U.S. as a neutral and that its purpose was defensive, not aggressive.

> This is not inconsistent in any sense with our status of peace. Still less
> is it a threat against any nation. It is an epochal and far reaching act of
> preparation for continental defense in the face of grave danger.

Resorting to the same historical analogy he summoned up to try to persuade Senator Walsh, he described the deal as "the most important
action" taken to bolster the national defense since the Louisiana
Purchase, which had been consummated without asking Congress in
advance. This transaction, as Roosevelt did not need to remind Capitol
Hill, was another executive agreement concluded without prior congressional approval. The President devoted a paragraph to the defensive value of the British bases, but he mentioned the destroyers only to
say they had been given to the British in exchange for the bases.

That Sunday afternoon, while the President's train took on a substantial contingent of congressional Democrats at Washington's Union
Station, Roosevelt turned various destroyer papers back to Hull with
only minor changes, along with a note of his own giving "my full and
cordial approval" to the exchange between Hull and Lothian.
Everything was signed and ready for release on Tuesday, September 3.

As events neared a climax, Roosevelt's mood was unsettled. Reporter
Doris Fleeson thought he seemed irritable. And to financier and adviser Bernard Baruch, a guest on the train, he appeared to be "brooding
about something." Twice he mentioned to Baruch that "he might get
impeached for what he was about to do."

But when he lunched on board the train with Secretary Ickes and his
wife, Jane, who had come along because the trip would include dedication ceremonies for the Great Smokey Mountain National Park, he
betrayed no unease. Roosevelt told the couple that before the trip was
over he would "give out a story" that would be "sensational." He would
not say what it was even to Ickes, who from the beginning had been one
of the destroyer deals most ardent supporters. But when the Secretary
and his wife returned to their drawing room, Ickes told her that he "had
no doubt" but that FDR was going to announce the transfer of fifty
destroyers to the British.

Before that announcement on Labor Day morning the presidential
train rumbled into Chattanooga for the dedication of the huge new
Chickamauga Dam nearby, the latest in the series of public power pro-
jects that had transformed the South and made the Tennessee Valley
Authority one of the crown jewels of the New Deal. Here, and everywhere else along his way, Roosevelt made sure to present himself not
just as chief executive but as Commander in Chief. A military guard of

honor met him at the Chattanooga station and motorized cavalry from nearby Fort Ogelthorpe stood guard along his route to the dam. If he needed inspiration, he surely derived it driving through the streets of Chattanooga, where throngs bearing Roosevelt and Wallace posters lined his route three deep.

Ickes was troubled because Secret Service chief Starling had over-ruled the original plans for the President to speak from a barge on the river below the dam, in full view of the huge crowd at the site. Instead, Roosevelt spoke from his car, where, Ickes complained, "Practically no one could see him." All could hear him over the public address system, though. Hatless in the broiling sun, with the sweat soaking through his seersucker suit, the President contrasted the vast benefits brought to this region by TVA with Republican standard-bearer Willkie's well-known opposition to public power. Not that he ever mentioned Willkie's name. That would have made this a political speech, which FDR had vowed he would not deliver.

There are those, he noted, who would say that all that TVA had wrought was not a proper activity for the federal government. "As for me," he said, "I glory in it as one of the great social and economic achievements of the United States. . . ." Melding the domestic achieve-ments of his presidency and the dangers facing America from abroad into one unifying theme, he warned his countrymen against "a time of peril unmatched in the history of the nations of all the world." Even so, he pledged the struggle for prosperity and progress at home would not be abandoned. "We are seeking the preparedness of America not against the threat of war or conquest alone," he declared, "but . . . to assure Americans a peace that rests on the well-being of the American people."

Roosevelt returned to this point, after the eleven-car train wound its way to Newfound Gap to the dedication of another New Deal achieve-ment, the 200,000-acre Great Smoky Mountains National Park, half of it in Tennessee, half in North Carolina. From a mile-high rocky bluff he recalled for a throng of some 25,000 the rigors of the American past, the days of "the old frontier that put the hard fiber in the American spirit and the long muscles on the American back." Those hardships had been conquered but new threats loomed. "The arrow, the tomahawk and the scalping knife have been replaced by the airplane, the bomb, the tank and the machine gun," Roosevelt declared. Confronted by "the greatest attack that has ever been launched against freedom of the individual," the President asserted that "Americans must prepare beforehand—for the simple reason that preparing later may and probably will be too late." As he spoke of "a thousand ways" that preparation must go forward, he provided a large hint of the announcement planned for the next day. "New bases must be established and I think will be established," he said, "to enable our fleet to defend our shores."

Roosevelt maintained his martial tone the next morning during a "sentimental pilgrimage" to an almost deserted naval ordinance factory in Charleston, West Virginia. He recalled that as assistant secretary of navy he had helped launch construction of the plant, which the government had then abandoned in 1921 after investing $30 million in it. The President also recalled he had rejected plans to sell the installation three years earlier because, he claimed, he sensed the time would come when it once again would be needed. The government had ordered remodeling of one part of the plant to produce big guns for America's two-ocean navy, now on the drawing boards; another section was already turning out armorplate for the fleet's new battleships.

Returning to the train, which would take him and his retinue back to the capital, Roosevelt gave no indication that anything more would be in the offing. Then, as the long grey cars wound their way along the mudlined banks of the Kanawha River, about forty-five minutes out of Charleston and shortly before noon, press secretary Steve Early summoned the twenty-three correspondents on board to make their way back through the swaying train to the president's car, the *Roald Amundsen*. There Roosevelt awaited them in a corner of the room, crisp in his blue summer suit, smiling and nodding greetings as the sun slanted through the half-shaded windows. Henry M. Kannee, the White House stenographer, sat at his right on the only other lounge chair in the room, while to his left Early perched on a radio, dangling his legs. As his guests filed into the jerking little Pullman sitting room, furnished in mahogany-colored metal and buff summer slipcovers, they soon realized that the space was inadequate for the occasion. One correspondent calculated that the car was meant to hold no more than seven. They made do. Five squeezed on to a couch, three crouched on the floor, some found chairs, while others stood and two tried to hear from the adjoining corridor.

They soon discovered that the President had inflicted a greater handicap on them than the lack of space. In one final stratagem, Roosevelt had found a way, even as he finally allowed the details of the destroyer trade to come to light, to shield himself from having to explain his actions. He had arranged that all the relevant documents bearing on the destroyer trade, the exchange of notes between Lothian and Hull, the attorney general's opinion, and the President's own mes-

sage to Congress would be released in Washington with no copies available to the White House press corps on the train. Thus handicapped,
these correspondents, the only ones who could question him at this
portentous moment, would have little basis for analyzing the complexi-
ties which for weeks had absorbed the best minds of two governments.

To add to their frustration and confusion, the President at first treated his announcement as if it were part of an inside joke. "I have today
nothing for you as news from here, although I have something for your
information," he said slyly. "It is a Washington story that will be out
there in 22 minutes, so that story will come from Washington. I cannot
add to it but you ought to know about it because it will probably get all
kinds of flashes."

The reporters would be told by their editors, Roosevelt predicted:
"For God sakes, to get some news." He added: "Well there isn't any
news."

Then tapping on his chair for emphasis, he stressed his favorite
point: "It is probably the most important thing that has come for
American defense since the Louisiana Purchase."

After Roosevelt read quickly through the text of his message to
Congress, he was asked to explain the distinction between the two sets
of bases—Newfoundland and Bermuda which he had described as gifts
and the others listed as acquired in exchange for the destroyers. "Oh all
kinds of things that nobody here would understand, so I won't mention
them," FDR said airily of the crucial provision. "It is a *fait accompli*; it
is done this way."

Asked about Attorney General Jackson's opinion, FDR gave much
the same response: "It is all over," he said. "It is all done."

Rather than discussing specifics, the President embarked on a
lengthy recounting of his version of the circumstances surrounding
Jefferson's purchase of Louisiana from the French. As Roosevelt told
the story, illustrated by vigorous flourishes of his ivory cigarette holder:

> France had a very weak army down there in Louisiana. . . . We were
> scared to death that there might be . . . some danger of some power
> going in there and going up the valley to connect with Canada . . . There
> was an awful lot of discussion about it and everybody was yelling, "For
> God sakes protect us," all over the country, "by acquiring if you can, this
> mouth of the Mississippi."

When Jefferson found Napoleon receptive to an offer, knowing that "to
put the thing up to Congress would have involved a delay," he went
ahead with the purchase, and later asked Congress to appropriate the

money to cover the cost, as Roosevelt told the story. "It was a *fait accompli*," the President, said repeating the phrase. "There was never any treaty, there was never any two-thirds vote in the Senate."

Actually there had been a treaty, as Roosevelt's own Attorney General had noted in his opinion justifying the destroyer deal, although it was drawn up and ratified after the fact. Asked if Jackson's opinion had cited the Louisiana Purchase as a historical precedent, Roosevelt said: "I think that is mentioned in it." Jackson actually stated that as a precedent for the destroyer deal, the Louisiana purchase was not "strictly pertinent."

For the most part, the President was elaborately nonchalant. At one point he paused to ask reporters whether to stress the second or third syllable in pronouncing the word "epochal." When a reporter pressed him to explain Jackson's opinion, which he professed not to have with him, Roosevelt said: "I stopped being a lawyer twelve years ago." Nor did he want to discuss the long-term implications of his action. "I would stick to this," he said. "You have all this information. In other words don't say this is a forerunner of this or a forerunner of that. You might hit but the chances are ten to one you would miss."

On one point he was quite clear. Asked if Senate ratification was required, he read briefly from his message and said: "It is all over; it is all done."

In addition, Roosevelt called attention to the restatement of Churchill's pledge not to surrender the British fleet, which also would be released in Washington. "Is that part of the deal?" he was asked.

"No," the President said, "it happens to come along at the same time."

"Fortuitously?" a reporter suggested.

The President liked that way of putting it. "Fortuitously," he agreed. "That is the word."

When someone asked him about the value of the destroyers, Roosevelt sought to put the transaction in a larger context. "In a great emergency, remove pure figures from your mind," he advised. Some would say it was a good deal, while others would disagree. "You can take your money and take your choice," he said. "Personally I think it is a damned good trade."

After three tortuous months the President had completed his performance and also graded it. Now the audience and critics would be heard.

# "An Openly Hostile Act"

Writing to Brendan Bracken, Churchill's parliamentary private secretary, a week before the announcement of the destroyer deal, Colonel Donovan provided a Republican's view of the presidential election campaign just getting under way. "The trend against Roosevelt is pretty strong, mostly on his domestic and third term issues," he reported. "The thing that gives him strength, strange as it may seem, has been his position on the war." He noted, though, that on this the President himself would probably not agree. "He says, however, that he will lose the election on the destroyers, but still feels that it should be done."

Roosevelt made much the same point to his secretary, Grace Tully, as they worked at Hyde Park on the final changes in the documents announcing the trade. "Congress is going to raise hell about this, but even another day's delay may mean the end of civilization," she later recalled him saying. "Cries of 'war monger' and 'dictator' will fill the air, but if Britain is to survive we must act."

Setting aside the rhetorical flourishes, the meaning of the words is consistent with the way Roosevelt depicted himself, publicly as well as privately—as a bold leader willing to risk his own political future for the sake of principle and his country's best interest. This, however, was not the way he actually played out his role. His dedication to helping the British cause varied greatly from time to time, depending on the fortunes of war abroad and the direction of the political winds at home. He told Grace Tully that "another day's delay" on the destroyers could be disastrous. Yet he put off action for many a day while he waited for the confluence of circumstances and events that would minimize the chances of political damage and maximize the opportunity for political gain.

He watched the opinion surveys which were just emerging as an important factor in politics, with an eagle eye, even suggesting questions for pollsters to ask. It was at Roosevelt's behest, as George Gallup later revealed, that the public was queried about whether it was in favor of transferring destroyers to Britain. In addition to monitoring the

Gallup and *Fortune* polls, which were publicly reported, as he neared the time for a decision on the destroyer issue, he scrutinized a series of private studies conducted by two Princeton University professors, who, he was told by his go-between, political aide Lowell Mellett, "welcome suggestions for questions." In one of their surveys, 59 percent of those interviewed thought it more important for the United States to stay out of war than to help England win, at the risk of getting into war. But 85 percent favored sending more food and arms to England to save her from defeat and 50 percent thought it more important that England win than their personal choice for president be elected in November, against only 40 percent who felt the other way. Though the data did not differ significantly from what was available publicly, the exclusiveness of the information appealed to Roosevelt's fondness for secretiveness. "These confidential polls are extremely interesting," he wrote Mellett. "I think you can think up some additional questions for them."

When Roosevelt told Donovan that the destroyer deal could cost him the election, poll results, based on his own question, that showed three out of five Americans in favor of selling destroyers to the British, contradicted this calculation. Roosevelt's worries, however, went beyond whether he would have a healthy majority on his side, which seemed assured. More than a majority, he wanted a broad consensus that would spare him from having to explain his actions. This he was able to achieve by presenting the acquisition of the naval and air bases as the deal's main thrust, thus transforming the transaction from a potential liability into a major triumph. As Richard Strout of the *Christian Science Monitor* wrote after the press conference on board his railroad car, "It was inevitable that under the circumstances he must have been thinking of the tremendous point he had scored over Wendell Willkie, his political antagonist." Though, as Strout added: "Mr. Roosevelt would have indignantly refused to comment if that point had been raised."

Part of the advantage the President gained came simply from the broad public impact of the announcement. Sweeping in scope, unprecedented in nature, Roosevelt's forceful action heartened Americans at a moment when it appeared that only the Axis powers could act decisively. The destroyer deal elevated FDR above the status of candidate and, more than any other event of his presidency until then established him as Commander in Chief.

The *New York Times* bannered the announcement in a three-line headline across eight columns of its front page, the same display given to the fall of France in June:

ROOSEVELT TRADES DESTROYERS FOR SEA BASES;
TELLS CONGRESS HE ACTED ON HIS OWN AUTHORITY;
BRITAIN PLEDGES NEVER TO YIELD OR SINK FLEET

Prominently displayed on its front page, along with six separate stories on the trade, was a map of the Atlantic coast showing the eight British bases, captioned: "U.S. Acquires Defense Bastions." On its editorial page the *Times*, using the word Roosevelt had trouble pronouncing, hailed the transaction as "epochal," adding that Great Britain and the U.S. "now place at the disposal of one another instruments of which each has special need in the defense of the Atlantic world against aggression." The *Christian Science Monitor*, which only the week before had urged the President to get on with the deal, predicted history would record this event "as the beginning of the ebb of the totalitarian tide."

While rejoicing in the boost for Britain's naval defenses, the pro-British press also carefully underscored the reciprocal advantage gained for the United States. Thus the *New York Herald Tribune*, Joseph Alsop's home base and a prime advocate of aid for Britain, called the bases "a stockade of steel" on America's eastern flank. *Time* contended the acquisition of the bases "may alter the course of history by preventing enemies from attacking the U.S., making possible their defeat if they attempt it."

Even more impressive were the accolades from the other side in the impassioned debate over U.S. response to the war abroad. By acquiring the bases, Roosevelt had gained an objective which had long been close to the hearts of isolationists and thus shielded himself from charges that he was stripping U.S. defenses for the sake of the British. Even the *Chicago Tribune*, the sounding board of Midwestern isolationism, trumpeted praise: "Any arrangement which gives the United States naval and air bases in regions which must be brought within the American defense zone is to be accepted as a triumph." From his retirement headquarters in San Francisco, Herbert Hoover called the naval and air bases the U.S. would soon get "important contributions to our defense." On Capitol Hill, other voices in the opposition party joined in the chorus of commendation heard from Democrats. "We've got to defend ourselves," said Republican Senator Ernest Gibson of Vermont. "We certainly need those bases." "A fine deal," said the GOP's Rep. Ralph Gamble of New York, who termed the naval and air bases "vital factors" in bolstering U.S. defenses.

Among critics, the *St. Louis Post Dispatch* issued the most vehement assault. In an editorial reprinted as a full-page advertisement in the *New York Times*, the *Post Dispatch* likened Roosevelt's unilateral action to "the edicts forced down the throats of Germans, Italians and Russians by Hitler, Mussolini and Stalin." The consequences could be "the shedding of blood of millions of Americans," the paper declared. "If Congress and the people do not rise in solemn wrath to stop Roosevelt now—at this moment—then the country deserves the stupendous tragedy that looms right around the corner." The *New York Daily News* warned: "The United States has one foot in the war, and one foot on a banana peel." Recalling the "nightmare" of World War I, the *News* grumbled ominously: "Once again we seem to have given England a blank check, to draw on as needed. The outlook is dark indeed." Most criticism focused on the President's failure to clear the deal with Congress in advance, a point that even some supporters of the transaction lamented. "It must be said that the present agreement would be even more desirable if it had the formal stamp of Congressional approval on it," the *New York Times* acknowledged. Unhappy lawmakers were less restrained. "There is no longer any need for Congress," Michigan Republican Congressman Paul Shafer sardonically complained. "A legalistic subterfuge," charged New York Republican Congressman Clarence Hancock. "A long step toward war," said Representative George Tinkham, a Republican who had been elected to the House the same year World War I began. "There is no difference between his action from either Hitler, Mussolini or Stalin."

The opposition party's standard-bearer, Wendell Willkie, whose reaction to the deal had once been considered so critical, was hamstrung by his own tacit endorsement of aid for Britain in his acceptance speech, wrung from him with the help of William Allen White. Now he could find nothing ill to say of the trade, which he acknowledged "the country undoubtedly will approve," except to question the way the President had gone about it. He called it "regrettable" that the President did not first ask for Congressional approval.

That sounded too much like mush to Senator Vandenberg and other old-line Republican isolationists, who prodded their nominee into making another statement on September 6 in which he tried to compensate for his laggardliness with the ferocity of his rhetoric.

> Leaving out of account the advantage or disadvantage of the trade, the method by which that trade was effected was the most arbitrary and dictatorial action ever taken by any President in the history of the United States. It does us no good to solve the problems of democracy if we solve

them with the methods of dictators or wave aside the processes of democracy.

In reality, though, the argument was all but over. "The President acted," Roosevelt critic Arthur Krock wrote. "Mr. Willkie could only talk." Balanced against the prospect of bolstering national defense by gaining the British bases, the concern over Congress's prerogative was too pale a banner to rally many Americans. Willkie tried to argue that what was in jeopardy was not just some legalism but rather a fundamental democratic principle. But for the case against presidential overreaching to impress the public, the combination of influential journalists, prestigious law firms, and corporate interests, who made up what would later come to be known as the American Establishment, needed to muster their prestige behind that cause. In this particular situation, their zeal to aid the British so absorbed these high-minded forces that they exhibited little concern about how this was accomplished.

On Wednesday, September 4, when the House returned to session after its Labor Day recess, the *New York Times* reported that "only a handful" of members spoke out against the President. While the Senate was still on holiday, the Democratic congressional leadership, after meeting with the President and expressing their own enthusiasm, could confidently say that they detected no "important" opposition. Of hundreds of telegrams received, the White House reported, only a dozen were critical.

With all the good news, something still gnawed at FDR. Following his announcement of the trade, some critics had pointedly recalled his public statement only three weeks previous that the negotiations with Britain over bases had nothing to do with destroyers. "I see some of our old friends said that I had not told the truth," he remarked at his September 6 press conference. When all the details of the negotiations could be disclosed, Roosevelt maintained, "they will find that as of the day that I made that statement in press conference, it was literally true."

When would this disclosure be made, one reporter asked. "The State Department rule is ten years," the President replied.

"Well, that is not going to help in this campaign," the broadcaster Earl Godwin drily observed.

"What has the campaign got to do with national defense?" Roosevelt demanded with no hint of irony.

Most politicians could see an obvious connection. The candidacy of Wendell Willkie "is undergoing a rather definite slump," as Turner

Catledge of the *New York Times* reported the next day, citing as a major reason Roosevelt's "dramatic, highly personal handling of the presently popular deal" for destroyers and bases. Two weeks later a Gallup poll confirmed that Roosevelt had assumed a commanding lead over his challenger who not long before had been ahead of the incumbent. By Gallup's reckoning, if Roosevelt won all the states in which he was currently leading he would collect 453 electoral votes to only 78 for Willkie, a veritable landslide.[*]

Across the Atlantic, the British public was "jubilant." In the government, the sense of elation was mixed with relief that the prolonged negotiations at last seemed to be over and, for officials and ordinary citizens alike, tempered by the realization that the Americans had indeed driven a hard bargain. "Uncle Sam has remained Uncle Sam," Britain's World War I Prime Minister David Lloyd George grumbled to Soviet Ambassador Ivan Maisky. ". . . He hasn't been very generous. . . . For this old iron we have had to pay with several very important bases on our territory. . . . But what could we do? There was no other way out." For many Britons the terms of the destroyer deal only exacerbated the general resentment that colored attitudes toward U.S. aid under the provisions of the Neutrality Act. "It is widely realized that the support we are getting from America is paid for in hard cash," Churchill's secretary, John Colville, wrote in his diary on the day before the deal was unveiled.

Also dampening British spirits was the Luftwaffe, which on the day the transaction was announced in Washington had been pounding the island with flights of as many as 600 bombers for ten straight days. Indeed, Churchill had to delay his speech officially announcing the deal on September 5, because a German raid sent M.P.s to their basement shelters. Relying on what he later described as "the language of understatement," Churchill reported that "the memorable transactions" involving the destroyers and bases had been completed to "the general satisfaction" of both Britons and Americans. With tongue firmly planted in his cheek, he added: "Only very ignorant persons would suggest that the transfer of American destroyers to the British flag constitutes the slightest violation of international law or affects in the smallest degree the non-belligerency of the United States."

As for Britain's side of the bargain, he deftly sought to justify the granting of the bases on grounds of self-interest. "I have no doubt that

---

[*]Those figures were remarkably close to the final tally which gave Roosevelt 449 to 82 for Willkie.

Herr Hitler will not like this transference of destroyers," he said. "And I have no doubt that he will pay the United States out if he ever gets the chance." This prospect, Churchill said, made him glad that U.S. defenses in the Atlantic had been bolstered by bases that "will enable them to take danger by the throat while it is still hundreds of miles from their homeland."

For their part, the British would lose no time in exploiting their hard-earned prizes, Churchill said. British crews were already meeting the destroyers at the ports where they would be delivered. "You might call it the long arm of coincidence," he said, "I don't think that there is any more to be said about the whole business at the present time," he said, except to offer members of the House this closing advice: "When you have got a thing where you want it, it is a good thing to leave it where it is."

Actually, though Churchill did not choose to mention this to Parliament, the destroyer deal was still far from where the British wanted it, mostly because of Welles's failure to advise Hull of the war material that the British had been promised in addition to the destroyers. When the "very much disturbed" Lothian had first raised this problem with Morgenthau, the Treasury Secretary responded with a sarcastic brushoff.

"No, I'm not going to ask the President, 'Mr. President had you forgotten a promise or something?' " Morgenthau told Lothian. "Take it up with him yourself," he advised the ambassador.

Lothian did so, urged on by his own government. On September 5, the same day that Churchill addressed Parliament, he sent an "action this day" message to Halifax, recommending a cable of thanks to Lothian, but more urgently inquiring about the torpedo boats, flying boats, aircraft and rifles the U.S. had pledged to deliver. "I consider we were promised all the above and more too. Not an hour should be lost in raising those questions," he declared. " 'Beg while the iron is hot.' "

But it was no use begging for the torpedo boats, which had run afoul of the tangled legal theorems the U.S. had used to justify pushing through the deal without congressional approval. The British would have to wait to receive torpedo boats from the U.S. until March of 1941, when twenty-eight were transferred to them on the day Roosevelt signed the Lend-Lease Act.

The 250,000 Enfield rifles were less of a problem, though complicated nonetheless. Since the U.S. could no longer link them to the destroyers, as part of an exchange for bases, they had to be certified separately as not essential for defense. Finally the Army cleared the rifles for shipment on September 21 and none too soon. The next day, an impatient

Churchill, unaware that the problem had been solved, pleaded with Roosevelt that the weapons were "mostly urgently needed" and asking for their shipment "even if no ammunition is available."

The Navy had less trouble dealing with the five old patrol bombers promised the British, simply agreeing to turn over every new bomber that came off the assembly line for the next few months. The five B-17 Flying Fortresses were a bigger headache because they were in short supply. The President had been stunned when General Marshall reported to him that aside from units assigned to the Canal Zone and Hawaii, the U.S. had only forty-nine of the big new bombers in service-able condition. "His head went back as if someone had hit him in the chest," Stimson recorded in his diary. Under an impromptu arrange-ment, the Army Air Corps substituted for the Flying Fortresses another four-engine bomber, the B-24 Liberator. The British agreed to provide the U.S. with 120 airplane engines to equip B-17s, which were, Stimson noted, "without engines and without any possibility of getting them for a long time." In return, Roosevelt ordered that henceforth the British would receive every other new B-24 manufactured, an improvement over the one in three they had been receiving.

As it turned out, these experiences foreshadowed the delay and frus-tration that marked the culmination of the two main parts of the deal, the transfer of the destroyers and the leasing of the bases. Guns uncov-ered, depth charges at the ready, the first dozen of the fifty ships, eight from Boston harbor and four more from Philadelphia, departed September 5 for Halifax where British crews waited to board them. They found the storeroom crammed with such forgotten amenities as coffeemakers, China, silver, and tablecloths, a dowry so generous it may have helped to foster an initial access of enthusiasm among the Royal Navy officers. "They are simply magnificent ships," declared Rear Admiral S. S. Bonham Carter, chief of British naval operations in the North Atlantic. "They are in perfect condition."

In the weeks to come, the Admiral would have ample reason to reflect on those words. In truth, many of the ships, known as "Town Class" destroyers, because almost all were named after towns common to both the U.S. and Great Britain, had nearly outlived their usefulness. Age had eroded their seaworthiness, and the differences between British and American naval construction magnified their defects. One American officer was supposed to have said that the hulls of the gift ships were barely thick enough "to keep out the water and small fish." A multitude of problems soon struck. Each ship was equipped with four torpedo tubes instead of two, as in newer models; the two extra tubes projected over the side, causing the destroyers to dip in even the slightest swell of the sea. The ships could not turn at the high speeds required for attack without risking damage and they lacked the deck space for the antisubmarine weapons needed to carry out the main mission the British had in mind for them. Finally, the stresses of combat duty on the high seas on the poorly designed steering gear produced frequent collisions.

One of the new additions to His Majesty's navy, H.M.S. *Chesterfield*, vividly demonstrated this drawback when she rammed a sister ship, H.M.S. *Churchill*, in the stern, backed away, and then rammed into the unfortunate ship again. H.M.S. *Georgetown* collided with the former U.S. ship, H.M.S. *Hamilton*, and after repairs *Georgetown* ran aground at New Brunswick. Another idiosyncrasy, the tendency of the four-inch guns, when loaded and fully elevated, to fire themselves, wasted considerable ammunition until the British learned to correct for it. British officers argued among themselves as to whether the twin propellers were too far apart or too close together, but all agreed their positioning was gravely flawed.

With all these shortcomings, weeks were spent refitting the ships for service, and after three months, only thirty of them had arrived in British waters. In mid-December Churchill, mustering as much tact as he could, reported to the President that the British had "so far only been able to bring a very few of your fifty destroyers into action on account of the many defects which they naturally develop when exposed to Atlantic weather after having been laid up so long." To better help the U.S. Navy ready its own ships for action, Churchill promised to send a long list of recommended "preparations and renovations" based on the Royal Navy's harsh experience.

By the spring of 1941, six months after the closing of the deal, the British had called nearly all the destroyers to active service on a broad range of missions. Six went to the Canadian Navy for escort duty in Canadian waters. Most of the rest were assigned convoy or mine-laying duty, warding off the German U-boats' assaults on Britain's American lifeline. As age and service took an increasing toll, a number were converted to target ships. And in 1944 eight were transferred to the Soviet Navy, but only after intensive inspections and extensive repairs undertaken at the insistence of the skeptical Russian admirals. Certainly the most spectacular mission of all the Town Class ships was performed by H.M.S. *Campbelltown*, formerly U.S.S. *Buchanan*, in March of 1942, after the U.S. had entered the war. Fitted out to look like a German destroyer, bearing a strike force of commandos and loaded with explosives, *Campbelltown* rammed the huge *Normandie* dock at St. Nazaire, built to service the passenger liner of that name. This was the only Atlantic Coast facility large enough to accommodate the German battleship *Tirpitz*, pride of Hitler's fleet, which the British feared would ravage their shipping. Nearly half *Campbelltown*'s crew were killed on the mission, and her captain, Lt. Commander S. H. Beattie, was taken prisoner. While in a German prison camp, he learned he had won the Victoria Cross.

Some statistics suggest the destroyers' overall value. In June of 1941, when the Royal Navy had only about 200 destroyer and destroyer escorts fit for duty, the Town Class ships accounted for approximately one-fifth of the total, enough margin of safety to help stave off Hitler's total domination of the North Atlantic shipping lanes. Their contribution, as near as could be measured, was roughly proportional to their numbers. Of the 27 submarines sunk by surface ships, former U.S. destroyers played a part in five.

The Royal Navy's judgments of their performance varied widely. Admiral of the Fleet Lord Toveny called them "the worst destroyers I had ever seen, poor seaboats with appalling armament and accommodation." Admiral of the Fleet Sir James Somerville said, however, that had these ships not been available, "the outcome of the struggle against the U-boats and the subsequent outcome of the European war itself might have been vastly different." Admiral of the Fleet Sir Philip Vian, himself a destroyer commander, delivered the most balanced verdict. Though the hand-me-downs were "tactically of the lowest order," he said, "their mere presence thrashing about in the water around the convoys afforded some sort of deterrent against the U-boat at a time when the escort forces we ourselves could provide were almost an *objet de rire*."

Just as the value of the destroyers to the British did not measure up to advance expectations, so did the usefulness of the bases fall far short of the ballyhooed claims made by supporters of the deal. To be sure, some cautionary voices were heard at the very beginning. After its initial outburst of enthusiasm, the *New York Times* soberly reminded its readers that "when planes and ships are insufficient in number or quality, bases cannot help much." While the destroyers-for-bases deal "is good publicity," Major General Henry H. "Hap" Arnold, commander of the U. S. Army Air Corps, told his fellow military chiefs a few days after the deal was announced, "it does not amount to nearly as much as it appeared, because the bases we have obtained are no good and will require millions of dollars for development."

Events would bear out Arnold's assessment. For that matter, the U.S.

had two other potential base sites of its own in the Caribbean, the neglect of which should have sent up a warning signal about the shortage of resources which would diminish the value of the much-heralded new coastal bastions. At Guantanamo Bay on Cuba, the state of the facilities reflected, according to an official Navy history, "the period of strict Naval economy between the wars, having been relegated to practically inactive status." Similarly on Puerto Rico, the total military establishment in September of 1939 consisted of one wireless station and one hydrographic station. By the fall of 1940 the Navy had contracted for construction of an airfield but had not even planned for any sort of naval base.

Meanwhile, though the Navy's patrol duties had increased, from Charleston to the Panama Canal it could not offer its ships a single drydock, nor, except for limited facilities at Guantanamo, any sites for repairs, fuel, and supplies. The Navy's struggles to fulfill expectations for the President's much-vaunted neutrality patrol illustrated its shortcomings. The scope of the proposed assignment flabbergasted the admirals. To patrol the designated area they would need 290 ships, equivalent to almost the entire U.S. fleet, and from 3,000 to 4,000 planes, about triple their total number of existing aircraft. They were told the President would settle for a "token" patrol.

The local conditions to which Roosevelt had alluded when he told Mackenzie King that the U.S. would not want the West Indies islands even as a gift posed another obstacle. Economic hard times, combined with racial tensions and political discord, had fostered widespread discontent and intermittent violence, and the colonial governments naturally viewed with anxiety any potentially aggravating new development. Having had little chance to consider the implications of the leases beforehand, they "made an effort afterward to assert what they felt were their rights," as the official army history put it. Consequently, as this account continues in a striking example of understatement, "it became evident that rapid progress could not in every case be expected." As squabbles developed between the U.S. military and the local officials about site selection and other matters, Americans complained that the British did not have "a clear picture" of the arrangement. For their part the British feared the Americans had in mind nothing less than a takeover of the British West Indies. Thus, the Bermuda House of Assembly, which had originally applauded the agreement, alerted King George VI that Bermudians were "deeply disturbed" that the development of the bases might affect Bermuda's status as part of the British Commonwealth.

With characteristic enthusiasm, Roosevelt personally plunged into the site selection process during a post-election vacation cruise in the Caribbean. After a brief inspection tour of some of the sites, he explained what he viewed as the underlying strategic theory behind the choice of bases. "It is obvious that the further you can keep a potential attack against the American continent from the continent . . . the safer it is for the continent," he said. "That means we want to be as far away as we can." As negotiations dragged on with the British, he chided the White House press corps "about the stuff, the awful nonsense being written about those bases." Site selection negotiations with the British had seriously bogged down only at Newfoundland, Trinidad, and the Bahamas, Roosevelt insisted in late December. But enough problems in enough places kept Churchill and the new U.S. ambassador John Winant from signing the final bases agreement until March of 1941, more than six months after the announcement of the trade.

The Navy put up its most significant installations on Bermuda, Trinidad, and Newfoundland at Argentia, using the other sites mainly as staging areas. But by the time these outposts were ready for action, the need for them had dissipated. In midsummer of 1940, with Britain seemingly on the verge of collapse, U.S. commanders had envisaged the new bases assuming a key role in the new Rainbow Four strategy, stressing hemisphere defense. By the spring of 1941, however, Britain's ability to hold off Hitler had transformed U.S. strategy so that it "now seemed to lie in buttressing Great Britain as the remaining bulwark against the military might and unprincipled leadership of Nazi Germany."

Not until after Pearl Harbor, when Hitler unleashed his submarine wolfpacks against American shipping, did the U.S. Atlantic coast again emerge as a strategic sector in the war. In this critical struggle the U.S. found most useful the base at Argentia on Newfoundland, on which it had spent $45 million. Planes flying out of Argentia scored the first two U.S. submarine kills of the war and provided extra protection for the lumbering Britain-bound convoys.

The Navy benefited less from its $35 million investment in Bermuda, which was largely bypassed by the struggle against the wolfpacks. Ships and planes based on Bermuda recorded only 24 attacks on submarines during 1942 and sank only a single U-boat. By contrast, as the official Naval history records, "U-boats showed their utmost insolence" around Trinidad, which guarded the Gulf of Paria, one of the region's most important routes of commerce. Despite its two army air fields and its massive naval installation, including four piers and twenty large ware-houses, Trinidad could dispatch only two converted yachts, two patrol craft, and four Catalina flying boats to battle the wolfpacks. Later the Navy assigned a 110-foot submarine chaser as the flagship of this ragtag fleet.

No wonder, then, that the subs prowled Trinidad's waters relatively immune from attack. They sent their first Allied ship to the bottom in February, right on the edge of the island's harbor, an ominous harbinger of future devastation. During June of 1942 German submarines sank more ships in the Caribbean, the Gulf of Mexico, and their approaches than they could claim the world over in any previous month. In November of that year, when the Allies lost twenty-five ships to subs in the bottom of the Caribbean, most went down within 300 miles of Trinidad. As a result the Trinidad forces spent more time picking up survivors of sunken ships than attacking the submarines that caused the damage.

With these depredations at their height, one of "Betty" Stark's admirals wrote the Chief of Naval Operations lamenting the loss of the destroyers traded to Britain, which presumably would otherwise be guarding against submarine attacks in U.S. coastal waters. Because of the trade with Britain, Stark replied, these ships have been combating subs for a year longer than they would have otherwise.

The full significance of the deal, however, could not be measured in tangible terms, as Churchill had pointed out to the War Cabinet, referring to the "long step" taken by the U.S. toward belligerency. The British were reluctant to stress this point too openly, given traditional American attitudes. "Tell people in England not to talk about an Anglo-American alliance," Lothian wrote Lady Astor. "That always means entanglement in Europe to the U.S.A. Strengthening the defence of both is a better line." Whether or not Americans understood the change in their position in the world, Churchill believed Hitler would recognize its import. "The effect of the proposal as a whole on Germany would be immense," he contended. And the members of the Cabinet, while resentful of the aggressive bargaining by the Yankees, also saw the transaction in a larger context, as "the first step in constituting an Anglo-Saxon bloc or indeed a decisive point in history."

As Churchill had anticipated, Berlin reached much the same conclusion. The impact was all the greater because this was a peril Hitler had foreseen many years before in *Mein Kampf*. In explaining the relentless German quest for *lebensraum*, he described most European states "like pyramids stood on their heads," because their area in Europe was "absurdly small in comparison to their weight in colonies, foreign trade, etc." By contrast, he pointed to the United States whose vast area on its own continent gave it "immense inner strength" and also provided a potential source of strength for Great Britain. "The position of England," Hitler wrote, "if only because of her linguistic and cultural bond with the American union can be compared with no other state in Europe." Now that Britain had taken advantage of her unique position, Germany would have to react. Earlier, Berlin had considered issuing an advance warning to the U.S. against the transaction. "We have as is known, so far accepted without opposition the numerous violations of neutrality by the American government," Secretary of State Ernst von Weizsäcker cabled the German chargé d'affaires Thomsen in Washington on August 8, after Pershing's speech seemed to rally support for the destroyer transfer. "But if the American government should now take serious steps to place naval vessels at the disposal of England, this would bring up the question of whether the American government should not be officially warned against such an action."

Thomsen strongly advised against the idea, contending that Roosevelt would not be able to get approval from Congress or from the Navy to turn over the destroyers to the British. Any negative statement from Berlin, he warned, could be used to whip up support in favor of a deal and thus do more harm than good.

The *Wilhelmstrasse* also considered filing a formal protest after the fact, charging a violation of neutrality, but instead fell back on the cautious course of merely minimizing the British benefit from the transaction. Following explicit instructions from propaganda minister Goebbels, the German press proclaimed that the British willingness to yield so much in the trade demonstrated the desperation of Hitler's last remaining foe. The official foreign office statement established the tone:

> For the first time since George Washington's war of liberation England is retreating in the Western Hemisphere. The United States is about to take over the power of hegemony, not with force this time but as an heir.

Echoing the party line, the *Hamburger Fremdenblatt* jeered: "In this deal, which stands alone in history, Great Britain with one stroke sacrifices every one of her strategic key points in the northern half of American history." But despite Berlin's *diktat*, the U.S. perfidy did not go entirely unmentioned. "A flagrant breach of neutrality," complained the *Deutsche Allgemeine Zeitung*, which asserted that the U.S. was taking advantage of the war to "overhaul Britain just as in the last war it took the chance of attaining parity with the Empire."

In their private deliberations, the leaders of the two Axis powers also saw the analogy with World War I all too clearly. "In Berlin a great deal of excitement and indignation," Count Galeazzo Ciano, Mussolini's son-in-law and Italy's foreign minister, recorded in his diary on September 4, the day after the trade was announced. "The Duce on the other hand says he is indifferent." In truth, Mussolini was keenly aware of the implications of this Anglo-American collaboration. Anticipating the consummation of the deal, he had issued a warning to Hitler the week before it was announced. Setting aside the possibility of some sudden change, which he acknowledged was always possible with an erratic people like the Americans, Mussolini wrote that direct U.S. intervention could confront Axis might on any day now.

The Germans had arrived at much the same conclusion, compelling a major change in their strategic thinking. Despite FDR's occasional bursts of bellicosity, as in the June 10 speech at Charlottesville, Hitler had believed that the U.S. would avoid direct involvement in the war, as long as there was no immediate threat to the Americas. Convinced that American war production would be hampered by labor stoppages and the like, he believed he could finish off Britain before the U.S. supplies could count for much. By September of 1940, though, he had realized that the British, thanks to Churchill and the Royal Air Force, were putting up a stiffer fight than he had anticipated, and that their resistance had encouraged the Americans to a boldness he had not foreseen.

Hitler's top naval commander, Grossadmiral Erich Raeder, underlined this new outlook in a meeting with the Führer and with General Alfred Jodl, Chief of Staff of the Armed Forces High Command, on September 6. They spent much of the session pondering difficulties confronting Operation Sealion or "Seelöwe," as the Germans dubbed the contemplated cross-Channel invasion. Already the Navy had begun minesweeping to prepare for troop landings, but bad weather had interfered. Raeder pointed to the great importance of air superiority, but in any event, he warned, "the crossing itself will be very difficult."

Turning to the Third Reich's other problems, Raeder called attention to the destroyer deal. This, he said, "represents an openly hostile act against Germany" and the prelude to "the closest cooperation between Britain and the U.S.A." The situation required "an examination of the possibilities for *active* participation in the war on the part of the U.S.A." and of the German response to that event.* One option, which Hitler considered "expedient and feasible" was for Germany to occupy the

*The emphasis is in the original.

Azores and the Canary Islands before the U.S. seized those outposts. Hitler's own comments were not recorded. But later on, in his lengthy declaration of war against the U.S., the Führer made a point of citing the destroyer deal in the course of a review of FDR's provocative conduct: "In September 1940 he [Roosevelt] draws still nearer to the war. He turns over to the British fleet fifty destroyers of the American Navy in return for . . . several British bases in North and South America."

Actually Hitler had already begun to pursue other and far more ambitious options. He had turned to the East, where for months Germany and Italy had been conducting off-again, on-again negotiations with their anti-Comintern pact partner Japan looking toward a broader treaty. Late in August, realizing that the destroyer deal was about to be concluded, Berlin resumed talks with Japan. Hitler's motives for a military alliance with the Japanese were twofold. Both reflected the new realities of the war in the West, shaped by Britain's surprisingly strong resistance and by the destroyer deal. By acquiring the militant Japanese as their ally, the Germans hoped mainly to force the U.S. to hesitate about extending its involvement in Europe. Hitler also saw a long-range benefit having to do with the Soviet Union. While Britain stubbornly clung to resistance, it might make sense for Hitler to eliminate once and for all the potential threat from his unlikely ally in Moscow. And if he attacked the Soviet Union, he wanted the Japanese on his side, and poised at Stalin's back.

This was the gist of Foreign Minister Von Ribbentrop's message when he arrived in Rome to break the news of the treaty with Japan to the Italians. "He thinks that such a move will have a double advantage against Russia and against America, which under the threat of the Japanese fleet will not dare to move," Foreign Minister Ciano recorded in his diary on September 19. But Ciano disagreed in part. "The anti-Russian guarantee is very good," he told his German counterpart. "But the anti-American statement is less appropriate, because Washington will increasingly favor the English."

The destroyer deal had also obliged the Japanese to revise their strategic thinking, particularly about a possible alliance with Germany. Earlier that summer, the Japanese could see no need or advantage to such a connection. After Hitler had ground the military might of the Western democracies in the dust, the Japanese saw the world situation presenting "a golden opportunity," for fulfillment of her own ambitions in Asia. "The German victories have gone to their heads like strong wine," Ambassador Joseph Grew had reported to the State Department. The French and Dutch were left too weak by the defeats to

defend their own possessions in Asia, and the beleaguered British hardly seemed able to stand in Tokyo's way. What the Empire of the Rising
Sun wanted in Asia it could take for itself, or so it seemed.

Moreover, the Japanese had cause to be wary of involvement with
Germany. Such a connection, they feared, would antagonize the U.S.,
perhaps triggering a confrontation they did not yet want. Also, the
Japanese had learned not to depend on Hitler. The German Soviet
nonaggression pact of 1939 which stunned the whole world had special
and painful impact for Tokyo. Germany along with Italy and Japan had
signed the 1936 anti-Comintern pact which aimed at combating the
spread of communism, a purpose contradicted by Hitler's rapproche-
ment with Moscow. Not only that, but the pact signed in Berlin in
August 1939 came just as the Japanese were suffering a humiliating
defeat at the hands of the Red Army in border fighting in Mongolia.
This betrayal by Hitler and the surprising strength shown by Stalin suggested to the Japanese, who had joined the Allies in World War I, that
they might be well advised to watch World War II from the sidelines.

Additionally, it was by no means clear that Hitler was ready to give
the Japanese a free hand in Asia because of Germany's own interests in
the region and his desire to stay on good terms with the Soviet Union,
which would naturally be threatened by any sign of Japanese aggression.
For example, in March 1940 when Mussolini, eager to placate Tokyo,
recognized the new Chinese puppet government installed in Nanking
by the Japanese under Wang Ching-Wei, a long-time Chiang Kai Shek
rival, Hitler objected out of concern for the reaction of the Soviets.

Then came the RAF's strong showing in the Battle of Britain and the
destroyer deal. The Japanese could no longer count on a quick German
victory causing the coveted Dutch and French possessions to fall into
their laps. German recognition of Japan's sweeping agenda for Asian
conquest coupled with warnings that the U.S. and Britain might
arrange another similar trade for U.S. warships, this time involving
bases in the Pacific, both found a susceptible audience in the army-
dominated government in Tokyo. The newspaper *Asahi* saw additional
reason for anxiety in Churchill's reassurance to the U.S. that the Royal
Navy would not be surrendered or scuttled. In Japanese minds, this
raised the possibility that in the event of a British defeat their fleet
would be sent to Singapore, where it would menace Japan's hopes of
expansion. "It is now obvious that the United States, having completed
defense of its front door, will consolidate the defense of its backdoor on
the Pacific," *Asahi* concluded. "Together with America's huge naval
program this must arouse our deepest concern."

In both Berlin and Tokyo the reasons to stand apart had been replaced by powerful incentives for combining forces. On September 27, 1940, German, Italy, and Japan signed the Tripartite Pact in Berlin. Although government officials celebrated in Hitler's capital, Ciano, on hand as Italy's representative, was uneasy. "Even the Berlin street crowd, a comparatively small one, composed mostly of school children, cheers with regularity but without conviction," he wrote in his diary. "Japan is far away. Its help is doubtful. One thing is certain: that the war will be long."

The treaty was brief and succinct. Its main clauses granted Japan dominance in "Greater East Asia," and recognized Germany and Italy as the leaders of a "New Order" in Europe. The three powers pledged to come to each other's aid if either of them were attacked "by a power at present not involved in the European War or the Sino-Japanese Conflict." Since the agreement specifically stated that the pact did not affect relations with the Soviet Union, that left only one country to which this ominous provision could be relevant. The treaty was a dagger aimed at the United States. Fifteen months after the pact was signed, Hitler's new ally drove the blade home at Pearl Harbor.

# Breach of Trust

"That destroyer arrangement seems to have worked out perfectly," Roosevelt wrote King George VI, two weeks after his reelection to a third term. "There is virtually no criticism in this country except from legalists who think it should have been submitted to the Congress first. If I had done that, the subject would still be in the tender care of the Committees of the Congress!"

The letter, with its cavalier view of the law, reflected the devotion to political expediency which, from start to finish, informed Roosevelt's management of the destroyer deal. At each critical step along the convoluted path to consummation, nearly everyone involved always held the end to justify whatever means came to hand. No one can accurately measure how much the trade contributed to Great Britain's ability to resist its foes and to the ultimate victory over the Axis. But whatever the benefit, a high price was paid in undermining the rule of law.

The "legalists" whom Roosevelt so readily dismissed found the precedents cited in Attorney General Jackson's opinion defending the deal too shaky to support the broad claims that he advanced for executive power. "The destroyers have by now been transferred," wrote Cornell University's Herbert W. Briggs, an editor of the *Journal of International Law*. "But let no one say that it was accomplished legally."

Jackson relied heavily on the Supreme Court's 1936 ruling in *U.S. v. Curtiss-Wright*, upholding Roosevelt's authority to prevent arms sales to two warring South American countries. This opinion, however, included the caveat that the President's power in foreign affairs "must be exercised in subordination to the applicable provisions of the Constitution." In any event the *Curtiss-Wright* case pertained to the presidential exercise of power delegated to him by joint resolution of Congress, unlike the destroyer deal in which Congress had not acted at all nor even been consulted. Beyond all this, as Edwin Borchard, a Yale specialist in international law, wrote: "There are constitutional understandings which require that agreements of great importance, particularly involving the question of war and peace, shall not be concluded by executive power alone."

Jackson was also accused of misreading the two key statutes standing in the way of the deal—the espionage act of 1917 and the Walsh amendment. The Attorney General interpreted the espionage act's prohibition on sending warships from the U.S. to a warring power to apply only to ships that had initially been built for service with that country. But the statute had been drafted by the Department of Justice to bring the U.S. criminal code into conformity with accepted provisions of international law, which explicitly banned the *sending out* of a warship to a foreign power, not the *building* for a foreign power.[*]

Similarly, Jackson also adopted a conveniently narrow view of the Walsh amendment's restrictions on the transfer of military material. Initially, the amendment had required certification that the material was not only "not essential," but also "cannot be used" for the national defense. The elimination of the phrase "cannot be used," the Attorney General asserted, showed Walsh's willingness to allow his amendment to be given a flexible interpretation. But if Walsh wanted to accomplish anything at all with his amendment, it was to prevent the Navy giving up any of its ships. Walsh made the change in language, as the Senate record showed, only so as not to interfere with the transfer of surplus planes, rifles and the like—not ships. He later remarked that his Committee had put in the bill "every conceivable precaution against the limitation or reduction in the size of our Navy."

When these dubious statutes and precedents were set aside, Jackson's case rested almost entirely on the President's role as Commander in Chief, about which the Constitution is notably vague, and on his even more elliptically defined power in foreign relations. In a lengthy letter to the *New York Times*, the eminent political scientist Edward S. Corwin pointed out that Jackson's opinion overrode the power specifically delegated to Congress to dispose of government property, in this case, the fifty destroyers, with the hazy authority claimed for the President. To take that argument to its logical conclusion, Corwin asked: "Why may not any and all of Congress's specifically delegated powers be set aside by the President's 'executive power' and the country be put on a totalitarian basis without further ado?" Corwin,

---

*The two provisions are the Treaty of Washington of 1871, under which the U.S. was awarded $15.5 million from the British for damage down by the British-built Confederate raider Alabama, and Article VIII of Hague Convention XIII of 1907 (Briggs at page 576).

who had served as a consultant to Jackson's predecessor, Homer Cummings, concluded: "No such dangerous opinion was ever before penned by an Attorney General of the United States."

In addition to exceeding his powers by neglecting to seek congressional approval and transgressing on congressional authority, the critics charged that Roosevelt did not meet the most fundamental obligation imposed upon a Chief Executive by the Constitution, "to take care that the laws be faithfully executed." To the contrary, as a latter-day critic, Democratic Senator Daniel Patrick Moynihan of New York, argued in his book, *On the Law of Nations*, Roosevelt, "actually subverted the law" and "was clearly subject to impeachment."

But nothing of the sort happened. Instead, Congress ultimately approved appropriations for building the bases leased from the British. Despite some fierce huffing and puffing by isolationists, the most serious form of reprisal they advocated was an investigation of the "propaganda engine" which had foisted the destroyer deal on the country. The explanation for this behavior was certainly understood by Roosevelt and had been forecast beforehand by Acting Solicitor General Townsend: It was politics, not law, that determined the destroyer deal's reception. "If the great weight of public opinion favors the release and sale of over-age destroyers to the British government," Townsend had predicted, "a construction of the statutes permitting this to be done, even though somewhat legalistic, will receive general public endorsement, and should it reach the Courts will, I think, be approved by them."

The flaw in the President's conduct is not that he took political considerations into account, but rather in the values and goals from which he derived his politics. Just as the Constitution and the federal laws govern the president's exercise of his power as Chief Executive, an implicit social contract establishes the standard for judging his behavior as a politician. Voters bestow upon a president vast authority over decisions that will control their lives. They must wait four years to render judgment on his performance. The system's success depends on the extent to which voters can trust the president during this interval to deal with the choices before the country openly and candidly. In implementing the destroyer deal, Roosevelt followed a pattern of manipulation and concealment that breached that trust.

To avoid being held accountable, he relied whenever he could on proxies, at the cost of delay and confusion. He maneuvered Willkie into a corner, leaving him to deal with William Allen White, who had no official role in the Roosevelt Administration and no authority to speak for it. He arranged for Ambassador Lothian to negotiate with three different officials, Hull, Knox, and Welles, each of whom had a different agenda.

The President inhibited informed public discussion of the deal by prevailing upon Willkie to refrain from criticism and by publicly denying any linkage between negotiations for bases and the destroyer deal. In his presentation of the completed transaction he contrived to have the idea of aid to Britain seem to have been all but subsumed by the British assurances about their fleet and their grant of bases, both political feathers in his cap.

But the promise about the fleet was of dubious value since, as Churchill had pointed out, whatever agreement he might make would not be binding on his successor at 10 Downing Street. As Halifax remarked about Roosevelt's relentless pressure about the fleet: "It is indeed most unfortunate that the Administration should not have tackled the question in a different way, i.e., by explaining to their people that there was no chance of any substantial portion of the British fleet ever reaching American shores, that if we were defeated U.S.A. were bound to be Hitler's next victim, and that their best chance was therefore to help us now."

As for the bases, by emphasizing their acquisition as "a far-reaching act of preparation for continental defense" while scarcely mentioning the destroyers, the President helped to carry out the greatest deception of all: concealing from the public the extent to which the destroyer deal set the U.S. on the road to war. According to Breckinridge Long's contemporary account, the President saw much greater danger from the transaction than he let on to the public. "Germany may take violent exception to it and declare war on us," Long wrote in his diary on August 31, three days before the deal was announced, after talking with Secretary of State Hull. "Cordell realizes that—specifically said he did, and says the President does, too."

Long after the Japanese attack on Pearl Harbor brought an end to America's uneasy peace between the wars, Roosevelt's critics continuously accused him of misleading the nation near the climax of the 1940 presidential campaign by promising American mothers and fathers that "Your boys are not going to be sent into any foreign wars." More than ten years later, Sam Rosenman, who had helped to write the speech that contained that pledge, cited the destroyer deal in the president's defense:

> The President did many drastic things after the election to meet dangers from abroad; but none was more drastic in intent than the exchange

*before the election* of United States destroyers for British bases.* The people who voted for him in November 1940 had been fully informed by this act alone—in addition to all he had said and done before—just how far he was prepared to go to make ready to repel any attack."

But the question was not how far FDR was prepared to go to repel attack. Americans understood that if the United States was attacked the Commander-in-Chief would order the armed forces to strike back. The more pertinent question about the destroyer deal and Roosevelt's other actions was the extent to which they created circumstances in which attack became inevitable. And this was an issue which the President dealt with through evasion and obfuscation.

Roosevelt's conduct of the destroyer trade reflected the increasing personalization of his presidency, harking back to his 1936 reelection campaign, at the outset of which he had told Raymond Moley: "There is one issue in this campaign, it's myself." Increasingly frustrated by the political system, lacking the patience to construct alliances, and without the intellectual discipline to formulate a meaningful framework for his policies, the President increasingly relied on the force of his personality. More and more he made guile and secrecy the favored weapons in his political arsenal. His disregard for the checks on his authority in the destroyer deal was of a piece with his early offers to the British to mount blockades against the Japanese and the Germans in violation of international law, and in the absence of congressional sanction.

Moreover, despite his lighthearted shrugging off of his critics in his letter to King George, evidence from his own lips suggests that Roosevelt understood the gravity of his conduct. As noted previously, in the fall of 1938 when he told British Ambassador Lindsay of his plan circumvent the neutrality act's ban on selling arms to belligerents so that he could ship arms to the allies, the President cautioned the diplomat that if word of his scheme leaked out "he would almost certainly be impeached." Two years later, on the eve of announcing the destroyers-for-bases trade, he again mentioned, this time to Bernard Baruch, his concern about impeachment. Even allowing for a certain measure of characteristic over-dramatization, it is clear the President himself felt his behavior contravened the standards to which he publicly paid allegiance.

In the aftermath of the destroyer deal, emboldened by its approval

*The emphasis is in the original.

and his own reelection, Roosevelt at times addressed the issue of aid to Britain more forthrightly. In one of his most memorable phrases, in December of 1940, he proclaimed the U.S. to be "the arsenal of democracy" and declared that the country confronted "an emergency as serious as war itself." Responding to yet another desperate appeal from Churchill, this one for financial help, Roosevelt conceived of and pushed through Congress the Lend-Lease program, allowing Britain to get billions of dollars' worth of arms without having to put up the cash it no longer had. To simplify the scheme, the President borrowed a metaphor Ickes had used on behalf of the destroyer deal, saying it amounted to nothing more than lending a garden hose to help put out a neighbor's fire before it spread. Lend-Lease in effect repealed the Neutrality Act's requirement for cash payments, although the prohibition on U.S. ships carrying arms abroad remained in force.

For the most part, though, the President continued to follow his long-established pattern of calculated ambiguity. As the U.S. commitment to Britain expanded, Roosevelt tried to ease concerns of other neutral nations, particularly in the Western Hemisphere. Among the U.S.'s "good neighbors" he tried to forge a united front against the Axis in the face of still smoldering resentment of past strong-arm Yankee diplomacy. Assigned to reassure the Latin Americans, Attorney General Jackson redefined international law to fit U.S. policy. Addressing the Inter-American Bar Association in Havana in March, Jackson acknowledged that "weighty names and even heavier texts" had been mustered to contend that international law prohibited the destroyer trade and other U.S. aid to Britain. Jackson also conceded that nineteenth-century rules, which demanded impartial behavior by a neutral, lent credence to this criticism. But these rules, Jackson argued, had been "superseded" by events since World War I. The Attorney General contended that the modern version of international law embodied in the covenant of the League of Nations not only allowed but actually obligated neutral nations to engage in "active discrimination" against aggressor nations while providing "active assistance" to their victims.

All of what Jackson had to say, the *Hartford Courant* observed, could have been condensed into two sentences: "The United States holds the Axis to be the aggressor in the present war. We will do whatever we can to defeat it, regardless of accepted principles of international law." The *Courant* added: "We might as well face the fact frankly rather than attempt to create new legal principles to fit our convenience."

Frankness was not a luxury the President felt he could afford, even as he steered the country closer to war. In the spring, he ordered U.S.

troops to occupy Greenland, using the newly leased base on New-foundland as a staging area, and extended the so-called neutrality zone patrolled by American ships far out into the Atlantic. In July he deployed the Marines to Iceland, replacing British troops, and informing Congress after the decision was made.

To Ickes, who joined Roosevelt for a fishing trip off the Florida coast in March, the President seemed spoiling for a fight. "Things are coming to a head," Roosevelt told his guest at dinner one night. "Germany will blunder soon." Ickes had no doubt of Roosevelt's "scarcely concealed desire" for a submarine attack or some other incident that would allow the U.S. to declare war against Germany or at least to convoy merchant ships on their way to Britain.

Yet through the spring Roosevelt resisted pressure from the British and from the hawks in his own cabinet—chiefly Stimson and Knox—to have the U.S. Navy convoy British merchant ships across the submarine-ridden Atlantic, believing that Congress would reject any such proposal. In midsummer, with the law makers embroiled in a fierce battle whether to renew the 1940 selective service law which was due to expire in October, Stimson and Marshall had to prod Roosevelt into publicly endorsing an extension. Even then, and despite the challenge to an essential pillar of his defense policy, Roosevelt shied away from speaking directly to the country. He settled instead for a message to Congress in which he warned that a failure to extend the law would lead to "disintegration" of the Army. In August Congress approved an eighteen-month extension, but the margin of victory in the House was only one vote. Not until late in the fall of 1941 after German torpedoes had battered one U.S. destroyer, the *Kearny*, and sunk another, the *Reuben James*, with heavy loss of life, did Roosevelt ask Congress to amend the Neutrality Act to permit the arming of U.S. merchantmen. The change went through only three weeks before Pearl Harbor.

In the midst of the destroyer negotiations in the summer of 1940, Roosevelt had told Lothian he thought it "probable" the U.S. would enter the war. As the months passed, that belief seemed to grow firmer. By late October of 1941, according to Sam Rosenman, the President "was convinced that American entry into the war was almost unavoidable." Many Americans felt the same way, judging by some of the President's mail, which was turned over to Sam Rosenman for speech-writing fodder. Typical was the letter from a St. Louis banker urging the President to tell Americans "the whole truth about the terribly dangerous situation we are in." The letter added: "Tell them now. Lead us. We will follow you as we always follow you."

Of course, as Roosevelt realized, plenty of Americans bittterly disagreed with that view and he was unwilling to test their strength. In an open letter to the President in late October, Robert E. Wood, head of the America First Committee, which had emerged as the most powerful group battling aid to Britain, challenged him to ask Congress for a declaration of war. Wood candidly stated that America First would fight against the resolution and, he believed, help defeat it. He hoped to end Roosevelt's policy of "subterfuge," as Wood called it, by daring Roosevelt to draw the issue between war and peace. If Congress voted to declare war, Wood pledged that America First "and all other patriotic Americans would respect that decision." Stimson, Ickes, and the other hawks in the Administration wanted Roosevelt to take up Wood's challenge, believing that the President could rally the public on his side. Persuaded otherwise, Roosevelt did not even answer the letter.

"The very fact that such a demand now came from an important spokesman for isolationism," Sherwood wrote later, "provided Roosevelt with sufficient confirmation of his conviction that, were he to do this, he would meet with certain and disastrous defeat." This was a remarkable judgment from a man who had three times been elected to the presidency, and who was considered one of the most effective molders of public opinion the nation had ever seen.

What accounted for the President's unwillingness to match his power, prestige and skill against the forces of isolationism? One reason stemmed from his difficulties with Congress, due not only to the Madisonian checks and balances built into the system but also to the personal antagonism against Roosevelt which had mounted, during two terms, in both parties. General Marshall, called upon to shepherd military appropriations legislation through Capitol Hill in the frantic spring of 1940, found Republicans willing to help him because they could tell their constituents they were following his advice, not Roosevelt's. "He had such enemies that otherwise members of Congress didn't dare, it seemed, to line up with him," Marshall later recalled. "And that was true of certain Democrats who were getting pretty bitter."

Indeed party discipline, never enforced vigorously in the U.S. Congress, seemed to be crumbling completely. On the critical vote to extend selective service, members of Roosevelt's own party cast 64 of the 202 opposition votes. A variety of motives inspired the balky lawmakers in both parties. Some, like Democratic Senator Walsh of Massachusetts, were fiercely protective of their particular interests and constituencies. Probably more numerous were those like Willkie's running mate, Republican Senator Charles McNary, who, by promising

Roosevelt he would not object to the destroyer deal if the President bypassed Congress, hoped mainly to avoid political injury.

Another reason for Roosevelt's reluctance to be more forthcoming with the public about the likelihood of war was the supposedly irresistible strength of isolationist sentiment. However powerful this attitude was, Roosevelt had to be held responsible for contributing to it by his unwillingness to challenge it. Thus, in seeking revision of the Neutrality Act and repeal of the arms embargo in the fall of 1939, the President decided to rest his case on the misleading claim that his proposals would keep the nation out of war. If, instead, he had chosen to make the argument that repealing the embargo would help Britain and France and thus strengthen the security of the U.S., he not only would have been more honest, he would also have helped to pave the way for future assistance to the Allies. Afterward Cordell Hull argued that even though he and Roosevelt realized that a German victory over Britain and France would leave the U.S. in "utmost danger," they also believed that "with isolationism still powerful and militant in the U.S. it would have been the peak of folly to make aid to the democracies an issue in connection with neutrality legislation." Herbert Agar, a Roosevelt admirer and sometime confidante, observed: "It seems a pity to say that the peak of folly would have been to tell the truth." Roosevelt assumed, he noted, that "an uproar would have been the price of truth telling. Such an assumption raises questions about the durability of democracy."

But what FDR's behavior called into question was not the quality of democracy, but the quality of Roosevelt's leadership, which much of the time made the avoidance of "an uproar" its supreme objective. His zeal to suppress disagreement often led him to conceal realities because they were bound to be disturbing. "My problem," Roosevelt had explained to William Allen White in December of 1939, "is to get the American people to think of conceivable consequences without scaring the American people into thinking that they are going to be dragged into this war." The "one thing we don't want to do," is to "frighten the American people at this time or any time," Roosevelt confided to the senate Military Affairs Committee in early 1939.

Roosevelt's passion for secrecy and distaste for public debate inhibited him from using the White House's bully pulpit to full advantage. Polling data suggest that in his prolonged competition with the isolationists, the President had more strength than he realized, or was willing to use. Thus, during the debate over revision of the neutrality law in September of 1939, opinion favoring the Administration's proposal for repeal and for sending war material to the Allies jumped sharply following the President's speech on the subject on September 21, innocuous as that address was. But Roosevelt's rhetoric served only as "a temporary hypodermic," a contemporary analysis of the data in *Public Opinion Quarterly* concluded. His support faded when he failed to follow up.

Even in the summer of 1940, when Hitler's stunning conquests shocked Americans into the awareness of the dangers they faced abroad, Roosevelt remained cautious. As the General Staff met to consider how much it would cost to ready their troops for the crisis that was already upon them, word went out from the White House that the President wanted a $4 billion ceiling on Army appropriations for the next fiscal year. "I can sell the American people a bargain for $3,999,900,000, a lot more easily than one for $4,000,000,000." Sure enough, the Army's request for $5.8 billion was pared back to $3.9 billion.

The President staged a similar retreat in May of 1941, after a powerful speech explaining his decision to extend the range of the Navy's neutrality patrol to a point half way across the Atlantic. Pledging "every possible assistance to Britain," he added: "All additional measures necessary to deliver the goods will be taken." He declared "an unlimited national emergency" which required, he said, "the strengthening of our defense to the extreme limit of our national power and authority."

Afterward Roosevelt invited Robert Sherwood, who had drafted the speech, and his guest that evening, Irving Berlin, to the Monroe Room on the second floor of the White House, where he insisted that Berlin play and sing "Alexander's Ragtime Band," and many other of his hits. Still later, when Sherwood went to Roosevelt's bedroom to bid him good night, he found him sitting in bed surrounded with what seemed Sherwood to be a thousand telegrams. "They're ninety-five percent favorable!" Roosevelt exclaimed. "And I figured I'd be lucky to get an even break on this speech." Just as favorable, Sherwood noted, was the response of the press.

Yet at his press conference the next day, to Sherwood's astonishment and dismay, Roosevelt retreated. He dismissed any notion of ordering the Navy to convoy merchant ships or asking Congress to change the neutrality law. Hopkins, who supposedly knew Roosevelt as well as anyone, could not account "for this sudden reversal from a position of strength to one of apparently insouciant weakness." Sherwood blamed the backtracking on the "long and savage campaign" waged against the President by isolationists, even though their tactics "had failed to blind American public opinion." Having gained public approbation, Roosevelt was content to rest on his laurels, rather than exploit his advantage and run the risk of clashing with the isolationists.

His determination to avoid "scaring the people," as he had termed it to William Allen White, inhibited the President from spurring the pace of the military buildup. In 1940, he had cut the Army's budget request by one-third, to make it easier for him "to sell to the American people" as "a bargain." Later that summer he heard General Powell complain to him about troops using broom sticks and drain pipes in place of machine guns and mortars. Still the President was reluctant to sound the alarm that would have helped to speed defense production. In the spring of 1941 as the country moved closer to war, Detroit was turning out new cars at a record rate, consuming scarce materials that could have been used for tanks and planes. But when some in the Administration's defense program called for cutbacks in auto production, the manufacturers resisted. Eleanor Roosevelt mildly suggested that Americans "begin thinking" about doing without new cars. Roosevelt himself said nothing on the issue, either to the public, or to the auto industry.

Roosevelt's gravest sin as a leader was not that he was too political but that he lacked the courage to use his political skills to promote his own convictions. "He ought not to have done it," Daniel Moynihan writes of the President's flouting of the law to carry out the destroyer deal. "He probably could have gotten the law changed."

But this was not Roosevelt's way. As Ben Cohen put it approvingly in a retrospective look at FDR's leadership style, Roosevelt "instinctively refrained from committing himself definitely or completely to a specific course of action, whether it was executive action, national legislation or international engagement until he had some idea of the support he might expect or the strength of the opposition he might encounter."

Henry Stimson saw this trait differently from Cohen. He could not help comparing Franklin Roosevelt with his cousin Theodore who had first brought Stimson into public service. As McGeorge Bundy describes Stimson's thinking:

> From what he knew of both men, he was forced to believe that in the crisis of 1941 T.R. would have done a better and more clean cut job than was actually done. . . . Franklin Roosevelt was not made that way. With unequaled political skill he could pave the way for any given specific step, but in so doing he was likely to tie his own hands for the future, using honeyed and consoling words that would return to plague him later.

In critiquing the destroyer deal, Professor Corwin urged the President to concede that he was standing on dubious constitutional ground and

suggested that he ask the Congress to ratify the transaction *post facto*.
In that way, not only would the President "largely atone for his ill-con-
sidered procedure," Corwin contended, but he would also forestall "its
furnishing justification for future acts of a similar or even more extreme
character."

Roosevelt of course did no such thing, for the same reasons he did not
seek congressional authorization in advance. He wanted no part of a
procedure that would inevitably raise questions he did not want to
answer, both about the origins of the destroyer deal and its implications.

The country stood to benefit from a full-scale debate in Congress
over the destroyer deal, however. A discussion could have shed light on
such questions as the value of the much-vaunted British bases, the
resources the U.S. Navy would need to develop them, and the expected
reaction of the Axis powers. The answers would have furnished
Congress and the public with a clearer understanding of their choices,
as the President walked a tightrope between war and peace.

As for the problems created by the expansion of his authority,
Roosevelt preferred to leave their solution until after the war was over.
"When the war is won," he promised in a speech given in 1942, "the
powers under which I act automatically revert to the people of the
United States—the people to whom those powers belong."

Yet that is not what happened. Instead, all through what John
Kennedy called "the long twilight struggle" that was the sequel to
World War II, the reach of the presidency lengthened and broadened.
After a harrowing examination of the Iran–Contra scandal, which
shocked the nation nearly half a century after the destroyers-for-bases
deal, the historian Theodore Draper warned that a "a long process of
presidential aggrandizement, congressional fecklessness and judicial
connivance . . . had put the constitution in danger by fostering the concept of nearly total presidential domination of foreign policy."

Roosevelt was certainly not the first such presidential offender. The
custom of chief executives enlarging their authority in foreign policy
could be traced at least as far back as Jefferson's purchase of Louisiana,
a transaction Roosevelt himself was quick to cite as precedent for his
own conduct.

Over the years, when opportunity presented itself, other presidents
readily fell into the same freewheeling pattern, among them the first
Roosevelt in the White House. Long after he had disregarded traditional congressional prerogatives in creating the Panama Canal, TR defended himself with reasoning strikingly similar to President Franklin
Roosevelt's comments to King George about the destroyer deal:

If I had acted strictly according to precedent I should have turned the whole matter over to Congress. In which case Congress would be debating it at this moment, and that Canal would be fifty years in the future."

But Roosevelt's destroyer deal marked a watershed in the use and abuse of presidential power, foreshadowing a series of dangerous and often disastrous adventures abroad. After expanding presidential power to forge the New Deal's domestic reforms, Roosevelt demonstrated how this same power could also be used to work his will abroad. Just as importantly, the destroyer deal eliminated isolationism and thrust the U.S. forward in the world to a position of unrivaled responsibility and influence, and also, as Roosevelt's successors often pointed out, alarming vulnerability.

In announcing the destroyer deal, Roosevelt described it as an act of defense taken "in the face of grave danger." Four months later, in his annual message to Congress, he declared the moment to be "unprecedented in American history," because, he averred, "at no previous time has American security been as seriously threatened from without as it is today." This alarm would be sounded again and again by chief executives over the next half century as they defended their exercise of power, often with only dubious legal or constitutional sanction, without congressional approval, and with little or no public debate.

Just as FDR negotiated with the British with one eye on the campaign calendar, his successors have been attentive to their own political agendas. Just as Ben Cohen and Robert Jackson found a way around the law for Roosevelt, more recent presidents imaginatively created legal rationales for their own conduct. They also have been aided and abetted, like Roosevelt, by the passive compliance of Congress. Moreover, history being cumulative, each of these episodes has served as a precedent for the next.

Particularly noteworthy is the tendency of postwar Presidents to draw on the prewar experiences of Roosevelt as a basis for action in very different circumstances. "The fateful events of the nineteen-thirties, when aggression unopposed bred more aggression and eventually war, were fresh in our memory," President Harry Truman told Congress, in defending his decision to intervene after war broke out between North and South Korea. Relying on this recollection, Roosevelt's immediate successor presented the country with the specter of an attack instigated by the Soviet Union, bent on world conquest. That judgment was open to question. But with Republicans savaging him for being "soft" on communism, and for "losing China"

Truman knew his own prestige was at stake and could not afford to seem passive in the face of aggression. As Truman historian Robert Donovan wrote: "Vicious domestic political repercussions, damaging to the President, would have been inevitable if the 'loss' of China were to be followed by the 'loss' of Korea."

Without asking either the advice or approval of the Congress, Truman committed the United States to the defense of South Korea, claiming that he was fulfilling U.S. obligations under the U.N. Charter. In fact, the U.S. was not legally obligated; the U.N. had only "recommended" that member states give help to the South Koreans.*

A State Department memorandum listing 87 instances in which Truman's predecessors had ordered U.S. forces into battle without congressional sanction furnished additional justification. But most were brief, minor episodes aimed at protecting American lives and property, from pirates and the like. None compared to Korea, for which nearly 6 million Americans were mobilized for more than three years of fighting costing more than 130,000 casualties, the fourth bloodiest war in U.S. history until Vietnam.

Congress would probably have approved Truman's actions, just as it probably would have endorsed FDR's destroyer deal. But like his predecessor Truman had reasons for bypassing Congress. On Capitol Hill the Korean issue likely would have touched off an embarrassing debate on his Administration's past actions and utterances, such as Secretary of State Dean Acheson's statement excluding South Korea from the list of nations whose frontiers the U.S. felt bound to defend. It also would lead to questions about Truman's ultimate goals in intervention, and what price he would pay to achieve them, inquiries which Truman would much rather have avoided since he had not fully considered them himself. Because he failed to set out U.S. objectives in Korea, and rally the public behind them, Truman was forced to bear alone the political burden of fighting a frustrating conflict that stirred massive discontent at home and wrecked hopes for domestic reform and progress.

In 1958 when President Dwight Eisenhower dispatched 15,000 Marines to Lebanon in the midst of civil unrest he saw no need for approval from Congress, whose leaders were notably unenthusiastic when he informed them of his intentions. He cited no authority beyond his own as Commander in Chief, the same authority that Attorney General Jackson asserted not only empowered but also obligated the

*The U.N. Charter stipulates that special agreements must be negotiated with individual nations before they can be required to send forces.

President to act to preserve national security. "The issue was clear to me," Eisenhower said later, in words emblematic of the post-Roosevelt presidency. "We had to go in." To drown out criticism, Eisenhower rang the by now familiar Klaxons of the Cold War. He warned that "tiny Lebanon" was ripe for Communist takeover and compared its vulnerability to Greece, Czechoslovakia, and China. In reality, though, the unrest in Lebanon threatened neither its government nor the interests of the U.S. No shots were fired and the Marines, with little to do, withdrew after four months. Apparently Eisenhower intended mainly to deter Egyptian leader Nasser from fomenting trouble in the Mideast by demonstrating U.S. willingness to commit its forces in the region. Ike had a political motive, too: He wanted to rebut Democratic criticism that the U.S. defense establishment was top heavy with strategic weapons and lacking in the flexibility to wage brushfire wars. At any rate the expedition exacerbated resentment of the U.S. throughout the Arab world.

The Cuban missile confrontation in October of 1962 represented the ultimate in the unilateral exercise of presidential power, since it brought the U.S. not merely to the brink of war but to the edge of nuclear holocaust without so much as a gesture in the direction of Congress. In ordering the Navy to blockade Cuba, President John Kennedy made a point of calling his action a "quarantine," a term he believed had been legitimized by FDR. At any rate Kennedy did not even attempt to propound a legal rationale, relying instead on what he depicted as the graveness of the danger. He described the missiles as "an explicit threat to the peace and security of all the Americas," though of course the U.S. all along had been in danger from Soviet missiles sited elsewhere.

By themselves the placement of Soviet missiles in Cuba "did not substantially alter the strategic balance *in fact*. . . . But that balance would have been altered *in appearance*," as Theodore Sorensen acknowledged.[*] Appearances mattered greatly in the political arena, where the Republicans had proclaimed Cuba the dominant issue of the 1962 campaign; they warned that with Soviet help, Castro was staging a dangerous military buildup, a contention that Kennedy denied. When the evidence showed the Republicans to be right, Kennedy feared an election day disaster. More fundamentally, Kennedy worried that if he failed to act, then his ability to govern, certainly to have his words taken seriously on national security, would have been permanently crippled.

The crisis ended in peace and triumph for Kennedy thanks to Soviet leader Khrushchev's irresolution and to good fortune. Dean Acheson,

---

*The emphasis is in the original.

one of the small circle of advisers consulted by Kennedy during the crisis, congratulated him on his "firmness and judgment." But he thought
the President had been reckless and offered this verdict in private:
"Plain dumb luck."

The conclusion to the Cuban missile crisis contrasted with the consequences of Kennedy's decision to expand U.S. involvement in
Vietnam. These were only beginning to emerge when Lyndon Johnson
succeeded to the presidency.

As with Harry Truman and Korea, President Lyndon Johnson's
approach to Vietnam was greatly influenced by his interpretation of
Franklin Roosevelt's experience in the 1930s. "Our policy in Vietnam . . .
springs from every lesson that we have learned in this century," he
declared in an address in Chicago, the same city where, as he recalled,
Roosevelt had delivered his celebrated call to quarantine the aggressors. "The country heard him but did not listen," he said. "And then we
saw what happened when the aggressors felt confident that they could
win while we sat by."

Unfortunately Johnson, a Roosevelt protégé, took the wrong lesson
from the quarantine speech. It was not the country that let Roosevelt
down, it was his own political courage that failed. Johnson had fears of
his own, mostly for his cherished Great Society programs. "I knew from
the start," Johnson would say later, "that if I left the woman I really
loved—the Great Society—in order to get involved with that bitch of a
war on the other side of the world, then I would lose everything at
home." But Johnson was equally convinced that if he abandoned the
anti-Communist cause in Indochina the Great Society would be
doomed, because its progenitor would lose credibility.

Torn by this political dilemma, Johnson smothered debate. He exploit-
ed the murky circumstances of the Tonkin Gulf episode in the summer of
1964 to stampede Congress into adopting a resolution approving "the
determination of the President . . . to take all necessary measures to
repel any armed attack against the forces of the United States and to prevent further aggression" in Southeast Asia. With this resolution as a legal
shield, Johnson furtively escalated the war, increasing American involvement by stealthy increments. He could not conceal, however, the human
and economic cost. Forced to decide between the Great Society and the
war in Indochina, Lyndon Johnson's sin was not that he made the wrong
decision but that he refused to make any honest decision at all. As a result
he lost not only the Great Society but also the White House to Richard
Nixon and ultimately the country lost the war.

Having campaigned for the presidency on the promise that he would end the war, President Nixon set about to accomplish that, but in a way intended to preserve U.S. credibility, allowing him to open diplomatic relations with the Chinese and promote détente with the Soviet Union. Meanwhile, at home, Nixon used the war to strengthen his electoral base by appealing to the patriotism of middle-class Americans and driving a wedge between them and the antiwar protestors.

As legal grounding for his decisions, Nixon cited his responsibility as Commander in Chief "to take the action necessary to defend the security of American men," using the term "Commander in Chief" repeatedly, as Arthur Schlesinger pointed out, "as if it were an incantation." Nixon eventually had his way in Vietnam, but at a terrible cost to Vietnam, to his own country, and to his presidency. Faced with opposition at home, Nixon extended his abuse of power into the domestic arena, leading ultimately to his forced resignation under threat of impeachment.

In response to Nixon's Vietnam policies, and after more than a quarter of a century of inaction, Congress passed the War Powers Resolution of 1973 to curb further abuses of presidential power. But presidents have often ignored its weak and cumbersome provisions and Congress has failed to enforce them. President George Bush's massive military buildup in the Persian Gulf, undertaken without congressional authorization, demonstrated the law's inadequacy. Not until he was ready to go to war in January of 1991 did Bush ask for congressional backing, and at that time he asserted that he did not even need it.

Despite the Cold War's end, Bush still relied on the hoary claim of national security. Following Iraq's swift conquest of Kuwait, he tried evoke recollections of World War II, frequently likening Iraqi ruler Saddam Hussein to Hitler. "America stands where it always has, against aggression, against those who would use force to replace the rule of law," Bush told the Veterans of Foreign Wars. Yet the postwar world had seen an array of other aggressions, from Goa to Afghanistan, to which the U.S. had not responded on a scale comparable to Operation Desert Shield. More explicitly and practically, Bush warned that the Iraqi invasion imperiled "the world's great oil reserves," thus endangering "our way of life, our own freedom and the freedom of friendly countries." And he hoped that this overblown rhetoric would drown out recollections of how much the Bush Administration had coddled Saddam, whom it had valued as a bulwark against Islamic extremism and as a multibillion-dollar trading partner.

In legal terms, Bush offered no rationale beyond the assertion of Secretary of State James A Baker, III, echoing and expanding on what Acheson had said during Korea, that presidents had used armed force

more than 200 times and that war had only been declared five times.
But, as in Acheson's case, nearly all these earlier episodes were touched
off by minor disputes, and offered no analogy to the vast U.S. commitment in the Gulf. The swift and relatively easy triumph of Operation
Desert Storm was tarnished by Bush's willingness to allow the justly
maligned Saddam to remain in power. With his military success soon
overshadowed by the economic recession that ended his presidency,
the ultimate mockery of Bush's Gulf adventure was provided by a
bumper sticker: "Saddam still has his job. What about you?"

In another vain attempt to check the abuse of executive power,
Congress adopted the Boland amendment.* Designed specifically to
block President Ronald Reagan's administration from supporting efforts
to overthrow the leftist Sandinista regime in Nicaragua, its wholesale
covert violation was the heart of the Iran–Contra scandal. In the spirit of
past presidencies, advocates of the Contra cause within the Reagan
Administration devised ways to circumvent the law by channeling aid to
the anti-Sandinista Contra guerrillas through the National Security
Council and by tapping into private or "third country" funds. The Boland
amendment, they claimed, did not technically apply in these areas. The
linkage of these activities to the equally underhanded efforts by the
National Security Council staff to sell arms to Iran in the hope of freeing
American hostages ultimately led to disclosure of both operations.

Unlike his predecessors who shied away from public debate of their
foreign policy goals, Reagan, employing his vaunted skills as communi-
cator, tried to build public support for aid to the Contras. But when he
lost the debate, as Congress and the public rejected his appeal, Reagan
allowed his policy to be pursued anyway, outside the law. The doctrine
of absolute presidential supremacy, firmly held by the President and
other key figures in the skullduggery, undergirded the Iran–Contra
conspiracy. Marine Lt. Col. Oliver North summed up this belief in the
course of defending his escapades on behalf of the Contras as a
National Security Council staff member. "As I understand it," North
said in describing the President's role, "he is the person charged with
making and carrying out the foreign policy of this country." If Congress
had a part to play, North did not acknowledge it.

The revelation of this high-level chicanery shook the nation's confidence
in President Reagan, even stirring fears among his advisors that he would

*The Boland amendment was actually a series of several amendments to appropria-
tion acts adopted between 1982 and 1986, as Congress sought in vain to tighten the
screws against covert aid for the Contras.

be impeached. Yet one of the most disturbing aspects of Iran–Contra was the failure of the various agencies which investigated it to comprehend its scope or meaning or to find any correctives. "The Iran–Contra affair resulted from the failure of individuals to observe the law, not from deficiencies in existing law or in our system of governance," declared the congressional select committees that probed the case. Its findings "pointed to the fundamental soundness of our constitutional process," the report concluded. Similarly, General Brent Scowcroft, one of three members of the special review board appointed by the President, asserted: "The problem at the heart was one of people, not process."

But this is like attributing a series of crashes by the same type of airplane to pilot error. The American model of government has crashed repeatedly over the past years, making it clear that the problem has to do with more than the shortcomings of individual personalities.

Defenders of the political system speak of its ability to correct itself. But that has not happened. In the case of the destroyer deal, and often since, Congress has been reluctant to challenge the President's use of excessive authority. In September 1994, when President Bill Clinton claimed authority to invade Haiti without congressional sanction, many lawmakers disagreed. But none could find a way to stop him until the decision by the island's military rulers to step down turned the planned assault into a relatively peaceful occupation. Congress's most dramatic response, the attempt to impeach Richard Nixon, occurred after the fact, and Iran–Contra demonstrated that whatever deterrent effect this action might have had has diminished. Other measures, such as the Boland amendment and the War Powers Resolution, have been flouted or ignored. Nor has the judicial system been of much help. Reluctant to become involved in what many jurists consider political disputes, courts have generally avoided pleas to check executive power. In the Iran–Contra case, the best efforts of independent prosecutor Lawrence Walsh were of little avail. Trial juries found the two most important figures he moved against, Oliver North and Rear Admiral John M. Poindexter, Jr., the President's national security advisor, guilty of felonies. But their convictions were later reversed when an appellate court found their protection against self-incrimination had been violated by their testimony before Congress. The pardons granted by Reagan's successor, Bush, in the closing days of his presidency to former Reagan Administration officials involved in the Iran–Contra case further undercut respect for the law and the principle of accountability. The pardons not only exempted these officials from prosecution but shielded Bush himself against investigation of his role in the scandal.

The nature of the process by which presidents are selected compounds the flaws in the governing system that have led to presidential excess. In an editorial assessing Richard Nixon's guilt in Watergate, the *New York Times* pointed out:

> To become President requires calculation, singlemindedness, and ferocity, qualities which can abruptly become far less admirable after an election, depending on the character of the man. Even if the electorate judges character wisely, not even the most upright President can wholly immunize himself against the compulsions of office.

In fact, both the political and governing process tend to work against the goals of accountability and debate. Yet no quick solution presents itself. Fundamental reform is a long way off. It lacks an established constituency and no one can be sure that the risk will be worth the benefits.

The best chance for improvement begins with a better understanding of the shortcomings of the system. This will at least bring more realistic expectations to our judgments of presidential behavior and more forceful demands for full debate of presidential decisions. In the meantime, the defects of the political system should not be allowed to excuse presidential misconduct, particularly lying and deception. This rationale, often heard from Roosevelt's defenders, was expressed with unusual candor by the historian Thomas Bailey:

> Franklin Roosevelt repeatedly deceived the American people during the period before Pearl Harbor. . . . He was like the physician who must tell the patient lies for the patient's own good. . . . Because the masses are notoriously shortsighted and generally cannot see danger until it is at their throats, our statesmen are forced to deceive them into an awareness of their own long-run interests.

In reality, when Roosevelt and other presidents lied, they did it mainly for their own good, or what they believed to be their own good. But they were often mistaken because they have tended to be at least as shortsighted as the masses. Presidential lying is not only immoral, it is also impractical. As the record of the White House illustrates, presidents have done themselves, as well as the country, far more harm than benefit by hiding the truth. Prospective presidents who think otherwise should say loudly and clearly at the outset of their campaigns that they will sometimes betray the public trust to protect the Republic from its enemies. If a candidate providing such a disclaimer wins election, at least the country will know what to expect.

Until that happens, it should be kept in mind that the chief lesson from the past forty years of presidential excess is the importance of open discussion and debate. While chief executives are fond of citing national security as a reason for secrecy, experience suggests that not much of what has been concealed would have offered significant aid and comfort to foreign foes. The most likely disadvantage of full disclosure and debate would be inconvenience and awkwardness for chief executives. This cost to them seems small compared to the price the country has paid for their abuse of power. The great lengths to which everyone involved in the destroyer deal went to manipulate public opinion serves as a heartening reminder of the power that can be wielded by a citizenry enlightened enough to understand and look after its own interests.

Increased candor and accountability will neither shrink nor shackle the presidency. To the contrary, the defining of presidential purposes for the benefit of the public can generate support and strengthen the office. Leaders are not much without followers. ". . . If we are to go forward we must move as a trained and loyal army willing to sacrifice for the good of a common discipline," Franklin Roosevelt told Americans in his first inaugural, "because without such discipline no progress is made, no leadership is effective." It needs to be remembered, though, that discipline is good not just for followers, but also for leaders.

# Notes

*Abbreviations used in notes:*

| | |
|---|---|
| CR: | *Congressional Record* |
| CSM: | *Christian Science Monitor* |
| FDRL: | Franklin D. Roosevelt Library |
| FRUS: | *Foreign Relations of the United States.* State Department Series, 1938–40. Cited by year and volume. |
| LC: | Library of Congress |
| NYHT: | *New York Herald Tribune* |
| NYT: | *New York Times* |
| PC: | *Complete Presidential News Conferences* (of Franklin Roosevelt) |
| POQ: | *Public Opinion Quarterly* |
| PL: | *Personal Letters* (of Franklin Roosevelt) |
| PPA: | *Public Papers and Addresses of Franklin D. Roosevelt* |
| PSF: | President's Secretary's File, Franklin D. Roosevelt Library |
| WP: | *Washington Post* |

## CHAPTER ONE: "I WANT TO GET MY HAND IN NOW"

15   The path of the cable: Whalen, p. 310, based on correspondence with Tyler Kent. See also Kimball, pp. xvii—xxi

15   The text of the telegram: Kimball, p. 37. There are several other sources for the telegram, but Kimball is the most complete and I have relied on this work throughout for the text and timing of the Roosevelt–Churchill cables.

17   "invaded by a foreign foe" *PPA*, 1933, No.1, 15.

18   "how glad I am": Kimball, p. 89. Also see Reynolds, *Creation*, pp. 84 ff and Leutze, pp. 47–48 for Foreign Office reaction to this correspondence.

18   More a troubleshooter: Ward, *Temperament*, p. 433.

18   An instant dislike: Beschloss, pp. 200, 230. Ward, *Temperament*, pp. 392–93. Churchill did not recall the encounter.

19   Churchill's drinking: A. A. Berle Diary, May 5, 1940. FDRL; Ickes Diary, May 12, 1940. LC.

19   Economic relapse: Parmet and Hecht, p. 13.

19   Wage comparisons: *Historical Statistics of the United States*, U.S. Department of Commerce. Washington, 1975. p. 163.

20   Mrs. Roosevelt's new approach: *WP*, May 15, 1940.

20   The baseball season's start: *NYT*, May 15, 1940.

20   The movies of 1940: *Time Capsule/1940.* pp. 209–215.

20   Nylon's arrival: *NYT*, May 15, 1940.

21  The controversy over *There Shall Be No Night*: BLI, June 13, 1940, citing *New York World-Telegram*, June 13, 1940. FO 371/24240, A3427/131/45

21  Times Square scene: *Time*, May 20, 1940.

21  10 million horses: *WP*, May 15, 1940.

22  "Holland will never cease": *NYT*, May 15, 1940.

22  "leave America isolated": *NYT*, May 15, 1940.

22  "The surest way": *NYT*, May 13, 1940.

22  Poll findings: *POQ*, March 1940.

23  FDR's boyhood: Maney, p. 6 and Tugwell, p. 27.

23  "My first black mark": *PL, Vol. 1*, pp. 96–98.

24  The *Crimson* editorials: Tugwell, p. 33.

24  Lippman's warning: Steel, pp. 291–92.

24  "A good trip": Moley, p. 52.

25  Football analogy: Hurd, p. 164.

25  Holmes's judgment: Burns, p. 157.

25  "Psychoanalyzed by God": Leuchtenburg, William E. "The First Modern President," in Fred I. Greenstein, ed.: *Leadership in the Modern Presidency*. Cambridge, Mass.: Harvard University Press, 1988.

25  On James and Sara: Maney, pp. 2, 4.

26  Snubbing Vanderbilt: Freidel, *Apprenticeship, p. 12;* Maney, p. 2.

26  Franklin confided: Freidel, *Apprenticeship*, p. 86.

27  Nominating Smith: Gallagher, pp. 60–62.

27  "A vagrant beam": Stimson diary, Dec. 18, 1940.

27  "Frictionless command": Freidel, *Ordeal*, p. 66.

28  "No one could tell": Tugwell, p.66.

28  Old flame revived (FN): Maney, p. 21

28  "I was a goose": Freidel, *Destiny*, p. 31.

28  Concealing disability: Maney, p. 26, Seale, p. 916. Gallagher treats the issue at length and in detail.

28  Pool reporters knew: Gallagher, p. 103.

29  "For me or against me": Moley, p. 342.

29  Waging the campaign: Moley, p. 350.

29  The last campaign address: Burns, p. 283.

29  The Court confrontation: There are many sources but Burns offers the most concise analysis, pp. 291–315.

30  The doomed purge: Burns, p. 377.

30  Millis's verdict: Burns, *Deadlock of Democracy*, Englewood Cliffs, N.J.: Prentice-Hall, 1963, p. 166, citing Millis, Walter, "The President's Political Strategy," *Yale Review*, Sept. 1938.

30  The *Fortune* survey: *Fortune*, March 1940 (press release in Joseph Alsop papers, LC).

## CHAPTER TWO: THE CORKSCREW TRAIL

31  Room 1702: Rollins, pp. 4–5.

31  "He is dying": Stiles, p. 178.

31  Howe's efforts: Stiles, pp. 178–183.

32  Trouble loomed: Moley, p. 30.

32  Baker ready: Martin, pp. 191 ff.

32  "A gone goose": Rosenman, p. 70.

33  Hearst the key: Swanberg, p. 497.

33  Getting word to Hearst: Whalen, p. 124.

33  Sealing the deal: Martin, p. 191; Swanberg, p. 518.

33  "The cat that swallowed": Rosenman, p. 72.

33  "Good old McAdoo": Tully, p. 51; Martin, p. 199.

34  Sacrificing the League: Beard, pp. 65 ff.

34  Hearst denounced: Swanberg, p. 516.

34  "The old Tom Watson element": Democratic National Committee files, box 131, Georgia, FDRL.

34  Hearst's empire: Beschloss, p. 70.

34  "This is bad ball": Freidel, *Triumph*, 250.

35  Baker's statement: Beard, p. 70, citing *NYT*, Jan. 27, 1932.

35  Hearst unimpressed: Freidel, *Triumph*, p. 250.

35  FDR caves in: *PPG*, 1932. pp. 550 ff.

35  "The shortest distance": Martin, p. 138.

35  A harsh view: Beard, p. 81, citing *NYHT*, Feb. 4, 1932.

36  "Your most ardent . . . friends": Freidel, *Triumph*, citing House to FDR, Feb. 10, 1932. Democratic National Committee files, New York City, FDRL.

36  Kudos from the West and South: Beard, pp. 82–83.

36  Kennedy's meeting with Roosevelt: Beard, p. 99, citing *NYT*, May 9, 1932.

36  Hearst gave Kennedy to understand: Whelan, pp. 122–25, Beschloss, pp. 71–72.

37  The debt he established: Whalen, pp. 126–29; Farley, *Behind the Ballots*, 149.

37  Moley recalled: Moley, 63.

38  FDR's background: Langer and Gleason, p. 1; Lindley, Ernest K. "Statesman's Progress." *WP*, Oct. 15, 1939.

38  The sea captured his imagination: Ward, *Trumpet*, p. 160, Lash, *Roosevelt and Churchill*, p. 37.

38  He tried to run away: *Ibid*.

38  "How could you expect me?": Moley, p. 95.

38  TR's influence: Lash, *Roosevelt and Churchill* p. 37.

39  FDR's bragging: Freidel, *Ordeal*, pp. 81–82; Schlesinger, *Crisis* pp. 364–65; Ward, *Temperament*, 534–35.

39  Not a comma: Ward, *Temperament*, p. 324.

40  The promise was kept: Ward, *Temperament*, p. 348 n.

40  Went all out: Beard, p. 47, Burns, pp. 70, 75.

40  Weariness with Wilson: Freidel, *Ordeal* p. 89.

40  Democrats backed away: Beard, p. 52.

40  "The principal agency": Roosevelt, Franklin D., "Our Foreign Policy."

40  "Ideals do not change": Freidel, *Triumph*, p. 253.

41  Isolationist backing: Cole, *Isolationists*, pp. 22–25.

41  Rooted deep: Chadwin, p. 4.

41  The social reformers: Lubell, p. 140.

41  A silent partner: Beard, p. 148; Cole, pp. 187ff.

41  Johnson Act: Cole, pp. 89–94.

42  Confided to Johnson: Cole, p. 123.

43  "If God is against war": Cole, p. 125.

43  The World Court message: *Vital Speeches of the Day*, Vol. I, Jan. 28, 1935, p. 258; Cole, pp. 121–24.

43  Nye's probe: Langer and Gleason, p. 14.

43  Nye's beliefs: Lubell, pp. 137–41.

44  Nye saw opportunity: Detzer, p. 154; Cole, p. 144; Lubell, p. 146.

44  He told the Senate: Hull, p. 400; Cole, p. 149

44  "Tangled our relations": Hull, p. 404.

44  Democratic platform: *Guide to U.S. Elections*, p. 83; Divine, p. 31.

45  New Deal lost momentum: Divine, p. 60; Cole, pp. 291–92.

45  "An act to preserve": Lubell, p. 41.

46 Quarantine speech: *PPA*, 1937, Oct. 5, pp. 406–11.
46 "An end to shilly shally": Moffat, 154–55.
46 Press reaction: Borg.
46 Roosevelt scotched the idea: *PC*, 1937, No. 400. 10: 245–54.
46 A different view (FN): Reynolds, p. 30.
47 A plan for peace: Hull, p. 546; Langer and Gleason, p. 22.
47 Chamberlain dragged his feet: Reynolds, p. 19; Langer and Gleason, p. 26.
47 A joint blockade: Reynolds, p. 30.
48 Once again, a plan: Reynolds, p. 35; Lash, *Roosevelt and Churchill*, p. 25.
48 Warning to Lindsay: Reynolds, p. 35; Cole, p. 300. Lash.
48 Assurance to Hitler: Cole, p. 286. *FRUS*, 1938, Vol. 1 pp. 675–80; pp. 684–85. *PPA*, 1938, Sept. 27, No. 121, 535–37; Divine, p. 58.
48 "Good man": Wood, p. 197.
48 "The greatest opportunity": Divine, p. 58; Langer and Gleason, p. 35.
48 Assurance to Chamberlain: Cole, p. 301; Reynolds, p. 47.
49 "Methods short of war": *PPA*, 1939, p. 3
49 Negotiations with the French: Cole, *Isolationists*, pp. 297–303; *FRUS*, 1938, Vol. 2 pp. 297–314. Blum, pp. 64–71, Transcript of White House Conference with the Senate Military Affairs Committee, January 31, 1939, Box 118, Folder 1-P, PPF, F.D.R.L.
50 Roosevelt denounced the report: *PC*, 1939, Feb. 3.
51 Fondness for alcohol (FN): Lothian tel. No. 1149, June 28, 1940 FO 371/24240.
51 Roosevelt told Connally: Connally, p. 226.
51 The last-ditch meeting: Alsop and Kintner, pp. 44–46, Seale, p. 984, Divine, p. 66.
53 "Even a neutral": *PPA*, 1939, pp. 460–63.
53 Sherwood would concede: Sherwood, p. 125.
53 Remarks to Cabinet: Navy Secretary Edison's recollections of Roosevelt's remarks, Sept. 2, 1940 Navy Department File, Charles Edison Folder, PSF, FDRL.

## CHAPTER THREE: "A GOOD STIFF GROG"

55 "Years younger in New York": Reynolds, *Lord Lothian*, p. 3; Butler, p. 227.
55 "Know-it-all": Reynolds, *Lothian*, p. 8; the uncharitable official was Lord Vansittart, famous for his acid tongue.
55 "To make them understand": Butler, p. 227.
55 Lothian's early view of Hitler: Butler, p. 215; Ickes, *The Inside Struggle*, p. 571.
56 Lothian's metaphor: Ickes, *Ibid*.
56 "We who are about to die": Box 32, Diplomatic Correspondence, Great Britain, 1939, PSF, FDRL.
56 Somewhat embellished (FN): Reynolds, *Lothian*, pp. 7–8.
57 "He had no objection": Reynolds, *Lothian*, p. 7.
57 "Best and safest": Reynolds, p. 16.
58 Traced back to World War I: *Ibid*, pp. 10 ff.
58 "Notoriously inaccurate": *Ibid*, p. 36.
58 Roosevelt's bond: Lindley, "Statesman's Progress."
58 "Rather than Tories": Roosevelt memo to Stephen Early, Oct. 19, 1939, p. 942, *PL*, Vol. 4.
58 "Trouble with the British": Farley, p. 199.
59 The secret arrangement: Baptiste.
59 Adams had ordered: Howarth, pp. 60–61.
59 Lindsay "aghast" and other details on leases: Baptiste.
61 Welles's address: Langer and Gleason, pp. 209–10.
61 Roosevelt told George VI: Reynolds, p. 67.
61 As Roosevelt explained: Baptiste.

61   A ship was sunk: *Almanac*, p. 40.
61   She was hunted down: Hull, p. 690.
61   The Admiralty rejected: Langer and Gleason, p. 213.
62   "Allowed to die down": Kimball, p. 28, C-3x.
62   "Tremendously interesting": *Ibid* p. 33, R-2X.
62   The Foreign Office suspected: Reynolds, p. 79.
62   FDR renewed his efforts: Cole, pp. 321–23; p. *CR*, Sept. 21, 1939, pp. 10–12, *NYT*, Sept 22, 1939
62   Vandenburg's reaction: Cole, p. 328, citing Vandenberg Diary, Sept. 15, 1939.
63   Would seem contrived: Cole, p. 327.
63   White's organization: Chadwin, 21, Johnson, *WAWA*, p. 517.
63   "A high wall around ourselves": Roosevelt to Sir Alan Lascelles, Nov. 13, 1939, *PL*, Vol. 461 p. 955.
63   A note of gratitude: Chamberlain to FDR, Nov. 10, 1939, Great Britain Folder, PSF, FDRL.
64   "A starving farmer": Minute by Undersecretary David Scott, Feb. 29, 1940, FO 371 24238 A 1857/131/45.
64   "The general feeling": Kimball, p. 33, R-2x.
64   Chamberlain's complaint: Reynolds, p. 78.
64   British analysis of mail: FO 371, A1541/131/45.
65   Scott's memo: Reynolds, p. 80.
65   "I must frankly admit": Langer and Gleason, p. 363.
65   Welles drew some hope: Welles, p. 88.
65   "We will all go down": *Ibid*, 108–09.
65   "Window dressing": Long, pp. 64–65, Welles, p. 121.
65   "In front of the fire": Welles report, March 12, 1940, PSF, FDRL
66   One point Churchill stressed: Welles, pp. 133–34.
66   Welles's views on Churchill and Mussolini (FN): Reynolds, *Creation*, p. 91; Ickes, pp. 464–65.
66   Cadogan's comment: Reynolds, p. 327, n91.
66   No hope for peace: Hull, p. 740.
66   As Welles later wrote: Welles, p. 119.
66   Action far removed: Langer and Gleason, p. 371; T. North Whitehead minute, April 4, 1940, FO 371 A371/24239.
66   "Could not do any harm": Long, pp. 64–65.
66   "Of the greatest value": *PPA*, 1940, No. 23, 111.
66   "The most outrageous thing": *MPD*, April 10, 1940, FDRL.
67   A vague sop: *PPA*, 1940, No. 35, p. 166.
67   Glum forecast: *MPD*, April 29, 1940, FDRL.
67   "With American sympathy": Minute by T. North Whitehead, April 11, 1940 FO 371/24239 A 2756/131/45.
68   Press reaction: BLI No. 27, May 4, 1940, FO 371/24239 A3171.
68   "Depends on the dictators": Lothian to Halifax, April 29, 1940, FO 371 24239 A 3202/131/45.
68   "A profound impression": Halifax to Lothian, May 13, 1940. FO 371/24239 A 3242/131/45.

## CHAPTER FOUR: "THOSE BLOODY YANKEES"

71   Early allied orders: Reynolds, p. 90.
71   Knox's call: *Time*, May 20, 1940.
71   Some warned: Krock, Arthur. "Are we nearer war," *NYT*, May 12, 1940.

72 "Gloomy stuff": BLI report No. 244, May 29, 1940, FO 371/24240 A 3427/131/45.

72 FDR's May 10 address: *PPA* 1940, No. 42, pp. 184–90; *NYT*, May 14, 1940.

73 $2 billion for defense: *PPA*, 1940, No. 148, pp. 198–212; *Time*, May 20, 1940, *Newsweek*, May 27, 1940.

73 "Silent and hostile": Ickes, p. 179.

74 U.S. destroyer strength: Alden, 1; Hague, 7; Greenberg, Memorandum from Admiral Harold Stark, June 9, 1940, Navy Folder, May-June 1940, Box 58, PSF, FDRL; Hall, p. 141.

74 It would take six or seven weeks: Kimball, p. 38, R-4x.

74 FN: Bullitt to Hull, May 15; Hull to Bullitt, May 16. *FRUS*, 1940, Vol. 1, pp. 222-24, 243–44.

75 "Send it off tonight": Colville, p. 136.

75 The fleet might take up harbor: Reynolds, *Lothian*, p. 18.

75 "You must not be blind": Kimball, p. 40, C-11x.

76 "No comment requested": *PC*, 1940, No. 645, Vol. 15 pp. 351–53.

76 The resolution rejected: Lothian to Foreign Office, May 25, 1940. FO 371 24240 A 3242 131/45.

76 "A thousand miles away": Rosenman.

76 Mainly reassurance: *PPA*, 1940, No. 52, pp. 233–40.

76 "Down a rat hole": *Newsweek*, May 27, 1940.

77 "Not much enthusiasm": BLI No. 244, May 29, 1940. FO 371/24240. A/3427.

77 "No inclination to lead": *Time*, June 3, 1940.

77 Went out of his way: *PC*, 1940, No. 647, Vol. 15, pp. 383-384.

77 Churchill's May 15 cable: Kimball, 37, C-9x.

78 Morgenthau's coordinating role: Blum, 94–103, 109.

78 Longer and better: Graham and Wander, 265.

78 "To Henry": Blum, *Years of Urgency*, p. 34.

79 "More than anyone else": Schlesinger, *Coming of the New Deal*, p. 541.

79 FDR's complaint: Farley, p. 212.

79 Roosevelt annoyed: Farley's diary, March 8, 1940, LC.

79 Woodring opposed aid: Graham and Wander, 461.

79 "You've got to do something": MPD, April 26, 1940, FDRL.

79 "But makes no move": Ickes, p. 207.

79 Hopkins's suggestion: *Ibid*, p. 193.

79 "Dear Harold": *Ibid*, p. 198.

80 "Do it today": Marshall, p. 211.

80 "You did a swell job": MPD, Vol. pp. 2,531–534, FDRL.

80 "Let General Marshall": Marshall, p. 214.

80 "If I was the president": Blum, p. 150.

81 "A drop in the bucket": Blum, p. 151.

81 Marshall's list: *Ibid*, Langer and Gleason, pp. 487–88.

81 The basis of the list: Watson, pp. 188, 309.

81 "How's your conscience": Blum, p. 151.

81 "Only by the President": *FRUS*, Vol. 3, p. 3, Welles memorandum, May 23, 1940.

81 Purvis background: Goodheart, p. 46.

82 A tenacious negotiator: Blum, p. 110.

82 "What is the difficulty?": MD, transcript of May 29 meeting, FDRL.

82 Inventing a legal basis: *PC*, 1940, No. 650, June 8. Vol. 15, pp. 542–546; Blum, p. 153, Watson 310; Langer and Gleason, 488. *FRUS*, Vol. I, 1940, p. 237, Hull to Bullitt.

82 What the Army could sell: *PC*, No. 650, June 8, 1940, Vol 15, p. 548.

83 "The whole damned lot": Blum, p. 153.

83 "An extra push: Blum, p. 155.

83 "Not talking about it": *PL*, Vol. 4, p. 1037.

83 The Navy disclosed: *NYT*, June 7, 1940.

83  In service only three months: *Newsweek*, June 17, 1940.
83  "Darned fast": *PC*, 1940, No. 650, June 8, Vol. 15, p. 548.
84  "Backdoor strategy:" *NYT*, June 8, 1940.
84  Some newspapers disagreed: BLI Report No. 273, June 10, 1940. FO 371 A3427/131/45.
84  "A buyer's market": *PC*, 1940, No. 650., June 8, Vol. 15, pp. 545–46.
84  FDR took the bait: Moffat, p. 310.
85  Reynaud's comment: *FRUS*, Vol. 1, p. 244. Bullitt to Hull.
85  "The hand that held the dagger": *PPA*, 1940, No. 58, pp. 259–64.
85  Drafting of speech (FN): Hull, pp. 784–85.
85  "An audible gasp": BLI No. 267, June 13, 1940. FO 371 24270 A 4327/131/45.
85  Lothian's suggestion: Lothian to Churchill, June 17,1940, FO/371/24240, A3582.
86  Warning against hysteria: FO 371/24239 A3316.
86  List of priorities: MD, Vol. 267, p. 189, FDRL.
87  Stark needed every ship: MD, Vol. 269, p. 58.
87  Recommissioning cost: *PC*, 1940, Vol. 15, 339–40, May 17, 1940.
87  Lunch with Ickes: Ickes, pp. 199–200.
87  The Navy's view: *NYT*, June 25, 1940.
88  "Do what I told you": Ickes, p. 202.
88  "On the fence": FO 371/24239 A 3312/26/45.
88  "We must be careful": Churchill, p. 115.
88  Time to replace equipment: Gilbert, p. 478.
88  "A storm in public opinion": Balfour to Halifax, June 13, 1940 FO 371 24239 A 3242/131/45.
88  The triggering episode: *CR*, Senate, June 21, 1940, p. 8774ff.
89  Edison's note: Box 58, Navy Folder, May–June, 1940, President's Secretary's File, FDRL.
89  "Weigh my words": Kimball, p. 50, C-17x.
90  "The most effective thing": Churchill to Lothian, June 17, 1940, FO 371/24240 A 3582.
90  Walsh's appearance and background: Wayman, pp. 101, 113, 132, 141, 151, 181–82, 234, 275.
91  Walsh's warning: *NYT*, June 20, 1940.
91  Hopkins's advice: Memo, June 20, 1940, Robert Jackson papers, LC.
92  "Suffered a humiliation": *CR*, Senate June 21, 1940, pp. 8797–98.
92  Walsh the dominant figure: *Ibid*, pp. 8774 ff.
92  A sweeping restriction: *Ibid*, p. 8828.
93  "Not a single plane": *Ibid*, p. 8830.
93  Jackson's ruling: *NYT*, June 25, 1940.
93  "No other option": Lothian tel. June 27,1940 FO 371/24240 A 3583.


## CHAPTER FIVE: "HE'S FIXED IT SO NOBODY ELSE CAN RUN"

95  Farley's Papal audience: Farley, p. 194.
95  Fall back plan: Appleby.
95  The war made it easier: Farley, p. 248.
96  British press survey: BLI report No. 301, June 27, 1940, FO 371/24240 A 3427/131/45.
96  Whitehead's advice: FO 371/24238 A 3312/26/45.
96  The King's letter: King George VI to Roosevelt, June 26, 1940. Box 38, Great Britain/King and Queen Folder, PSF, FDRL.
97  Churchill gave up: Kimball, pp. 53–54, C-20x.
97  "One in three": Farley, p. 252.
97  Third term tradition: Parmet and Hecht, pp. 2 ff.

97 FDR's view: Farley, p. 251.
97 "Can any citizen hesitate?": Lash, *Dealers*, p. 361 ff.
98 Corcoran's mission: *Ibid*, p. 366.
98 Chatting with Hopkins: Sherwood, pp. 93–95.
98 Hopkins background: Graham and Wander, pp. 183–85.
98 Tax and tax: Sherwood, p. 102.
98 Hopkins's illness: McJimsey, p. 118; Sherwood, p. 92.
99 "You make the best speeches": Cummings diary, July 4, 1938, Alderman Library.
99 "You'll be in my chair": Hull, p. 856.
99 Advice to LaGuardia: Berle, p. 194.
99 "That little wop" (FN): Cummings diary, July 4, 1938, p. 86 Alderman Library.
100 "A nice long rest": Farley, pp. 74–76.
100 "Put on the dunce cap": *PC*, 1937, June 29, No. 377. Vol. 9, pp. 465–466.
100 "Too old or too young": Farley, p. 72.
100 "I did not rise to the bait": MD, May 24, 1937, FDRL.
100 "Wallace could not make a speech": Cummings diary, 85, Alderman Library.
100 "Margin of doubt": Sherwood, p. 94.
101 "Admitted the difficulty": Ickes, *The Inside Struggle*, p. 394.
101 Relationship with Farley: Graham and Wander, p. 125.
101 "Even if no one lifts a finger": Farley, p. 6.
101 "Issues aren't my business": Moley, p. 36.
101 All signed with a flourish: Freidel, *Triumph*, p. 173.
102 "Not his social equals": Farley, p. 68.
102 Thumbs down: *Ibid*, p. 184.
102 "Don't pass this on": *Ibid*, p. 186.
103 Third term opposition declines: *NYT*, June 5, 1940.
103 "A day to day basis": Farley, p. 196.
103 Wallace's speech: *Ibid*, p. 208.
103 Time and place of the convention: *Ibid*, pp. 211, 224.
104 "The greatest asset": *Time*, Jan. 15, 1940.
104 "A horse's hair": Farley, p. 207.
104 "A grand idea": Farley, pp. 222–24.
104 Lindley's story: *WP*, March 4, 1940.
104 Instead of refuting: *PC*, 1940: Vol. 15, pp. 181-85.
105 "Into the cradle": Farley, p. 229.
105 "Out of whole cloth": *PC*, Vol. 15, pp. 204–206.
105 Growing up in homespun: Hull, pp. 10–14
106 Starting off with FDR: *Ibid*, pp. 150, 158.
106 "Straight to hell": Hull, 856.
106 "Still in the picture": Long, 73.
106 "A lot to do soon": Hull, p. 856.
107 The German view: Thomsen telegram to the Foreign Ministry, April 19,1940, *DGFP*, Series D, Vol. IX, p. 207, No. 139.
107 Poll findings: *NYT*, June 5, 1940.
107 "Nobody else can run": Farley, p. 237.
107 Farley dragged his feet: *Ibid*, pp. 196, 211.
107 Landon contended: *NYT*, May 23, 1940.
108 "The reason for the move": *NYT*, June 23, 1940.
108 Woodring's charge: *CR*, Senate, June 21, 1940, p. 8791.
108 Added to the confusion: Parmet and Hecht, p. 116.
109 "No longer qualified": *NYT*, June 21, 1940.
109 Willkie's reaction: Parmet and Hecht, p. 116.
109 "Best engineered": Smith, Richard Norton, p. 306.

109   Packing the galleries: Neal, p. 105.

109   Luce leads the way: *Ibid*, p. 76.

110   The platform writers intended: *Ibid*, p. 86.

110   The Nazi role: Thomsen to the Foreign Ministry, July 3, 1940. DGFP Series D Vol. X, Berlin Rogge, pp. 262–63, Friedlander, pp. 101–02.

110   The GOP platform: *Election Guide*, pp. 64–65; Parmet and Hecht, p. 139

110   "This is no time": Smith, Richard Norton, p. 304.

111   Dewey's problems: *Ibid*, pp. 303–04.

111   Dewey and the destroyers: Parmet and Hecht, p. 120.

111   "Walking in its sleep": Sherwood, p. 174.

111   The British view: *BLI No. 302* June 26, 3427/131/45 FO 371 24240. *NYT*, June 25, 1940.

112   "Every whale": *NYT*, June 26, 1940.

112   Thompson's suggestion: Smith, Richard Norton, p. 306.

112   "Maybe you'll get him": Neal, p. 115.

112   A brief speech: *NYT*, June 29, 1940.

112   "Unfortunate" news: Thomsen to Berlin, June 28, 1940, No. 1296. *DGFP*, Series D, Vol. X, Friedlander, p. 101.

113   "He would be elected": Farley, p. 252.

113   Farley's bland reply: *Ibid*, p. 247.

113   "I don't want to run": *Ibid*, p. 248.

114   "All right with me": Hull, p. 861.

114   Rosenman's role: Rosenman, p. 204 ff.

114   Hopkins in Chicago: Farley, p. 261.

114   Another confidant: Sherwood, p. 176.

114   Anti-third term sentiment: *Election Guide*, p. 37.

115   A full scale battle: Rosenman, p. 211.

115   The German role: Thomsen to the Foreign Ministry, July 19, 1940, No. 190. DGFP. Rogge, pp 262-63, Friedlander, pp. 101–02.

115   Wheeler credited: Masland.

115   Hull complained: Hull, p. 862.

115   FDR's compromise: Rosenman, p. 212.

115   "We want Roosevelt": *Time*, July 29, p. 14. Sirevag, p. 89. *NYT*, July 17, 1940.

116   Reaction to Wallace: Farley, p. 302.

116   "A call to service": *PPA*. 1940, No. 70 pp. 293–302.

## CHAPTER SIX: "SOMEBODY'S NOSE IS OUT OF JOINT"

117   Donovan at the gate: *NYT*, July 15, 1940.

117   Churchill brooded: Gilbert, p. 650.

117   Lothian's cable: Lothian to FO tel. No. 1311, FO 371/24237, A3542/90/45.

118   Donovan to be taken seriously: Lothian to FO, tel. No. 1316, FO 371/24237, A3542/90/45.

118   Lothian elaborated: Lothian to FO, tel. No. 1366, A3542/90/45.

118   "Wide-ranging enthusiasm": Smith, R. Harris. pp. 3–6.

119   Donovan's upbringing: Ford, p. 15.

119   "My old friend": *Ibid*, p. 75.

119   Life in Buffalo: Troy, p. 24.

120   World War I exploits: Donovan biographical outline, Donovan papers, Military History Institute.

120   Father Duffy's advice: Troy, p. 25.

120   "He won't be satisfied": Ford, p. 71.

120  Donovan's nickname (FN): John Mosedale, *The Greatest of All*. New York: Dial, 1974. pp. 15–16.
120  Donovan's career at Justice: Pringle.
121  Moving to Wall Street: Troy, 25–28.
121  Roving abroad: *Ibid*.
122  "Bill is not happy": Wilson, p. 322.
122  Luxury at the front: Pringle.
122  Donovan's demeanor: Polmar and Allen, Winks.
122  Appealing to women: Dunlop, p. 196.
123  "We cannot afford to be a sissy": *NYT*, Nov. 12, 1939.
123  Knox's recommendation: Knox to Roosevelt, Dec. 15, 1939, Navy Folder, PSF, FDRL.
123  "Might be misunderstood": Roosevelt to Knox, Dec. 29, 1939, *PL*, Vol 4, p. 975.
123  "A skinny kid": Stevenson, p. 5.
123  "Burning urgency": Dunlop, vii.
124  "Transcends other questions": *NYT*, June 22, 1940.
124  FDR approves: Hyde, p. 36.
124  "The real assignment": Mowrer, p. 315.
125  Kennedy at Harvard: Whalen, p. 25.
125  He promised himself: Graham and Wander, p. 225.
125  "Broke down and cried": Whalen, p. 49.
126  "Exactly what you think": *Ibid* p. 157.
126  Kennedy grumbled: *Ibid*, p. 174.
126  "He laughed so hard": Beschloss, pp. 153–54.
126  "He's done more for me": Whalen, pp. 282–84.
127  "Joe has been taken in": Farley, p. 199.
127  "He understood completely": Whalen, p. 252.
127  "Had a good laugh": Ickes, *The Inside Struggle*, p. 712.
127  "The slightest bit of good": Langer and Gleason, p. 252.
127  Friendship cools: Beschloss, p. 192.
128  "I'll eat my hat": Moffat, p. 303.
128  Tyler Kent episode: Whalen, pp. 309–20.
128  "It is appalling": Long, p. 114.
129  Relations with British: Whalen, p. 278.
129  Kent case details (FN): Gerald Nye Papers, Box 14, Tyler Kent Folder, Hoover Library.
130  "I think it is stronger": *NYT*, March 8, 1940.
130  Nicholson's rejoinder: Whalen, p. 287.
130  JFK's thesis: Whalen, pp. 295–96.
130  Luce's foreword: Elson, p. 428.
130  "If we had to fight": *FRUS*, 1940, Vol. 3. p. 29. Kennedy to Hull, May 15, 1940
131  "The height of nonsense": Welles to Roosevelt, July 12, 1940. Box 62, Navy Department-Knox Folder, PSF, FDRL.
131  "Straighten it out": Roosevelt to Knox, July 13, 1940, Box 62, Navy Department-Knox Folder, PSF, FDRL.
131  On board the *Sequoia*: Dunlop, p. 204, citing Frank Knox to his wife, July 14, 1940. Knox papers, LC.
131  Gauging British determination: Leutze, p. 100.
131  Dinner at the Embassy: Dunlop, p. 208.
132  "To bare their breasts": Dunlop, p. viii.
132  Kirk's warning: Leutze, p. 101.
132  Defeatist views: Victor Cavendish-Bentinck memo, Aug. 2, 1940. FO 371/24240.
132  Visit to the palace: Dunlop, p. 209; Stevenson, p. 114.
132  Churchill's command post: Stevenson, p. 125.
133  British show of strength: Ford, p. 91.

133 Meeting with Mowrer: Leutze, p. 100; Mowrer, pp. 314–17.
134 "Mr. Kennedy is rather particular": Kirk to Donovan, July 25, 1940; Donovan Papers.
134 "Dear Wild Colonel": Cooper to Donovan, July 29, 1940. Donovan Papers, U.S. Army Military History Institute.
134 Lee's background: Lee, xiii, 19.
134 "I would have been in a corner": *Ibid*, pp. 28 ff.
134 Donovan's return: *NYT*, Aug. 5, 1940.
135 Roosevelt not communicative: *PC*, Aug. 6, 1940, Vol. 16: 96-97 *Ibid*. Aug. 9, 1940, Vol. 16, pp. 103–104. *Ibid*, Aug. 10, 1940, Vol. 16, pp. 111–112.
135 Lothian reported to London: Lothian Telegram No. 1641, Aug. 7, 1940, FO 371/24237 A 3542D90/45.
135 Fifth Column articles: *NYT*, Aug. 20–24.
135 Donovan's meeting with FDR: Leutze, p. 100, citing Donovan summary to John Balfour and T. North Whitehead, Dec. 21, 1940 in F.O.A. 5194/4925/45.
136 Donovan's lobbying: Stimson Diary Aug. 6, 13; Langer and Gleason, p. 716; Donovan letters of Aug. 27 to Brendan Bracken, Rear Admiral J. H. Godfrey, Sir Cyril Newall, and Captain Alan G. Kirk, Donovan Papers, MHI.

## CHAPTER SEVEN: THE OTHER BATTLE OF BRITAIN

137 "Public opinion itself": Lothian to Foreign Office, Feb. 15, 1940. FO 371 24238, A1190/131/45.
137 "Stop Hitler Now": *NYT*, June 11, 1940, reprinted in Johnson, *Battle*, p. 85, which is a chronicle of the White committee's activities.
138 Villard's response: Sherwood, p. 167.
138 "A great piece of work": *PC*, 1940, June 11, Vol. 15, pp. 556–57.
139 FDR's acceptance speech: *PPA*, 1940, July 19, p. 302.
139 The dominant sentiment: BLI Report No. 274. June 11, 1940. FO 371/24240 A3427/131/45.
139 Demanding all-out aid: *Philadelphia Inquirer*, June 2, 1940.
139 One emotion dominated: BLI No. 316, July 3, 1940, FO 371/24241, A3628.
139 Public equallly divided: *POQ*, December 1940, 711.
139 Everything for England but war: *Ibid*, September 1940, 391.
140 Anti-war sentiment: BLI report No. 284, FO 371 24240 A3427/131/45.
140 "No islands anymore": *NYT*, June 14, 1940.
140 "Lead us not into war": *Time*, June 24, 1940.
140 Wheeler's warning: *NYT*, June 13, 1940.
140 "They are going fast": White Papers, LC.
140 "Lost his cud": Johnson, *Battle*, 100.
140 Fear of Hitler: Thomsen to Foreign Ministry, May 16,1940 *DGFP*, Series D, Vol. IX, p. 350, No. 253.
141 Wiegand's warning: Wiedemann to Weizaeker April 17, 1939. DGFP series D Vol. VI, p. 272.
141 Investigators later learned: Rogge, 234–36.
141 Thorkelson's insert: *Ibid*, 236–37.
141 Roosevelt's muted response: *PC*, 1940, June 14, Vol. 15, pp. 567–68, No. 652.
142 Talking to business editors: *PC*, 1940, No. 652-A, Vol. 15, pp. 571–73.
143 "Time to turn": Lindbergh, "Aviation, Geography and Race."
143 Lindbergh's assessment: Cole, *Lindbergh*, p. 54. Mosley, p. 225, p. 229.
143 Impact of Lindbergh's views: Cole, *Lindbergh*, p. 53. Hull, p. 590.
143 "This amiable man": Rogge, pp. 275–76.
143 Reaction to FDR: Lindbergh, *Journals*, p. 184.

143  (Lindbergh's medal) (FN): Mosley, p. 234.
143  Not numerically inferior (FN): Bullitt, pp. 424–25.
144  FDR's offer: *Ibid*, p. 259.
144  "We need fear no invasion": *NYT*, Sept. 16, 1939.
144  No danger of invasion: *NYT*, May 20, 1940.
144  Rallying the isolationists: BLI Report, May 27, 1940. A 3427/131/45.
144  "A blind young man": *NYT*, May 21, 1940.
144  "Wrong way Corrigan": *Ibid*. In 1938 Douglas P. Corrigan, a 31-year-old Los Angeles
      stunt pilot, was denied permission to fly the Atlantic from New York by the Federal
      Bureau of Air Commerce. The agency did not think his 1929 Curtiss-Robin monoplane
      with a top speed of 95 miles per hour, no radio, and no instruments but a compass was
      up to the trip. Corrigan bought 320 gallons of gas, took off, and 27 hours later landed in
      Dublin, where he earned his nickname by claiming he thought he had been headed
      back home to California. *Time*, July 25, 1938.
145  Lindbergh is a Nazi: Freidel, *Rendezvous*, p. 301 citing MD, May 20,1940, FDRL.
      Others held that view, too, including the U.S. ambassador to Paris, William Bullitt. That
      same month, when Lindbergh was considering traveling in Europe, the British made
      informal inquiries of U.S. diplomats about the appropriateness of granting him a visa to
      visit England. Bullitt told his colleague, the British ambassador, that he regarded
      Lindbergh "as a Nazi agent," whose arrest he would recommend to the French govern-
      ment if he chose to visit that country. Tel. No. 409. Sir R. Campbell to Foreign Office.
      May 25, 1940, FO 371/24239, A 3295/90/45. Lindbergh did not make the trip.
      Lindbergh, *Journals*, p. 347.
145  German reaction: Rogge, pp. 277–78; von Boetticher to the Foreign Ministry, May 24,
      1940, *DGFP*, Vol. IX, No. 311.
145  Lindbergh's June 15 speech: *NYT*, June 16, 1940.
145  Pittman's response: *NYT*, June 17, 1940.
145  Summing up the quandary: BLI No. 295, June 21, 1940, FO 371/ 24240, A3427/131/45.
145  "A grand job": Johnson, *Letters*, p. 400.
145  "Just the rooster": Johnson, *WAWA*, p. 520.
146  Gannett's appraisal: *Ibid*, p. 79.
146  "A middle class product": Parrington, *Main Currents in American Thought*, New York:
      Harcourt, 1927, 1930, Vol.2, p. 374.
146  "We don't care to build up": Johnson, *WAWA*, p. 94.
146  "No man has waged": *Ibid*, p. 210.
146  View on other GOP presidents: Allen, Frederick Lewis. *Only Yesterday*. New York:
      Harper, 1964, pp. 125, 150. Johnson, *WAWA*, p. 425.
146  "For the New Deal": *Ibid*.
147  Advice on Winrod: Roosevelt to White, June 8, 1938; White to Roosevelt, June 10,
      1938. William Allen White papers, Series C, box 290; LC. *NYT*, July 31, 1938.
147  "Watch out for your health": White to Roosevelt, February, 1938; Roosevelt to White,
      Oct. 13, 1938; William Allen White papers, Series C box 290; LC.
147  "Bothering with Venezuela": Johnson, *WAWA*, p. 251.
148  "The devil's joke": *Ibid*, p. 510.
148  Repealing the arms embargo: *Ibid*, pp. 516–18.
148  Roosevelt's "problem": Roosevelt to White, Dec. 14, 1939; White to Roosevelt, Dec. 22,
      1939; William Allen White papers, Series C, box 290. LC.
148  An emergency appeal: Johnson, *Battle*, p. 69.
149  The Committee's activities: BLI No. 279, June 12 1940, A 3427/131/45 FO 371/24240.
149  "Nowhere to go": *Ibid*.
149  "Morganatic relationship": Johnson, *Battle*, p. 91.
149  A specific goal: *Ibid*.
149  The July 23 appeal: *Ibid*, p. 100.

149   "We must show him": Johnson, *WAWA*, p. 532.
150   "Between us and Hitler": *NYT*, July 30, 1940.
150   Miller's manifesto: *NYT*, June 10, 1940.
150   Opposed to war: *POQ*, Sept. 1940, p. 553.
150   Century Group members: Miller, p. 94.
151   Anglo-Saxon origins: Chadwin, p. 70.
151   Forming the National Policy Committee: Miller, p. 82.
151   "Some personal responsibility": Miller to Baruch, Feb. 10, 1937, National Policy Committee papers, LC.
151   "The people do not realize": Miller to White, July 18, 1940, William Allen White papers, LC.
152   He was able to report: Chadwin, p. 41.
152   The group agreed: Miller Papers, Alderman Library.
152   "A great deal still to be done": Chadwin, p. 76.
152   More thought and more legwork: Chadwin, pp. 75–76; Rogge, pp. 181–82.
152   Luce's dinner at the White House: Elson, p. 435; Herzstein, p. 15, Kobler, p. 122, Miller, p. 98, Chadwin, p. 81.
153   "The WASP ascendancy": Alsop, pp. 18, 48–49.
153   Alsop's report: Memorandum of Meeting, July 25, 1940, Miller papers, Alderman Library.
154   Agar's view: Agar, 145.
154   Roosevelt non-committal: Chadwin, 87.
155   Get Pershing: Agar, pp. 147–48.
155   Efforts to get Pershing: Miller, pp. 99–101.
155   Pershing's view: Agar, 147.
156   Pershing's speech: *NYT*, Aug. 5, 1940.
156   Page one photograph: *NYHT*, August 5, 1940.
157   "Now is the moment": Lothian to Churchill, July 30, 1940. FO 371/24240 A3582.
157   "A thing to do now": Kimball, p. 57, C-20x.

## CHAPTER EIGHT: BELLING THE CAT

159   FDR in shirt sleeves: *Time*, August 5, 1940.
159   "The grievous action": *NYT*, July 4, 1940.
159   Boost from the press: BLI No. 333, July 19,1940,FO 370 24240, A 3628/131/45
160   Whitehead's conclusion: FO 371/24241 A 3628/131/45.
160   Poll figures: Cantrill, "America Faces the War."
160   "If that's all we mean": *NYT*, July 31, 1940.
161   *Dallas News* editorial: quoted in *Time*, August 12, 1940.
161   *Time* charged: *Time*, August 5, 1940.
161   "One navy and two oceans": Lothian, p. 112.
161   Reaction to speech: Butler, p. 291; BLI Report No. 357, August 1940, A 3628 FO 370/24241.
162   Knox's background: Schlesinger, *Upheaval*, pp. 529–30; Graham, p. 226.
162   Neither as mean nor as narrow: In 1935, in the course of his unsuccessful pursuit of his party's presidential nomination, Knox's denunciations of Roosevelt were so outlandish, and therefore so counterproductive, that the President was asked at his press conference if Knox, and Herbert Hoover, then engaged in similar assaults, were on the Democratic payroll. "Strictly off the record, it is a question of how much longer we can afford to pay them," Roosevelt wisecracked. "They have been so successful that they are raising their prices." PC 1935, No. 212.
162   Knox heard Lothian: The most complete account of Knox's conversation with Lothian and

of the August 2 cabinet meeting is provided in a memorandum written for Morgenthau, who was absent, by Assistant Treasury Secretary Daniel Bell and filed with the Morgenthau diary at the Franklin D. Roosevelt Library for the date of August 2. Except as otherwise indicated, this account of the Cabinet meeting is based on that memorandum

162  Lothian "almost tearful": Ickes, p. 283.
162  Prior conversation about bases: Tel. No. 1307. Lothian to Foreign Office. July 11, 1940. FO 371/24255.
163  Hull's persona: Langer and Gleason, pp. 7–9.
164  "Who would take Hitler's word?": Watkins, p. 668.
164  Cohen had been approached: Ickes, p. 233.
164  Ickes sent a memorandum: *Ibid*, p. 271.
164  "Well nigh desperate": *Ibid*, pp. 282–83.
165  "God on his side": *Ibid*, p. 266.
165  "If I could be of help": *Ibid*, p. 284.
165  Cabinet room description: Rosenman, pp. 1–3.
165  The Pan American conference: *NYT*, Aug. 1, 1940.
166  "The one thought on the Hill": Ickes, p. 292.
166  Forcing Willkie's hand: *Ibid*.
166  Farley's plans: Farley, pp. 318 ff.
166  "Really a big man": Stimson diary, Aug. 2, 1940.
167  "All have confidence": Ickes, p. 293.
167  FDR's memo: *PL*, Vol 4, p. 1050.
168  "We made real progress"; *PL*, Vol. 4, II, p. 1053.
168  White's difficulties: *NYT*, Aug. 1, 2, 1940; Chadwin, pp. 94–96.
168  "Done us dirt": Chadwin, p. 95.
168  "He didn't blow up": Langer and Gleason, p. 754, citing *Chicago Tribune*, Nov. 30, 1940.
169  Poll findings on FDR v. Willkie: Cantrill.
169  Cheers in Norfolk: *NYT*, July 30, 1940.
169  "Grass roots stuff": Neal, p. 122.
170  Willkie conquers New York: Barnard, p. 191, *Newsweek*, July 15, 1940.
170  "Politics makes strange bedfellows": Neal, p. 144.
170  She cheered him up: Papers of Irita Van Doren, LC.
171  "Everybody knows about us": Neal, pp. 43–44. But in reality Willkie was not always so forthright. When Washington columnist Marquis Childs confronted him with the rumors about himself and Van Doren, he claimed they were just "good friends." Neal, pp. 43–44. Later he tried to laugh the matter off by telling a group of reporters that Childs had accused him of having five mistresses.
171  "The dolly letters": Neal, p. 145.
171  The Guru letters: Schlesinger, *Coming of the New Deal*, p. 32; Macdonald, pp. 120 ff; Davis, p. 616.
171  "Sick at heart": Douglas, p. 339; Michelson, p. 197.
171  Roosevelt told Mellett: Butow. Mrs. Willkie's appearances at her husband's side made FDR think back to the defensive measures taken by an earlier political figure, New York's playboy mayor Jimmy Walker, who had come under investigation for corruption in 1932. The legislative probe of Walker, a fellow Democrat, who had nominated Roosevelt for governor in 1928, caused intense embarrassment for then Governor Roosevelt. He was obliged to preside at the inquiry into the charges against Walker and feared the whole mess would divide his party and hurt his chances for the presidency. It was well known that Walker had a mistress, a showgirl named Betty Compton with whom he lived for years. But when he was under fire in 1932, as Roosevelt told the story, he paid his estranged wife $10,000 to spend the weekend with him in Albany and attend Mass on Sunday at the Albany Cathedral. "Now Mrs. Willkie may not have been hired, but in effect she's been hired to return to Wendell and smile and make this cam-

paign with him," Roosevelt told Mellett. "Now whether there was a money price behind it, I don't know, but it's the same idea."

171  Roosevelt's taping (FN): Butow
172  To the bitter end: Willkie.
172  "And so you Republicans": *NYT*, June 29, 1940.
172  Joining the party: *Newsweek*, July 15, 1940.
172  Willkie's strategy: *Ibid*.
172  Appeal to Democrats: *NYT*, July 30.
173  The Willkie clubs: Parmet, p. 205.
173  Minimal civility: *NYT*, Aug. 12; Barnard, 216, 551–52; John C. O'Laughlin memorandum, August 15, 1940; O'Laughlin correspondence, Herbert Hoover Library.
173  "Avoid conflicts": Martin, p. 110.
174  "If we want to get into a war": Langer and Gleason, *Chicago Tribune*, Aug. 6, 1940.
174  "It's not my baby": Smith, Gene, pp. 216–207; Moley, pp. 72–78
174  Willkie's revenge: *NYT*, August 10, 1940.
175  "The attitude would justify it": Stimson diaries, August 8, 1940.
175  A reassuring telegram: White papers, Box 347, series C, LC.

## CHAPTER NINE: GETTING AROUND THE LAW

177  "Ambition must counter-act ambition": Fairfield, p. 160.
177  Dies's lament: Burns, p. 339.
178  McNary sent word: Cohen, p. 27.
179  Cohen background: Lasser, Lash, *Dealers*, pp. 36–53.
179  "Corcorandcone": Louchheim, p. 114.
179  Overused tactic: Moley, pp. 183 fn.
180  "Go to the movies": Louchheim, p. 113.
180  Playing for time: *Ibid*, p. 115.
180  Morgenthau's concern: Blum, *Roosevelt and Morgenthau*, p. 258.
180  Cohen approached on his own: *Ickes*, p. 233.
180  Cohen memorandum: Cohen to Roosevelt, July 19, 1940, PSF, FDRL.
182  Off base: Ickes, p. 271.
182  He broke out in hives: Ward, *Temperament*, pp. 30–31.
183  Cohen's arguments lacked force: *PL*, Vol. 4, pp. 1048–49.
183  Another memo: Hackworth memorandum for Hull, August 2, 1940, PSF, FDRL.
184  Developments in the war: *Almanac*.
184  Only one sentence: *NYT*, Aug. 3, 1940.
184  Willkie's lead in the polls: *Ibid*, Aug 4, 1940.
184  FDR Jr. on duty: *Ibid*, Aug. 3, 1940.
184  Seeking Frankfurter's help: Lash, *Dealers*, p. 409; Murphy, p. 210; Lasser.
185  Sums from Brandeis: Murphy, pp. 40–45.
185  "A plague of lawyers": Peek.
185  "If it weren't for him": Louchheim, p. 56.
185  "A patriarchial sorcerer": Moley, p. 285.
185  Lobbied hard for him: Murphy, p. 187.
186  Jews called on FDR: Freedman: pp. 481–82.
186  Frankfurter solved the problem: Murphy, p. 197.
186  Depicting FDR: Freedman, p. 533.
187  "I do not regret": *PPA*, 1940, No. 70, pp. 301–03.
187  Had no hesitation: Lash, *Dealers*, p. 409; Lasser.
187  An old friend in Acheson: Murphy, p. 210; Lasser.
188  "If confirmed, please send": Interview with Philip Kurland, June 12, 1993.

188  Frankfurter's hearing: *NYT*, Jan. 13, 1939; Acheson, p. 209; Baker, p. 210.
189  "A real sportsman": Acheson, pp. 193–94.
189  The Cohen-Acheson letter: *NYT*, August 11, 1940.
189  Survey of the Senate: Ben Cohen Papers, LC.
189  Acheson's first choices: Acheson, p. 222.
190  "No part preparing": Lash, *Dealers*, p. 411.
190  "That was not the purpose": Acheson, p. 222.
191  The President "might be interested": Cohen to LeHand, August 12, 1940, Destroyers-for-Bases Folder, PSF, FDRL.
191  "Somewhere in midair": Alsop to Helen Reid, Aug. 13, 1940, Joseph Alsop papers, LC.
191  "Filled with anxiety": Stimson diary, Aug. 13, 1940.
192  When to tell Congress?: Blum, p. 180.

## CHAPTER TEN: "A RATHER HARD BARGAIN"

193  "He usually gets 80 percent of the deal": Reynolds, 25, citing MD, Vol. 22, p. 155, April 29, 1936, FDRL.
193  "Invariably demanded 90 percent": Young.
193  Overworked and overwrought: Reynolds, *Lothian*, p. 29.
193  "Entirely satisfactory": Nicolson, p. 104; Colville, p. 198.
194  Lothian warned Churchill: Tel. No 1579, Lothian to Churchill, Aug 1, 1940 FO 371/24240 A 3582/131/45.
194  Roosevelt summoned Lothian: Tel. No. 1606, Aug. 3, 1940 FO371/24241 A 3670/141/45
194  A gesture of good will: War Cabinet Paper (40) No. 276. FO 371/24241 A3600/2961/45; Reynolds, *Lothian*, p. 29n; Leutze, pp. 107–111.
195  Early interest in bases: Conn and Fairchild, Vol. 12, p. 354; Rogge, pp. 152–54; Cole, pp. 472–74.
195  "We want to make it difficult": Reynolds, p. 54.
195  No immediate threat: Greenfield, p. 25.
195  The German expedition: Conn and Fairchild, Vol. 1, pp. 47–48
195  Congress galvanized: *NYT*, June 4, 1940.
196  Davies urges: Conn and Fairchild, Vol. I, 47
196  Several papers supported: BLI Report, Survey of American Press, June 14, 1940. FO 370/24240 A 3373/131/45.
196  "A gracious thing" *Ibid*.
196  Plan for repurchase: *New Republic*, June 3, 1940.
196  The Steuben Society's complaint: *NYT*, June 25, 1940.
196  Instead of waiting: Tel. No. 814, Lothian to Foreign Office, May 27, 1940, FO 371/24255, A3297/2961/45.
197  The War Cabinet meeting room: Simkins.
197  Churchill opposed: Balfour minute, May 28. FO 371/24255.
197  "Practically no help": Extract from War Cabinet Conclusions, No. 146(40) May 29, FO 371/24255 A3297/2961/45.
198  Reviving the idea: Tel. No. 1086, June 24, 1940, Lothian to Foreign Office. FO 371/24255.
198  Mixed reaction: Balfour minute on Paper L, July 1, 1940. FO 371/24255 A3600/2961/45; Balfour minute on Paper D, July 30, 1940. FO 371/24255 A3600/2961/45.
198  Halifax sums up: Memorandum July 18, 1940. FO 371/24255 A3600/2961/45.
199  Outlining more exensive grant: Tel. No. 1579, Lothian to Churchill, Aug. 1, 1940. FO 371 A3528/131/45
199  Churchill's bold front: Kennedy to Hull, May 15, 1940, *FRUS Vol 3, 1940*, pp. 29–30.

200  "The vital interests": Balfour memo, Aug. 8, 1940, FO 371/24240.

200  "Rather like blackmail": Leutze, p. 77.

201  "If their fright is justified": Berle diaries, Box 211, FDRL.

201  A blunt reply: Leutze, p. 281 n10, citing Cordell Hull papers, box 47, Folder 113, LC.

201  Churchill's June 4 address: Gilbert, p. 468.

201  Lothian's distress: Lothian to Churchill, Tel. No. 932, June 7, 1940. A3316 FO 371/24239.

201  "It is not for us": Lothian, p. 101.

201  Churchill reply: Churchill to Lothian, Tel. No. 1038, June 9, 1940. A3316, FO 371/24239.

202  His first obstacle: Tel. No. 1610, Lothian to Foreign Office. Aug. 4, 1940. FO 371/24241 A3640.

202  Such procedures move slowly: Hull, p. 833.

202  Meeting with Welles: Tel. No. 1616, Lothian to Foreign Office, Aug. 5, 1940. FO 371/24241 A3640.

203  "The world would dissolve": Ickes, *The Inside Struggle*, p. 640.

203  "Swallowed a ramrod": Ward, p. 473n.

203  Despite his demeanor (FN): *Ibid*, Bullitt, p. 517, *NYT* Sept. 25, 1943.

204  "Ambiguous and ill drafted": Churchill to Halifax, Aug. 6, 1940. FO 371/24241.

204  In this nautical company: Leutze, pp. 110–11.

204  "Pray make it clear": Unsent telegram, Churchill to Lothian, August 7, 1940.

204  "The argument with the most effect": Lothian Tel. No. 1629, Aug. 6, 1940. A3670 FO 371/24241.

204  Churchill turned to Halifax: Churchill to Halifax, Aug. 7, 1940. A 3670 FO 371/24241.

204  The unsent cable (FN): *Their Finest Hour*, pp. 405–06. Leutze, p. 286, n75.

205  "Very great difficulties": Halifax to Lothian, No. 1827, Aug. 8, 1940. FO 371/24241.

205  Haziness about the bases: Halifax to Lothian, No. 1828, Aug. 8, 1940. FO 371/24241.

205  British desiderata: Lothian to Welles, August 8, 1940. *FRUS*, Vol 3, p. 64; Tel. No. 1653 Lothian to Foreign Office, Aug. 8, 1940. FO 371/24241 A3670

205  "Implied no commitment": Welles to Roosevelt, Aug. 8, 1940. State Department files, Welles Folder. PSF, FDRL.

205  "Entirely unsatisfactory": Welles to Kennedy, Aug. 14, 1940. *FRUS*, Vol. 3, p. 66.

205  He would act on his own: Lothian to Foreign Office, Tel. No. 1660, Aug. 9, 1940. FO 371/24241, A3670.

206  "Admirable shape": Stimson diary, Aug. 13, 1940.

206  FDR's offer: Kimball, 58, R-8x.

206  London should bear in mind: Lothian to Foreign Office, Tel. No. 1703, Aug. 13, 1940, FO 371/24241; Balfour minute, Aug. 14, 1940, FO 371/24241, A3793G.

206  "Russia's demands on Finland": Colville, p. 223.

207  "Not a neutral action": Extract from War Cabinet Conclusions, 227(40); Aug. 14, 1940. A3793G, FO 371/24241.

207  "How grateful I feel": Kimball, p. 60, C-21x.

207  An aura of nonchalance: *PC*, No. 671 Vol. 16, pp. 123–27.

208  Smarter not to campaign: Moffat, p. 325.

208  "Broom sticks and rain pipes": *Time*, Aug. 26, 1940; *NYT*, Aug. 18, 1940.

209  "The important thing": *PC*, No. 672, Vol. 16, pp. 131–32.

209  "Willkie is lost": Moffat, p. 325.

209  "A very happy mood": Pickersgill, p. 131.

209  O'Laughlin's advice: O'Laughlin memorandum, Aug. 15, 1940. John C. O'Laughlin correspondence, Hoover Library.

210  "Like a piece in a jig saw puzzle": Pickersgill, p. 131.

210  "Find some other way": *Ibid*, 132.

210  Even as a gift: *Ibid*, p. 135.

210  Arms in addition to the destroyers: Conn and Fairchild, Vol. I, p. 57; Welles to
     Roosevelt, June 19, 1940. Navy Department July–December 1940 Folder, PSF, FDRL.
210  All seemed in readiness: Welles to Roosevelt, Aug. 20, 1940. PSF, FDRL.
211  Churchill's problems: Reynolds, 287.
211  "A rather hard bargain": Kennedy to Hull, *FRUS 1940 Vol. 3*, pp. 67–68.
211  "Rights, powers and authority": Welles to Roosevelt, Aug. 19, 1940. State Department
     Folder, 1940, PSF, FDRL.
211  "Very advantageous bargain": Churchill, p. 408.
212  Churchill's speech: *NYT*, Aug. 21, 1940.
212  He sang "Old Man River": Colville, p. 227.


# CHAPTER ELEVEN: "TWO FRIENDS IN DANGER"

213  Kennedy listened: *NYT*, August 21, 1940.
214  "They were ready to pull away": Pickersgill, p. 140.
214  "A strange mixture": Colesville, p. 128.
214  Lee's impressions: Lee, p. 37.
215  More like a cleric: Morison, p. 41.
215  Silence for assent: Abbazia, pp. 66–67; In the wake of Pearl Harbor Stark gave up his
     post as Chief of Naval Operations and became Commander of U.S. Naval Forces
     Europe. Graham and Wander, p. 401.
215  Did not yield the conn: Goodheart, p. 64.
215  "Do run over": Harold Stark Papers, Correspondence File, Box 23, U.S. Naval
     Historical Center.
215  "My only objection": *Ibid*.
216  Filled with misgivings: Leutze, p. 118, citing Stark to Knox memorandum, Aug. 17,
     1940. CNO files, Destroyers-for-Bases Folder, Naval Archives. Also Sutphen, p. 68. The
     original of the document was apparently lost in the transfer of records from the U.S.
     Naval Historical Center to the National Archives.
216  The Townsend memorandum: Papers of Robert H. Jackson, Legal File, Box 88. LC.
216  "Around this table": *Hearings on Emergency Supplemental Appropriations Bill*.
     Committee on Appropriations, Subcommittee on Naval Appropriations. U.S. House of
     Representatives, 76th Congress, Nov. 28, 1939. pp. 141–154.
216  Marshall's view (FN): Perish, p. 154; Conn and Fairchild, *Framework*, p. 57.
217  "Ready in case of need": *Supplemental Hearing—U.S. Navy Appropriation Bill, 1941*.
     Committee on Appropriations, Subcommittee on Naval Appropriations, U.S. Senate,
     76th Congress. Tuesday, May 21, 1940.
217  He would have to comply: Leutze, p. 119; Sutphen, p. 70.
217  Backed the court plan: Gerhart, pp. 109–14.
218  "Not that kind of bird": Gerhart, pp. 221–22.
218  Jackson's opinion: Jackson to Knox, Aug. 17, 1940. PSF, Destroyers-for-Bases Folder, FDRL.
219  "A feller needs a friend": Stark memorandum for the President, Aug. 21, 1940. Navy
     Folder, PSF, FDRL.
219  "A pretty good job": Stimson diary, Aug. 21, 1940.
219  Stimson's ties to Frankfurter: Stimson and Bundy, p. 7; Murphy, p. 36.
219  Frankfurter's view: Stimson diary, Aug. 16, 1940.
220  Walsh wrote FDR: Walsh to Roosevelt, Aug. 19, 1940. David Walsh Papers, College of
     the Holy Cross, Worcester, Mass.
220  FDR did not give up: *PL*, Vol. 4, p. 1056.
220  Churchill underlined determination: Kimball, p. 63, C-22x.
221  A new list: Lothian to Welles, Aug. 22, 1940. Box 58, Navy Folder, July–October 1940,
     PSF, FDRL.

221  No deal without "molasses": Lothian to Foreign Office, No. 1789; Aug. 23, 1940. PREM 3/462/2/3/ Westminster College.
222  "Rather incensed": Cadogan, p. 23.
222  Churchill proposed: Leutze, p. 122.
222  "Empires don't bargain": Gerhart, p. 217.
223  "Grand policy": Stimson diary, Aug. 23, 1940.
223  Hull sounded a harsher note: Hull, pp. 835 ff.
223  Yet another cable: Kimball, p. 66, c-23x.
223  Hackworth's answer: Hull, p. 837.
224  Churchill adamant: Kimball, p. 67, c-24x.
225  "Political life at stake": Lothian to Foreign Office, Tel. No. 1857, Aug. 28, 1940. Premier File 3/462/2/3.
225  Hull's memorandum and final details: Hull, pp. 839–41.
225  "I do not enjoy being a dummy": Beschloss, p. 211.
226  "You are essential": Roosevelt to Kennedy, Aug. 28, 1940. Box 37, J. P. Kennedy Folder, July 1939–1940, PSF, FDRL.
226  No way mollified: Kennedy to Hull, Aug. 29, 1940. 71, *FRUS*, 1940, Vol. 3.
226  The new cable: Kennedy to Hull, Aug. 29, 72, FRUS, 1940, Vol. 3.
227  FDR asked pointedly: Kimball, p. 69, R-10x.
227  "It certainly does": Kimball, p. 69, C-26x.

## CHAPTER TWELVE: *"FAIT ACCOMPLI"*

229  "Awfully well": *NYT*, Sept 1, 1940.
230  Labor Day Message: *PPA*, 1940, No. 86.
230  Evidence of the risk (FN): Reynolds, p. 104.
231  Nye declared: *NYT*, Sept. 2, 1940.
231  The destroyer poll: Gallup poll, Aug. 17, 1940, cited in "Gallup and Fortune Polls, *POQ*, Dec. 1940, p. 713.
231  A less scientific study: *NYT*, Sept. 1, 1940.
231  The three documents: These three documents, along with Jackson's opinion, are in *PPA*, 1940, No. 91, pp. 391–407.
232  Welles's oversight: Conn and Fairchild, Vol. 1, p. 59; Stimson diary, Sept. 10, Sept. 14, 1940.
233  Altered the punctuation: Cf U.S. Statutes at large, 65th Congress, Vol. 40, Ch. 30, 1917, Title V, Section 3.
233  Jay's defense: Fairfield, p. 188.
234  "Germany might take umbrage": Long, p. 125.
235  "My full and cordial approval": Destroyer Bases Folder, PSF, FDRL.
235  Fleeson's and Baruch's impressions: Goodwin; p. 147.
235  "Sensational" story: Ickes, p. 313.
236  The trip to Tennessee: *NYT*, Sept. 3, 1940; *Time*, Sept. 9, 1940.
236  Ickes troubled: Ickes, p. 310.
236  "I glory in it": *PPA*, 1940, No. 88, p. 363.
237  Americans must prepare: *Ibid*, No. 89, p. 370.
237  "Sentimental pilgrimage": *NYT*, Sept. 4, 1940.
237  The press conference scene: *CSM*, Sept. 4, 1940; *Time*, Sept. 16, 1940, Davis, p. 105.
238  "For God sakes": The complete transcript of the press conference is in *PC*, 1940, No. 677, Vol. 16: pp. 173–190.

## CHAPTER THIRTEEN: "AN OPENLY HOSTILE ACT"

241  "The thing that gives him strength": Donovan to Bracken, Aug. 27, 1940, U.S. Military History Institute.

241  "Congress is going to raise hell": Tully, p. 244.

241  As Gallup revaled: Smith, Richard Norton, p. 329.

242  Access to private polls: Mellett to Roosevelt, Aug. 7, 1940. Folder No. 4721, PPF, FDRL.

242  "Extremely interesting": Roosevelt to Mellett, Aug. 12, 1940. Folder No. 4721, PSF, FDRL.

242  As Strout wrote: *CSM*, Sept. 4, 1940.

243  The *Times*'s coverage; *NYT*, Sept. 4, 1940.

243  "The beginning of the ebb" *CSM*, Sept. 4, 1940.

243  "A stockade of steel": *NYHT*, Sept. 4, 1940.

243  *Chicago Tribune* trumpeted praise: Quoted in *NYT*, Sept. 4, 1940.

243  Hoover's reaction: *Public Statements of Herbert Hoover*, 1940. No. 2687, Hoover Library.

243  Congressional reaction: *NYT*, Sept. 4, 1940.

244  "The outlook is dark": cited in *CR*, Sept. 26, 1940, p. 12647.

244  "Would be more desirable": *NYT*, Sept. 4, 1940.

244  "Regrettable": *Ibid*.

244  Prodding Willkie: Barnard, p. 229.

245  Willkie's second thoughts: *NYT*, Sept. 7, 1940.

245  "Willkie could only talk": *Ibid*, Sept. 5, 1940.

245  "Only a handful": *Ibid*.

245  "It was true": *PC*, 1940, No. 68, Vol. 16, p. 197.

245  Willkie's slump: *NYT*, Sept. 8, 1940, Sept. 20, 1940.

246  British "jubilant": *Ibid*, Sept. 4, 1940.

246  Lloyd George grumbled: Lash, *Roosevelt and Churchill*, p. 217.

246  "Hard cash": Colville, p. 238.

246  Ten straight days: Gilbert, p. 758.

247  Churchill's speech. *NYT*, Sept. 6, 1940; Churchill, p. 415.

247  The broken promise: Stimson Diary, Sept. 14, 1940; Langer and Gleason, p. 769; Conn and Fairchild, Vol. 1, p. 59.

247  "Take it up yourself": MD, Vol. 304, Sept. 4, 1940.

247  "Action this day": Churchill, p. 666.

247  Until Lend-Lease: Hall, p. 145.

248  Arrangements for the other material: Stimson diaries, Sept. 10, Sept. 27, Oct 1; Churchill, p. 672; Conn and Fairchild, Vol. 1, p. 60.

248  Destroyers depart: *NYT*, Sept. 8, 1940.

249  Defects of destroyers: Goodheart, pp. 194–96, 206, 213–214; Hague, pp. 7–8; Churchill, p. 606.

250  *Campbelltown*'s mission: Goodheart, p. 210; Greenberg.

250  Grading their performance: Goodheart, pp. 208, 236–37.

250  Early skepticism: *NYT*, Sept. 5, 1940; Conn and Fairchild, Vol. 1, pp. 60–61.

250  Past neglect: Building the Navy's Bases in World War II, pp. 5–13.

251  A "token" patrol: Abbazia, p. 66–67.

251  Rapid progress not expected: Conn and Fairchild: Vol. 12, p. 366.

251  British concerns: Goodheart, p. 218.

252  "It is obvious": *PC*, 1940, No. 700, Vol. 16, p. 342.

252  "Awful nonsense": *Ibid*, No. 703, Vol. 16, pp. 369–70.

252  Strategic shift: Conn and Fairchild, Vol. 1, p. 67.

252  After Pearl Harbor: Morrison, pp. 144–45, 248; Goodheart, pp. 228–34.

253  Stark's reply: Morrison, p. 36.

253 "Tell people in England": Butler, p. 298.
253 A peril foreseen: Edmonds, p. 197; Hitler, p. 139.
254 Berlin considered: Von Weizsacker to Thomsen, Aug. 8, 1940, No. 312, p. 442, DGFP, Vol. X.
254 Thomsen strongly advised: *Ibid*, Thomsen to Von Weizsacker, Aug. 10, 1940, No. 1685.
254 Following explicit orders: Friedlander, p. 125; *NYT*, Sept. 4, Sept. 5, 1940.
255 Private deliberations: Ciano, p. 290; Friedlander, p. 124, citing *Les Lettres Secrètes Échangées par Hitler et Mussolini*, Paris: Editions du Pavois, 1946, p. 79.
255 Germans change their thinking: Friedlander, p. 125. Langer and Gleason, pp. 774–75, citing State Department interrogations of former German representatives in the U.S.
255 Raeder's reaction: *Führer Conferences on Matters Dealing With the German Navy, 1939–45*. Sept. 7, 1940. U.S. Department of the Navy, Office of Naval Intelligence.
256 Hitler's reaction: Bailey and Ryan, p. 93.
256 Berlin resumed talks: Friedlander, p. 131.
256 Hitler's motives: Lash, p. 220; Ciano, p. 293.
256 Grew's view: Grew, *Peace and War*, p. 92. *Turbulent Era*, p. 1225.
257 Betrayal by Hitler: Ciano, p. 229.
257 Fear of another destroyer deal: Lash, p. 220.
257 *Asahi* concluded: quoted in *NYT*, Sept. 6, 1940.
258 "The war will be long": Ciano, p. 296.

## CHAPTER FOURTEEN: BREACH OF TRUST

259 "Worked out perfectly": Roosevelt to King George VI, Nov. 22, 1940, *PL*, Vol. 4, p. 1084.
259 *Curtiss-Wright* case: *United States* v. *Curtiss-Wright Export Corp. et al.*, 299 U.S. 304.
259 Unlike the destroyer deal: Draper, p. 585.
260 Walsh's intent: *CR*, Senate, June 21, 1940, p. 8774.
260 Corwin's critique: *NYT*, Oct. 13, 1940.
260 Treaty of Washington provisions (FN): Briggs.
261 "Subject to impeachment": Moynihan, p. 72.
261 Attacking the "propaganda engine": *CR*, *Senate*, 76th Congress, 3rd session, Sept. 26, 1940, p. 12646. Also see Ross, Charles G. "Inside Story of 'Propaganda Engine' to Send U.S. Army and Navy Equipment to Britain." *St. Louis Post-Dispatch*, Sept. 22, 1940.
261 Townsend predicted: Memorandum for the Attorney General from Newman A. Townsend, Acting Solicitor General, Aug. 13, 1940, Jackson papers, LC.
261 A social contract: In *Breach of Faith*, (New York: Atheneum, 1975), pp. 329 ff. Theodore White condemns Richard Nixon for violating the American faith that no one, not even a president, stands above the law. The understanding referred to in this chapter is broader in that it is based on the political creed implicit in the Constitution as well as the explicit language of its provisions and of federal statutes.
262 "Not into foreign wars": *PPA*, 1940, No. 122, p. 517.
262 "Many drastic things": Rosenman, p. 237.
262 Evidence from his own lips: Goodwin, p. 14.
264 "Arsenal of democracy": *PPA*, 1940, No. 149, p. 643.
264 Yet another appeal: Kimball, p. 102, C-43x.
264 Jackson's speech: *NYT*, March 28, 1941.
264 "Face the fact": *Hartford Courant*, March 31, 1941.
265 Spoiling for a fight: Ickes, p. 466.
265 Resisted pressure: Cole, p. 425.
265 Shied away: *PPA*, 1941, No. 66, pp. 272–77.
265 Only three weeks before Pearl Harbor: Cole, p. 444.
265 Roosevelt convinced: *PPA*, 1941, No. 104, p. 444.

265  "Lead us": Rosenman, p. 296.
266  Roosevelt did not answer: Cole, p. 450.
266  "He would meet with defeat": Sherwood, p. 382.
266  "He had such enemies": Marshall, p. 214n.
266  Democrats cast 64 No votes: Cole, p. 439.
267  Misleading case: *PPA*, 1939, No. 130, p. 518.
267  "The peak of folly": Hull, p. 684.
267  "Raises questions": Agar, p. 137.
268  A contemporary analysis: Jacob.
268  A $4 billion ceiling: Watson, pp. 179–80.
268  "An unlimited emergency": *PPA*, 1941, No. 45, p. 181.
268  He insisted Berlin play: Sherwood, pp. 298–99.
268  A similar retreat: *PC*, 1941, No. 745, Vol. 17, pp. 367–70.
269  "Instinctively refrained": Cohen.
269  Stimson's view: Stimson and Bundy, p. 366.
270  "Automatically revert": Buhite, p. 235.
270  "A long process": Draper, p. 582.
271  "Fifty years in the future": Address at University of California, Berkeley, March 23, 1911, Moos.
271  "Fresh in our memory": Donovan, p. 201.
272  Political consequences: Donovan, p. 202.
272  U.S. not obligated: Glennon, pp. 205–06.
272  State Department memorandum: *Department of State Bulletin*, Vol XXIII, July 31, 1950, pp. 173–78.
273  "The issue was clear": Eisenhower, p. 272.
273  Cold War alarms: Lyon, p. 824.
273  Eisenhower's real motives: Ambrose, p. 472.
273  The term quarantine: Roger Hilsman, *To Move a Nation*. New York: Doubleday, 1967.
273  "*In appearance*": Sorensen, p. 678.
273  Kennedy worried: Riccards, p. 90.
274  "Plain dumb luck": Brinkley, pp. 170–73.
274  "The country heard him": Public Papers of President Lyndon B. Johnson, 1966, Vol. 1, p. 288.
274  "I would lose everything": Kearns, p. 263.
274  Johnson smothered debate: Berman, pp. 31–32.
275  Nixon appealed to middle class: Safire, p. 138.
275  Nixon warned: Public Papers of President Richard M. Nixon, Nov. 3, 1969, pp. 369–75.
275  As legal grounding: Schlesinger, *Imperial Presidency*, p. 188 n21, citing Nixon, *New Road for America*.
275  Presidents have ignored: Draper, p. 13. Glennon, *Constitutional Diplomacy*, pp. 87–122.
275  "America stands where it always has": *NYT*, Aug. 21, 1990.
275  Bush offered no rationale: Glennon, "The Gulf War and the Constitution."
276  Circumventing the law: Draper, p. 27.
276  North's view: Draper, p. 181.
276  The Boland amendment (FN): Glennon, *Constitutional Diplomacy*.
277  Findings of the probes: Select Committees' Report, *NYT*, Nov. 19, 1987; Scowcroft's View, *NYT*, Feb. 27, 1987.
277  Best efforts to no avail: Walsh, pp. 561–66.
278  Assessing Nixon's guilt: *NYT*, May 6, 1977.
278  "The masses are shortsighted": Bailey, pp. 12–13.
279  "A common discipline": *PPA*, 1933, Vol. 2, No. 1, 14.

# Bibliography

## BOOKS

Abbazia, Patrick. *Mr. Roosevelt's Navy*. Annapolis: Naval Institute, 1973.

Acheson, Dean. *Morning and Noon*. New York: Houghton Mifflin 1965.

Acheson, Dean. *Present at the Creation*. New York: Norton, 1969.

Agar, Herbert. *The Darkest Year*. New York: Doubleday, 1973.

Allen, Frederick Lewis. *Only Yesterday*. New York: Harper, 1964.

Alsop, Joseph, with Adam Platt. *"I've Seen the Best of It."* New York: Norton, 1992.

Alsop, Joseph and Robert Kintner. *American White Paper*. New York: Simon and Schuster, 1940.

Ambrose, Stephen E. *Eisenhower the President*. New York: Simon and Schuster,1984.

Bailey, Thomas. *Man In the Street*. New York: Macmillan, 1948.

Bailey, Thomas and Paul B. Ryan. *Hitler vs. Roosevelt: The Undeclared War*. New York: Free Press, 1979.

Barnard, Ellsworth. *Wendell Willkie*. Marquette Mich.: Northern Michigan University Press 1966.

Beard, Charles. *American Foreign Policy in the Making*. New Haven: Yale, 1946.

Berle, Beatrice Bishop and Travis Beal Jacobs. *Navigating the Rapids, 1918–1971*. New York: Harcourt, 1973.

Berman, Larry. *Planning A Tragedy: The Americanization of the War in Vietnam*. New York: Norton, 1983.

Beschloss, Michael R. *Kennedy and Roosevelt*. New York: Norton, 1980.

Blum, John Morton. *From the Morgenthau Diaries: Years of Crisis. 1928–1938* Boston: Houghton Mifflin, 1967.

Blum, John Morton. *From the Morgenthau Diaries: Years of Urgency. 1938–1941*. Boston: Houghton Mifflin, 1967. (Cited in Notes as Blum).

Blum, John Morton. *Roosevelt and Morgenthau*. Boston: Houghton, Mifflin, 1972.

Buhite, Russell D. and David W. Levy. *FDR's Fireside Chats*. Norman: University of Oklahoma, 1992.

Bullitt, Orville. *For the President: Personal and Secret*. Boston: Houghton Mifflin, 1972.

Brinkley, Alan. *Dean Acheson: The Cold War Years*, New Haven: Yale University, 1992.

Burns, James MacGregor. *Roosevelt: The Lion and the Fox*. New York: Harcourt, 1956.

Butler, J. R. M. *Grand Strategy*. Vol II. London: Macmillan, 1957.

Butler, J. R. M. *Lord Lothian*. New York: Macmillan, 1960.

Brown, Anthony Cave. *The Last Hero*. New York: Times Books, 1982.

Cadogan, Sir Alexander. *Diaries*. New York: Putnam, 1972.

Cantril, Hadley. *Public Opinion 1935–1946*. Princeton: Princeton University, 1951.

Chadwin, Mark. *The Hawks of World War II*. Chapel Hill: University of North Carolina, 1968.

Churchill, Winston. *Their Finest Hour*. Boston: Houghton, Mifflin 1949.

Ciano, Galeasso. *The Ciano Diaries*. Edited by Hugh Gibson. New York: Doubleday, 1946.
Cole, Wayne. *America First*. New York: Octagon, 1971.
Cole, Wayne S. *Roosevelt and the Isolationists*. Lincoln: University of Nebraska, Press 1983.
Colville, John. *The Fringes of Power*. New York: Norton, 1985.
Conkin, Paul. *The New Deal*. Arlington Heights, Ill.: Harlan Davidson, 1967.
Conn, Stetson, and Byron Fairchild. *The United States Army in World War II: Vol. XII, Part 1, The Framework of Hemisphere Defense*. Washington: Office of the Chief of Military History, 1960.
Conn, Stetson, and Byron Fairchild. *The United States Army in World War II: Vol XII, Part 2, Guarding the United States and its Outposts*. Washington: Office of the Chief of Military History, 1964.
Connally, Tom. *My Name Is Tom Connally*. New York: Crowell, 1954.
Dallek, Robert. *Roosevelt Diplomacy and World War II*. New York: Holt, Rinehart.
Davis, Kenneth S. *FDR: Into the Storm*. New York: Random House, 1993.
Davis, Forrest and Ernest Lindley. *How War Came*. New York: Simon & Schuster, 1942.
Detzer, Dorothy. *Appointment on the Hill*. New York: Holt, 1948.
Divine, Robert A. *The Reluctant Belligerent*. New York: John Wiley, 1979.
Donovan, Robert. *Tumultous Years: The Presidency of Harry S. Truman, 1949–1953*. New York: Norton, 1982.
Douglas, William O. *Go East Young Man*. New York: Random House, 1974.
Draper, Theodore. *A Very Thin Line*. New York: Hill and Wang, 1991.
Dunlop, Richard. *Donovan: America's Master Spy*. Chicago: Rand McNally, 1982.
Eisenhower, Dwight D. *Waging Peace*. New York: Doubleday, 1965.
Elson, Robert T. *Time, Inc*. New York: Atheneum, 1968.
Edmonds, Robin. *The Big Three*. New York: Norton, 1991.
Fairfield, Roy. *The Federalist Papers*. New York: Anchor, 1966.
Farley, James. *Jim Farley's Story*. New York: McGraw-Hill, 1948.
Feis, Herbert. *The Road to Pearl Harbor*. Princeton: Princeton University Press, 1950.
Ford, Corey. *Donovan of OSS*. Boston: Little, Brown, 1970.
Freedman, Max. *Roosevelt and Frankfurter: Their Correspondence*. Boston: Little, Brown, 1967.
Freidel, Frank. *Franklin D. Roosevelt: A Rendezvous with Destiny*. Boston: Little, Brown, 1990.
Freidel, Frank. *FDR: Launching the New Deal*. Boston: Little, Brown, 1973.
Freidel, Frank. *FDR: The Apprenticeship*. Boston: Little, Brown, 1952.
Freidel, Frank. *Franklin D. Roosevelt: The Ordeal*. Boston: Little, Brown, 1954.
Freidel, Frank. *FDR: The Triumph*. Boston: Little, Brown, 1956.
Friedlander, Saul. *Prelude to Downfall*. London: Chatto and Windus, 1967.
Gallagher, Hugh. *FDR's Splendid Deception*. New York: Dodd Mead, 1985.
Gerhart, Eugene C. *America's Advocate: Robert H. Jackson*. Indianapolis: Bobbs-Merrill, 1958.
Gilbert, Martin. *Finest Hour*. Boston: Houghton, Mifflin 1983.
Glennon, Michael. J. *Constitutional Diplomacy*. Princeton: Princeton University Press, 1990.
Goodheart, Phillip. *Fifty Ships that Saved the World*. New York: Doubleday, 1965.
Goodwin, Doris Kearns. *No Ordinary Time*. New York: Simon & Schuster, 1994.
Graham, Otis Jr. and Meghan Robinson Wander. *Franklin D. Roosevelt. His Life and Times*. New York: Da Capo, 1990.
Grew Joseph. *Ten Years in Japan*. New York: Simon & Schuster, 1944.
Grew, Joseph. *Turbulent Era*. Johnson, Walter, ed. Boston: Houghton Mifflin, 1952.
*Guide to U.S. Elections*. Washington: Congressional Quarterly, 1975.
Hagan, Kenneth J. *This People's Navy*. New York: Free Press, 1991.
Herzstein, Robert E. *Henry R. Luce*. New York: Scribner's, 1994.
Hitler, Adolf. *Mein Kampf*. Boston: Houghton Mifflin, 1971.

Howarth, Stephen. *To Shining Sea: A History of the United States Navy*. New York: Random House, 1991.

Hull, Cordell. *The Memoirs of Cordell Hull, Vol. 1*. New York: Macmillan, 1948.

Hurd, Charles. *When the New Deal Was Young and Gay*. New York Hawthorn, 1965

Hyde, Montgomery. *Room 3603*. New York: Farrar, Straus and Giroux, 1962.

Ickes, Harold. *The Inside Struggle*. New York: Simon and Schuster, 1954.

Ickes, Harold. *The Lowering Clouds*. New York, Simon and Schuster, 1955. (Cited in Notes as Ickes)

Johnson, Lyndon. *The Vantage Point*. New York: Holt, Rinehart, and Winston, 1971.

Johnson, Walter. *The Battle Against Isolation*. Chicago, ILL.: University of Chicago Press, 1984. (Cited in notes as *Battle*)

Johnson, Walter. *William Allen White's America*. New York: Henry Holt, 1947. (Cited in Notes as *WAWA*)

Johnson, Walter, ed. *Selected Letters of William Allen White*. New York: Henry Holt, 1947. (Cited in notes as *Letters*)

Kearns, Doris. *Lyndon Johnson & the American Dream*. New York: New American Library, 1976.

Kimball, Warren, ed. *Churchill and Roosevelt: Complete Correspondence*, Vol.I Princeton: 1984.

Langer, William L. and Everett Gleason. *The Challenge to Isolation*. New York: Harper, 1952.

Lash, Joseph P. *Roosevelt and Churchill*. New York: Norton, 1976.

Lash, Joseph P. *Dealers and Dreamers*. Doubleday: New York, 1988. (Cited in Notes as *Dealers*)

Leigh, Michael. *Mobilizing Consent*. Westport, Conn.: Greenwood, 1976.

Leuchtenburg, William E. *Franklin D. Roosevelt and the New Deal*. New York: Harper, 1963.

Leutze, James R. *Bargaining for Supremacy*. Chapel Hill, N.C.: University of North Carolina Press, 1977.

Lindberg, Charles A. *Wartime Journals*. New York: Harcourt, 1970.

Long, Breckinridge. *War Diary*. Fred Israel, ed. Lincoln: Univerity of Nebraska Press, 1966.

Louchheim, Katie, ed. *The Making of the New Deal*. Cambridge: Harvard, 1983.

Lubell, Sam. *The Future of American Politics*. New York: Harper, 1952.

Lyon, Peter *Eisenhower: Portrait of the Hero*. Boston: Little, Brown, 1974 p. 824.

Lukas, J. Anthony. *Nightmare: The Underside of the Nixon Years*. New York: Viking, 1976.

Macdonald, Dwight. *Henry Wallace*. New York: Viking, 1947.

Marshall, George C. *Papers Vol. 2* Larry Bland, ed. Baltimore, Md.: Johns Hopkins University Press, 1986.

McJimsey, George. *Harry Hopkins*. Cambridge: Harvard University Press, 1987.

McLachlan, Donald. *Room 39*. New York: Atheneum, 1968.

Michelson, Charles. *The Ghost Talks*. New York: Putnam, 1944.

Miller, Francis P. *Man from The Valley*. Chapel Hill: University of North Carolina Press, 1971.

Moffat, Jay Pierrepont. *The Moffat Papers*. Nancy Harrison, ed. Cambridge: Harvard, University Press 1956.

Moley, Raymond. *After Seven Years*. New York: Da Capo, 1939.

Morgan, Ted. *FDR: A Biography*. New York: Simon & Schuster, 1985.

Morison, Samuel Eliot. *History of U.S. Naval Operations in World War II, Vol. 1. The Battle of the Atlantic*. September 1939–May 1940. Boston: Little, Brown, 1947.

Mosley, Leonard. *Lindbergh*. Garden City, N.Y.: Doubleday, 1976.

Mowrer, Edgar Ansel. *Triumph and Turmoil*. New York: Weybright and Talley, 1968.

Murphy, Bruce. *The Brandeis-Frankfurter Connection*. New York: Oxford University Press, 1982.

Neal, Steve. *Dark Horse*. Garden City, N.Y.: Doubleday, 1984.

Nixon, Richard. *RN: The Memoirs of Richard Nixon*. New York: Groset & Dunlap, 1978.

Parish, Thomas. *Roosevelt and Marshall*. New York: Morrow, 1989.

Parmet, Herb. *Never Again*. New York: Macmillan, 1968.

Parrington, Vernon L. *Main Currents in American Thought*. 3 volumes. New York: Harcourt, 1930.

Pickersgill, J. W. *The Mackenzie King Record. Vol. 1. 1939–41*. Toronto: University of Toronto Press, 1960.

Polmar, Norman and Thomas B. Allen. *World War II: America at War*. New York: Random House, 1991.

Rauch, Basil. *Roosevelt From Munich to Pearl Harbor*. New York: Creative Age, 1950.

Reynolds, David. *The Creation of the Anglo-American Alliance*. Chapel Hill, N.C.: University of North Carolina Press, 1981.

Reynolds, David. *Lord Lothian and Anglo-American Relations*. Philadelphia: Philosophical Society, 1983.

Rogge, O. John. *The Official German Report*. New York: Yoseloff, 1961.

Rollins, Alfred B., Jr. *Roosevelt and Howe*. New York: Knopf, 1962.

Roosevelt, Elliot, ed. *FDR: His Personal Letters*. 4 Vols. New York: Duell, Sloan, and Pearce, 1947, 1948, 1950.

Roosevelt, Elliot and James Brough. *A Rendezvous with Destiny*. New York: Putnam, 1975.

Roosevelt, Franklin D. *Complete Presidential Press Conferences*. 9 Vols. New York; Da Capo, 1972.

Rosenman, Sam. *Working with Roosevelt*. New York: Harper, 1952.

Royal Institute of International Affairs. *The American Speeches of Lord Lothian*. July 1939 to December 1940. London: Oxford University Press, 1941. (Cited in notes as *Speeches*)

Russet, Bruce M. *No Clear and Present Danger*. New York: Harper and Row, 1972.

Schlesinger, Arthur. *The Crisis of the Old Order*. Boston: Houghton, 1957.

Schlesinger, Arthur. *The Coming of the New Deal*. Boston: Houghton, 1959.

Schlesinger, Arthur. *The Politics of Upheaval*. Boston: Houghton, 1960.

Seale, William. *The President's House*. Washington: White House Historical Assocation, 1986.

Sherwood, Robert E. *Roosevelt and Hopkins*. New York: Harper, 1948.

Sirevag, Torbjorn. *The Eclipse of the New Deal*. New York: Garland, 1985.

Smith, R. Harris. *OSS: The Secret History of America's First Central Intelligence Agency*. University of California Press: Berkeley, Calif.: 1972.

Smith, Richard Norton. *Thomas E. Dewey and His Times*. New York: Simon & Schuster, 1982.

Sorensen, Theodore C. *Kennedy*. New York: Harper and Row, 1965.

Smith, Gene. *The Shattered Dream*. New York: Morrow, 1970.

Steel, Ronald. *Walter Lippmann and the American Century*. New York: Vintage, 1980.

Stiles, Lela. *The Man Behind Roosevelt*. New York: World, 1954.

Stimson, Henry L. and McGeorge Bundy. *On Active Service in Peace and War*. New York: Harper and Brothers, 1947.

Swanberg, W. A. *Citizen Hearst*. New York: Bantam, 1967.

*Time. Time Capsule, 1939*. New York: Time Life, 1967.

*Time. Time Capsule 1940*. New York: Time Life, 1967.

Troy, Thomas. *Donovan and the CIA*. University Publications: Lanham, Md., 1981.

Tugwell, Rexford G. *The Democratic Roosevelt*. Baltimore: Penguin, 1957.

Tully, Grace. *FDR: My Boss*. Chicago: People's Book Club, 1949.

Ward, Geoffrey C. *A First Class Temperament*. New York: Harper, 1989.

Ward, Geoffrey. *Before the Trumpet*. New York: Harper, 1985.

Young, Peter, ed. *The World Almanac Book of World War II*. New York: World Almanac, 1981.

Watkins, T. H. *Righteous Pilgrim*. New York: Holt, 1990.

Watson, Mark S. *The United States Army in World War II. Chief of Staff: Prewar Plans and Preparations.* Washington, D.C.: Center of Military History, United States Army, 1991.

Welles, Sumner. *The Time for Decision.* New York: Harper, 1944.

Wheeler, Burton. *Yankee From the West.* Garden City, N.Y.: Doubleday, 1962.

Whelan, Richard. *The Founding Father.* New York: New American Library, 1964.

Wilson, Hugh. *Diplomat Between Wars.* New York: Longmans, Green, 1941.

Winant, John Gilbert. *Letter from Grosvenor Square.* Boston: Houghton Mifflin, 1947.

Winks, Robin W. *Cloak & Gown.* New York: Morrow, 1987.

Wood, Edward Frederick Lindley, 1st Earl of Halifax. *Fullness of Days.* New York: Dodd, Mead, 1957.

## ARTICLES

Baptiste, F. A. "The British Grant of Air and Naval Facilities to the United States in Trinidad, St. Lucia and Bermuda in 1939 (June-December). *Caribbean Studies.* Vol. 16, No.2 (1976)

Borchard, Edwin. "The Attorney General's Opinion on the Exchange of Destroyers for Naval Bases." *American Journal of International Law,* Vol. 34, October 1940.

Borg, Dorothy. "Notes on Roosevelt's 'Quarantine' Speech." *Political Science Quarterly.* Vol. 72, September, 1957.

Briggs, Herbert W. "Neglected Aspects of the Destroyer Deal." *American Journal of International Law,* Vol. 34, October 1940.

Cantrill, Hadley. "America Faces the War." *Public Opinion Quarterly.* Vol. 4, No. 3, September 1940.

Cohen, Benjamin V. et al. "Presidential Responsibility and American Democracy. *The Prospect for Presidential- Congressional Government.* Berkeley Calif.: University of California, Institute of Governmental Studies, 1977.

Corwin, Edward. "Executive Authority Held Exceeded in Destroyer Deal." *New York Times,* Oct. 13, 1940. (letter to the editor)

Davenport, Russell W. "The Ordeal of Wendell Willkie." *Atlantic Monthly.* November 1945.

Glennon, Michael. "The Gulf War and the Constitution." *Foreign Affairs,* April 1991.

Jacob, Philip. E. "Influences of World Events on U.S. Neutrality Opinion." *Public Opinion Quarterly,* March 1940.

Lindbergh, Anne. "Prayer for Peace." *Reader's Digest.* January 1940.

Lindbergh, Charles. "Aviation, Geography and Race." *Reader's Digest.* September 1939.

———. "What Substitute for War?" *Atlantic.* March 1940.

Moos, Malcolm. "The American Presidency in Contemporary Statesmanship." In Cohen et al. The Prospect for Presidential-Congressional Government.

Peek, Jerome. "In and Out, the Experiences of the First AAA Administrator." *Saturday Evening Post.* May 16, 1936.

Pratt, Lawrence. "The Anglo-American Naval Conversations on the Far East of January 1938." *International Affairs.* Vol. 47 No 4, October 1971.

Pringle, Henry F. "Exit 'Wild Bill.' " *Outlook,* January 9, 1929.

Riccards, Michael P. "The Dangerous Legacy." In Paul Harper and Joann Krieg, eds., John F. Kennedy: *The Promise Revisited.* Westport, Conn: Greenwood Press, 1988.

Roosevelt, Franklin D. "Our Foreign Policy: A Democratic View." *Foreign Affairs.* July 1928.

Stromberg, Roland N. "American Business and the Approach of War." *Journal of Economic History.* Winter, 1953.

Waymack, W. H. "The Middle West Looks Abroad." *Foreign Affairs."* Vol. 18 No. 3. April 1940.

Willkie, Wendell. *Democratic Party's Share in Isolationism. The United States News.* Sept. 8, 1944.

Young, Lowell T. "Franklin Roosevelt and America's Islets: Acquisition of Territory in the
    Caribbean and the Pacific." *The Historian* 35, 1973. pp. 205–20.


## GOVERNMENT DOCUMENTS

*Building the Navy's Bases in World War II*. History of the Bureau of Yards and Docks, U.S.
    Government Printing Office, Washington, 1947.
Department of State. *U.S. Documents on German Foreign Policy, 1918–1945, vols. IX and X*
    Washington: Government Printing Office, 1957. (Cited in Notes as DGFP)
Department of State, U.S. *Peace and War: U.S. Foreign Policy 1931–1941*. Washington,:
    Government Printing Office, 1942. (Cited in Notes as *Peace and War*)
Germany. Kriegsmarine. Ober Kommando. *Fuehrer Conferences on Matters Dealing with the
    German Navy, 1939–1945*. Wilmington, Del.: Scholarly Resources, 1983.
Roosevelt, Franklin D. *Complete Presidential Press Conferences*, 1933–41. New York: Da
    Capo, 1972.
Roosevelt, Franklin D. *Public Papers and Addresses 1933–1941*. New York: Macmillan.
    (Cited in Notes as *PPA*) by year.
Walsh, Lawrence E. *Iran-Contra: The Final Report*. Vol. I. New York: Times Books,1994.


## MANUSCRIPT COLLECTIONS

Alderman Library, University of Virginia, Charlottesville, Va.: Diary of Homer Cummings,
    Papers of Francis P. Miller.
College of the Holy Cross Library, Worcester, Mass.: Papers of David Walsh.
Franklin D. Roosevelt Presidential Library, Hyde Park, N.Y.: President's Secretary's File,
    Morgenthau diaries (cited in notes as MD), Morgenthau Presidential Diaries (cited in
    notes as MPD), general correspondence, and records relating to the destroyers-for-bases
    trade.
Herbert Hoover Library, West Branch, Ia: Papers of Gerald Nye.
Library of Congress, Manuscript Division: The British Foreign Office microfilmed records
    of communication between its Washington Embassy and London covering governmental,
    political, and economic developments in the U.S., for the years 1938–1941 (cited in the
    Notes as FO 371 files). Also includes records of the British Library of Information (cited
    in notes as BLI). Also the papers of William Allen White, Joseph Alsop, Ben Cohen,
    James Farley, Cordell Hull, Robert Jackson, and Frank Knox.
Yale University Sterling Library, New Haven, Conn.: Diary of Henry Stimson, microfilm.
U.S. Military History Institute, Carlisle, Pa: Papers of William Donovan.
U.S. Naval Historical Center, Washington, D.C.: Papers of Harold R. Stark.


## SCHOLARLY PAPERS

Lasser, William. "The Destroyers for Bases Agreement and the Origins of the Imperial
    Presidency." Paper delivered at the American Political Science Association Meeting,
    Washington, D.C., September 1993.
Dellinger, David Worth. "Destroyers for Bases: An End to the Illusion of Neutrality." Master
    of Arts dissertation. Georgetown University, May 1967.
Sutphen, Harold J. "The Anglo-American Destroyers-Bases Agreement." Ph.D. Thesis.
    Fletcher School of Law and Diplomacy. April 1967.

# Index